LOUIS DIAT

FRENCH COUNTRY COOKING FOR AMERICANS

D1536995

DOVER PUBLICATIONS, INC.
NEW YORK

To my mother, Annette Alajoinine Diat, who guided the early years, inspired the later ones and whose memory is still a spur.

Mon appréciation la plus sincère à Helen Ridley qui, en traduissant mes pensées, a vraiment accomplit l'esprit de ce livre.

—L. D.

Published in Canada by General Publishing Company, Ltd., 30 Lesmill Road, Don Mills, Toronto, Ontario.

Published in the United Kingdom by Constable and Company, Ltd., 10 Orange Street, London WC2H 7EG.

This Dover edition, first published in 1978, is an unabridged republication of the work originally published in 1946 by J. B. Lippincott Co., under the title *Louis Diat's French Cooking for Americans, La Cuisine de Ma Mère.*

International Standard Book Number:
0-486-23665-X
Library of Congress Catalog Card Number:
78-51530

Manufactured in the United States of America
Dover Publications, Inc.
180 Varick Street
New York, N.Y. 10014

Contents

[iii]

Foreword

As an American I have for the past several years deplored the growing lack of imagination and discriminating knowledge in my country in the matter of eating. I can remember the good old days of the Nineties and the Nineteen Hundreds when my father, always very much the gourmet, took great pains to instruct his children in the savouring and enjoying of all kinds of comestibles. He was impatient of any stubbornness on our part which tended to favor any particular kind of food to the detriment of other kinds. Nothing enraged him more than a silly remark such as: "I don't like fish," "I can't abide turnips," "I never eat game!" Such proscriptions were anathema to him. His tastes were all-embracing, for he was a true epicure.

I believe that in the privacy of the homes of America such sensible latitude still prevails. But I find it alarming to view the growth of a sort of snobbery whenever the meal becomes in any sense a social affair—formal dinners or luncheons given at home or in places of public entertainment. I like to characterize such tendencies as "Polite Feeding." The imagination of most of us, when ordering food in public, seems to be increasingly timid. Steak, lamb, chicken, peas, string beans, and if the pocketbook allows, asparagus or broccoli. This is being "polite." The less conventional duck, veal, tongue, or fish, with the humble potato, cauliflower, corn, onions, eggplant, or carrots are, in some curious way, considered rather "common." And as for such admirable but homely delicacies as pork, goose, mutton, boiled fowl, kidneys, etc.—well, they are only to be whispered to a snobbishly horrified waiter to the accompaniment of a conciliatory leer.

This is, to my mind, a sad state of affairs. So, when a man of Monsieur Diat's recognized authority in the realm of culinary art, encourages the housewives and diners-out of America to make the most of all and sundry foods; to shun none and to accept everything edible with gratitude and enthusiasm, it is a lesson devoutly to be learned and remembered. This lesson he manages adroitly to teach by his careful

[iv]

description of the famed home cooking of his native France, stressing the splendid economy and skill, due to which the French people have been for centuries renowned as the best fed people in the world.

We in America owe a debt of gratitude to Monsieur Diat for his efforts.

MONTY WOOLLEY.

Preface

It is the simple but delicious cookery of the French countryside that I bring you in this, my second book. In it I hope to recapture the spirit of the French home cuisine, that spirit which makes the heart of every *Maitresse de maison* swell with pride and satisfaction when she has prepared a delectable meal for an appreciative family.

For many years now I have catered to the *haut monde* in the great kitchens of Ritz hotels. It has been my privilege to prepare world-famous dishes for world-famous people. Yet never have these years dimmed my memories of the food that was served in my boyhood home —and in thousands of French homes like my own—where even the simplest cooking was fine cooking because it was done with patience and loving care. It was, in fact, in homes such as these that the discerning tastes of France's great chefs—and the famous gourmets who have inspired and honored them—sprouted and flourished.

French cooking, like American, is to an extent regional. Just as in America, different sections take great pride in their specialties and I have included recipes for many of the important dishes served in various parts of France. But for the most part this is a collection of Bourbonnais recipes—dishes served in that small province in the center of France that borders on the Allier River, because that is where my home was and the dishes are the ones my mother served there. It was her skillful and discriminating cookery, her unforgettably delicious meals that were my first inspiration and which decided my career.

My Mother's Kitchen

My mother's kitchen with its well-scoured stone floor, whitewashed walls and small-paned casement windows was as French as the tricolor that waved over the town hall. It was far, indeed, from the efficient compactness of a modern American kitchen—but, oh, so cheerful! I remember how the sunshine streamed in through the windows on bright days, marking off big, sunny squares on the floor, how the copper pots gleamed, and how, even on dull days, the whiteness of the walls seemed to chase away any gloom. French kitchens like ours had an inviting coziness, a warmth always pungent with tantalizing smells.

The cheeriness of our kitchen was due, however, only in part to the streaming sunshine and the comfortable warmth of the big, black stove. More important was the spirit of my smiling, friendly mother who was the queen of this little domain. Pictures of her bustling in her kitchen —her capable hands on the rolling pin flattening out a fat ball of pastry, or carefully skimming the *pot-au-feu*, or perhaps carrying a soufflé to the table, carrying it so very gently lest its magic puffing collapse too soon—these pictures have been constantly before me as the recipes for this book—her recipes—have gone down on its pages. Perhaps my memory now serves me so well because all these kitchen activities were fascinating to me, a continual lure. Her love of fine food made the daily meal-getting a delight and a challenge and turned us children into little gourmets with our first solid food.

Our kitchen lacked the vast array of equipment that seems so important today; for instance, we did not even have a meat grinder and an egg beater. Sharp knives minced and chopped to every degree of fineness, wire whips whisked to any desired lightness. Our bowls were of old-fashioned mustard colored earthenware and we mixed with wooden spoons. Copper was used for cooking vegetables and sauces; black iron for frying, sautéing, and general cooking; and brown earthenware casseroles, in several shapes and sizes, for soups, stews and all kinds of baking. Our stove was heated by coal or wood, had no con-

venient gas cocks or electric switches and no thermostat to regulate—
or thermometer to tell—the oven's heat. Cooking was quickened or
delayed by moving the pots nearer or farther from the hot center and
the oven was judged by the feel of its heat on the hand—judged, I
might add, with great accuracy.

Ours, I know, was a typical French kitchen and the fine cooking that
was done in it was typical, too. My mother, like most French women,
had learned to cook when a girl by watching her mother, grandmother,
aunts and friends. She was given small tasks at first, then took on more
complicated ones until she had trained all her five senses on this very
important and, to her, delightful occupation. She learned the feel of
foods, such as the lightness of brioche dough when ready for the oven
or the resistance meat gives the fork when not quite done; she knew
how foods should look, how fine the meat should be chopped for
hachis or how coarse the vegetables for hors d'oeuvres; she could tell
freshness by smell; and determine the heat of fat by the sputtering
sound of chicken or fish frying in it. But above all, she learned to taste
with discrimination—that never-ending tasting that warned her just
when to remove the faggot or advised an extra ten minutes' cooking.
Using the senses so constantly makes them keener and keener and
cannot fail to make a better and better cook. The way a French housewife does use her senses instead of depending entirely upon recipes
and mechanical aids is, I think, one reason why women like my mother
thought of cooking as a creative art, never a tiresome chore.

Simple Foods but Delicious Meals

I see in every American market the same fruits and vegetables, the same meat and fish that filled our country market baskets. That is, with a few exceptions—no veal, for example, has quite the same whiteness and delicacy of French veal. But, on the other hand, we were not lucky enough to have the profusion of out-of-season foods that appear so regularly in American markets nor the canned and packaged goods that make cooking almost child's play.

Mother's cookery-skill and thrift started with her marketing. Not a sou left her purse for anything second rate. With her keen eyes and sensitive fingers she judged the plumpness of this, the firmness of that, the crispness of something else. I can't imagine her marketing by phone—even if she had had one to use. Nor can I picture her wasting any of the food she bought so carefully. The waste common in this country would have left her completely bewildered. To spend precious francs and sous for food and then throw half of it in the refuse pail! She would have been as likely to have thrown the actual coins there.

We Bourbonnais may have been a bit lavish with dairy foods because milk and cream, butter, cheese and eggs were plentiful. But they were used carefully and regularly, rather than extravagantly. There is a difference. Never, for example, at the end of a heavy meal would great spoonfuls of whipped cream be ladled over a rich dessert. On the other hand, never were the few spoonfuls of cream, needed to bring a soup or a sauce to a final point of delectability, left out. And to risk a poor result by being stingy with butter or eggs would have seemed the strangest kind of economy in our home.

Now nutritionists tell me that dairy foods are one of the best and least expensive ways of obtaining vital nutrients—a better and cheaper way than getting them in pills. They say, too, that to throw away food that can be used in the soup pot or salad bowl is to throw away health. My mother would have understood them.

[ix]

In the France that I knew, butter was an indispensable staple in cooking, used by even the poorest families. But few people ate it on bread at the table, and I, for one, still prefer my bread plain. Cream soups and sauces never lacked its fine, rich flavor and the only pastry in which anything but butter was used was the pastry for meat pies. In summer, butter was plentiful and cheap and enough was preserved for the winter months.

One way of preparing it for storage was to melt it very slowly, to avoid scorching, and pour off the clear, melted fat into crocks which, when well covered, were stored in the cold cellar. (The residue in the pan was browned just the least bit and spread on bread for us children to eat with milk for a between-meal snack.) This particular butter was used for cooking vegetables and fish, for sauce Meunière or wherever melted butter was required.

The other way of preparing butter for storage was to knead out all the drops of liquid, then wash it well and continue kneading to remove every trace of buttermilk. A little vinegar was then put in the bottom of a crock, and a layer—about an inch—of butter spread over it, more vinegar and another layer of butter and so on until the crock was filled, ending with a layer of vinegar. It was pressed down firmly, covered closely and stored in the cellar. At any time a portion could be spooned out and washed with fresh water. This was reserved for making cream soups and sauces, for pastries and other delicacies.

We had to depend upon fresh foods that were in season, and consequently, we enjoyed all the more the special bounty of each season as it rolled round. But we did preserve some perishables for winter use, salting vegetables like green beans and drying fruits like plums and cherries.

Did mother have some special tricks up her sleeve that turned this simple provender into monuments of good living? If the wise use of dairy foods is an up-the-sleeve trick, then I can say "yes." And I can add "yes indeed," if the way she distributed seasonings and herbs through her sauces and soups, and enhanced their flavors with red and white wines are tricks. To "boil in salted water" and let it go at that was not her idea of how to prepare food.

The seasonings and herbs, in fact, which give fresh, new meanings to plain foods are as much a part of a French home and garden as the flagged walk which leads to the door. Everyone with a patch of ground, no matter how small, has neat rows of parsley, chives and chervil, bushy clumps of tarragon and thyme and the pungent odor of drying herbs permeated our kitchens every year in late summer.

In summer when freshly picked herbs were dropped in the pot, the dishes tasted just a little different from those in winter when the dried ones were used. That adds another bit of variation. City housewives without gardens could always find a market that sold herbs—fresh ones in summer, dried ones in winter—because they shopped until they did find one.

Wine which has that quality of making a sauce the perfect complement to a particular food was always at hand, too. Wines, such as the "pinard" that average Frenchmen drink every day, are so inexpensive that they are as cheap a flavoring as lemon juice in this country. I think that America's good, native wine also should be used more in cooking and I hope my recipes will encourage it.

During the last thirty-odd years, visits to my mother's home in France have been infrequent. But each one confirmed my boyhood memories of her cooking, of the food that always looked and smelled so appetizing, and tasted so delicious. On my last visit I said, "This is the cooking about which Americans should know more," and I knew then that sometime I would write this book.

CONVERSION TABLES FOR FOREIGN EQUIVALENTS

DRY INGREDIENTS

Ounces	Grams	Grams	Ounces	Pounds	Kilograms	Kilograms	Pounds
1 =	28.35	1 =	0.035	1 =	0.454	1 =	2.205
2	56.70	2	0.07	2	0.91	2	4.41
3	85.05	3	0.11	3	1.36	3	6.61
4	113.40	4	0.14	4	1.81	4	8.82
5	141.75	5	0.18	5	2.27	5	11.02
6	170.10	6	0.21	6	2.72	6	13.23
7	198.45	7	0.25	7	3.18	7	15.43
8	226.80	8	0.28	8	3.63	8	17.64
9	255.15	9	0.32	9	4.08	9	19.84
10	283.50	10	0.35	10	4.54	10	22.05
11	311.85	11	0.39	11	4.99	11	24.26
12	340.20	12	0.42	12	5.44	12	26.46
13	368.55	13	0.46	13	5.90	13	28.67
14	396.90	14	0.49	14	6.35	14	30.87
15	425.25	15	0.53	15	6.81	15	33.08
16	453.60	16	0.57				

LIQUID INGREDIENTS

Liquid Ounces	Milliliters	Milliliters	Liquid Ounces	Quarts	Liters	Liters	Quarts
1 =	29.573	1 =	0.034	1 =	0.946	1 =	1.057
2	59.15	2	0.07	2	1.89	2	2.11
3	88.72	3	0.10	3	2.84	3	3.17
4	118.30	4	0.14	4	3.79	4	4.23
5	147.87	5	0.17	5	4.73	5	5.28
6	177.44	6	0.20	6	5.68	6	6.34
7	207.02	7	0.24	7	6.62	7	7.40
8	236.59	8	0.27	8	7.57	8	8.45
9	266.16	9	0.30	9	8.52	9	9.51
10	295.73	10	0.33	10	9.47	10	10.57

Gallons (American)	Liters	Liters	Gallons (American)
1 =	3.785	1 =	0.264
2	7.57	2	0.53
3	11.36	3	0.79
4	15.14	4	1.06
5	18.93	5	1.32
6	22.71	6	1.59
7	26.50	7	1.85
8	30.28	8	2.11
9	34.07	9	2.38
10	37.86	10	2.74

Hors d'Oeuvres

⟨⊐ ❖ ⊏⟩

Hors D'OEUVRES, as I remember them in my mother's home, were usually served on special occasions like holidays, and at company meals, or in summertime for Sunday dinner. Not little snacks made by spreading fish and cheese pastes on tiny crackers, but real food served at the table either for the first course of dinner or the main course of luncheon. They were good, filling food and if eaten for the first course could be depended upon to make the more expensive main dish go farther. At luncheon, when served with a salad or preceded by our favorite Onion Soup, a generous platter of hors d'oeuvres was hearty enough for the main part of the meal.

Here was food economy in the French fashion, for hors d'oeuvres used up small amounts of leftover vegetables, meat and fish. And when there was a sudden abundance of some vegetable in the garden, my mother was not long in fixing up the surplus in a spicy, cold sauce for hors d'oeuvres.

In addition every town of any size had a *charcuterie* which sold oddments of cold meat specialties not usually made at home. From this *charcuterie* came delicious sausages of many kinds (cold sausages somewhat like bologna here), pork's head (headcheese), liver paste and so on. These when served with our homemade beef salad, pickled fish, marinated beets, cabbage and so on, made as tasty a combination as anyone could ask for. In little towns that were too small to have a *charcuterie*, the farmers who took the local eggs, butter, cheese, and chickens to the market always carried with them the orders from the housewives to the *charcuterie* and brought back the specialties.

My mother put the homemade hors d'oeuvres into small wooden bowls with just enough of the sauce to moisten, but not enough to make them soupy looking. Then around the edge of each would go a bright green border of freshly chopped parsley. Whenever we had delicacies from the *charcuterie* they were carefully sliced and neatly arranged on a platter. Everything was then placed on the dining table and passed around. Thick slices of crusty French bread and a bottle of dry white wine—we had never heard of cocktails—completed the course.

ARTICHOKES A LA GREQUE
(Artichauts à la Grecque)

12 *tiny artichokes* (*or 3 medium*)	*½ teaspoon salt*
3 *cups water*	1 *branch fennel, minced* (*optional*)
juice from ½ lemon (*or 2 tablespoons*	1 *stalk celery, minced*
vinegar)	*few coriander seeds*
½ cup olive oil	4 *peppercorns*

Use very tiny young artichokes about 1 to 1½ inches in diameter. Mix together the lemon juice (or vinegar), water, oil and seasonings and bring to a boil. Add artichokes and cook for 15 to 20 minutes. If artichokes are small enough there will be no choke to remove. But if tiny artichokes are unobtainable and larger ones must be used, cut each in quarters, remove the prickly choke and trim the leaves so that they are about 1 inch long. Cool in the cooking liquid and serve the artichokes in it.

BEET SALAD
(Salade de Betterave)

Beets, one of the *racines* (root vegetables) which we stored and used all winter, were made into this Beet Salad which was served not only as an hors d'oeuvres but also as an accompaniment for cold meats. It is delicious with cold Beef à la Mode or with the end of the beef that has been cooked in the Pot-au-Feu.

Wash 6 medium beets and bake in a moderately hot oven of 375 degrees about 40 minutes or until done. Peel, cool and cut in julienne or mince not too finely. Boil an onion for 15 minutes, drain, cool and dice—or chop enough spring scallions to make about ½ cup. Mix together and combine with Sauce Vinaigrette (page 35) or Cream Mustard (page 33).

RED CABBAGE WITH VINEGAR
(Choux Rouge au Vinaigre)

Cut cabbage in julienne, sprinkle with salt and let stand for about 1 hour. Then squeeze out all the water. (Or cut in julienne, cover with boiling water, boil 5 or 6 minutes, drain and rinse with cold water, a method which takes out the bitter taste.) Put the well-drained cabbage in a bowl, sprinkle top with a little salt, a few peppercorns, a bay leaf and a whole clove of garlic and then cover with boiling vinegar. Cool, cover closely and leave in the refrigerator for two days. When ready to serve, remove garlic and bay leaf and add 2 green apples, peeled, cored and thinly sliced and 3 tablespoons of olive or salad oil. Toss all together. Serve from a small salad bowl with a border of chopped sour pickles on top.

MARINATED CARROTS
(Carottes Marinées)

1 *lb. new spring carrots*	1 *tablespoon sugar*
1 *glass of white wine*	5 *tablespoons salad oil or olive oil*
1 *cup water*	*a faggot made of 2 sprigs parsley, a*
1 *clove garlic, crushed*	*little thyme, 1 bay leaf and 2*
½ *teaspoon salt*	*stalks chervil*

Scrape carrots and cut in quarters. Put remaining ingredients in saucepan and boil 5 minutes. Add carrots and cook until medium done. (They should be a little firm.) When cool, moisten with a little of the cooking liquor and serve from a small bowl. Sprinkle top with chopped chervil and parsley. ½ teaspoon dry mustard may be added to the cooking liquor if the flavor is liked.

CELERY WITH APPLE
(Céleris et Pommes d'Arbre)

Make a fine julienne of celery, about 1½ cups, put in cold water (or ice water) for 35 to 40 minutes to crisp. Drain. Put in a bowl and add 1 sour apple peeled, cored and finely minced. Mix with Sauce Vinaigrette with Mustard (page 35), Cream Mustard (page 33), or prepared mustard.

MARINATED CUCUMBERS
(Concombres Marinés)

Peel cucumbers, cut in half lengthwise and remove seeds. Chop the pulp fine, spread on a plate, sprinkle with salt and let stand 1 hour. Drain, press in a towel to remove all the moisture and mix with Sauce Vinaigrette (page 35). If desired, sliced radishes and sliced tomatoes and watercress may be mixed with the cucumbers.

KNOB CELERY WITH MUSTARD

Peel 6 medium celery knobs and cut in julienne. Spread on a platter and sprinkle generously with salt. Leave for ½ hour. Drain and press

[5]

out all the moisture with a towel. (Or cover the julienne of celery knob with boiling water, cook for a minute, drain and rinse with fresh cold water.) Combine with Sauce Vinaigrette with Mustard (page 35) and serve from a small salad bowl with chopped parsley or chervil sprinkled on top.

MARINATED FRESH HERRING
(Harengs Marinés)

½ cup olive or salad oil
12 small fresh herring (about 1½-2 lbs.), well cleaned
½ pint dry white wine
1¼ cups vinegar
1 medium carrot, thinly sliced

2 medium onions, sliced into thin rings
4 sprigs parsley, cut in small pieces
1 bay leaf
6 peppercorns

Put the oil in a flat saucepan and lay the fish on top. In another pan cook remaining ingredients gently 12 to 15 minutes. Pour this over the herring and cook all together very gently another 12 to 15 minutes. Cool. Serve the herring in a small hors d'oeuvres dish with the marinade poured over them and garnished with slices of lemon.

HEADCHEESE, COUNTRY STYLE
(Tête de Porc, Fermière)

Headcheese is ordinarily purchased from the *charcuterie* by housewives in average French homes. But country people who have farms where they raise hogs always make their own headcheese. People in this country who have farms where they raise pigs for food—even if only one or two each year—should know how to use the head for this delicacy. To prepare the head before cooking it, the hair should be scraped or singed off the skin, then the head is split in two and brains removed. The brains can be cooked and served just like calves' brains.

1 small pork head (5-6 lbs.)
½ lb. fresh pork skin
2 large carrots
2 large onions, each studded with 1 clove

a faggot of 6 sprigs parsley, some thyme and 2 stalks celery
¼ teaspoon freshly ground pepper
a pinch of Parisian spice (optional)
salt

Split head in two lengthwise, remove tongue and brains. (The brains can be cooked and served like calves' brains.) Parboil head and clean well. Cut each half in two again. Rub each piece and the tongue with Parisian spice and ground pepper, rubbing it in well, and put in a bowl with the fresh pork skin. Sprinkle well with salt and leave in a cold place for 2 to 3 days. Remove from the salt, dry pieces with a towel and put them (but not the pork skin) in a saucepan large enough so they can be well covered with water. Add carrots, onions and faggot, bring to a boil and skim well. Cook slowly for about 1 hour, then add pork skin and cook another 1½ hours or until meat is tender. Remove meat from stock and separate it from the bones. Cut all the meat, ears, tongue, etc., in large dice and put in a bowl. Correct the seasoning of the stock and strain 1 cup or a little more of it over the meat. Use the pork skin to cover the bottom of a round bowl and add meat mixture. Cover with a piece of white paper, put a plate on top with a weight on it to press the meat and leave in a cold place 24 hours. Remove weight and plate, invert pressed meat on a plate and cut in slices to serve.

LEEK SALAD
(Poireaux en Salade)

Although I suggest cooking the leeks in water for your convenience, actually we never did this at home. They were always simmered in soup—there always seemed to be soup on the stove to simmer them in—and removed as soon as tender. The leeks improve the flavor of the soup and the soup flavors the leeks. Leave about an inch of the white end uncut when cutting lengthwise and simmer the leeks very gently. This helps hold the leaves together and makes the dish more attractive and easier to serve.

Use large plump leeks and cut lengthwise into quarters before washing in order that the sand which collects between the leaves will come out easily. Simmer in salted water 45 minutes to 1 hour or until tender. Drain and cool. Serve either warm or cold, with Sauce Vinaigrette (page 35). Sprinkle with finely chopped tarragon and chives, if obtainable.

SPICED PORK
(Rillettes de Porc)

This is an inexpensive type of pâté that can be, and is, used like Pâté de Foie Gras. The flavor is of delicately spiced pork and the texture fine and smooth, yet its cost is negligible. At home we were not sparing with Rillettes de Porc when we sat at table and spread it on our crusty French bread—always to the accompaniment of a good bottle. We drank a dry white wine, but it is just as delicious with a dry sherry or a dry cocktail.

The secret of making good rillettes is to chop—or grind—the cooked

[7]

meat very, very fine. If you have old Pâté de Foie Gras crocks—or similar crocks—pack the rillettes in them, then you can scrape off the fat from the top and serve it right from the crock. But lacking them use jelly glasses and when ready to serve, take off the half inch layer of fat which covers the top and serve as much of the pâté as desired on a plate.

1½ lbs. lean pork, end of rib if possible	1½ teaspoons salt
	a pinch of Parisian spice (optional)
2 lbs. fresh pork fat	1 bay leaf
a little pepper	1 cup boiling water

Cut meat and fat into small dice and mix with pepper, salt, spice and bay leaf. Put in a saucepan that has a heavy bottom so that fat will melt and water will reduce slowly. Stir occasionally. When water is all cooked away and meat starts to brown add fat dice watching them carefully as they become brown and crisp. Remove meat and fat dice and put in a colander to drain. Save fat which drains out, put it back with that left in the pan and turn off the heat under the pan. Remove bay leaf and mince—or grind—the meat very fine. Put in a bowl and gradually mix in the hot fat, reserving about 1 cup of the fat. Pack the rillette mixture into small jars and pour the reserved fat over it to the depth of about ½ inch. Store in refrigerator until ready to use.

OYSTER PLANT A LA GRECQUE
(Salsifis à la Grecque)

This was a favorite dish of my mother's. She was so fond of oyster plant when fixed for hors d'oeuvres that when she was preparing them to be sautéed or à la crème, she always cooked enough extra to set aside for this Oyster Plant à la Grecque. After the preliminary boiling, oyster plant keeps well, much better than other cooked vegetables.

20-24 oyster plant (2 bunches)	½ teaspoon salt
3 cups water	1 branch fennel, minced
juice from ½ lemon or	1 stalk celery, minced
2 tablespoons vinegar	few coriander seeds
½ cup olive or salad oil	4 peppercorns

Peel oyster plant and cut into 1½ inch lengths. (Oyster plant darkens very quickly after peeling unless put in a bowl of water containing lemon juice or vinegar, using juice of ½ lemon or 3 tablespoons vinegar for 1 quart of water.) Drain, cover with boiling, salted water and boil

20 minutes. In the meantime, put water, lemon juice, vinegar, oil, salt and seasonings in a saucepan, bring to a boil, and add the oyster plant which has been cooked and drained. Cook all together 25 minutes. Cool in the liquid. Moisten with some of the cooking liquor and serve in a small salad bowl.

PORK LIVER PATE
(Pâté de Foie de Porc)

A very delicious pâté can be made from pork liver to take the place of the more expensive pâté de foie gras. In a good refrigerator a well-cooked pâté should keep for at least a week or ten days. It can be cut in slices for the hors d'oeuvres tray or can be served alone with French bread as a first course. As a matter of fact, in France we never started a meal with a fruit cup—that would be the dessert—but usually had some sort of a piquant appetizer such as this Pâté de Foie de Porc.

2 *lbs. pork liver*	*a pinch of thyme*
¾ *lb. lean pork*	1 *bay leaf, powdered*
¼ *lb. fat salt pork*	2 *shallots, finely chopped (or 1 small*
1 *tablespoon flour*	*finely chopped onion)*
2 *eggs*	1 *teaspoon chopped parsley*
½ *teaspoon salt*	¼ *lb. salt pork, cut in thin slices*
a pinch of Parisian spice (optional)	

Chop liver, lean pork and fat salt pork very finely or run through a meat grinder. Put in a bowl, add flour and work all together with a wooden spoon for about 5 minutes. Add eggs one at a time, mixing well after each is added. Add seasonings, shallots (or onions) and parsley. Line bottom and sides of a bread pan or baking dish with the thinly sliced salt pork and pack in the mixture. Cover top with sliced salt pork. Set in a pan of boiling water and bake in a moderate oven of 375 degrees for 1½ to 1¾ hours. Cool, unmold and serve in slices.

RICE SALAD

⅔ *cup cooked rice*	1 *tablespoon minced green pepper*
(grains must be whole and flaky)	1 *small onion, chopped*
⅓ *cup leftover cooked meat, or fowl*	*Sauce Vinaigrette* (page 35)
or fish	

Put rice, meat or fowl or fish that has been cut in small pieces, pepper and onion in a bowl and add enough Sauce Vinaigrette to moisten well. Toss all together carefully, using a fork to avoid crushing the rice. Correct the seasoning before serving.

Soups

THE soup pot in our home had little chance to get cold. Something was always gently bubbling in it, because soup was eaten every day and at any meal, breakfast included. The idea, however, that everything is dumped into a soup kettle which boils on endlessly like a witches' brew is all wrong, at least in the homes I knew. Only flavors that would go well together were combined and soup making received all the care and thought given any other cooking. When the soup casserole was empty it was washed out like any other utensil, ready for fresh ingredients.

It always seems to me that the thrift of the French reaches a peak in the marmite, that tall earthenware casserole used for soup making. Small amounts of this and that, inexpensive cuts of meat, fowl and vegetables, and everything flavorful that has no other use, like celery tops, find their way into the marmite. Put on the back of the stove, unhurried cooking releases all the goodness of its contents into the soup.

Very few housewives start the marmite with water. Part or all of the liquid which forms the base of a soup—or for that matter, a sauce—is stock. It adds that indescribable "something" to the flavor. Water can be substituted for the stock called for in recipes, and is used when stock is not available, but the flavor suffers. My mother always had stock on hand in a jar and it cost practically nothing because it was made from scraps of leftover meat that she could not use for anything else, from meat trimmings and from the extra bones she asked for—and received—from the butcher with each meat order. These with carrots and onions and a faggot were slowly simmered in water until all their flavors were extracted, after which the liquid was strained. Gentle cooking and careful skimming produced clear, tasty stock.

We kept the stock made from chicken and veal separate from that made from beef. The former was used as part of the liquid in cream soups and in white sauces, the latter went into soups such as Pot-au-Feu, Oxtail or Onion, and in more highly flavored sauces. I can't see any reason why a home where meat is served regularly would not have enough bones, trimmings and leftovers to have stock always on hand for cooking.

Soup in France, of course, is more often the whole meal than it is just one course. Not always the same kinds of soup, however, are eaten in all parts of the country. We Bourbonnais were partial to a good potage like St. Germain or Leek and Potato but I know other sections where the popular ones were clear soups with a bouillon base to which vegetables and vermicelli were added. But everywhere that I have been the two most universally popular were the Pot-au-Feu and Onion Soup.

To go with our soup we had crusty French bread fixed in various ways. For simple hearty soups, particularly the kinds that were not strained and were generously strewn with vegetables, we liked *croûte de pain*—bread crusts—which were nothing more or less than the crust of the loaf cut off in small thin slices and lightly toasted. (The center of the loaf was used for bread crumbs or croutons.) Another favorite for stock soups, always for Petite Marmite, were one-quarter inch slices of small crusty rolls. Cream soups usually had croutons served in them and these were small dice cut from the center part of the loaf and either fried in butter or toasted in the oven. And finally there were the thick slices of bread, sprinkled with cheese, that were floated in the tureen (or our individual bowls) of Onion Soup, having been browned in the oven and coming sizzling hot to the table.

CARROT SOUP
(Potage Purée de Carottes)

4 *or* 5 *medium carrots, minced*	½ *cup rice*
1 *medium onion, minced*	6 *cups white stock* (page 297)
3 *tablespoons butter*	*or water*
1 *teaspoon salt*	1 *cup hot milk, top milk preferred*
1 *tablespoon sugar*	*bread crusts* (page 293)

Put carrots and onion in a saucepan with 2 tablespoons butter, the salt and sugar. Cook slowly 15 minutes, mixing from time to time. Add rice, 4 cups of the stock (or water) and cook slowly until carrots are well done, about 45 minutes. Strain through a fine sieve, return liquid to pan and add remaining 2 cups stock (or water). Bring to a boil,

[11]

skim, if necessary, and add the milk with the remaining tablespoon of butter. Serve from a soup tureen with crusts of bread floating on top.

BEAN (WHITE OR BLACK) SOUP

There are dozens of different varieties of beans in France and all are used in making soup. After all, anything that can be kept as easily as dried beans can always be put to good use in the soup pot when other foods are scarce. But of all the good bean soups I ate at home I remember particularly the one we had each fall when the last beans of the garden were just starting to get a little dry on the vines. These were shelled and cooked for that delicious dish, Haricots à la Bourbonnaise, at which time my mother always saw to it that there would be enough left in the water to make into soup for our supper.

2 *cups dried beans*	2 *leeks, minced*
1½ *quarts water*	1 *onion, chopped*
1 *teaspoon butter*	¼ *lb. salt pork or a ham bone*
1 *tablespoon salt*	1 *faggot* (page 294)
1 *carrot, diced*	*a little pepper*

Clean and wash beans and soak 1 to 2 hours in enough cold water to cover. Drain, cover with the 1½ quarts water, add salt, bring to a boil and skim well. Melt butter in a saucepan, add carrot, leeks and onion and cook until golden brown. Add to beans. Add salt pork and faggot. Cook slowly until beans are well done, about 1 to 2 hours, the time needed to make them soft depending upon the beans. Discard faggot. Remove pork and reserve. Drain beans, reserve the liquid and rub the beans through a sieve. Return beans to the pan and add enough of the cooking liquid to make the soup the desired thickness. Correct the seasoning, add a little pepper and bring to a boil. If soup is too thick, thin it with a little milk. Slice or dice the pork and serve with the soup or save to serve with other foods. Croutons may be sprinkled on top if desired. Serves 6.

CABBAGE SOUP COUNTRY STYLE
(Soupe aux Choux)

Cabbage Soup is a real country dish and a favorite winter meal because it consists of all the vegetables that are stored for the winter to be used when fresh vegetables are not available in places far removed from big city markets. As you can see, this is a whole meal, the soup to be served first followed by the meat and vegetables.

2-3 *lbs. salt pork*
1 *ham bone*
1 *garlic sausage (if desired)*
3 *carrots*
2 *turnips, yellow or white*
4 *quarts water*
3 *onions*

4-5 *leeks*
2 *medium heads cabbage, Savoy or*
  winter, parboiled 10 *minutes*
5-6 *medium potatoes*
1 *teaspoon salt*
pepper

Put pork in a deep kettle, cover with water and boil 10 minutes. Drain and plunge into cold water. Drain. Replace pork in kettle with water, boil a few minutes, add salt and cook 1½ to 2 hours. Add sausages and all vegetables except potatoes. Cook ¾ to 1 hour, add potatoes and cook 30 minutes longer or until pork is well done. Correct seasoning and add a little pepper. Strain soup, skim off fat and serve with crusts of bread in it. Serve the salt pork and the sausage cut in slices and arranged in a serving dish around the cooked vegetables. Serves 5 to 6.

CREAM OF TOMATO SOUP
(Crème de Tomate)

2 *tablespoons butter*
1 *onion, chopped*
1 *carrot, chopped*
3 *tablespoons flour*
1 *quart chicken stock or water*
1 *small clove garlic*
2 *leeks, if obtainable*

4 *white peppercorns*
1 *teaspoon salt*
1 *tablespoon sugar*
6 *fresh tomatoes*
1 *cup canned tomatoes*
chicken bones, if available
1 *cup top milk or cream*

Melt butter in deep saucepan, add onion and carrot and cook slowly until golden brown. Add flour and mix. Add stock (or water), garlic, leeks, white peppercorns, salt, sugar, tomatoes and chicken bones (if used). Let cook over a low heat from 1 to 1½ hours, skimming as needed. Rub through a fine strainer, combine with the top milk and correct the seasoning. If the soup is too thick add a little more milk or stock to give desired consistency. Serve with cubes of bread which have been fried in butter or with cooked rice. Serves 4 to 6.

CROUTES AU POT

Croûtes au Pot, one of our very common French soups, is merely the stock from the Pot-au-Feu served with the carrots, turnips and leeks— cut in pieces an inch long—that were cooked in it. When the stock was skimmed to remove the fat, a little was always left in for Croûtes au Pot, just enough to make tiny glistening beads all over the surface of the soup. Served separately with it were always pieces of the crust of French bread spread with marrow taken from the pieces of bones that were cooked in the Pot-au-Feu.

LENTIL SOUP

Follow recipe for Bean Soup (page 12) substituting lentils for beans. Lentils need extra care in cleaning because there are always many little stones mixed in with them. They do not, as a rule, take as long to cook as beans, and usually will be done in an hour.

LEEK AND POTATO SOUP
(Potage Parmentier)

One of my earliest food memories is of my mother's good Leek and Potato Soup made with plump, tender leeks I pulled myself from our garden. They were much larger than any I can buy here, but I am glad to get leeks at all because when I first came to this country I actually couldn't find any—and what Frenchman can make soups without leeks? I finally persuaded one of my vegetable suppliers to find someone who would grow leeks for me. Now, fortunately for exacting cooks, every green-grocer sells them.

There are two variations of Leek and Potato Soup, *Potage Parmentier* which is strained and sometimes finished with eggs, and *Soupe Bonne Femme,* a less elegant version which is not strained and to which eggs are never added. My mother never fried croutons for the simple Bonne Femme version but cut the crisp crusts from the French bread and floated them on top.

4 *leeks (white part), minced*	3 *cups water*
1 *onion, finely minced*	1 *teaspoon salt*
2 *tablespoons butter*	3 *cups hot milk*
4 *potatoes, pared and chopped*	

Put leeks and onion in a saucepan with 1 tablespoon of the butter. If leeks are not available, substitute 2 onions, finely chopped. Cover and cook slowly a few minutes until they are soft, but do not allow them to become brown. Add potatoes, water and salt. Bring to a boil and cook slowly 30 to 35 minutes or until potatoes are very soft. Strain through a fine sieve. Return the strained purée to the pan, bring to a boil and add milk and remaining tablespoon of butter. Correct the seasoning. Serve with Croutons (page 294) if desired. Serves 4 to 6.

For a richer soup mix two egg yolks with ½ cup cream and combine with the hot soup. Bring to boiling point but do not allow to boil after adding the egg yolks.

LEEK AND POTATO SOUP
(Soupe Bonne Femme)

4 *leeks (white part), minced*	2 *teaspoons salt*
1 *small onion, finely minced*	4 *potatoes, peeled and minced*
2 *tablespoons butter*	2 *cups hot milk*
1 *quart water*	bread crusts (page 293)

Put leeks and onion in a saucepan with 1 tablespoon of butter. Cover and cook slowly a few minutes until they are soft, but do not allow to become brown. Add water, salt and potatoes. Cook slowly 40 minutes. When ready to serve, add milk and remaining tablespoon of butter. Correct the seasoning. Serve from a soup tureen with crusts of bread floating on top. Serves 4 to 6.

ONION SOUP
(Soupe à l'Oignon)

The French love to sit down to a meal of Onion Soup and never seem to tire of it. At home the earthenware casserole in which it was cooked was brought to the table and the soup dished from it into our pottery soup bowls. That is a custom worth adopting if you like, as we did, to come back for more of the rich bouillon with its succulent slices of onions. Sometimes my mother would make Onion Soup Gratiné and then she put the soup in the individual bowls, placing them in the oven to brown the cheese-topped crusts before the bowls were brought to the table.

2 *large onions, minced*	1 *teaspoon salt*
2 *tablespoons butter*	*little pepper*
1 *tablespoon flour*	bread crusts (page 293)
5 *pints stock* (page 297) *or water*	

Put onions in saucepan with the butter and cook slowly until golden. Add flour, mix and cook a few minutes. Add stock, salt and pepper and boil gently for 10 minutes. Serve from a soup tureen with bread crusts floating on top. If desired, sprinkle with grated cheese.

If preferred, this soup may be strained. It may also be made with half water (or stock) and half milk, in which case, heat the milk and add it to the soup just before serving. Serves 6 to 8.

[15]

ONION SOUP GRATINE
(Soupe à l'Oignon Gratiné)

Follow recipe for Soupe à l'Oignon. When soup is ready to serve, turn it into an oven-proof casserole, put crusts of bread on top and sprinkle them with grated Parmesan or Swiss cheese. Put in a hot oven until the cheese has melted and browned.

PANADES

A *panade* is a potage thickened with bread and finished with egg— the egg gives richness and seems to make the texture just right. It is a very tasty soup but one which I have never seen served in any but French homes. Panades were considered especially good breakfast soups. My mother's recipes all call for half a pound of bread because she bought her bread by the pound. One-half pound equals about 8 slices of the average American baker's sliced bread.

PANADE WITH CELERY

Follow recipe for Panade with Sorrel (below) substituting 2 cups finely diced celery for the sorrel. Add 3 tablespoons of water to the butter and cook the celery slowly in it until soft but not brown, then proceed as for the Panade with Sorrel recipe. Serves 6.

PANADE WITH LEEKS

Follow recipe for Panade with Sorrel (below) substituting 2 cups white part of leeks, finely minced, for the sorrel. Cook the leeks slowly in the butter until they are soft but not brown, then proceed as for the Panade with Sorrel recipe. Serves 6.

PANADE WITH SORREL

2 *cups sorrel, well cleaned and shredded*	½ *lb.* (8 *slices) stale white bread, cut in pieces*
2 *tablespoons butter*	2 *cups milk (part cream, if available)*
1 *quart warm water*	1 *large or 2 small eggs, lightly beaten*
1 *teaspoon salt*	

Put sorrel in saucepan with 1 tablespoon of the butter. Cover and cook slowly until sorrel is cooked down to about ½ cup. Add water, salt and bread. Mix well so that bread will become thoroughly soaked, then bring mixture to a boil, stirring all the time. Let cook slowly for a half hour longer, stirring from time to time. At this point beat briskly with a whip to make the mixture smooth. Add the milk to the eggs and combine with the hot mixture and add the butter. Bring back to boiling point, but do not allow to boil. Correct the seasoning and serve immediately. Serves 6.

OXTAIL SOUP
(Potage de Queue de Boeuf)

1 *oxtail (about 2 lbs.) cut in 1-inch sections*
2 *tablespoons beef fat*
1 *medium onion, sliced*
1 *faggot made of 1 leek, 2 sprigs parsley, 2 stalks celery*
½ *cup diced (or round) carrots*
2 *tablespoons flour*

2 *teaspoons salt*
2 *quarts water or stock*
½ *cup diced (or round) turnips*
1 *teaspoon dry herbs, mixed marjoram, rosemary, sage, basil, thyme and ½ bay leaf*
1 *glass sherry or Madeira (optional)*
4-5 *peppercorns*

Parboil oxtail for 2 or 3 minutes, drain off water and wipe the sections dry. Put fat in saucepan and when melted add oxtail, sliced onion and carrot and cook until all are golden brown. Add flour, mix well, add stock (or water), salt, peppercorns and faggot. Bring to a boil, skim well and simmer for about 4 hours, skimming as needed. Tie carrots and turnips in cheesecloth and cook during last hour or cook them in a separate pan. Strain the soup through cheesecloth on which the herbs have been placed, pouring carefully to prevent any sediment in the bottom of the pan from clouding it. The pieces of oxtail will remain in the bottom of the pan and should be removed with a spoon to the tureen. Correct the seasoning of the strained soup, add the cooked carrots and turnip, add the wine (if used) and pour over the oxtail. Serves 6.

PEA SOUP
(Potage St. Germain)

Pea Soup was seldom called "Potage de Pois" but usually "Potage St. Germain." The reason is that exceptionally good green peas grow abundantly in St. Germain, a place not very far from Paris and the French like to honor a town that has some special virtue by naming a dish for it.

You will find the flavor and color of this soup made of dried peas greatly improved if a cup of fresh green peas (or the pods of very young tender peas) which have been cooked until soft and then rubbed through a sieve are added to the soup after it has been strained. The pods, if young and tender, are particularly good. We would have this soup the day before or after we had Leek and Potato Soup because it uses up the green part of the leeks that are left.

[17]

2 cups split peas
5 cups water
1 teaspoon salt
2 tablespoons butter
½ cup fat salt pork, finely chopped
1 medium onion, chopped
1 medium carrot, chopped

2 leeks, green part
1 bay leaf
a little thyme
1 cup spinach leaves or green lettuce
    leaves
bread croutons (page 294)

Soak peas in water to cover about 1 hour. Drain, put in a saucepan with 4 cups of water and salt. Bring to a boil, skim, cover and cook slowly while preparing the following: melt 1 tablespoon butter in a saucepan, add salt pork and onion and cook until it melts and starts to brown. Add carrot, leeks, spinach or lettuce leaves, bay leaf and thyme and cook for a few minutes. Add to the split peas. Continue cooking all together for about 1 hour or until peas are soft. Rub through a sieve, add remaining cup of water (or a cup of bouillon or stock) if the soup is very thick. Bring to a boil, skim, correct the seasoning, adding a little sugar if desired. Add remaining tablespoon of butter. Serve with croutons. Serves 6.

POT-AU-FEU

No book on French cooking could be written that disregarded the Pot-au-Feu, the one dish that for centuries has regularly appeared, usually on Sundays, in every French home. Its savory fragrance and robust flavor is loved alike by the poor and the rich, and by city folk as much as by their country cousins. And the tall clay casserole called a *marmite* in which the Pot-au-Feu is cooked is as essential in a French kitchen as a stove on which to cook.

As a rule, enough meat and vegetables are put in the Pot-au-Feu to last two meals and there is usually stock left for the base of soups or sauces to follow on other days. Rump of beef, fresh plate or chuck— from ½ to ¾ pound of meat with bone for each quart of water—are the best cuts of meat for Pot-au-Feu. Then in addition every good housewife saves the carcasses of chickens she may have served and adds them to the pot. Or if chicken salad, vol-au-vent or other cooked chicken dish is planned for another day, the fowl is cooked in the Pot-au-Feu because the chicken flavor makes the stock extra delicious.

In serving Pot-au-Feu, some like slices of the meat, the vegetables and the soup put all together in the soup bowl. Others prefer to eat the soup separately and follow it with the sliced meat and vegetables.

But always very, very thin slices of small dry crusty rolls are eaten in the soup.

3-3½ *lbs. meat and bone (rump or*	5-6 *leeks*
fresh plate of beef)	2 *stalks celery*
4½ *quarts water*	1 *onion*
2 *tablespoons salt*	*a little thyme*
2-3 *carrots*	½ *bay leaf*
1 *turnip*	1 *clove*
1 *small parsnip*	

Cover meat and bones with water, bring to a boil and parboil 5 minutes. Remove meat and bones, discard water and clean pot. Put back the meat, bones, the 4½ quarts water and salt and bring very slowly to a boil, skimming all the time until the scum stops rising to the top. Boil very gently for 1½ hours, add vegetables (which have been cleaned and cut in pieces of any desired size) and cook for 2½ hours longer. Skim off the fat and correct the seasoning. Remove as much bouillon as desired for serving, remove meat, slicing enough for serving, and the vegetables. Strain remaining bouillon through cheese-cloth or fine sieve, let cool and keep in refrigerator for use in soups or sauces. To make the bouillon a good brown color, brown an onion, sprinkled with a very little sugar, in butter in a frying pan and add to the soup.

Instead of parboiling the meat and bones, they may be started in the cooking water reserving 2 cups of the water to be added after the soup has begun to boil. This brings the scum more quickly to the top. Done this way the soup stock, however, will not be quite as clear. Serves 6.

POTATO AND SORREL SOUP
(Potage à l'Oseille)

Follow recipe for Potato and Leek Soup (page 14) adding 2 cups sorrel which has been cleaned and shredded. Cook the sorrel with the onion and leeks until it is well cooked down then proceed as for Potato and Leek Soup. Or add 1 tablespoon Preserved Sorrel (page 200) to each 2 cups Potato and Leek Soup.

PUMPKIN SOUP
(Potage de Potiron)

Pumpkin Soup is another one of those dishes that are extremely popular in many parts of France and seldom seen on American tables.

[19]

At home my mother used pumpkin exclusively for soup. Oddly enough, I never saw a pumpkin pie until I came to this country.

2 *cups pumpkin, pared and cut in*
  dice
2 *cups water*
1 *tablespoon sugar*

2 *tablespoons butter*
½ *teaspoon salt*
3 *cups milk*

Put pumpkin, water, 1 tablespoon butter, sugar, and salt in a saucepan, bring to a boil and cook 15 minutes or until pumpkin is soft. Rub through a sieve, add milk and bring back to a boil. Correct the seasoning, and add remaining tablespoon of butter. Serve with tapioca that has been cooked in it or with crusts of bread on top. Serves 4 to 6.

SHEPHERD'S SOUP
(Soupe Bergère)

1 *tablespoon butter*
½ *cup fat salt pork in small dice*
1 *small turnip, pared and minced*
2 *leeks (white part), minced*
1 *onion, minced*

1 *carrot, minced*
5 *cups stock (or water)*
3 *potatoes, pared and minced*
12-18 *slices of bread, toasted*

Melt butter in a saucepan, add salt pork and cook until it is melted and starts to brown. Add turnip, leeks, onion and carrot and cook very slowly about ½ hour. Add stock (or water) and potatoes, bring to a boil and cook slowly about 35 minutes or until potatoes are soft. Correct the seasoning and serve in a tureen with toasted bread floating on top. Serves 6.

SORREL SOUP
(Soupe à l'Oseille)

1 *cup well-cleaned and shredded*
  sorrel
2 *tablespoons butter*
1 *tablespoon flour*
1 *quart water*

½ *teaspoon salt*
2 *cups milk (part cream, if available)*
1 *large or 2 small eggs, slightly*
  beaten
bread crusts (page 293)

Put sorrel in saucepan with 1 tablespoon butter. Cover and cook slowly until sorrel is cooked down to about ½ cup. Add the flour, mix all together, then add water and salt and cook slowly 15 minutes. Mix together milk and eggs and combine with the soup. Add remaining butter and bring back to boiling point, stirring constantly, but do not allow to boil. Correct the seasoning. Serve from a soup tureen with the crusts of bread floating on top. Serves 4 to 5.

TURNIP AND POTATO SOUP
(Soupe de Rave)

We grew a special kind of white turnip, called *"les raves,"* which were never hard nor woody. They grew so very fast that they matured in only a month and had a delicate and unusually sweet flavor. If, however, your turnips do not break away to a pulp when you make this soup strain it before adding the milk.

3 *young white turnips, pared and minced*	1 *teaspoon salt*
	5 *cups water*
3 *medium potatoes, pared and minced*	2 *tablespoons butter*
	1½ *cups milk*

Put turnips, potatoes, salt, water and 1 tablespoon of butter in saucepan. Bring to a boil and cook over a brisk fire ½ hour or until the potatoes are soft. Remove from fire and if the vegetables have not broken into a pulp, mash them or run the mixture through a sieve. Add milk, bring back to a boil, correct the seasoning and add remaining tablespoon of butter. Serves 4 to 5.

Sauces

❖

SAUCES, like soups, are part and parcel of everyday French home cooking. Without them the small amounts of meat and the odds and ends of leftovers which are the backbone of so many French meals would never stretch over the plates that must be filled each meal. It is her knack with sauces which makes the *bonne ménagère* able to turn any inexpensive cut of meat into a real delicacy and to produce sauced specialties every bit as good as the ones served in popular restaurants.

Essentially a sauce—that is, the kind which this chapter covers—is nothing more than a thickened liquid. Actually, making a sauce requires all possible skill and ingenuity to produce a combination which is delicious in itself and at the same time brings out the best flavors of the food it accompanies. But even that is not enough. A good sauce must have good texture, too. It must have just the right thickness and always be smooth. *Pas de grumeaux.* Lumps? But never. My mother would have been as ashamed of a lumpy sauce as of a dirty kitchen.

Most sauces start with a roux which is a mixture of fat and flour—as a rule equal parts of each. The flour is cooked in the fat, moving it around in the pan all the time to prevent scorching. The first few minutes of cooking, before there is any change in color, produces a white roux; longer cooking, to the point where it just starts to turn golden, makes a blond roux; further cooking, in which it takes on a good brown color, results in a brown roux. Each has its place in cooking, depending upon the liquid it thickens. Each can be made up and kept in a covered jar in the refrigerator for a week or more. I remember, for example, that when my mother bought fresh butter she would use what was left in the crock from the previous supply to make up some roux to have on hand for sauces.

Some sauces are thickened with Manié Butter which is made by creaming—instead of cooking—together the butter and flour, usually twice as much butter as flour. This is used when it is desirable to add the thickening at the end of cooking, often in stews and fish dishes.

Different fats—meat fats and vegetable shortenings—may be used in sauces, but for the most part butter is preferred and in delicately flavored sauces is considered essential. The kind of fat will not affect the texture but will change the flavor and it is the butter flavor which French people always want; fooling them with other fat flavors is almost impossible. But for the base of a sauce dozens of different liquids can be used—milk, tomatoes, stock made from meat or fish, meat juices, liquor from cooking vegetables and combinations of these liquids.

You will probably notice how much more liquid, usually twice as much or more, is called for in these French recipes for sauces than in American ones. And if you could watch the sauce being made you would see how much more time goes into its making because all the surplus liquid must be reduced by longer cooking. It is this concentration and blending of ingredients that develops the fine rich flavor.

Sauces of the Mayonnaise and Hollandaise type are a little out of the ordinary because they are not thickened in the conventional way with flour. They depend upon an emulsion of egg yolks and oil or butter to give the right consistency. They require somewhat more care and precision in mixing since good results depend upon adding the oil —or butter, as the case may be—very slowly.

Anyone who has mastered the technique of making good sauces, who has acquired that subtle sense of taste which recognizes the difference between good and poor texture and flavor in a sauce, has gone far on the road to good cooking. Care, patience and constant trying for perfection in combining ingredients will develop this quality, more than stilted recipes.

Hot Sauces

AU GRATIN SAUCE

¾ cup white wine
1 teaspoon finely chopped shallot
½ cup Brown Sauce (page 24)
   (or Tomato Sauce, page 31)

2 tablespoons Duxelles (page 185)
1 teaspoon chopped parsley

Cook wine and shallots until reduced to about 3 tablespoons. Add

Brown Sauce and Duxelles and boil 5 minutes. Add chopped parsley. Au Gratin Sauce is used for fish or vegetables.

BECHAMEL SAUCE

Béchamel Sauce, a simple combination of butter, flour and milk, is a foundation sauce which everyone should know how to make. An onion cooked in it gives added flavor, and other seasonings such as mustard are often added. For a richer sauce it can be combined with eggs, cream, cheese and so on. Béchamel Sauce, or any of its variations, is served on vegetables, fish, hard-cooked eggs, poultry and other cooked foods.

⅓ cup butter	1 teaspoon salt
½ medium onion, minced	few grains white pepper
⅓ cup flour	2 sprigs parsley
3 cups hot milk	a little nutmeg

Melt butter in a saucepan, add onion and cook until onion becomes very light brown. Add flour, cook a few minutes longer, add milk and seasoning, stirring vigorously. Cook gently 25 to 30 minutes, stirring constantly until sauce is thick and smooth and then occasionally for the remaining time. Strain. If sauce is not to be used immediately, stir occasionally as it cools to prevent a crust forming on top.

BORDELAISE SAUCE

¾ cup red wine	1 cup Brown Sauce (below)
1 tablespoon chopped shallots	1 tablespoon butter (or butter and
a little thyme	substitute)
1 bay leaf	½ cup fresh beef marrow
3 peppercorns	chopped parsley

Cook wine, shallots, thyme, bay leaf and peppercorns until reduced to about 2 tablespoons. Add Brown Sauce and boil gently for 10 minutes. Strain. Add butter. Cut marrow in small pieces and poach in boiling salted water for 1 or 2 minutes and add to sauce. Add chopped parsley just before serving.

BROWN SAUCE
(Sauce Brune)

Brown Sauce is another foundation sauce which if kept on hand can be added to stews, leftover dishes and to many sauces. It thickens them and at the same time gives a full rich flavor. To brown the bones, put them in a shallow pan in a hot oven and leave until they have taken on a good, brown color. Any gravy left over from a roast can be used as part of the stock. This sauce may be kept for a week in a covered jar in the refrigerator. To keep it longer, boil it up again, and wash the jar well before putting the sauce back in it.

⅓ cup fat (*beef or veal preferred*)	1 *stalk celery*
1 *onion, chopped*	1 *bay leaf*
1 *carrot, diced*	*a little thyme*
⅓ cup flour	1 *clove garlic*
3 *cups brown stock*	½ *teaspoon salt*
1 *cup canned* (*or* 3 *fresh*) *tomatoes*	3 *or* 4 *peppercorns*
2 *sprigs parsley*	

Prepare stock by cooking browned bones (and meat, if available) in water, or use bouillon cubes and water. Melt fat, add onion and carrot and cook until golden brown. Add flour and cook until a good deep brown. Add stock and tomatoes and boil, stirring all the time, until flour and fat are combined with the liquid. Add herbs, garlic, salt and peppercorns and cook gently, skimming when necessary, for about 2 hours, when there should be about 2 cups of sauce left. Strain, let cool and use as needed.

CAPER SAUCE
(Sauce Câpres)

1 *tablespoon capers*   1 *cup Cream Sauce* (below)
1 *teaspoon chopped parsley*

Add capers and parsley to hot Cream Sauce.

CREAM SAUCE
(Sauce Crème)

2 *cups Béchamel Sauce* (page 24)   ½ *tablespoon lemon juice*
1 *cup top milk or cream*

Cook Béchamel Sauce until reduced to about 1 cup. Add the top milk (or cream) and lemon juice. Cook, stirring constantly, until it just starts to boil. Use with fish, chicken, poultry, eggs and vegetables.

DEVIL SAUCE
(Sauce Diable)

Devil Sauce is particularly good if meat gravy left over from roast beef or veal or poultry is used instead of the stock called for in the recipe. Unless, however, the stock—or the gravy—is of good flavor and color I think it is better to use tomatoes.

1 *shallot, chopped*

3 *tablespoons vinegar (with tarra-*
gon, if available)

½ *cup stock (or ½ cup canned*
tomatoes)

1 *tablespoon butter*

1 *tablespoon flour*

a little salt and pepper

a little cayenne

½ *teaspoon chopped parsley, tarra-*
gon and chervil

Put shallots and vinegar in saucepan and reduce to almost nothing. Add stock (or tomatoes), bring to a boil. Thicken with Manié Butter, made by creaming together butter and flour and adding to sauce. Bring to a boil, stirring constantly. Correct the seasoning and add parsley, tarragon and chervil.

EGG SAUCE
(Sauce aux Oeufs)

2 *tablespoons butter*

1½ *tablespoons flour*

1 *cup hot milk*

salt and pepper

a little nutmeg

1 *hard-boiled egg, cut in small*
pieces

chopped parsley

Melt butter in saucepan, add flour and cook, stirring until it starts to turn a golden brown. Add milk and cook, stirring constantly, until thickened. Add egg and parsley.

HOLLANDAISE SAUCE

There are three rules which can never be overlooked in making Hollandaise and Béarnaise Sauces. One is to stir briskly all the time; the second is never to have the fire too hot or, if a double boiler is used, never allow the water to boil in the bottom of it; and the last is to add the butter slowly, making sure it is thoroughly combined and smooth after each addition. Disregard any of these rules and nine chances out of ten you will have scrambled eggs instead of Hollandaise.

3 *egg yolks*

1 *tablespoon water*

½ *lb. melted butter*

Cook water and egg yolks in a double boiler stirring briskly with a wire whip or slotted spoon until creamy. Remove top of double boiler to a warm place (or add a little cold water to that in the bottom of

the double boiler) and add butter very slowly, stirring all the time.
To make the sauce lighter, add 1 tablespoon hot water. Season to taste.
Strain through a fine sieve or cheesecloth. Add lemon juice to taste
when serving this sauce with fish.

BEARNAISE SAUCE

Bearnaise is merely a highly flavored Hollandaise, and the same care
used in making Hollandaise must be followed in making Béarnaise.

¼ cup tarragon vinegar
2 shallots, chopped
3 sprigs tarragon
4 peppercorns, crushed
¼ cup white wine (optional)

3 egg yolks, slightly beaten
½ lb. melted butter
½ teaspoon salt
cayenne pepper

Remove leaves from stems of tarragon and chervil. Mix together
vinegar, shallots, chopped stems of tarragon and chervil, peppercorns
and wine and cook until reduced to a thick paste. Mix egg yolks with
1 tablespoon water and combine with the paste. Whip together like
Hollandaise over very low heat (or in the top of a double boiler with
water kept just below the boiling point). When creamy, add butter
very slowly, stirring constantly. Add a very little cayenne pepper and
the salt. Strain through a fine sieve or cheesecloth and add the chopped
leaves of the tarragon and chervil.

ITALIAN SAUCE
(Sauce Italienne)

Follow recipe for Au Gratin Sauce replacing white wine with
Marsala and adding 2 chopped tomatoes and, if available, 2 tablespoons chopped ham. Use for sautéed meat and poultry.

MADEIRA SAUCE
(Sauce Madère)

2 cups Brown Sauce (page 24)   ½ cup Madeira (or sherry)

If Brown Sauce is thin, cook until it is reduced to about 1½ cups.
Add wine and bring to the boiling point but do not allow to boil. Boiling spoils the flavor of Madeira Sauce. Use for roast ham, ox tongue,
filet of beef or sautéed meats.

MANIE BUTTER
(Beurre Manié)

Manié Butter is not really a sauce. It is a convenient thickening that

[27]

can be added at the end of the cooking. It is used for example in making a sauce from the liquid in which fish has been poached. Or a stew or fricassee that requires thickening when it is about done. I remember my mother often added a bit of Manié Butter to the few spoonfuls of water left when peas or green beans were done just before she took the vegetables off the fire. This was tasty and the cooking liquor wasn't wasted. A chef uses Cream Sauce for the final thickening of many of his sauces because he always has it ready on the back of his stove but a housewife can substitute Manié Butter with excellent results and much more conveniently.

It is difficult to give exact amounts of Manié Butter needed but you will soon learn about how much is required for different amounts of liquid. Use discretion, of course. A thick pasty sauce is never desirable. And remember that after Manié Butter is added the mixture is brought to the boiling point only, not allowed to boil.

Rub together until smooth and creamy equal parts of butter and flour; or twice as much butter as flour; or three times as much butter as flour. The proportion used depends upon how much butter went into the mixture at the beginning.

MINT SAUCE

2 teaspoons fresh or dried mint,   ½ cup vinegar (preferably white)
    chopped fine   4 tablespoons hot water
1 tablespoon sugar   a little salt and pepper

Mix all together and stir until sugar is dissolved. Serve with Roast Lamb.

MORNAY SAUCE
(Sauce Mornay)

Mornay Sauce is used especially for eggs, fish, and vegetables au gratin. In using Mornay Sauce on top of a dish to be browned, it is greatly improved if a tablespoon of whipped cream is folded into the ½ cup of sauce which is spread over the top of the dish. The top will then have an even golden brown glaze all over it.

2 cups Sauce Béchamel (page 24)   ½ cup grated Parmesan or Gruyère
2 egg yolks   cheese
                                   1 tablespoon butter

Heat Béchamel Sauce and combine with egg yolks. Stir constantly
[28]

and remove from fire as soon as it starts to boil. Add cheese and butter and stir until all is thoroughly mixed. This sauce cannot be boiled or it will curdle and lose its good flavor.

MUSHROOM SAUCE
(Sauce aux Champignons)

3 *tablespoons butter or salad oil*
6 *mushrooms, cleaned and chopped*
1 *teaspoon finely chopped shallots*
½ *cup white wine*
1 *cup Brown Sauce* (page 24)

1 *medium tomato, fresh or canned,*
  chopped
1 *teaspoon chopped parsley, chervil,*
  and tarragon
1 *tablespoon butter*

Put butter (or oil) and chopped mushrooms in saucepan and cook gently until mushrooms start to turn golden. Add shallots and cook a few seconds longer. Add wine and cook until reduced to about one-half the original quantity. Add Brown Sauce and tomatoes and boil gently for 5 or 6 minutes. Remove from fire, add the remaining butter and herbs.

MUSTARD SAUCE
(Sauce Moutarde)

1 *tablespoon butter*
1 *tablespoon flour*
1 *cup hot milk*
1 *slice onion*

a little salt
a little pepper
1 *teaspoon prepared mustard*
few drops lemon juice

Melt butter in saucepan, add flour and cook until it just starts to turn golden. Add milk, onion, salt and pepper and cook, stirring constantly until it thickens, then continue cooking, stirring occasionally until reduced to about two-thirds the original quantity. Add mustard and lemon juice. Strain the sauce or remove the onion before serving.

PIQUANTE SAUCE

You may often wish to make Piquante Sauce at a time when you do not have any Brown Sauce on hand. In that case substitute the same amount of canned tomatoes and thicken with Manié Butter made by creaming together two tablespoons butter with 1 tablespoon flour.

½ *cup vinegar*
1 *tablespoon finely chopped shallots*
  (*or onion*)
1¼ *cups Brown Sauce* (page 24)

3 *tablespoons chopped sour pickles*
1 *teaspoon chopped parsley*
a little chopped tarragon, if available

[29]

Cook vinegar and shallots in saucepan until reduced to about 3 tablespoons. Add Brown Sauce and boil gently for 10 minutes. When ready to serve add chopped pickles, parsley and tarragon, but do not allow to boil after adding pickles and herbs.

PROVENCAL SAUCE FOR MEAT
(Sauce Provençale)

2 tablespoons butter
1 onion, chopped
3 shallots, chopped (if available)
2 tablespoons flour
½ glass white wine (if available)
1 cup meat stock

2-3 tomatoes, peeled, seeded and chopped (or ½ cup canned)
1 clove garlic, crushed
1 faggot (page 294)
¼ cup chopped cooked ham
½ teaspoon horseradish

Melt butter in saucepan, add onion and cook until golden. Add shallots and flour and cook just a minute or two. Add wine and stock and bring to a boil, stirring until smooth. Add tomato, garlic and faggot and cook slowly about 30 minutes. Strain, rubbing everything through the sieve. Return to fire, bring to a boil and add ham and horseradish. Correct the seasoning and pour over sliced meat.

RAIFORD SAUCE

3 tablespoons grated horseradish
½ cup stock (or water)
1 tablespoon butter
1 tablespoon flour
½ cup boiling water
½ teaspoon salt

3 tablespoons fresh bread crumbs
3 tablespoons cream (or top milk)
1 egg yolk, beaten
2 tablespoons vinegar
a little pepper
1 teaspoon prepared mustard

Cook horseradish slowly in stock (or water). Melt butter, add flour and cook a few minutes. Add boiling water and cook, stirring until smooth. Add salt, horseradish mixture, bread crumbs and cream (or top milk). Boil a few minutes, stirring everything together. Mix egg yolk with vinegar and combine with sauce, but do not boil. Correct seasoning, add pepper and mustard. To keep warm put in top of double boiler over hot water.

SHALLOT SAUCE
(Sauce Echalote)

¾ cup white wine
1 tablespoon chopped shallots
1½ cups Velouté (page 32)

2 tablespoons butter
1 teaspoon lemon juice

Cook wine and shallots until reduced to about 2 tablespoons. Add

Velouté Sauce and boil gently for 5 minutes. Remove from fire, add butter and lemon juice.

RAVIGOTE SAUCE

Sauce Ravigote is used for fish and poultry. It is especially good for leftovers or for meat specialties like brains.

4 tablespoons vinegar (tarragon vinegar, if available)
4 tablespoons white wine (optional)
1 tablespoon finely chopped shallots
2 cups Velouté (page 32)

2 tablespoons butter or butter substitute
1 teaspoon chopped chervil, tarragon and chives

Cook vinegar, wine and shallots until reduced to about 2 tablespoons. Add Velouté and boil gently for 5 to 6 minutes. Remove from heat and add butter and herbs.

ROBERT SAUCE

Follow recipe for Sauce Piquante, replacing shallots with chopped onion and slicing instead of chopping the pickles. Add 1 tablespoon prepared mustard before serving.

TOMATO SAUCE

Tomato Sauce is a foundation sauce and one that is used in many, many dishes. Anyone who does much cooking will want to keep it on hand. It can be kept in the refrigerator in a covered jar for a week and like Brown Sauce can then be cooked up again and put in a clean jar to keep it longer.

2 tablespoons butter
1 small carrot, chopped
½ onion, chopped
a little thyme
1 bay leaf
⅓ cup flour

2 cups canned tomatoes (or 4 or 5 fresh)
1½ cups stock or water
½ teaspoon salt
a little pepper
1 teaspoon sugar
2 cloves garlic, crushed

Melt butter, add carrot, onion, thyme and bay leaf and let cook until golden brown. Add flour and cook until it is golden. Add tomatoes, stock, garlic, salt, pepper and sugar. Boil, stirring constantly until it thickens, then cook slowly for about 1 to 1½ hours. Strain. Bring back to a boil and cook 4 or 5 minutes more, stirring constantly.

VELOUTE

Velouté is another foundation sauce which acts as the base of many other sauces. It can also be used in making croquettes. Like Brown and Tomato Sauce it, too, can be kept covered in the refrigerator for a week and then boiled up and put in a clean jar to keep it longer.

⅓ *cup butter*
⅓ *cup flour*
3 *cups white stock* (*part of this may be liquid in which mushrooms were cooked*)

½ *teaspoon salt*
2 *or 3 peppercorns*
1 *sprig parsley*
few gratings nutmeg

Prepare stock by cooking veal or chicken bones (and meat if available) in water or use chicken bouillon cubes and water. Melt butter (or substitute), add flour and cook, but do not let brown. Add stock and cook, stirring all the time until flour and fat are combined with the liquid. Add remaining ingredients and cook gently about 1 hour when there should be 2 cups of sauce. Strain, cool and use as needed.

POIVRADE SAUCE FOR GAME

Mix together 8 crushed peppercorns with ½ cup vinegar and cook until reduced to ¼ cup. Add 1 cup Brown Sauce (page 24) (or leftover thickened gravy). Boil slowly ½ hour and add 2 tablespoons red currant jelly. Strain and serve with game.

Butter Sauces

Butter sauces are the simplest and easiest sauces to make and are particularly appropriate on sautéed foods. In making Brown Butter or Polonaise Sauce there is a hazard in the fact that butter burns very easily. This means that in making either one of them you must keep your eye on it every minute because once scorched, it develops a bitter flavor and is ruined.

BROWN BUTTER SAUCE
(Beurre Noisette)

Noisette means hazelnut. Melt butter and cook gently until hazel-

[32]

nut brown in color. Serve with sautéed fish or meat or any "Meunière"
dish.

MAITRE D'HOTEL BUTTER

½ cup butter　　　　　　　　　　½ teaspoon salt
1 teaspoon chopped parsley　　　　juice of ½ lemon

Mix together all ingredients, stirring until creamy.

POLONAISE SAUCE

2 tablespoons butter　　　　　　　1 tablespoon fine, fresh breadcrumbs

Melt butter and cook gently until hazelnut brown in color, add
bread crumbs and cook until the crumbs are brown. The butter will
stop bubbling when it is ready to serve—will "fall down." Serve with
meat, fish or vegetables, with or without finely chopped parsley and
a few drops of lemon juice sprinkled over the top. For asparagus,
cauliflower, etc., chopped hard-boiled egg may also be sprinkled over
the top.

SHALLOT BUTTER SAUCE

3 tablespoons finely chopped shallots　½ cup butter
1 glass white wine

Cook shallots in wine until the liquid is reduced to almost nothing.
Add this to the butter, crushing the shallots as they are combined so
that the mixture will be smooth.

Cold Sauces

Most of the cold sauces—with the exception of Mayonnaise—are very
highly flavored and seasoned. Acids such as vinegar and lemon juice,
also herbs, capers and mustard are commonly used ingredients because cold sauces are so often served on cold, bland foods which need
their spicy sharpness. Any of the following are good with fish.

CREAM MUSTARD

1 teapsoon prepared mustard　　　few drops lemon juice
a little salt　　　　　　　　　　½ cup cream
a little pepper

Mix together mustard, salt, pepper and lemon juice. Add cream little by little, stirring vigorously until well combined.

GREEN SAUCE FOR FISH

leaves from 15 watercress sprigs
2 cups Mayonnaise (below)
12 leaves of spinach

8 parsley tops
a little tarragon and chervil

Wash all the leaves well. Cover with boiling salted water and let stand 5 or 6 minutes. Drain, put in cold water and drain again, pressing out all the surplus water. Rub the wilted leaves through a fine strainer and combine with mayonnaise. Mix well. Add seasoning to taste, if needed.

GRIBICHE SAUCE

3 hard-boiled eggs
½ teaspoon salt
1 teaspoon mustard
a little pepper
1½ cups olive oil or salad oil
½ cup vinegar

3 small sour pickles, finely chopped
    (about ⅓ cup)
1 tablespoon mixed, chopped pars-
    ley, chervil, tarragon and chives
    (if obtainable)

Separate eggs and crush yolks in a bowl to make a smooth purée. Add salt, mustard and pepper. Add oil little by little, stirring vigorously as in making mayonnaise. Add vinegar, and when thoroughly combined, add egg whites which have been cut into fine dice, the well drained pickles, parsley, chervil, tarragon and chives.

MAYONNAISE

Mayonnaise must be mixed very carefully or it will separate. The trick lies in adding the oil very, very slowly. And I have found that having both the eggs and the oil at room temperature when you start to mix it helps hold it together. If mayonnaise is to be kept for several days, another safeguard is to add a tablespoon of boiling water after mixing. Mayonnaise also separates if stored in an automatic refrigerator which is so cold that the oil solidifies.

4 egg yolks
½ teaspoon salt
a little pepper

1 tablespoon vinegar (or ½ teaspoon
    lemon juice)
1 pint olive or salad oil
1 teapsoon dry mustard

Rinse a bowl in hot water and dry thoroughly. Put in egg yolks, salt, pepper and mustard and a few drops of vinegar. Mix well. Add oil drop by drop, mixing all the time until 5 or 6 tablespoons have been added. Add a few more drops of vinegar and then more oil, little by little, until all is added, putting in remaining vinegar as the dressing thickens.

REMOULADE SAUCE

2 *sour pickles, finely chopped (about* ½ *cup)*
2 *tablespoons capers, finely chopped*
1 *tablespoon prepared mustard*

1 *tablespoon mixed, chopped parsley, tarragon and chervil*
2 *cups mayonnaise*

The pickles and capers must be very finely chopped and all moisture pressed out of them. Combine all ingredients and mix well.

TARTAR SAUCE
Same as Rémoulade Sauce.

VINAIGRETTE SAUCE

1 *tablespoon vinegar*
3 *tablespoons olive or salad oil*

a little salt and pepper
a little dry mustard

Combine all ingredients and mix well.

VINAIGRETTE SAUCE WITH FINES HERBES

1 *tablespoon vinegar*
3 *tablespoons olive or salad oil*
¼ *teaspoon prepared mustard*

1 *teaspoon mixed chopped parsley, tarragon, chervil and chives*

Combine all ingredients and mix well. To serve with calf's-head, brains, etc., add ½ onion finely chopped.

VINAIGRETTE WITH MUSTARD

1 *teaspoon prepared mustard*
a little salt
a little pepper

1 *teaspoon lemon juice or 1 tablespoon vinegar*
4 *tablespoons olive or salad oil*

Mix together mustard, salt, pepper, and lemon juice (or vinegar). Add oil little by little, stirring vigorously until well combined.

Substitute Sauces

The following sauces are good substitutes for Béarnaise and Hollandaise when butter is scarce or too expensive to use in large amounts. In the substitute Béarnaise Sauce the tarragon flavor is essential.

[35]

If fresh or dried tarragon is not available, then use tarragon vinegar. A little chopped parsley, however, may be substituted for the chervil.

Sauce Blanche should never be allowed to boil because this always seems to give it a floury taste. When used with vegetables like asparagus or broccoli, including lemon juice or not is a matter of taste, the French preferring it plain and Americans liking the lemon flavor. But when it is to be used with fish the lemon juice is necessary.

SUBSTITUTE BEARNAISE

2 *stalks tarragon*
2 *stalks chervil*
1 *teaspoon chopped shallots*
2 *tablespoons vinegar*

½ *cup Béchamel Sauce* (page 24)
1 *egg yolk, lightly beaten*
¼ *cup butter*

Remove leaves from tarragon and chervil stalks, chop leaves and reserve them to add later. Put stems and shallots in vinegar and cook until reduced to almost nothing. Add Béchamel Sauce and cook a few minutes. Combine with egg yolk but do not let boil. Add butter little by little, combining each addition thoroughly before adding the next. Strain through cheesecloth. Add finely chopped tarragon and chervil leaves.

SAUCE BLANCHE
(A Substitute Hollandaise)

1 *tablespoon butter*
1 *tablespoon flour*
1 *cup hot water*
½ *teaspoon salt*

a little pepper
2 *egg yolks*
2-3 *tablespoons* (*or more*) *butter*
1 *teaspoon lemon juice* (*optional*)

Melt 1 tablespoon butter in a saucepan, add flour and mix together without cooking. Add hot water and seasoning and mix well. Combine with egg yolks using a whip, and cook, stirring, until the boiling point is reached. Do not boil. Remove from the fire and stir in remaining butter. Add lemon juice, if desired.

SUBSTITUTE HOLLANDAISE

2 *egg yolks, beaten*
few drops lemon juice
1 *teaspoon cold water*

½ *cup hot Béchamel Sauce* (page 24)
¼ *cup butter*

Mix together egg yolks, lemon juice and water and combine with Béchamel Sauce. Heat slowly, stirring constantly, and remove from heat as soon as it starts to boil. Add butter a little at a time, combining each addition before adding the next. Correct the seasoning.

Fish

◁═ ✳ ═▷

FRENCH housewives make the most of fish because it is both delicious and cheap. They handle a fragile filet as if it were a precious trinket. They never send it to the table broken or other than perfectly cooked. And they give the sauces which, in cooking fish, are as important as the fish itself, as much thought and attention as goes into the most expensive delicacy.

Just as in this country, salt water fish are most popular in the sections of France near the coastline. Many favorite dishes like *Marseilles Bouillabaise* and *Filet de Sole Normande* are world famous. But people living in the inland sections must content themselves with fish from the local streams which, although smaller than many of the salt water kinds, have a certain fresh delicacy that is the joy of gourmets.

Fish is only good—and safe to eat—if it is fresh. The shorter the time from water to stove to table, the better. The one exception to this is skate, which I explain farther on—and excepting, of course, all salted and smoked fish. In buying fish, you judge its freshness by the brilliance of the eyes, the pink color of the gills, and the firmness of the flesh. And if you want the pick of the market, you should shop early. Take time, too, to chat with the fish dealer and you can learn from him what varieties are most plentiful in your locality and what are their best seasons. Those, obviously, are the ones to serve most frequently.

The fish recipes in this book are old, tried and true combinations which have stood the test of years in French homes. Read them carefully, especially if fish cookery has always been your *bête noire*. And look to your sauces. If the recipe calls for stock, ask the fish dealer for a few bones from which to make it, or make up a little mushroom stock; be sure to reduce the cooking liquid to the amount specified. Keep a bottle of white wine tightly corked in the refrigerator for fish sauces, and see what a difference that makes in your results.

[37]

BAKED FISH
(Poisson au Four)

Baking is one of the easiest ways of cooking fish, but is best for large fish. And let me suggest that you use an oven-proof earthenware or glass baking dish which can be brought to the table. It saves the awkward and always difficult job of transferring a large cooked fish from one dish to another.

To bake a fish, dip it—after cleaning and scrubbing off the scales—in milk and then in flour seasoned with salt. Put about ¼ inch of salad oil or good, freshly rendered fat in the baking dish and put in a hot oven of 450 degrees F. When the oil is hot, put the fish in the dish and bake from 10 to 20 minutes, depending upon its size, basting often with the oil. Drain off the oil before serving. Serve separately Mustard Sauce (page 29), Maître d'Hôtel Butter (page 33), or melted butter, and pieces of lemon.

BOILED FISH
(Poisson Poché)

To boil fish, cover it with Fish Stock (page 53), or Court Bouillon (page 54), or salted water to which has been added a few slices of lemon and a little milk. Wrapping the fish in a piece of cheesecloth will make it easier to remove from the water without breaking. Bring to a boil, then simmer 15 to 25 minutes, depending upon its size. Remove from cooking liquid and serve with Egg Sauce (page 26), Cream Sauce (page 25), or Hollandaise Sauce (pages 26 and 36).

BRAISED FISH
(Poisson Braisé)

Braising is another good way to cook a large fish. To do this, put a diced onion (some mushroom stems and peelings if available), a sliced carrot, a sprig of parsley, a bay leaf, a little thyme, one cup of fish stock or water, and ½ cup red or white wine in a pan large enough for the fish. Season the fish with salt and pepper and place on top. Cover pan and cook in a moderate oven of 375 degrees F., one-half to one hour, depending upon the size of the fish, basting often. Remove fish to serving dish and take off all the skin. Boil the cooking liquid until reduced to about one-third the original quantity. (If cooked in a dish that can be brought to the table, leave in the dish, pouring off the cooking liquid into another pan.) If red wine was used in braising, thicken the liquid with Manié Butter made by creaming together two tablespoons butter with one tablespoon flour. If white wine was used, thicken the liquid by adding one cup Cream Sauce (page 25) or Manié Butter as described above. Strain over the fish.

BROILED FISH
(Poisson Grillé)

Fish for broiling may be skinned and boned to make filets; or it may be opened up, laid flat, and the bones removed or not as desired; or a large fish like salmon may be cut into slices about ¾ inch thick. In any case dip in flour, season with salt and pepper and then brush with salad oil; then cook on a hot greased broiler about four to five inches from the heat. It will be done in 12 to 18 minutes, depending upon the thickness of the fish. Serve with pieces of lemon and melted butter, Maître d'Hôtel butter (page 33), or Mustard Sauce (page 29).

FISH SAUTE MEUNIERE
(Poisson Meunière)

This may be prepared as for broiling—that is, whole, in filets, or in slices, depending upon the size of the fish. Dip in milk and then in flour seasoned with salt and pepper. Put about ¼ inch of salad oil in a frying pan and heat very hot. Add fish and cook until golden brown on both sides. Remove to serving dish, sprinkle with a little pepper, a few drops of lemon juice, and a little chopped parsley. Place a slice of peeled lemon on top. For each serving cook one tablespoon butter until it is hazelnut brown in color and pour over the fish.

BROILED MACKEREL MAITRE D'HOTEL
(Maquereau Grillé)

If fish are small, broil whole; if large, cut into filets. Season with salt and pepper, brush with salad oil. Place on a hot grill and broil about 3 to 4 inches from a moderately hot fire, basting with oil or butter. Serve with Maître d'Hôtel butter (page 33).

SHAD MEUNIERE
(Alose Meunière)

Have fish boned, if desired, before cooking. Sprinkle with milk and with flour seasoned with salt and pepper. Put enough salad oil in a frying pan to cover the bottom of the pan, and heat until very hot. Place fish, flesh side down, in the pan and brown the skin side. Place pan under broiler (or in a hot oven) and cook about 15 to 20 minutes, or until fish is done, basting often. Serve with sliced lemon and butter cooked until hazelnut brown, and, if desired, sprinkle chopped parsley over the top.

TROUT

It was my brother who told me how Trout Meunière acquired the name. It seems that at Royat, which is very near Clermont-Ferrand, there was an inn in the early nineteenth century called *La Belle Meunière,* where the freshly caught trout were always served in the favorite local way, sautéed and dressed with brown butter. Once when Napoleon was in the neighborhood, he ate brook trout at La Belle Meunière and they were so delicious that he said trout prepared in this manner should always be called "Belle Meunière." And so they are to this day.

There are gourmets, however, who prefer to have trout cooked in court bouillon, and the dish is called "Truite au Bleu" because the fish takes on a blue tint. But however prepared, the fine flavor of trout depends upon its being freshly caught, almost, I'd say, jumping from brook to pan.

BROOK TROUT AU BLEU
(Truite au Bleu)

To prepare a brook trout this way, the fish should be alive. Clean them quickly and sprinkle with a little vinegar. Put about 2 inches, or just enough to cover the fish, of Court Bouillon (page 54) in a shallow pan or heatproof dish. Bring to a boil, and carefully drop in the fish. Turn down the heat so that they will only simmer, never boil rapidly, and cook 8 to 10 minutes. They will curl up and turn a bluish color. Serve from the dish in which the fish was cooked, or remove to serving dish and serve melted butter separately.

TROUT SAUTE MEUNIERE
(Truite Meunière)

Follow directions for Fish Saute Meuniere (page 39).

CADGERY

1½ *lbs. fish, fresh or leftover or both*	1½ *tablespoons butter*
½ *teaspoon salt*	1½ *tablespoons flour*
1 *medium onion, chopped*	1 *tablespoon curry powder*
3 *tablespoons butter*	2 *cups hot milk*
½ *cup rice*	3 *hard-boiled eggs, sliced or quar-*
1 *cup boiling water*	*tered (reserve one yolk for top)*

[40]

Boil fresh fish (page 38) or heat leftover fish by steaming it in a little salted water. Remove skin and bones and cut fish in pieces. Put onion with 2 tablespoons butter in saucepan and cook until onion is soft. Add rice and shake pan until all the grains are coated with butter. Add boiling water, cover, and cook 20 to 25 minutes in a hot oven of 425 to 450 degrees, or over very low heat on top of the stove. Turn out onto a hot dish and mix with 1 tablespoon butter, tossing the rice with a fork. In another pan melt the 1½ tablespoons butter, add flour, and cook until it starts to turn golden. Add curry powder and mix thoroughly. Add milk and cook, stirring constantly, until sauce is smooth and thick. Correct the seasoning if necessary.

To prepare the dish for serving, put a layer of half the cooked rice in a hot serving dish, then a layer of half the fish, a few slices of hard-boiled egg, and cover with half the sauce. Repeat, using the other half of the rice, fish, eggs, and sauce. Press reserved egg yolk through a fine sieve and sprinkle over the top. Serves 6.

DEVILED FISH AU GRATIN
(Poisson Diable au Gratin)

Follow recipe for Fish with Cream au Gratin (page 46), adding ½ teaspoon dry mustard to each cup of Mornay Sauce.

COD FISH COUNTRY STYLE
(Cabillaud Fermière)

1½-2 *lbs. cod fish in one piece*
salt and pepper
1 *medium carrot, sliced*
1 *onion, minced*
few sprigs parsley
a little thyme
1 *bay leaf*

4 *tablespoons salad oil*
1 *glass white wine (or juice ½ lemon)*
2 *tablespoons butter*
2 *tablespoons bread crumbs*
1 *teaspoon chopped parsley*
4 *potatoes, pared, quartered, and*
   cooked in salted water

Make slashes in the skin on both sides of the fish and season with salt and pepper. Put in a deep dish with carrot, onion, parsley, thyme, bay leaf, salad oil and wine (or lemon juice). Let stand 1 to 2 hours to marinate, turning fish often. Remove fish to an ovenproof earthenware or glass platter and strain the liquid over it. Spread 1 tablespoon of the butter on top. Bake in hot oven of 450 degrees, basting often, for 10 to 15 minutes. Sprinkle bread crumbs over the top and baste them with the liquid in the dish. Bake 15 to 20 minutes longer, or until fish is cooked and crumbs have formed a nice brown crust on top. Remove

[41]

from oven, sprinkle with parsley and a few drops lemon juice. Arrange potatoes around fish and pour other tablespoon butter (melted) over them. Serves 4.

FILET OF FRESH MACKEREL RAVIGOTE

6 *filets of mackerel*	*a little thyme*
3 *cups water*	1 *bay leaf*
1 *glass white wine (or ½ cup vinegar)*	5 *peppercorns*
½ *teaspoon salt*	*a little butter*
6 *slices carrot*	12 *freshly boiled small potatoes*
1 *medium onion, sliced*	*chopped parsley*
few sprigs parsley	1 *cup Ravigote Sauce* (page 31)

Make a Court Bouillon by cooking together water, wine, salt, carrot, onion, parsley sprigs, and seasonings for 12 to 14 minutes. Strain. Butter a shallow pan, lay filets in it, and cover with strained Court Bouillon. Poach filets in this by simmering them gently about 14 minutes. Remove them carefully to a serving dish and remove the skins and bones, if any. Arrange the potatoes around fish and sprinkle with chopped parsley. Cook 2 cups bouillon until reduced to one-third original quantity, combine with Ravigote Sauce, and serve separately. Serves 6.

FILET OF SOLE (OR OTHER FISH) AU GRATIN

6 *fish filets*	1 *teaspoon chopped parsley*
1 *shallot, chopped (or ½ medium*	½ *cup Brown Sauce* (page 24)
onion, chopped)	*or Tomato Sauce* (page 31)
2 *tablespoons butter*	*salt and pepper*
12 *mushrooms*	2 *tablespoons bread crumbs*
lemon juice	½ *glass white wine*

Put shallots (or onions) and 1 tablespoon butter in a saucepan and cook a few minutes. Slice 6 mushrooms (if very small, leave whole), cook about 5 minutes in a very little cold water with a few drops lemon juice, then put them aside to serve around fish. Chop stems and remaining mushrooms and add to butter and shallots. Cover and cook until water from mushrooms is just cooked away. Add a little of the chopped parsley, the Brown Sauce (or Tomato Sauce), and boil a few minutes. Spread bottom of an ovenproof serving dish with some of this sauce and place filets, seasoned with salt and pepper, on the sauce. Drain cooked mushrooms, place on filets, and cover with remaining sauce, which should be quite thick. Sprinkle with bread crumbs and remaining butter (melted) and wine. Put in an oven hot enough to brown the top and also to reduce the cooking liquor and to cook the fish all at the same time and in about 12 to 15 minutes. Remove from oven and sprinkle with a little lemon juice and remaining parsley. Serves 6.

FILET OF SOLE (OR OTHER FISH) BONNE FEMME

4 *fish filets*	1 *glass white wine* (*or fish stock or*
2 *tablespoons butter*	*water with lemon juice*)
2 *shallots, finely chopped*	½ *teaspoon flour*
¼ *lb. mushrooms, minced*	*lemon juice*
1 *teaspoon chopped parsley*	*salt and pepper*

Melt 1 tablespoon butter in a saucepan, spreading it over bottom of pan. Add shallots and half the mushrooms, place fish on top of them, then add remaining mushrooms. Season with salt and pepper, sprinkle one-half the parsley over top, then the wine (or stock or water and lemon). Cook in oven or on top of stove over a fairly quick fire so the liquid will reduce to about one-third original quantity. Cook 10 to 12 minutes, basting often. Remove fish to serving dish and thicken sauce with Manié Butter made by creaming together remaining butter and flour and adding it to the liquid in the pan. Bring to a boil, stirring constantly. Correct the seasoning, add a few drops lemon juice, and pour over the fish. Sprinkle top with chopped parsley. Serves 4.

FILET OF SOLE (OR OTHER FISH) MORNAY

6 *fish filets*	2 *cups Mornay Sauce* (page 28)
1 *cup fish stock* (page 53)	2 *tablespoons butter*
3 *tablespoons grated cheese*	1 *teaspoon salt*

Put 1 tablespoon butter in saucepan, add fish, seasoned with salt, and fish stock. Bring to a boil and cook slowly 10 to 12 minutes. Remove fish to serving dish. Cook the liquid in pan until reduced to one-third the original quantity, and add Mornay Sauce. Cover fish with sauce, sprinkle with cheese and remaining butter (melted). Put in a hot oven or under a very hot broiler and cook until brown. Serves 6.

FILET OF SOLE (OR ANY FISH) LILY

4 *fish filets*	½ *glass white wine* (*or fish stock or*
2 *tablespoons butter*	*water*)
1 *teaspoon chopped shallot*	½ *cup Béchamel Sauce* (page 24)
3 *or 4 mushrooms, sliced*	*chopped parsley*
2 *fresh tomatoes, peeled, seeded,*	½ *teaspoon salt*
and coarsely chopped	*a little pepper*

Put 1 tablespoon butter, chopped shallot, half the mushrooms and half the tomatoes in a saucepan. Lay fish on top, season with salt and pepper, put remaining mushrooms and tomatoes on top of fish, and pour the wine over. Bring to a boil and cook slowly 10 to 12 minutes. Remove filets to serving dish. Cook the liquid until reduced to about one-third the original quantity and add Béchamel Sauce. Correct the seasoning, add remaining butter, and pour over fish. Sprinkle top with chopped parsley. Serves 4.

FILET OF SOLE NORMANDE

6 *filets of sole*	12 *mushrooms* (*small*)
1 *pint mussels*	½ *teaspoon salt*
lemon juice	*a little pepper*
6 *oysters* (*optional*)	6 *slices French bread, fried in butter*
½ *cup butter*	½ *cup cooked shrimps*
1 *tablespoon flour*	*a few cooked crawfish* (*optional*)
2 *egg yolks*	*a few tiny fried fish* (*optional*)
½ *cup cream* (*or top milk*)	

Steam mussels in a little salted water containing a few drops of lemon juice until the shells open. Drain and save liquor. Cook mushrooms in 2 tablespoons water for a few minutes. Drain and save liquor. Poach oysters in their own juice for a few minutes. Put filets in a saucepan with 1½ cups of the mixed liquors from cooking the mussels and mushrooms. Bring to a boil and cook 10 to 12 minutes. Remove filets to serving dish and arrange mussels, mushrooms, and oysters over them. Prepare a roux by melting 2 tablespoons butter, adding 1 tablespoon flour and cooking until just golden. Add cooking liquid from filets, stirring with a whip to keep it smooth. Boil a few minutes. Mix egg yolks with cream and combine with sauce and bring just to the boiling point, stirring all the time, but do not let boil. Add remaining butter, correct the seasoning, and strain through a fine sieve over the fish. Garnish with crusts of bread, and, if used, the shrimps, fried fish, and crawfish. Serves 6.

FILET OF SOLE (OR OTHER FISH) WITH RED WINE SAUCE

6 *filets of sole*	*salt and pepper*
1 *large onion, finely chopped*	½ *teaspoon flour*
3 *tablespoons butter*	1 *glass red wine*

Cook onion in saucepan in 1 tablespoon butter until it starts to become golden colored. Add another tablespoon butter, the fish seasoned with salt and pepper, and wine. Cook about 10 to 12 minutes over medium heat, but hot enough to reduce the liquid to one-third the original quantity by the time the fish is done. Remove fish to serving dish. Thicken sauce with Manié Butter, made by creaming together remaining tablespoon butter with flour and adding it to the cooking liquid. Bring to a boil, stirring constantly. Correct the seasoning and strain through a fine sieve over the filets. Serves 6.

FILET OF SOLE (OR ANY FISH) WITH WHITE WINE SAUCE

4 *fish filets*
1 *shallot, chopped (or ½ medium*
  onion, finely chopped)
1 *teaspoon salt*
a little white pepper
½ *glass white wine*

¼ *cup fish stock* (page 53) (*or mush-*
  room stock or water)
2 *tablespoons butter*
2 *tablespoons flour*
egg yolk, lightly beaten
¼ *cup cream* (*or top milk*)

Put shallots (or onions) in saucepan with filets, seasoned with salt and pepper. Add stock (or water) and wine, bring to a boil, cover and cook slowly 10 to 12 minutes. In another pan make a roux by melting butter, adding flour and cooking until it just starts to turn golden. Remove fish from pan to serving dish and add liquid in which it was cooked to roux. Bring to boiling paint, mixing with a whip until perfectly smooth. Combine with egg yolk but do not allow to boil after yolk is added. Add remaining butter and cream and pour sauce over fish. If wine is not used, add a few drops lemon juice at the end. Serves 4.

FISH FILETS PAYSANNE

4 *fish filets*
2 *medium onions, sliced*
2 *medium carrots, sliced*
2½ *tablespoons butter*
1 *teaspoon flour*

½ *teaspoon salt*
a little pepper
½ *teaspoon chopped parsley*
1 *cup fish stock* (page 53) (*or white*
  wine or water)

Cook carrots and onions slowly in ½ tablespoon butter. Add 1 tablespoon butter, salt, pepper, parsley, and fish filets. Pour fish stock (or wine or water) over, bring to a boil, and cook slowly 10 to 12 minutes, then remove fish to serving dish. Cook the liquid until reduced to one-third its original quantity and thicken with Manié Butter made by creaming together remaining tablespoon butter and flour and adding it to hot liquid. Bring to a boil, moving the pan around instead of stirring the mixture to combine it. Pour over the fish. Serves 4.

FISH WITH CREAM AU GRATIN

1 *lb. cooked fish or shellfish*   2 *cups Duchess potatoes* (page 194)
a little salt   1½ *cups hot Mornay Sauce* (page 28)
1 *tablespoon melted butter*   2 *tablespoons grated cheese*

Remove skin and bones from fish and reheat by steaming with 2 tablespoons water, a little salt, and a little butter, cooking it until the water cooks away. Make a border of Duchess potatoes around the edge of a flat baking dish, using a pastry bag or a spoon. In the center spread enough Mornay Sauce to cover the bottom of the dish and place fish on top. Cover with remaining Mornay Sauce. Sprinkle grated cheese and a little melted butter over the top of both fish and potatoes. Cook in a hot oven or under broiler until golden brown. Serves 4.

FISH WITH TOMATO

4 *fish filets*   4 *fresh tomatoes, peeled, seeded,*
3 *tablespoons butter*   *and coarsely chopped*
1 *medium onion, chopped*   1 *teaspoon salt*
1 *shallot, chopped*   *a little pepper*
1 *clove garlic, crushed*   1 *teaspoon chopped parsley*
a little thyme   ½ *glass white wine* (*optional*)
½ *bay leaf, finely crushed*   ½ *cup tomato juice*
1 *tablespoon flour*

Put 1 tablespoon butter, onion, shallot, garlic, thyme, bay leaf and half the tomatoes in a saucepan. Lay fish on top, season with salt and pepper. Put remaining tomato and parsley on top, and pour wine and tomato juice over all. Bring to a boil and cook covered in a hot oven, or slowly on top of the stove, about 15 minutes. Remove fish to serving dish. Cook liquid until reduced to one-half the original quantity and thicken it by adding Manié Butter, made by creaming together flour and remaining butter and adding to reduced liquid. Bring to a boil, stirring constantly. Pour over the fish. Serves 4.

MARSEILLES BOUILLABAISSE

Bouillabaisse is a fish soup in which both fish and shellfish are combined, a dish which is famous all along the southern coast of France that skirts the Mediterranean. Each little seaport from Cape Cerbère to Menton has its own particular Bouillabaisse, and each Bouillabaisse is a little different from every other. All are delicious, but it is the Bouillabaisse made in Marseilles that is the most famous and the one which connoisseurs travel so far to eat.

[46]

There are many stories about the origin of Marseilles Bouillabaisse. One is that Venus originated it to serve to Vulcan to induce in him a drowsiness by which she wished to profit, a drowsiness supposedly caused by saffron, one of the essential ingredients of this dish. Another is that an abbess of a Marseilles convent created Bouillabaisse for Friday's fasts, a beginning which seems more logical to a literal-minded chef.

The characteristics of Marseilles Bouillabaisse are the intermingled flavors of tomato, garlic, and saffron, and the fact that olive oil, the common cooking fat in southern France, and never butter, is used in making it. Some also insist that Marseilles Bouillabaisse can only be made with fish and shellfish fresh from the sparkling waters of the Mediterranean, while others add that it never tastes quite right unless eaten some place on that sunny shorefront that runs from Marseilles to Toulon. Be that as it may, I have found that a delicious Marseilles Bouillabaisse with the characteristic flavors of tomato, garlic, saffron, and olive oil can be made from American fish and shellfish, a Bouillabaisse, in fact, that will make many a Frenchman homesick.

2 *live lobsters, 1½ to 1¾ lbs. each*	1 *lb. fresh tomatoes, peeled, seeded,*
1 *lb. fresh eels*	*and chopped (or 1 can)*
1½ *lbs. striped bass*	2-3 *cloves garlic, crushed*
1½ *lbs. sea bass*	2 *tablespoons chopped parsley*
2½ *lbs.Spanish mackerel or other fish*	1 *teaspoon saffron*
2 *doz. mussels*	1 *bay leaf*
2 *doz. clams*	*a little thyme*
½ *cup olive oil*	*a pinch of chopped fresh fennel tips*
3 *large leeks, chopped*	*(if obtainable)*
½ *lb. onions, chopped*	1 *can tomatoes (2¼ cups)*
2 *qts. water*	1 *tablespoon salt*
1 *large carrot, chopped*	*a little pepper*
	French bread cut in thin slices

Cut lobsters, eels, bass, and mackerel in slices about an inch thick. Scrub clams and mussels very thoroughly. Heat olive oil in a saucepan, add leeks, onions, and carrots, and cook until lightly browned. Add fresh tomatoes, garlic, parsley, saffron, fennel, bay leaf, thyme, salt, and pepper. Add tomatoes, water, lobsters (cut in pieces) and eels, and cook 15 minutes. Add striped bass, sea bass, and mackerel, and cook 10 minutes longer. Add clams and mussels and continue cooking until their shells open.

[47]

Dish up the fish with some of the cooking liquid in deep bowls and serve with the French bread slices. These may be plain, rubbed with garlic, or fried in olive oil. Serves 8 to 10.

MATELOTE

In our part of France almost every village had a fish pond, a low place in a field dammed to hold in water which was stocked with fish. Without these ponds we would have eaten very little fish and never had the occasional treats of matelote of which we were so fond.

The fish, breeding more quickly than they could be eaten, had to be thinned out every two or three years and this was done at pond drainings which became gala picnics for the neighboring farmers who shared the event—and the fish. After the dam was opened the water drained off rather slowly so our waiting lasted through the night. When the water became so shallow that the fish covered the entire surface the picnic ended abruptly. We worked feverishly with our nets to get the fish before they were sucked into the mud and soon were loading our tubs into the carts and driving off, some to sell their share of the catch in near-by villages, others to rural inns where tiny pools assured customers a continuous supply of fresh fish, while some of us took ours home, our mouths watering at the thought of the delicious matelote soon to come steaming to the table. A really good Matelote needs several kinds of fresh-water fish, so we had to wait for it until a pond draining because that was the only time my mother ever had the different kinds all at once.

MATELOTE MARINIERE

2 lbs. fish (eels, perch and others
   available)
white wine to cover
1 onion, minced
faggot of 1 sprig parsley, 1 bay leaf,
   a little thyme
2 cloves garlic
1 teaspoon salt

2 tablespoons butter
2 tablespoons flour
8-10 small white onions, cooked
8-10 small mushrooms, cooked
a few cooked shrimps (if available)
slices of French bread toasted or
   fried in butter

Clean fish well, cut in medium sized pieces, put in a saucepan and cover with white wine. Add minced onion, faggot, garlic, and salt. Bring to a boil and cook slowly for 12 to 15 minutes. Remove fish to serving dish. Strain the cooking liquid into another pan and add Manié Butter, made by creaming together butter and flour. Bring to a boil, stirring constantly. Correct the seasoning. Arrange onions and mushrooms over and around fish and pour sauce over it all. Garnish with shrimps (if used) and toasted bread. Serves 4 to 5.

HERRING WITH MUSTARD

Cut 2 or 3 gashes in the skin of 6 herrings and sauté 5 or 6 minutes in hot salad oil. Season with salt and pepper and drain well. Place in a hot serving dish and spread mustard which has been mixed with a little vinegar on top and sprinkle with chopped parsley. Melt 2 tablespoons butter in another pan and continue cooking until it becomes hazelnut brown. Pour over the herrings and serve. Serves 6.

MATELOTE WITH RED WINE

Follow recipe for Matelote Marinière, replacing white wine with red wine.

SALT CODFISH

Salt codfish, always very inexpensive, is sold everywhere and can be obtained in all seasons. Its convenience and low cost make it an ideal food in homes where these factors are important. It is unfortunate that many housewives don't use this food more often, because nicely prepared codfish makes a very delicious dish.

The quality of salt codfish does vary. Examine the codfish you buy and if the flesh has a silvery color and brown skin with fish fibers that are short and thick and in layers like leaves, then it is the best quality. When the flesh is yellow and the fibers dry and stringy-looking, the piece is old, tough, and poor flavored, or may even be rancid.

Preparing Salt Codfish

Salt codfish must be freshened by soaking in plenty of cold water for 10 to 12 hours. It is wise to taste a bit of it after this soaking, and if it still tastes very salty, change the water and soak a little longer. Remember that it will be too late to find this out after the fish is on the table ready to be eaten. Drain off the water in which the fish was soaked, cover with fresh cold water, and cook slowly for 15 to 20 minutes. Drain and serve with melted butter, Maître d'Hôtel Butter (page 33), or with any desired sauce and boiled potatoes.

PUREE OF SALT COD
(Brandade de Morue)

Brandade of Salt Cod is another one of the dishes which is common in French homes, but which I have never seen on American tables. It was popular in the interior sections where fresh fish was often unobtainable. I remember it coming to the table always in the same way, piled high in the dish with plenty of croutons at the base of the mound. The oil and garlic impart an unusual and rich flavor to this plebeian fish and its creaminess was offset, of course, by the croutons and the crustiness of the French bread eaten with it.

1 *lb. salt codfish*	3 *tablespoons boiling cream or top*
½ cup olive oil	*milk*
1-2 *cloves garlic, crushed*	*pepper*
salt if needed	*Croutons* (page 294)

Cover codfish with cold water, bring to a boil, and cook slowly 10 to 15 minutes to remove the salt. Drain and remove skin and bones, and break up fish into small flakes. Put one half the oil in a pan and heat it, but not quite as hot as for frying. Add fish and work up well with a wooden spoon, mixing and crushing the fish. Add garlic and remaining oil (which has been heated), adding the oil little by little and mixing thoroughly. Add top milk or cream gradually and beat all together until it is the consistency of mashed potatoes. Season as needed, using pepper generously. Pile into the serving dish and garnish with croutons fried in oil. Serves 4.

SALT CODFISH WITH SPINACH, HOUSEWIFE STYLE
(Morue avec Epinard à la Ménagère)

1½ *lbs. salt cod fish*	*½ teaspoon salt*
2 *lbs. spinach*	*a little pepper*
1 *medium onion, chopped*	*few gratings of nutmeg*
½ cup salad oil	1 *clove garlic, crushed* (*optional*)
1 *tablespoon flour*	*¾ cup milk*
2 *tablespoons bread crumbs*	

Follow directions for preparing Codfish (page 49). Clean spinach and cook in boiling water 8 to 10 minutes. Remove to cold water, then drain very thoroughly. Chop coarsely. Put onion and oil in saucepan and cook over hot fire until onion is golden brown. Add flour and when well combined, add spinach, salt, pepper, and nutmeg. Mix well over a hot fire for a few minutes, or until the spinach is dried out a bit. Add garlic and milk. Cook over low heat for about 15 minutes, stirring occasionally.

Separate the cooked fish into flakes and remove all bones. Mix with the prepared spinach and spread mixture in a shallow buttered or oiled baking dish. Sprinkle top with bread crumbs and cook in a hot oven or under broiler until brown. Serves 4 to 5.

SALT CODFISH FISHERMAN
(Morue des Pêcheurs)

1½ lbs. salt codfish
2 tablespoons butter
3 medium onions, minced fine
8 boiled potatoes, peeled and sliced

salt and pepper
1 teaspoon chopped parsley
2 tablespoons vinegar

Follow directions for preparing salt codfish (page 49). Separate into flakes and remove all the bones. Put butter and onion in a saucepan and cook over medium heat until golden brown. Add potato and cooked cod fish. Continue cooking about 5 minutes. Season with salt and pepper to taste. Add vinegar and chopped parsley and serve immediately. Serves 4 to 5.

SAUTEED SHAD ROE
(Oeuf d'Alose Sauté)

Dip shad roe in milk and sprinkle with flour. Put enough salad oil in frying pan to cover bottom of pan. Heat oil, but not too hot, and put in the roe. Cook slowly with the pan partly covered, turning roe when underside is brown. Cook until done, about 12 to 15 minutes, depending upon thickness. Shad roe is firm when done, but to be sure, make a little cut in the side of the piece with a sharp knife and if done the inside will not be red. Serve with a slice of lemon, some chopped parsley, and Brown Butter (page 32).

SKATE
(Raie)

Skate, a tasty and inexpensive fish, is very popular in France, though in this country one seldom sees it, except occasionally in restaurants. Although in season all the year, it is at its best in spring and summer.

Skate is different from other fish in that the body, which is quite small, is never eaten. The edible parts are the two circular sections attached to each side of the body and called the "wings." Usually they are already detached from the body when you buy them, so that you actually buy "skate wings," not skate. This fish also differs from other kinds of fish in that it is better not to eat it immediately after being caught. The flavor and texture of skate wings are improved if, after washing, they are left for a couple of days covered with salted water in the refrigerator.

To Cook Skate Wings

Put skate wings in a saucepan and cover with water to which has been added 1 minced onion, 1 sprig parsley, 1 small bay leaf, a little thyme, ½ tablespoon salt, and ¼ cup vinegar for each quart of water. Bring to a boil and boil slowly, covered, 20 to 25 minutes. Drain, place on a towel, and remove the skin from both sides of the wings and also the edges, which should slip off with the skin. Return to the cooking liquor until ready to use. If put in the refrigerator, the liquor will jell and the wings can be kept in this way for a couple of days.

SKATE WITH BLACK BUTTER
(Raie au Beurre Noir)

Drain freshly cooked skate wings (above) or reheat in their liquor those that have been kept in the refrigerator and then drain. Place in a serving dish and sprinkle with salt, pepper, chopped parsley, a few capers, 1 teaspoon of vinegar, and a few drops of lemon juice for each serving. Melt 1 tablespoon butter for each serving and continue cooking it until very brown, then pour over the fish. Serve very hot.

SMOKED HADDOCK, BROILED

Spread the haddock (or the filets) with salad oil and broil under a moderate heat 8 to 10 minutes, or until fish is heated through. Serve with melted butter.

SMOKED HADDOCK WITH EGG SAUCE

Place haddock in a pan and cover with cold water to which a few spoonfuls of milk have been added. (The milk will whiten the fish a little.) Add a little salt, bring to a boil, and let simmer 12 to 15 minutes. Serve with Egg Sauce (page 26).

SOUFFLE OF FISH
(Soufflé de Poisson)

1 cup cooked fish (leftover)	3 egg yolks, beaten
cod, halibut, or other white fish	½ teaspoon salt
3 tablespoons butter	a little pepper
3 tablespoons flour	4 egg whites, stiffly beaten
1½ cups milk	

Chop fish very fine and run through a coarse sieve. Melt butter, add flour, and cook until it just starts to turn golden. Add milk and cook, stirring constantly, until mixture thickens. Continue cooking gently, stirring occasionally, until reduced to about 1 cup. Combine with egg yolks by mixing a little of the sauce to the yolks and then turning this back into the sauce. Cook over a very low heat, stirring vigorously until it just starts to boil. Remove from fire and add salt, pepper, and fish. Fold in stiffly beaten egg whites. Turn into a buttered and floured soufflé mould, or deep casserole, and bake in a hot oven of 450 degrees for 15 to 20 minutes. Serve immediately. Serves 3 to 4.

TUNA FISH (OR SWORD FISH) PROVENCAL
(Thon [ou Poisson Épée] Provençale)

1½-1¾ lbs. fresh tuna fish in one piece
1 teaspoon salt
a little pepper
4 tablespoons salad oil
1 onion, chopped
3 tomatoes, peeled, seeded, and
    chopped (or 1 cup canned
    tomatoes)
1 clove garlic

1 glass white wine (or juice of
    1 lemon)
fish stock or water (about 1 cup)
a faggot of 2 sprigs parsley, 1 bay
    leaf, a little thyme, 1 stalk celery
1 tablespoon flour
1 tablespoon butter
1 tablespoon capers

Season fish with salt and pepper. Put oil in a saucepan and heat until very hot. Add fish and cook on both sides until golden in color. Add onion, tomatoes, and garlic, and cook slowly about 15 minutes. Add wine and enough stock (or water) to just cover fish. Add faggot, cover pan, and cook about 40 minutes in oven, or slowly on top of stove. When done place fish in serving dish, remove the faggot, and thicken liquid in pan with Manié Butter made by creaming butter and flour together and adding it to the hot liquid. Bring to a boil, stirring constantly. Pour sauce over fish and garnish with capers. Serves 4 to 5.

FISH STOCK
(Fumet de Poisson)

fish bones and head
water
mushroom peelings
a little thyme

1 bay leaf
2-3 sprigs parsley
salt
a few drops lemon juice

Put bones and head in a saucepan with enough water to cover. Add remaining ingredients and cook for 20 minutes. Strain and use for cooking fish or for fish sauces.

[53]

COURT BOUILLON FOR FISH

2 qts. water   1 tablespoon salt
½ cup milk   3 slices lemon, peeled and seeded

Combine all ingredients and pour over fish. Bring to a boil and let simmer until fish is cooked.

STOCK FOR FISH WITH VINEGAR

3 qts. water   6 sprigs parsley
½ cup vinegar   a little thyme
1 tablespoon salt   1 bay leaf
2 medium carrots, sliced   8 peppercorns
2 large onions, sliced

Combine all ingredients, boil about 30 minutes, and strain.

STOCK FOR FISH WITH WINE

2 cups water   a little thyme
1 glass red or dry white wine   1 bay leaf
1 onion, sliced   ½ teaspoon salt
2 sprigs parsley   4 peppercorns

Combine all ingredients, boil about 30 minutes, and strain.

Shellfish

I can't be too emphatic in impressing upon anyone who prepares shellfish how important it is for the fish to be fresh and in this instance freshness means actually being alive. Unless shellfish is alive up to the minute of cooking, it will not taste good, but of greater consequence is the fact that it may not be safe to eat because shellfish spoils more rapidly than any other food. Canned shellfish should be eaten as soon as possible after the can is opened and frozen shellfish immediately after defrosting.

When I was a boy, shellfish was not very common in the part of France where I lived, nor for that matter in any of the interior sections. It was sold in the cities to which trains could bring it quickly in tubs of ice, not in small country places inconvenient to the main lines. But along the coast line of France, just as here in America, shellfish dishes were served all the time and were very popular. Some of them, such as

Marseilles Bouillabaisse and Mussels Marinière, have lured and delighted gourmets from all over the world.

So I learned about shellfish actually after I had left my boyhood home and was off on my own career. The recipes which I am including in this book are not from my mother's kitchen but were selected because they are the ones which my friends have always enjoyed most and which I think you will, too.

CRAWFISH
(Ecrevisse)

Crawfish, one of the few fresh-water shellfish, are very plentiful in France, the small streams in the interior supplying all that are wanted even in a country where the people are as fond of them as the French are. Starting a good dinner with *Ecrevisse au Buisson* is as usual and popular as a shrimp or crabmeat cocktail is in this country. The crawfish there, however, are much larger than the American variety, the biggest and best coming from the river Meuse. American crawfish come from Green Bay, Wisconsin and from New Orleans. The season is a short one, starting in July and ending the last of October.

Crawfish look like tiny langouste-type lobsters and the part eaten is the flesh in the tail and claws. They are always served in the shell which the diner removes with his fingers.

In preparing crawfish, the end of the intestinal tract lying under the tail must be pulled out immediately before cooking. If this is left in, both the fish and the sauce will have a bitter taste. Wine is important in cooking crawfish because the best flavor of the dish is lost without it, but if wine is unavailable it is possible to substitute lemon juice.

CRAWFISH A LA BORDELAISE

24-36 *crawfish*	1 *pony cognac (if available)*
1 *carrot, diced very fine*	1 *glass white wine (or water and*
1 *onion, diced very fine*	*juice of ½ lemon)*
2 *shallots, chopped fine*	1 *teaspoon flour*
1 *sprig parsley*	3 *tablespoons butter*
1 *clove garlic, crushed*	1 *teaspoon salt*
a little thyme	1 *teaspoon chopped parsley*
a small bay leaf, pulverized	

Clean crawfish and remove end of intestinal tract under tail. Put carrot, onion, shallots, sprig of parsley, garlic, thyme, bay leaf and 2 tablespoons butter in saucepan. Cook very slowly until vegetables are soft, about 15 minutes. Add the crawfish and salt. Cook over a hot fire, shaking the pan all the time until fish turn red. Add cognac and white wine and cook over a hot fire 12 minutes. Remove crawfish to a deep serving dish. Continue cooking the liquid until it is reduced to ½ the original quantity. Then add Manié Butter, made by creaming together the flour and remaining tablespoon butter. Do not allow to boil after the sauce thickens. Correct the seasoning of the sauce and pour over the crawfish. Sprinkle with chopped parsley. Serves 4.

CRAWFISH A LA NAGE

Follow recipe for Boiled Crawfish in Vegetable Broth and just before serving add 2 tablespoons butter to it. If desired, the broth may be strained but this is not usual.

BOILED CRAWFISH IN VEGETABLE BROTH
(Ecrevisses au Court Bouillon)

24-30 *crawfish*	*a little thyme*
1 *carrot, thinly sliced*	1 *bay leaf*
2 *shallots, minced*	2 *glasses white wine* (*or water with*
1 *onion, thinly sliced*	*juice of 1 lemon*)
3 *sprigs parsley*	½ *teaspoon salt*

Put all ingredients, except crawfish, in a saucepan and cook slowly until vegetables are soft. Clean crawfish and remove the end of the intestinal tract under the tail. Put fish into the boiling broth immediately after cleaning them. Cover the pan and cook over a hot fire 12 minutes, shaking the pan from time to time. Serve with the broth in which they were cooked. Serves 4.

CRAWFISH EN BUISSON

This is a way of serving crawfish rather than a way of cooking them and a way that is very common in France. A buisson is a three-tiered dish with the top tier smaller than the middle one and the bottom tier the largest. The crawfish are cooked exactly as for Boiled Crawfish in Vegetable Broth, but are drained from the broth and then arranged on the tiers of the buisson. Then the dish is generously garnished with parsley, which is very effective against the pink fish. Mayonnaise is often served separately.

LOBSTER A L'ARMORICAINE

This very savory lobster dish gets its name from an odd coincidence of the similarity of two names and the fact that it has been so popular with American visitors to France. Lobster was first prepared this way many years ago in Brittany originally called "Armorique" in the days when France was known as Gaul. Hence "Lobster à l'Amoricaine" in tribute to the ancient name and times. For many decades it has been as popular in Parisian restaurants as in the inns of Brittany. Americans always ordered it and called it "Lobster à l'Americaine," a name that has clung to lobster prepared in this particular way, and the only name by which it is known in this country.

This recipe calls for the "homard" which is the French lobster that corresponds to our east coast variety. In using west coast lobsters— they correspond to the French "langouste"—the claws have to be disregarded because all the meat is in the tail. Sometimes only the tails are purchased. This means of course that you will have none of the tomalley (the greenish gray liver about the consistency of soft butter which is exposed in the body of the lobster when it is cut open) to thicken the sauce, so you take care of this omission by adding, at the end of cooking, a little Manié Butter, made by creaming together 1 tablespoon butter with 1 teaspoon flour. Bring just to a boil and stir constantly after adding it.

2 *live lobsters 1¾ to 2 lbs.*	1 *pony brandy*
1 *teaspoon salt*	½ *cup Tomato Sauce* (page 31) (*or*
¼ *cup olive oil*	*tomato juice*)
4 *tablespoons butter*	3 *tomatoes, peeled, seeded and*
1 *small carrot, finely chopped*	*chopped*
1 *small onion, finely chopped*	½ *cup fish stock* (*or dry white wine*)
a little thyme	1 *clove garlic, finely crushed*
1 *bay leaf*	½ *teaspoon chopped chervil*
1 *sprig parsley*	½ *teaspoon chopped tarragon*
2 *shallots, chopped*	*a little cayenne pepper*
1 *glass dry white wine*	½ *teaspoon flour*

Cut lobsters in pieces, claws first and the tail in 3 or 4 pieces. Set the tomalley aside. Season lobster with salt and sauté in the oil which has been heated very hot. Make a Bordelaise Mirepoix by putting 1 tablespoon butter in another pan, adding the carrots and onion and cooking them until lightly browned; then add thyme, bay leaf and parsley. Place the lobsters on the Bordelaise Mirepoix, add 1 tablespoon butter, the chopped shallots and white wine. Pour the brandy over and ignite it. Add Tomato Sauce, fresh tomatoes and fish stock (or extra wine). Cover tightly and cook 20 to 25 minutes. Remove the lobster and take the meat from the shell unless it is to be served in the shell. Strain the sauce through a large strainer and thicken by mixing in the tomalley blended with 1 tablespoon butter, the flour, a very little crushed garlic, the finely chopped chervil and tarragon. Combine thoroughly but do not allow to boil. Correct the seasoning, pour the sauce over the lobster and serve very hot with boiled rice or Rice Pilau (page 216). Serves 4.

MUSSELS FOR GARNISHING

Wash mussels, scrubbing them well. Put in a saucepan and add, for each quart of mussels, 1 chopped onion, 2 sprigs parsley, a little thyme, 1 bay leaf, a few peppercorns, ½ glass white wine. Cover and cook over a hot fire about 8 minutes. Remove mussels from shells and use for garnishing fish dishes. The cooking liquor may be strained and used for the stock in any fish sauce.

MUSSELS MARINIERE

18 *to* 24 *mussels*	2 *tablespoons butter*
2 *shallots, chopped*	½ *teaspoon flour*
1 *glass white wine*	1 *teaspoon chopped parsley*

Clean mussels, brushing them well. Put in a saucepan with shallots and wine. Cook about 6 to 8 minutes or until they open. Remove from pan and take off one shell from each mussel. Put in serving dish. Reduce the cooking liquor to ⅓ the original quantity and thicken with Manié Butter, made by creaming together the butter and flour, and adding it to the liquid. Correct seasoning, add parsley and pour over the mussels. If a richer sauce is desired, thicken by adding 2 tablespoons Cream Sauce instead of the Manié Butter. Serves 2.

MUSSELS POULETTE

Follow recipe for Mussels Marinière (above), adding minced mushrooms to the sauce and finishing with 2 tablespoons Cream Sauce (page 25).

OYSTER BROCHETTE
(Anges à Cheval)

Remove oysters from shell and roll each in a thin piece of bacon. For each serving, put six on a metal serving skewer. Place under broiler and broil about 4 to 5 minutes, or until bacon is half cooked, then sprinkle with fine brown or fried bread crumbs and a little cayenne pepper. Return to broiler and continue cooking about 4 or 5 minutes longer or until bacon is crisp. Serve on toast.

OYSTER CROQUETTES

1 cup oysters
¾ cup thick Béchamel Sauce
 (page 24)

2 egg yolks, slightly beaten
Anglaise Coating (page 293)

Poach oysters in their own liquor a few minutes, or until the edges curl. Drain well and if still moist dry them on a towel. Cut in small pieces. Cook oyster liquor until reduced to almost nothing and add to Béchamel Sauce, then combine with oysters. Add egg yolks, correct the seasoning and spread mixture on a platter. Chill until firm enough to handle, form into croquettes and coat à l'Anglaise (page 293). Fry in deep hot fat or sauté until brown. Serve plain with lemon or with Cream Sauce (page 25) or Tomato Sauce (page 31). Serves 4.

OYSTER PATTY

Allow 4-5 oysters and 1 mushroom for each patty. Poach oysters in their own liquor for a few minutes or until the edges curl. Remove from the liquor and reduce the liquor to ⅓ the original quantity and combine with about twice the amount of Béchamel Sauce (page 24). In the meantime, clean and slice the mushrooms and cook with a little salt, a little butter and a few drops of lemon juice for a few minutes in a covered pan over very low heat. Add the cooked mushrooms with their juice and the cooked oysters to the sauce. Serve in patty crusts.

Miscellaneous Fish

EELS
(Anguilles)

Generally we used eels—and most often along with other fish—in making Matelote, or in "Bouilliture d'Anguilles," a dish similar to Matelote but without the other fish. But we also liked them as an hors d'oeuvres either jellied or in a Vinaigrette Sauce. Unless they are very small and young, hence sure to be tender and without too much fat, it is not advisable to sauté them without first cooking them in a Court Bouillon. The larger and older eels always are very rich in fat, which many people find indigestible, and need the cooking liquid to draw out some of this fat (which can then be skimmed from the top of the liquid) and the extra cooking to make them tender.

Eels which you purchase come from the market skinned and cleaned. But those who catch them must do this themselves. It should be done immediately by cutting the skin just below the head and pulling it off in one piece. But since this is a knack that must be learned, some find it easier to cut them in sections of an inch and a half to two inches, clean them, and then grill them or put them in a very hot frying pan until they puff up. This loosens the skin as some of the fat cooks out and it can be easily peeled off. After skinning they are cleaned like any other fish.

There are a great many varieties of eels, both fresh and salt water, but in general those found in swiftly running water are better than the ones in still, murky waters. There are special varieties that are preferred for Matelote and also for Bouillabaisse, and of course people who are particularly fond of them often have individual preferences. Probably the most important point to remember, though, is that they must be cooked and eaten as soon as possible after catching them.

BOUILLITURE OF EEL

1 *eel* (2 *lbs.*) *skinned and cleaned*	3 *cloves garlic, crushed*
salt and pepper	1 *tablespoon flour*
3 *tablespoons salad oil*	*red wine*
1-2 *onions, chopped*	1 *faggot* (page 294)

Cut eel in 1½ to 2 inch pieces and season with salt and pepper. Heat oil and sauté eel in it until golden brown on all sides. Add onion and cook it until it is golden. Add garlic. Remove all to saucepan, sprinkle with flour, mix well, and add enough red wine and water (using half of each) to cover. Add faggot, bring to a boil, cover pan and cook slowly 20 to 25 minutes or until eel is tender. Discard faggot, skim fat from surface of liquid, and correct seasoning. Serves 3 to 4.

EELS IN MATELOTE

1 *eel* (2 *lbs.*) *skinned and cleaned*	½ *lb. mushrooms*
salt and pepper	2 *tablespoons butter*
8 *small onions, parboiled*	1 *tablespoon flour*
1 *faggot* (page 294)	*bread fried in butter*
red or white wine	

Cut eel in 1½ to 2 inch pieces, and season with salt and pepper. Put in saucepan with onions, faggot, and enough wine and water (using half of each) to cover. Bring to a boil, cover pan, and cook 25 to 30 minutes or until eel is tender. Five minutes before the end of the cooking time, skim off fat from surface of liquid and add mushrooms. Remove pieces of eel, onions and mushrooms to serving dish, after draining them well. Discard faggot. Cook the liquid until reduced to one-half the original quantity. Thicken with Manié Butter, made by creaming together butter and flour. Bring to a boil, stirring constantly, correct seasoning and strain over eel and vegetables. Serve garnished with bread fried in butter. Serves 3 to 4.

SAUTEED EELS

Cut very young eels in 1½ to 2 inch pieces. Season with salt and pepper, dip in milk, then in flour. Heat salad oil very hot in frying pan, add eels and cook about 6 or 7 minutes on each side or until tender and golden brown. Remove to serving dish, sprinkle with lemon juice and parsley. Pour off oil from pan and add butter to pan, allowing one-half tablespoon for each serving. Cook until hazelnut brown and pour over eels.

EELS VINAIGRETTE

1 *eel* (2 *lbs.*) *skinned and cleaned*	1 *clove garlic, crushed*
salt and pepper	1 *faggot* (page 294)
1 *tablespoon butter* (*or oil*)	*white wine*
1 *onion, sliced*	*Vinaigrette Sauce* (page 35)
1 *carrot, sliced*	

Cut eel in 1½ to 2 inch pieces and season with salt and pepper. Spread butter in bottom of saucepan and place onion and carrot on it. Add garlic and faggot and enough wine and water (using half of each) to cover. Bring to a boil, cover pan and cook 20 to 25 minutes or until eel is tender. Let cool in cooking liquid. Skim fat from surface of liquid, remove eel to serving dish, and combine with Vinaigrette Sauce.

If preferred, the eels may be chilled in the cooking liquid and served after the liquid jellies. Eels cooked this way can also be removed from the cooking liquid and then sautéed in oil and served with lemon and browned butter, or they can be dipped in Fritter Batter (page 90) or coated à l'Anglaise (page 293) and fried in deep hot fat or oil. Serves 3 to 4.

FROGS' LEGS
(Les Grenouilles)

The meat of frogs' legs is white, tender, and very delicate, much like

[61]

the white meat of a young chicken. Very large legs, however, are a gamble because they are sometimes tough. I have always found medium-sized ones—eight to ten to the pound—best. Although the small ones—eighteen to twenty to the pound—can be depended upon to be tender, there is little eating on them and one is buying practically all bone. It is impossible to tell which legs will be tough and which tender until they start to cook. After that it is very easy because as soon as the first heat reaches them the tough legs suddenly straighten out very stiffly, and the longer they cook the tougher and stringier the meat becomes. They are always too tough to serve. The joints of the tender ones, on the other hand, remain relaxed and the meat becomes tender during cooking.

To prepare frogs' legs, take off the skin, if not already done, and cut off the feet. Then soak them in very cold water, changing it occasionally, for about two hours to make them white and to plump up the flesh. After this they can be prepared in any of the following ways, allowing about a half-pound for an average serving.

FROGS' LEG FRITTERS

Clean frogs' legs, cut off feet, and soak in cold water two hours. Drain and dry well. Marinate in salt, pepper, chopped parsley and a little vinegar. When ready to serve, dry them well, dip in Fritter Batter (page 90) and fry in deep hot fat or oil until golden brown. Drain. Serve with Fried Parsley (page 189) and Tomato Sauce (page 31).

FROGS' LEGS PROVENCAL

Follow recipe for Frogs' Legs Meunière (below), adding a little finely chopped garlic to the hazelnut brown butter about half a minute before pouring it over the frogs' legs.

FROGS' LEGS MARINIERE

Follow recipe for Frogs' Legs Poulette (page 63), omitting mushrooms.

FROGS' LEGS MEUNIERE

Clean frogs' legs, cut off the feet, and soak in cold water two hours. Drain and dry well. Dip in milk, then in flour, and sauté slowly in hot oil about 6 to 8 minutes (depending upon size), or until brown on all sides. Put in serving dish and season with salt, pepper, and a few drops of lemon juice. Pour off the oil from the pan and add butter, allowing one-half tablespoon for each person. Cook until hazelnut brown in color and pour over frogs' legs. Sprinkle with chopped parsley and garnish with a piece of lemon for each serving.

FROGS' LEGS POULETTE

2 *lbs. frogs' legs*	*½ glass white wine (or a few drops*
½ lb. mushrooms	*lemon juice in water)*
2 *tablespoons butter*	1 *teaspoon flour*
2 *shallots, chopped* (*or* 1 *tablespoon*	*½ teaspoon salt*
onion)	*a little pepper*
½ cup cream (*or top milk*)	1 *teaspoon chopped parsley*

Clean frogs' legs, cut off feet, and soak in cold water two hours. Drain and dry well. Clean and chop mushrooms and put in a saucepan with 1 tablespoon butter, shallots, and frogs' legs. Add wine (or lemon juice and water), bring to a boil, and cook 10 to 12 minutes. Remove frogs' legs to serving dish. Cook liquid in pan until reduced to not more than ¼ cup. Add cream, bring back to the boil, and cook 2 to 3 minutes. Thicken sauce with Manié Butter, made by creaming together remaining butter and flour and adding to the liquid. Bring to a boil, stirring constantly. Correct seasoning, add parsley, and pour over frogs' legs. If Cream Sauce is on hand, ¾ cup can be substituted for the cream and Manié Butter. Serves 4.

SNAILS
(Escargots)

Snails are best in the fall, in fact connoisseurs don't, as a rule, like spring snails. Those which grow in the wine-grape sections are considered the most desirable and they should be gathered when they have receded within their shells.

The cleaning of snails is a very important part of their preparation. First they must be washed in cold water, changing the water several times. Then remove the little membrane that covers the opening of each shell. After the membranes are removed, put them in a large pail of salted water, using two handfuls of salt and one glass of vinegar for about 50 snails. Leave for two hours, shaking them from time to time so they will throw out their impurities. Wash again in salted water, changing the water two or three times until all impurities are washed out.

To cook snails, put them in a kettle with one bottle of white wine and just enough water to cover them, adding for each quart of liquor one teaspoon salt, one chopped carrot, one large onion studded with a clove, four minced shallots, four cloves of garlic, and a faggot made of five sprigs of parsley, two stalks of celery, one bay leaf, a little thyme, and five peppercorns. Bring to a boil and cook slowly about three to three and a half hours. Drain, remove each snail from its shell with a metal skewer and cut off the black spot at the end of each one. Put a little special Butter for Snails (below) in the bottom of each shell and cover with more of the butter. Put a few tablespoons of white wine in a flat round baking dish or in individual dishes. Arrange the snails on the dish and sprinkle each one with fine bread crumbs. Put in a hot oven or under the broiler for 7 or 8 minutes.

If desired, before returning the snails to their shells, they may be sautéed in a little butter to which some chopped shallots and crushed garlic have been added.

BUTTER FOR SNAILS
(For 50 Snails)

¾ *lb. butter*	1 *tablespoon chopped celery*
2 *teaspoons chopped shallots*	1 *teaspoon salt*
4 *cloves garlic, crushed to a fine*	*a little pepper*
paste	

Cream butter, add remaining ingredients, and mix all together thoroughly.

Eggs and Cheese

◄═❖═►

Eggs

I SELDOM saw eggs served at breakfast in the France that I knew. They were a plentiful food, especially in the spring, but we always ate them at lunch or dinner. They were a great favorite, too, and the ways which French housewives prepared them seemed numberless.

The mild flavor of eggs makes it possible, of course, to combine them with more foods than probably any other food we eat. Here in America bacon, ham and sausages are familiar accompaniments, but sometimes we forget the delicious combinations possible with such flavorful vegetables as tomatoes and spinach, and how many sauces there are that turn these amazing little packages of concentrated nourishment into excellent dishes for simple home dinners.

BOILED EGGS
Soft-Boiled

The softness or hardness of a boiled egg depends, of course, upon the length of time it cooks. There are two ways of preparing the soft-boiled ones. The way I prefer is to start them in boiling water and boil them for 3 minutes. The other way is to place them in cold water, bring to the boiling point, and boil for 2 seconds. These time periods apply to eggs at room temperature when put in the water.

Hard-Boiled

Although many people don't seem to realize it, a hard-boiled egg can be poorly cooked like any other food. It must not, for example, be cooked too long because then the yolk becomes dark-colored and has an unpleasant strong odor. Put the eggs in boiling water and simmer them for 10 minutes. Then remove from the water and plunge immediately into cold water. The sudden change from hot to cold condenses

[65]

a little of the steam between egg and shell, causing the shell to slip off like a charm.

OEUFS MOLLETS

The French prepare a kind of soft-boiled egg called Oeuf Mollet which is served with sauces or in any of the ways that poached eggs are served. To prepare Oeufs Mollets, put the eggs in boiling water, turn down the heat, and simmer them for 5 to 6 minutes. Plunge them into cold water, remove, and take off the shells. Keep the shelled eggs warm by leaving them covered with lukewarm salted water until ready to serve. The whites will be firm and the yolks soft, very much like poached eggs. For ways to serve Oeufs Mollets, follow any of the recipes suggested for Poached Eggs (pages 71 to 72).

EGGS BECHAMEL

6 *hard-boiled eggs*
1 *cup Béchamel Sauce* (page 24)

¼ *cup grated Parmesan or Swiss cheese*

Cut eggs lengthwise and remove yolks. Rub yolks through a fine sieve and mix with ½ cup Béchamel Sauce. Correct the seasoning if necessary. Spread about 2 tablespoons Béchamel Sauce in a china baking dish, place egg whites on it, and fill whites with egg yolk mixture. Cover with the remaining sauce, sprinkle with grated cheese, and brown in a hot oven or under the broiler. Serves 3 to 4.

EGGS IN COCOTTE

A cocotte is a small porcelain baking dish in which eggs are baked. Coat the cocotte with melted butter, break the egg into it and add 1 tablespoon of sweet cream. Place cocotte in a shallow pan of boiling water, cover, and bake in a moderate oven of 375 degrees, 6 to 8 minutes, or until white is congealed, or cook on top of stove 5 to 6 minutes. Sometimes a heartier dish is wanted. Then chicken or vegetables, such as tomato or asparagus, may be placed in the bottom of the cocotte; or a little Mornay Sauce (page 28) and grated cheese or some meat gravy may be put on top of the egg.

EGGS BOURGUIGNONNE
(Oeufs Pochés au Vin Rouge)

In every part of France where red wine is plentiful, and especially in the sections where a very light red wine is made, the kind with so little alcohol that it cannot stand shipping and must be consumed at home, the wine is used in many ways not common in other parts of the world. Eggs Bourguignonne, or Oeufs Pochés au Vin as they are often called, is one of these ways. The eggs are poached in a well-seasoned liquor the base of which is a light red wine. This recipe is very typical of our Bourbonnaise cuisine and one which my mother frequently served on Fridays or other fast days.

2 cups light red wine (or wine and water)	a little thyme
	slices of white bread fried in butter
2 tablespoons butter	(rubbed with a little garlic, if de-
1 tablespoon flour	sired)
6-8 poached eggs	1 teaspoon salt
2 shallots, chopped	a little pepper
1 bay leaf	1 sprig parsley

Boil wine in a saucepan with shallots, bay leaf, thyme, parsley, salt, and pepper. Poach eggs in this liquor and when done remove to another dish. Cook liquor until reduced to a third of its original quantity. Mix 1 tablespoon of butter with flour and add gradually to the liquor. Stir vigorously. Correct seasoning and add remaining butter. Strain. Serve eggs on fried bread with sauce poured over. Serves 3 to 4.

EGG CROQUETTES

6 hard-boiled eggs cut in fine dice	1 egg yolk
1 cup thick Béchamel Sauce (page 24)	½ teaspoon salt

Mix all ingredients together and chill. Divide into balls about the size of an egg and form into any desired shape, roll in flour, and coat à l'Anglaise (page 293). Cook in very hot deep oil or fat until brown. Serve with Tomato Sauce (page 31) or Cream Sauce (page 25) and with parsley that has been washed, dried, and fried in the same fat with the eggs. Serves 3 to 4.

DEVILLED EGGS, COLD
(Oeufs Diablés Froids)

3 hard-boiled eggs	2 tablespoons mayonnaise (page 34)
a little salt	Tartar Sauce (page 35)
½ teaspoon prepared mustard	paprika

Cut eggs in half lengthwise. Rub yolks through a sieve. Add salt, mustard, and mayonnaise. Mix well. Place whites on serving dish and fill them with egg yolk mixture. Coat them with Tartar Sauce (or mayonnaise) and sprinkle with paprika. Serves 3.

DEVILLED EGGS, HOT
(Oeufs Diablés Chauds)

3 *hard-boiled eggs*
½ *teaspoon prepared mustard*
2 *tablespoons Béchamel Sauce*
  (page 24)

a little salt
Mornay Sauce (page 28)
grated cheese
paprika

Cut eggs in half lengthwise. Rub yolks through a fine sieve, add mustard, Béchamel Sauce, and salt. Mix well. Arrange whites on heat-proof serving dish and fill them with egg yolk mixture. Cover with Mornay Sauce and sprinkle with grated cheese. Put in hot oven of 425 degrees or under broiler to brown. Sprinkle with paprika. Serves 3.

EGGS A LA TRIPE

6 *hard-boiled eggs*
2 *medium onions*
2 *tablespoons butter*
1 *teaspoon salt*

a little pepper
2 *tablespoons flour*
2 *cups hot milk* (*or half milk and*
  half cream)

Parboil onions for two or three minutes, drain, and place in a sauce-pan with the butter. Cook them slowly without letting them brown, then add flour, salt, and pepper, and mix all together well. Add milk gradually and cook one-half hour, stirring all the time at first and then occasionally. Slice the eggs and mix with the sauce. If desired, the onions may be strained out of the sauce before it is combined with the eggs. Serves 3.

FRIED EGGS

Melt butter in frying pan or use fat from fried bacon. Break the eggs in the pan and cook a few minutes or until the white is set. Or fry the bacon (or ham) first, then drop the eggs into the pan and finish cooking all together.

FRIED EGGS FRENCH STYLE
(Oeufs à la Française)

Break the egg on a plate and slide into a pan of oil heated very hot for deep fat frying. Roll the egg with a wooden spoon as it cooks so that it will have its original shape, but do this very carefully so the yolk will not break. Let fry until the egg is golden brown. Remove from the oil, drain off surplus fat, and season with salt. Serve with rice or with vegetables, or use them as a garnish for other foods. Parsley fried in the fat is usually served with these eggs, and Tomato Sauce.

OMELETS

A French housewife is never at a loss for a dish to serve her family or guest if she has a few eggs in the house—or out in the *poulailler*, that is, the hen house. Before you can turn around she has whisked up the eggs, and her long handled black iron omelet pan is heating on the stove, waiting to receive them. Her omelet pan, like her marmite, is as important a part of a French housewife's equipment as the stove on which she cooks. But it is a pan sacred to omelets; nothing else is ever cooked in it. Nor is it ever washed, but cleaned with a cloth and plenty of coarse salt. Using an omelet pan to cook anything else, or washing it with water, makes each succeeding omelet stick to the pan, an unheard-of occurrence which would make any French housewife blush with shame.

Mother made two kinds of omelets, the rolled ones that are familiar to all Americans and also a flat kind that is less often seen here but which is more common than rolled ones in many sections of France. Instead of rolling or folding the egg mixture when the bottom has set, a flat omelet is flipped over like a pancake, and these, let me tell you, can be made just as creamy inside and as tender as the rolled variety.

Our favorite all-year-round omelet, and a good hearty dish if there ever was one, was *Omelette Paysanne*, which combined salt pork or ham, potatoes, and herbs with the eggs. We also liked those that were made with tomatoes and onions. But in September when the fields were covered with mushrooms, mushrooms went into every omelet, until cold weather deprived us of that seasonal luxury. In really cold weather, an *Omelette au Rhum* was an occasional extra-special treat to end a light supper.

Medium-sized omelets are as a rule better than large ones, because an omelet made of too many eggs is difficult to make well. But most important to remember is that too much beating always makes a poor omelet, heavy and watery. The eggs should be well broken up, but that is all.

PLAIN OMELET

For 3 to 4 eggs, use ¼ teaspoon salt and 1 tablespoon butter. Mix the eggs lightly with a fork and add the salt. Be careful not to overbeat the eggs. Place the butter in an omelet pan and let it become hazelnut brown. Put the eggs in the butter and stir briskly with a fork to make sure that the eggs are not sticking to the pan at any point. They should congeal immediately upon contact with the hot butter. Roll the omelet by moving the skillet and folding both sides with a fork. Invert serving dish over pan, then turn pan and dish over to slip omelet onto the dish. Serves 2.

OMELET COUNTRY STYLE
(Omelette Paysanne)

6 eggs
⅓ cup diced salt pork (or bacon or cooked ham)
2 potatoes, finely diced
1 cup sorrel, cooked down and drained (optional)

a little chopped parsley
a little chopped chives (optional)
a little salt
2 tablespoons butter

Melt 1 tablespoon butter in omelet pan and add diced pork (or bacon or ham). When dice are brown, remove to a plate and reserve. Add potatoes to fat in pan and sauté until they are soft and golden brown. Add lightly beaten eggs mixed with salt, pork dice, sorrel, parsley, and chives. Shake pan and at the same time stir the ingredients with a fork. When eggs start to set around the edges, put remaining butter around the edges and under the omelet and move the pan gently in a circular motion to make sure the omelet is not sticking to the bottom. When the first faint odor of eggs just starting to brown is noticeable, flip over the omelet and let brown lightly on the other side. When that side has set and started to brown, slide omelet onto serving platter. Serves 3 to 4.

FLORENTINE OMELET

Cook fresh spinach and drain very thoroughly, but do not chop it. Mix with eggs, season with salt and pepper, and make into either a rolled or flat omelet.

MUSHROOM OMELET
(Omelette aux Champignons)

Clean and slice mushrooms, sauté in butter, and mix with eggs which have been slightly beaten. Cook, following directions for Plain Omelet (page 69).

OMELET PARMENTIER

Follow recipe for Omelet Paysanne (above), using only the potato, parsley, and chives in it.

OMELET WITH TOMATO

Peel, seed, and chop tomatoes (allowing one for each person), and cook until thick, like stewed tomatoes. Season with salt and a pinch of sugar. Make a plain rolled omelet (page 69). Before rolling the omelet, put one-half the cooked tomatoes in it, roll it up, and place on serving platter. Put remaining cooked tomatoes at either end as a garnish.

RUM OMELET
(Omelette au Rhum)

Make a plain rolled omelet or a rolled omelet with jam or jelly or marmalade in the center. While the omelet is cooking, heat a little rum in a saucepan. Turn the omelet onto a hot serving dish and sprinkle the top with sugar. Pour the hot rum over it, letting the rum run down on the plate and around the edges of the omelet. *Flambé*, that is, light the rum and spoon it over the omelet as it flames. Bring the dish to the table while the rum burns.

POACHED EGGS
(Oeufs Pochés)

In France poached eggs are seldom served for breakfast. Instead, they make the main dish of a lunch or supper. But they are not served plain, and usually have a vegetable such as spinach, or perhaps slices of ham, under them, and a sauce like Mornay or Hollandaise poured over them. Nor are they always served hot. Very frequently they are served cold, garnished with meat or vegetables and covered with a sparkling aspic jelly—a welcome treat on a hot day.

Eggs for poaching must be very fresh if the white is to congeal quickly and completely envelope the yolk. Unless an egg does this and so holds its shape during cooking, the white and the yolk separate.

To Poach Eggs

Put 1 quart of water and 2 tablespoons vinegar in a shallow pan and bring to the boil. Break egg on a plate and sprinkle a little salt on the yolk, then slide it gently into the boiling water. Let simmer over low heat about 3 to 3½ minutes, basting very gently with the surrounding water. When the white is set, remove egg with a perforated spoon or skimmer. Eggs can be poached an hour or so before they are to be served and kept warm—without changing their texture at all—by placing them in plain lukewarm water. If preferred, the vinegar may be omitted when poaching eggs.

POACHED EGGS A L'ANGLAISE

Poach eggs in plain boiling water (omitting the vinegar), and cook

[71]

them just before they are to be eaten. Serve plain on toast or with
bacon or ham.

POACHED EGGS FLORENTINE

Drain poached eggs, and place on a bed of cooked spinach leaves.
(Do not chop or cream the spinach.) Cover with Mornay Sauce
(page 28), spread a little melted butter on top, and brown quickly
in hot oven of 425 degrees, or under broiler.

POACHED EGGS MORNAY

Drain poached eggs, and place on slices of toast. Cover with Mornay
Sauce (page 28), spread a little melted butter on top, and brown
quickly in hot oven of 425 degrees, or under broiler.

POACHED EGGS SUZETTE

Bake a large potato and when done cut a circle out of the top large
enough to hold an egg. Remove potato pulp from shell, mash with 1
teaspoon butter, season with a little salt, and put back into shell, leaving enough space in it to hold a poached egg. Cover egg with Mornay
Sauce (page 28), sprinkle with grated cheese, and brown quickly in
hot oven of 425 degrees, or under broiler.

COLD POACHED EGGS

Follow directions for poached eggs, but allow an extra minute of
cooking time. Remove from boiling water and place in cold water to
prevent further cooking and also to chill them. Remove and serve in
either of the following ways: garnish with slices of ham, decorate with
leaves of tarragon or chervil, and cover with Aspic Jelly (page 293);
or garnish with slices of ox tongue, sliced tomatoes, and any spring
vegetables, and cover with Aspic Jelly (page 293).

SCRAMBLED EGGS
(Oeufs Brouillés)

Scrambled eggs must always be cooked at the last minute. People
should wait for them because they cannot stand and retain all their
delectable characteristics. Perfect scrambled eggs are smooth and
creamy, and this is done most easily by stirring them with a wooden
spoon as they cook.

If they should start to become too firm, a little butter or cream, or
the yolk of another egg, can be whipped in briskly and will bring back
their creaminess. It is very important to scramble eggs over a low heat,

for which reason a double boiler is often used, a method which maintains a low temperature all during the cooking and insures their smoothness and delicacy.

6 *eggs*   2 *tablespoons cream* (*optional*)
2 *tablespoons butter*   *salt and pepper*

Break eggs in a bowl and beat until well mixed but not too light. Melt 1 tablespoon of butter in a saucepan, add eggs, and cook over a low fire, mixing with a wooden spoon as they cook. Keep heat very low because too hot a fire will make the mixture lumpy. When eggs start to coagulate add remaining tablespoon of butter (and the cream, if used) and correct the seasoning. Serve plain or with cheese, mushrooms, tomatoes, asparagus, chopped chives and parsley, chicken livers, bacon, ham, or sausages.

SHIRRED EGGS
(Oeufs sur le Plat)

Use a special porcelain shirred-egg dish or cocotte which holds two eggs. Put one teaspoon melted butter in the dish and break two eggs into it. Place in a moderately hot oven of 375 to 400 degrees for two or three minutes, just long enough to have the white congeal. Serve plain or garnished with tomatoes, asparagus tips, bacon, ham, sausages, chicken livers, or kidneys. Or serve with black butter as follows: sprinkle with a few drops of vinegar, season with salt and pepper, and pour over the top some butter which has been cooked until very dark brown. In this case, do not have the eggs too well cooked because the hot butter will finish cooking them. Never sprinkle salt over shirred eggs before cooking them, as it gives them an unattractive speckled appearance.

SHIRRED EGGS WITH BACON AND CHEESE

2 *slices broiled bacon*   2 *eggs*
2 *thin slices Swiss cheese*

Put bacon in the bottom of a porcelain shirred-egg dish or cocotte and place the cheese on it. Drop the eggs on top, being careful not to break the yolks. Bake in a moderately hot oven of 400 degrees for two or three minutes, or until the whites are congealed. Serves 1.

SHIRRED EGGS WITH SPINACH

Put a little butter in a porcelain shirred-egg dish, spread cooked

[73]

spinach over the bottom of the dish and drop the eggs on top. Cook as for Shirred Eggs (page 73).

STUFFED EGGS AURORA
(Oeufs Farcis à l'Aurore)

Cut 4 hard-boiled eggs lengthwise and remove yolks. Rub yolks through a sieve or mash them. Add 1 tablespoon butter and 2 tablespoons thick purée of tomato and season with salt and pepper. Arrange whites on a heatproof serving dish and fill them with egg yolk mixture. Put in a moderate oven to heat, but don't allow to brown. Cover with a sauce made by mixing ½ cup very hot Béchamel Sauce (page 24) with 4 tablespoons thick Tomato Sauce (page 31). Serves 4.

STUFFED EGGS SURPRISE
(Oeufs Farcis Surprise)

Cut 4 hard-boiled eggs lengthwise and remove yolks. Rub yolks through a sieve or mash them. Add 1 tablespoon butter and season with salt and pepper. Add about ½ cup finely chopped leftover meat or Mushroom Duxelles (page 185) and a little chopped parsley. Arrange whites on a heatproof serving dish and fill them with the mixture. Cover with Mornay Sauce (page 28), sprinkle with grated cheese, and brown quickly in hot oven of 425 degrees or under broiler. Serves 4.

Cheese

CHEESE CROQUETTES

2 tablespoons butter	¾ cup cheese, cut in small cubes
3 tablespoons flour	½ teaspoon salt
1½ cups boiling milk	a little pepper
2 egg yolks or	
1 whole egg, beaten	

Melt butter in saucepan, add flour, and cook until it starts to turn golden. Add milk and cook, stirring constantly until thickened, then continue cooking, stirring occasionally until it is reduced to about 1 cup. Add the cheese and then the egg yolks (or egg) and mix well over low heat until thoroughly combined. Correct the seasoning, spread on a flat buttered dish, and let cool. When cold, form croquettes in any desired shape. Coat à l'Anglaise (page 293) and sauté in butter or fry in deep hot fat. Serve with Tomato Sauce (page 31). Serves 4.

CHEESE AND POTATO PIE

This is a very old-fashioned French recipe which both my mother and grandmother served often. Ours was a dairy section where milk was plentiful and cottage cheese was made so regularly, it was almost always on hand. So we used it in many ways, some of them a little unusual. This particular cheese pie was a main dish with which we ate a cooked vegetable and, in season, a green salad. What was left we ate cold the next day, usually after generous bowls of hot soup—and a good meal we thought it. For good texture in this pie, or any cheese pie or cake, break up the cottage cheese with a wire whip—or a slotted spoon—and then run it through a fine strainer so that it is very smooth, with no lumps.

2 cups cottage cheese	½ teaspoon salt
½ cup sour cream	a little milk
2½ cups freshly cooked potatoes, riced	1 tablespoon butter
	pastry for 9-inch pie (page 227)

Whip cheese until it is smooth and run through a fine sieve. Mix with sour cream and add potatoes while they are still warm. Add salt. Cover bottom and sides of 10-inch pan with pastry, rolling the edge to form a border. Fill with the cheese and potato mixture, brush top with milk, and dot with small pieces of butter. Bake in a medium oven of 350 to 375 degrees about 45 minutes or until brown. Serves 6.

CHEESE SOUFFLE

A soufflé to be good must be handled carefully and quickly. The yolks must be beaten very light and the whites beaten stiff, but not past the point where they lose their sheen and become dry. Combining the whites by "folding" them in is particularly important and is done by cutting through and turning the mixture over and over very lightly, until no masses of white are visible and the mixture is light and fluffy. Stirring mashes the air out of the whites and the delicacy of the soufflé vanishes. As soon as the whites are in, the dish must go in the oven immediately—every minute of delay gives the eggs a chance to go flat. And finally, everyone must be ready to eat the soufflé the minute it is done.

[75]

¼ cup butter	a little cayenne pepper
½ cup flour	a little nutmeg
4 egg yolks	¾ cup finely grated cheese
1½ cups hot milk	(Parmesan, dry Swiss, or Cheddar)
½ teaspoon salt	4 egg whites

Melt butter, add flour, and cook slowly until the flour just begins to turn golden. Add milk and cook five minutes, mixing with a whip or slotted spoon. Add seasonings. Beat yolks until light, turn a little of the hot mixture into them, and when well combined return to the hot mixture. Reheat to boiling point, stirring constantly, but do not allow to boil. Remove from fire and add cheese. Fold in egg whites, which have been beaten stiff but not too dry. Pour into a buttered deep baking dish and bake in a hot oven of 425 degrees about 20 minutes. Serves 4 to 5.

CHEESE TART

8 ozs. Swiss cheese	a little paprika
1½ cups hot milk	a little nutmeg
3 eggs, beaten	pastry for 9-inch pie (page 227)
½ teaspoon salt	

Line pie plate with pastry. Slice cheese into fine pieces and place over the pastry. Add milk to eggs, add seasonings, and pour over the cheese. Bake in a moderately hot oven of 375 degrees 35 to 40 minutes or until custard is set and top is brown. Serves 6.

QUICHE LORRAINE

tart pastry (page 227) for 8 to 10-inch pan	3 eggs and 1 yolk, beaten
	1 tablespoon flour
6 slices bacon, not too thin	½ teaspoon salt
6 ozs. Swiss cheese, thinly sliced	a little nutmeg
2 cups milk	1 tablespoon butter

Line an 8 to 10-inch pie plate with the tart pastry. Cut bacon slices in two and broil them. (If bacon is very salty, parboil it and drain before broiling.) Overlap slices of broiled bacon and cheese over the bottom of the pastry. Mix together eggs, flour, salt, and nutmeg, and combine with the milk. Melt butter and let it continue cooking until it starts to brown, then add it to the custard mixture and pour it all over the bacon and cheese. Bake in a moderately hot oven of 375 degrees until custard is set and brown on top, about 35 to 40 minutes. Serve warm. Serves 6.

Meat, Poultry and Game

⊲⊐ ✣ ⊏⊳

Rules for Roasting

ALTHOUGH each type of meat and poultry must be considered separately, there are some over-all rules for roasting them. The first thing to remember is that it is preferable to place the meat on a trivet or rack because even a little space under the meat gives the heat a chance to get all around it. Second, the meat, excepting pork and ham, should have plenty of fat spread over it in addition to its own fat—beef suet or fresh beef or pork drippings can be used for all meats, while slices of fat salt pork are especially good for poultry. With young spring chickens, however, some people prefer butter. Next, the pan should never be covered, and last, the meat should be frequently basted during roasting with the hot fat from the pan. Adding water to the pan is not necessary unless the fat, and the juice which drips into it, seem about to scorch. And then only a couple of spoonfuls are needed with more added—a very little at a time—as the water evaporates. Care must be taken in basting meat to skim off the fat and spoon it over and never to baste with any of the water.

Gravy is made the same way for all kinds of meat and poultry and in French cooking is never thickened with flour. To make gravy, skim off all the surplus fat from the pan, leaving just enough to flavor the gravy, then add a little water—or stock—and cook directly over the fire, stirring in all the brown crustiness that has formed around the pan. Season it, of course, with salt. If water is used, the true flavor of the particular meat is retained, whereas stock, which usually combines other meat and also vegetable flavors, adds other flavors.

In roasting dark meats, that is, beef and mutton, there are three degrees of doneness, namely, rare, medium and well done. An experienced cook can tell which point has been reached merely by touch-

[77]

ing the meat. If very soft it is not cooked enough, if a little springy it is rare to medium well done and if it is firm it is well done. Doneness can also be judged by pricking deeply with a two-tined kitchen fork or metal skewer and watching the color of the juice that comes out when the skewer is withdrawn. If the juice is blood-red the meat is rare, if pink it is medium done, if clear and colorless it is well done. But the average person gets the best results, particularly in roasting beef, by timing the cooking per pound of weight, as given below and on page 79.

In roasting white meats like pork, veal and very young lamb, it is almost impossible to set a truly accurate time because it will vary just a little with the shape and thickness of the cut, the size and distribution of the bones and the amount of fat. So the time table is a guide but your fork must be the final test. This same variation of bone and fat exists with beef but no harm is done if beef is a little more or less rare whereas white meats, never served rare, must be given sufficient cooking.

Finally, before roasting any meat it is well to make sure that it is suitable for roasting. Many times a piece of meat—a cut of pork, for example—will be old and thus apt to be tough, or a cut of beef, too fresh to be tender. Then braising is better than roasting.

TIME TABLE FOR ROASTING

BEEF

For a roast of beef with the bone in it, start the meat in a hot oven of 450 to 475 degrees and sear it to hold in the juices. When it is brown all over, probably in 15 to 20 minutes, turn down the heat to medium, 375 degrees, and finish the cooking. For the entire cooking time, that is, including searing and roasting, allow 12 minutes per pound for rare, 15 minutes per pound for medium and 15 to 20 minutes per pound for well done. For a boned roast allow an extra 5 to 7 minutes per pound. A whole filet of beef should first be larded with strips of fat pork and roasted in a hot even of 425 to 450 degrees during the entire cooking, allowing 8 minutes per pound.

MUTTON

A leg or loin of mutton—or lamb that is almost mutton—should be roasted in a hot oven of 400 to 425 degrees during the entire cooking time, allowing 12 to 15 minutes per pound. This brings it to the pink stage.

LAMB

The time required to cook a leg of lamb depends entirely upon its age. A very young, very small leg should be well done and is roasted in a hot oven of 400 to 425 degrees during the entire cooking, allowing 18 minutes per pound. But a larger leg that has come from older lamb is more delicious if removed from the oven while still a little on the pink side. For this, allow 12 to 15 minutes per pound.

VEAL

Loin or rack of veal requires a moderately hot oven of 375 to 400 degrees, allowing 18 to 20 minutes per pound. It must be well done, never showing the least tinge of pink. And when roasting the rump, it will be more tasty if the butcher has larded it with strips of fat pork.

PORK

Pork loin requires a moderately hot oven of 375 to 400 degrees, allowing 20 to 25 minutes per pound. It must be well done, never pink.

POULTRY
Chicken, Capon and Turkey

White-meat poultry like chicken, capon and turkey should be well done—but not cooked until dry—and should have a good brown color all over, following directions on pages 122 and 144. To find out when a bird is done, pierce the thick part of the second joint with a two-tined kitchen fork and make sure that the juice which follows the fork, when it is withdrawn, is clear and colorless. Or if the bird is not stuffed it can be lifted up to let the juice run out from the inside. The juice must be clear and colorless. In either case, more cooking is required if the juice has any pinkness at all.

DUCK

Duck, with the exception of wild ducks which are preferred rare, must be cooked "*à point*" which means just exactly right, not the least bit over-done or under-done. For a 5 to 6 pound duck, allow about an hour in a moderately hot oven of 400 to 425 degrees. For wild duck, use a hotter oven, about 450 to 475 degrees, and a very short time, not more than 10 minutes unless it is wanted medium rare which takes 15 to 18 minutes. The time varies a bit according to the size of the bird.

GAME
Small Feathered Game

All small feathered game like pheasant, guinea hen, partridge and quail must be well covered with slices of fat pork and will profit by being basted with added drippings of fresh pork fat. These birds require cooking in a hot oven of 425 to 450 degrees. The temperature and time required depend upon the size—the smaller the game the hotter the oven and the shorter the time to cook them without their drying out. A 2 pound guinea hen or pheasant takes 30 to 40 minutes, an average American partridge about 30 to 40 minutes—and I say "American" because the French partridge is a much smaller bird and takes only 12 to 15 minutes to roast. Quail—the French style of cooking is to roll them in grape leaves before covering them with fat pork slices—takes 12 to 15 minutes in an oven of 450 degrees.

Furred Game

Game, like venison and hare, or any other furred game, should be well covered with fat pork and large pieces of meat should be larded with strips of fat salt pork. Then the bottom of the roasting pan should be well covered with salad oil which must be heated very hot. The meat is put in this hot oil and roasted in a hot oven of 400 to 425 degrees, allowing 10 to 12 minutes per pound and turning it over in the oil so that it browns on all sides. Game is frequently marinated in wine, spices and herbs, as described in the recipes, and then it is very important to dry it well with a towel, not merely drain it, before cooking. Otherwise its moist surface will prevent it from browning.

Beef

Beef, in fact all meat, has never been too plentiful in the country sections of France. And although the beef that reached our home kitchens was good home-grown beef, it was seldom the very best because that went to the large cities—Paris, Lyons, and so on—where it brought higher prices. This fact seemed only to be a challenge to French housewives.

Most of our beef was made into dishes that take the long cooking which helps to make meat tender. Long cooking, of course, does not necessarily insure a delicious result; the cooking must also be gentle or else the meat is very apt to become stringy. If the dish is to be tasty, flavors and seasonings must be carefully considered in relation to the cut of meat and the length of time it will cook. *Bonnes ménagères* —good housewives—like my mother and grandmother were experts in making the toughest and least desirable cuts delicious. Sometimes they would let the meat stand in a marinade of wine, herbs and spices before it was cooked. They always watched the pot to make sure that it simmered so gently that it hardly bubbled. And never, absolutely never, can I remember either of them making a sauce that was floury-thick or tasteless. Instructions or recipes can only be a guide in this kind of cooking. The excellence of the result will still depend upon the carefulness and skill of the cook.

BEEF A LA MODE
(Boeuf à la Mode)

Beef à la Mode is a pot roast prepared the French way. Its special flavor—the reason why it is so delicious—depends upon the wine marinade in which it soaks before cooking. It penetrates the meat, is then used for the cooking liquid and finally goes in the sauce. If one is in a hurry these hours of marinating the meat can be omitted, in which case, the wine and spices are added to the pan after the meat has been browned. Do be particular, however, when you remove the meat from the marinade to wipe it as dry as possible—if it is wet it will not brown well. Be careful, too, about adding salt because as the liquid cooks down the salt in it becomes more pronounced. If you happen to have your oven going when the time comes to brown the meat, put it in the oven and baste it often with the fat. That gives it a fine even brown.

4-5 *lbs. rump of beef*
1 *tablespoon salt*
a little pepper
1 *pint wine (white or red)*
2 *tablespoons fat*
2 *tablespoons flour*
a veal bone (or calf's-foot)
   (optional)

5-6 *carrots, parboiled and cut in*
   pieces
12 *small onions (or 3 large cut in*
   quarters) browned in a little butter
1 *quart stock or water*
1 *cup canned tomatoes*
1 *clove garlic*
a faggot (page 294)

Have butcher lard beef with strips of larding pork. Season it with salt and pepper and put in a bowl with the wine. Let marinate in a cold place 5 to 6 hours, turning the meat over several times the better to absorb the wine. At the end of this time, put fat in saucepan and heat very hot. Remove meat from wine and dry it well all over, then brown in hot fat on all sides. When golden brown, drain fat from pan and sprinkle flour in bottom of pan and mix it with the brown juice which clings to the pan. Add bone, marinade, stock (or water), tomato, garlic and faggot. The meat should be just covered with liquid, but no more. Bring to a boil, cover pan and cook slowly on top of fire or in a moderate oven of 350 degrees about 2 hours. Remove meat from gravy and skim off all fat. Clean pan and put back meat with carrots, onions and strained gravy. Bring back to a boil and cook 1½ to 2 hours longer or until meat is tender. Test by piercing with a fork and if it offers no resistance it is tender. Remove veal bone (if used) or if calf's-foot is used cut meat in small pieces and serve with the beef. Correct the seasoning of the gravy, which should have reduced to about one half the original quality. May be served either hot or cold. If served cold, the veal bone should be included so that the gravy will become jellied. Serves 6 to 8.

BEEF EN DAUBE

2 lbs. rump of beef
1 teaspoon salt
a little pepper
1 glass red wine
2 shallots, chopped
¼ lb. fat salt pork, diced
3 or 4 slices of salt pork
3 tablespoons melted beef fat

beef or veal bones, browned in the oven
2 carrots, sliced
2 onions, chopped
2 cloves garlic, crushed
1 sprig parsley, 1 bay leaf and a little thyme tied in a faggot
2 cups stock or water
1 teaspoon chopped parsley

Have the butcher lard the meat with strips of larding pork. Cut meat into 12 pieces and season with salt and pepper. Put in a bowl with wine and shallots and leave for 2 hours, then drain and save the wine. Parboil salt pork dice, drain and sauté until brown. Heat beef fat in a frying pan until very hot and cook meat in it until well browned on both sides. Put browned bones in a casserole, add ½ the meat, ½ the carrots, the salt pork dice, ½ the onion, the garlic and faggot. Add remaining meat, carrots and onions. Add wine, and stock (or water). The meat should just be covered with liquid. Place salt pork slices on top.

Cover casserole and seal it with a roll of dough made by mixing 2 cups flour with enough water to make a stiff dough. Bring to a boil, then put in a slow oven of 325 degrees F. and cook 3 to 4 hours. Remove dough, uncover, skim off all fat and discard faggot. Serve from casserole. To serve cold, remove bones and chill in refrigerator until it jellies, then serve in slices. Serves 6.

BEEF HASH MENAGERE
(Hachis de Boeuf Ménagère)

With the kind of refrigeration we had in our homes, cooked meat could be kept much more safely than fresh. Therefore, when housewives bought their Sunday's meat they selected pieces large enough to make into leftover dishes for several days. Our beef was usually cooked in the Pot-au-Feu which, after all, is just boiled beef, delicious when hot but without too much flavor when cold—never juicy and flavorful like a piece of cold roast beef. But the dishes my mother made from this leftover boiled beef, especially the *hachis*—hash of various kinds—were such delicious tidbits that we enjoyed them as much as the original meat.

All sorts of flavorful ingredients, onions, herbs, tomatoes, and so on went into the hash. And our potatoes were so mealy and floury—like the Idaho variety in this country—that they gave the mixture a light, creamy consistency. The hash was baked—seldom fried—in a shallow earthenware dish, the brown kind of ware that we used for so many purposes.

1 *lb. leftover boiled or braised beef,*	½ *teaspoon salt*
chopped not too fine	*a little pepper*
2 *tablespoons butter or fat*	4 *medium potatoes*
1 *medium onion, finely chopped*	½ *cup hot milk*
1 *tablespoon flour*	1 *tablespoon butter*
1 *cup stock*	3 *tablespoons grated cheese*
½ *cup canned tomatoes*	2 *tablespoons bread crumbs*
chopped parsley	

Melt fat in saucepan, add onion and cook slowly until golden. Add flour, mix well and cook a few minutes. Add stock and tomato and cook, stirring until smooth. Add meat, parsley and seasoning and mix all together. Cook slowly 30 to 40 minutes, or longer if the mixture seems soft. Peel potatoes, cut in pieces and boil until soft, then drain and press through a ricer or sieve. Put the riced potatoes in a saucepan and stir with a spatula until very smooth, then add milk and butter little by little, mixing all the time. Correct the seasoning. This mashed potato should be rather thin. Put hash mixture in a heatproof serving dish and spread potato on top. Sprinkle with cheese and bread crumbs mixed together, and then with a little melted butter. Cook in a hot oven of 400 degrees or under the broiler until brown. Serves 4.

BEEF HASH A LA BOURBONNAISE
(Hachis de Boeuf à la Bourbonnaise)

2 cups leftover boiled, braised or roasted beef, chopped	½ teaspoon salt
2 tablespoons butter or fat	a little pepper
1 large onion, finely chopped	1 teaspoon chopped parsley
2 cups freshly cooked potatoes, chopped	fine bread crumbs

Melt butter, add onion and cook until golden. Remove from fire, add remaining ingredients and mix all together well. Spread in a well-greased flat earthenware dish and sprinkle top with fine bread crumbs and a little butter. Put in a moderately hot oven of 400 degrees F. and cook until brown on top. Serves 3.

BEEF HASH WITH CHESTNUTS

1 lb. leftover beef, cut in small dice	1 cup meat stock
2 dozen chestnuts	½ cup canned tomatoes
2 tablespoons butter	½ teaspoon chopped parsley
1 medium onion, finely chopped	½ teaspoon salt
1 tablespoon flour	a little pepper

Cook and peel chestnuts (page 174). Melt butter in saucepan, add onion and cook slowly until golden. Add flour, mix well and cook a few minutes, then add boiling stock and tomatoes. Stir until smooth and continue cooking until reduced to about 1 cup. Add meat, parsley and all the broken chestnuts. Add salt and pepper and bring to boiling point but do not allow to boil. Serve garnished with whole chestnuts. Serves 3.

BEEF MIROTON

1 lb. leftover boiled or braised beef	½ cup canned tomatoes
2 tablespoons butter or fat	a little salt and pepper
4 medium onions, minced	2 teaspoons vinegar
1 tablespoon flour	2 or 3 sour pickles, sliced
1 cup stock	1 teaspoon chopped parsley

Put butter in saucepan, add onion and cook slowly until golden. Add flour, cook a few minutes longer, add stock and tomatoes, salt and pepper and cook, stirring until it comes to a boil. Then continue cooking slowly 20 to 25 minutes. (For a sharper-tasting sauce, add ½ teaspoon dry mustard mixed with a little vinegar and 1 teaspoon grated horseradish). Add pickles. Do not boil after adding mustard, horseradish or pickles. Cut meat into thin slices and put in heatproof serving dish, pour sauce over meat and keep hot in oven until ready to serve, but do not allow to boil. Sprinkle parsley over the top. May be garnished with fried eggplant, or boiled potatoes sprinkled with bread crumbs and browned under the broiler. Serves 4.

BEEF SAUTE LYONNAISE

1 *cup leftover boiled beef cut in*	2 *tablespoons vinegar*
small thin slices	*salt and pepper*
1 *onion, sliced*	1 *cup sliced potatoes, sautéed*
2 *tablespoons butter*	1 *teaspoon chopped parsley*

Melt butter in frying pan and sauté meat quickly in it, until pieces are a little brown on both sides. Melt other tablespoon of butter in another pan and sauté onion in it until golden. Mix together beef, onion, vinegar, and season with salt and pepper. Then add potatoes, toss all together lightly and serve sprinkled with chopped parsley on top. Serves 3.

BEEF SALAD COUNTRY STYLE
(Salade de Boeuf Fermière)

1 *lb. leftover beef, thinly sliced*	1 *medium onion, finely chopped*
½ *cup fat salt pork*	1 *tablespoon mixed parsley, chervil*
½ *cup Vinaigrette Sauce* (page 35)	*and tarragon*
½ *cup warm stock*	½ *teaspoon salt*
2 *cups freshly cooked rice*	*a little pepper*
3 *tomatoes, peeled, seeded and*	2 *hard-boiled eggs*
thinly sliced	

Cut salt pork in small dice and sauté in pork fat until brown. Mix together Vinaigrette Sauce and stock. Add beef, salt pork and remaining ingredients. Serve garnished with sliced tomatoes and hard-boiled eggs arranged around the edge of the bowl. Serves 6.

BEEF STEW WITH VEGETABLES
(Ragoût de Boeuf)

When beef is fresh-killed and consequently less tender or when a cut of beef is a tough one, stew is about the best way of preparing it. The long slow cooking makes the meat tender. Other advantages are that stew is a delicious, nourishing and economical dish. The preparation of a really good stew, however, does take time and care—more than broiling a steak or chop takes—but the result is worth every bit of effort put into it. To my way of thinking a fine, flavorful stew is a treat and the sign of a good cook.

Any kind of meat can be made into a stew with many combinations of vegetables. When fresh vegetables are scarce, a combination of root vegetables—potatoes, carrots, turnips, onions, oyster plant or celery —can be used, or a combination of dried beans, potatoes, and onions. But when fresh beans and peas are in season, and therefore plentiful, that is the time to vary your stew by using them.

Making a good stew, like so many other things, depends upon know‑ ing and following a few simple rules. For good flavor it is essential to include some of the onion family, onions and garlic always, shallots if you have them, and to add a faggot for the special savor which it imparts. It is also important that the meat be well browned. This is accomplished by first wiping each piece of meat dry, then having good hot fat in which to brown the pieces and putting only a few pieces at a time in the pan. This procedure prevents the meat from steaming, which in turn would prevent browning. Finally a stew must never, never be hurried; instead, it must simmer gently, slowly. *"Mijoter"* is the French word we use to describe the gentle stewing which allows the mixture to barely bubble, a word for which I can find no English equivalent.

1¾ lbs. lean beef, cut in medium-
   sized pieces
1 teaspoon salt
a little pepper
6 small onions, sautéed
3 carrots, cut in pieces and parboiled
   5 minutes
1 clove garlic
2 tablespoons flour
enough water to cover the meat

3 sprigs parsley, 2 bay leaves and a
   little thyme tied in a faggot
½ cup Tomato Sauce (page 31)
2 or 3 tomatoes, peeled, seeded and
   chopped
1 tablespoon butter
1 heart of celery, cut in pieces
4 large potatoes, cut in pieces
1 teaspoon chopped parsley

Season meat with salt and pepper and fry in melted beef fat, along with 1 onion and 1 carrot until golden brown. Remove fat, add garlic and flour and mix well with a wooden spoon. Place in the oven for a few minutes to let the flour become brown. Add water, faggot and tomatoes, bring to a boil and cook slowly over low heat about 1½ hours. During this time sauté carrots in butter and prepare the other vegetables. Remove meat to another pan and place all the vegetables on top of it. Skim fat from gravy, correct the seasoning and strain over meat and vegetables. Add chopped parsley, bring to a boil and cook slowly for another hour or until meat is well done. Serves 4.

CARBONNADE DE BOEUF FLAMANDE

2 *lbs. beef (chuck or other lean beef)*
1 *teaspoon salt*
a little pepper
2 *tablespoons beef or veal fat*
2 *tablespoons flour*
1 *glass beer*
2 *tablespoons vinegar*

3 *cups stock (may be made from*
    bones, page 297)
1 *teaspoon sugar*
2 *tablespoons butter*
3 *large onions, minced*
1 *sprig parsley,* 1 *stalk celery, a little*
    thyme, 1 *bay leaf, tied in a faggot*

Have butcher cut meat into 12 slices and flatten them a little with a mallet. Season the slices with salt and pepper. Put fat in frying pan and when very hot sauté the meat, a few pieces at a time, until brown on both sides. Remove meat from pan, add flour to fat in pan and cook, stirring, until golden brown. Add beer, vinegar, stock and sugar and boil slowly, stirring until smooth. Melt butter in another saucepan, add onions and cook until golden. Put meat and onions in layers in a casserole, add faggot and strain the sauce over. Bring to a boil, cover and put in a hot oven of 425 degrees F. and cook 1½ to 2 hours or until meat is tender. Discard faggot, skim off all the fat from the top and serve from the casserole. If desired, the meat may be removed to a serving platter and the sauce strained over it to remove the onions. Serve boiled potatoes with this dish. Serves 6.

FRICADELLES OF BEEF

1 *lb. (or 2 cups) leftover cooked*
    beef, chopped
3 *large potatoes*
1 *large onion, finely chopped*
1 *tablespoon butter*

1 *egg, beaten*
1 *teaspoon chopped parsley*
salt and pepper
3 *tablespoons melted beef or veal fat*

Wash and bake potatoes. When done remove pulp, put in a bowl and crush and work up with a spoon until smooth. Cook onion in butter until golden and mix with meat. Then add potatoes. Add egg, parsley, salt and pepper and mix thoroughly. Divide the mixture into pieces about the size of an egg, roll in flour and flatten like hamburger cakes. Heat the beef fat in a frying pan and cook the cakes in it until brown on both sides. Then place pan in a moderately hot oven for 7 or 8 minutes. Serve with Tomato (page 31) or Piquante Sauce (page 29) and any desired vegetables. Serves 4.

SLICED BOILED BEEF MUSTARD

Cut leftover boiled beef in ¼ inch slices. Spread both sides of each slice with prepared mustard and dip in bread crumbs to coat both sides. Sprinkle top with a little melted butter and broil—or sauté—until both sides are brown. Put in a flat dish, season with salt and pepper and sprinkle with vinegar and chopped parsley. Let stand 15 to 20 minutes to absorb the vinegar. Dip in flour and then coat à l'Anglaise (page 293). Sauté in butter or fat until brown on both sides. Serve with Tomato Sauce (page 31).

BEEF KIDNEY SAUTE WITH MUSHROOMS

I have never subscribed to the idea that beef kidneys should be cooked a long time on top of the stove. Beef kidneys can easily become strong-tasting if they are over-cooked and may even become tough. If they seemed to be extra-strong-flavored kidneys, my mother put them in a colander and doused them up and down in boiling water a few times and drained them. Our way of cooking them—and I still follow it—was to cut them up into small pieces and sauté them quickly. Then they were drained in a colander while the sauce was made. The result was always delicate in flavor and tender.

1 *beef kidney*	⅓ *cup stock (or ½ cup canned*
4-5 *mushrooms*	*tomatoes)*
4 *tablespoons salad oil (or cooking*	½ *teaspoon salt*
fat)	*a little pepper*
3 *shallots, chopped*	2 *tablespoons butter*
1 *tablespoon flour*	½ *teaspoon chopped parsley*
⅓ *glass wine (red or white)*	

Wash and peel mushrooms and mince them. Put 2 tablespoons salad oil in a saucepan, heat very hot and add mushrooms. Cook slowly until brown. Add shallots and sprinkle the flour over all. Let cook, stirring all together, until the flour is golden. Add wine and stock, bring to the boil and cook slowly about 10 minutes. Meanwhile, remove skin from kidney, cut in half lengthwise and after removing fat and sinews, cut in thin slices or chop coarsely. Season with salt and pepper. Put remaining 2 tablespoons salad oil in frying pan and heat very hot. Add kidney slices and sauté for a few minutes on all sides. Turn into a colander and drain. Add them to the hot sauce, but do not let them boil. Add butter and chopped parsley. Serves 2 to 3.

BEEF BRAINS
(Cervelle de Boeuf)

Allow 1 brain for 2 to 3 people. Wash brains in cold water. Remove the membrane and blood which covers them, if there is any. Leave in cold water for several hours, changing the water often. Put brains in saucepan with enough cold water to cover, 2 tablespoons vinegar, 1 teaspoon salt, 5 peppercorns, ½ onion, sliced, 1 small carrot, sliced, and a faggot made of 4 sprigs parsley, a little thyme and a bay leaf. Bring to a boil, cover and simmer 25 to 30 minutes. Remove from heat. Leave brains in this cooking liquor until ready to prepare them for serving—never leave them unless covered with liquid.

BRAINS WITH BLACK BUTTER

Clean and cook brains (above). Remove from hot cooking liquid and cut to make 3 slices from each side of brain, 6 slices in all. Arrange on serving dish, season with salt and pepper, sprinkle with chopped parsley, about a dozen capers and a tablespoon of vinegar, Melt 3 tablespoons butter in a small pan and cook until almost black. Pour over the brains and serve very hot.

BRAINS RAVIGOTE

Clean and cook brains (above). Remove from hot cooking liquid and cut to make 3 slices from each side, 6 slices in all. Arrange on serving dish and pour Ravigote Sauce (page 31) over.

BRAINS VINAIGRETTE

Clean and cook brains (above). Remove from hot cooking liquid and cut to make 3 slices from each side of brain, 6 slices in all. Arrange on serving dish and pour over Vinaigrette Sauce (page 35) to which a chopped hard-boiled egg has been added. Sprinkle with finely chopped chives, tarragon and chervil. Serve either hot or cold.

BRAINS SAUTE

Clean and cook brains (above). Remove from hot cooking liquid and cut to make 3 slices from each side of brain, 6 slices in all. Dip in

[89]

flour. Sauté in hot oil or butter until brown on both sides. Serve with butter, melted and cooked until it is hazelnut brown, a slice of lemon and sprinkled with chopped parsley.

BRAIN FRITTERS
(Beignets de Cervelle)

It is important not to overwork the Fritter Batter. Mix until it is smooth, but still remains runny. If it is worked too much it will not cling to the slices of brains. A favorite garnish for Brain Fritters was parsley fried in the same fat that the fritters were cooked in. After washing and drying them, the clusters of parsley were dropped in the hot fat. After a few minutes they rise to the surface and then they are done.

Clean and cook brains (page 89). Remove from warm or cold cooking liquid and cut to make 3 slices from each side of brain, 6 slices in all. Season with salt and pepper and sprinkle with a few drops of lemon juice or vinegar, a tablespoon of olive oil and a little chopped parsley. Leave in this marinade about 20 minutes. Dip each slice of brain in Fritter Batter (below), drop in deep hot fat and cook until well browned. Remove and drain on towels. Serve with Tomato Sauce (page 31) and garnish with fried parsley.

FRITTER BATTER

¾ *cup flour*	¼ *cup warm water*
a little salt	*1 egg white, stiffly beaten*
2 tablespoons oil (*or melted butter*)	

Mix flour and salt with water. Add oil (or butter), mix smooth but do not overwork. Fold in the egg white.

BRAISED SMOKED OX TONGUE
(Langue de Boeuf Braisée)

Tongue must be soaked before cooking and the time required will depend upon how salty it is. Ask the butcher and if it is very salty, soak overnight, otherwise 3 to 4 hours is sufficient. To cook, cover generously with cold water, bring slowly to a boil and continue cooking slowly for 2 to 3 hours or until tender when pierced with a fork. Remove from the hot liquid and cut off tough end which contains bones and muscles. Peel off skin. Slice, arrange on serving platter and serve with Madeira Sauce (page 27) or Sauce Piquante (page 29).

COLD SMOKED OX TONGUE

Follow directions for soaking and cooking Braised Ox Tongue, but leave in the cooking liquid to cool. When cold remove from the liquid, cut away the tough end, peel off skin and slice as desired.

OXTAIL PARISIENNE
(Queue de Boeuf)

In making Oxtail Parisienne or any oxtail ragoût, I always prefer to start the cooking a day ahead and then to let it stand overnight in the refrigerator after the first four hours of cooking. This gives the fat a chance to rise to the surface and congeal and every single bit of it can be easily removed. An oxtail ragoût that has not been thoroughly skimmed is apt to be over rich in fat and too heavy for some digestions. Remember, however, that there must be enough liquid to cover the oxtails. If they poke up through the surface, it is almost impossible to get off all the fat.

1 *oxtail (about 2 lbs.), cut in sections*	1 *faggot* (page 294)
1 *teaspoon salt*	½ *glass white wine or sherry*
a little pepper	*(optional)*
3 *tablespoons beef fat*	1 *cup canned tomatoes*
3 *carrots, cut in large dice*	*stock or water to cover meat*
6 *small onions*	½ *cup sautéed mushrooms*
2 *tablespoons flour*	3 *medium potatoes, cut in pieces*
1 *clove garlic, crushed*	*chopped parsley*

Season oxtail with salt and pepper. Put fat in saucepan and when hot, add oxtail. Cook until all the pieces are golden brown all over. Add onions and carrots and let them brown. Pour off all the fat from the pan, add flour and garlic and mix well. Add faggot, wine, tomatoes and stock (or water), using enough liquid to cover the meat well. Bring to a boil, cover and cook slowly 4 hours. Skim off all the fat, then add mushrooms and continue cooking 35 to 40 minutes longer or until meat is tender. Meanwhile boil potatoes until done, drain and add. Correct the seasoning and serve sprinkled with chopped parsley. Serves 3.

TRIPE

Tripe is good only if it is fresh. For this reason it is always best to order it ahead, making sure that you are getting a fresh supply and not one that has been in the butcher shop any length of time.

In preparing tripe at home, be cautious in adding salt because some butchers use more salt than others in the parboiling. Remember, too, that tripe needs a long cooking to make it tender and that most people prefer a spicy or flavorful sauce with it. In France the favorite tripe dish is à la Mode de Caen, a dish that never tastes the same when prepared here because it is extremely difficult in this country to obtain some of the necessary ingredients. As a matter of fact, my experience has been that most Americans prefer Tripe à la Bordelaise or with Cream Sauce.

TRIPE A LA BORDELAISE

1 *lb. tripe, parboiled and cut in large julienne*
2 *medium onions, chopped*
1 *tablespoon butter*
1 *clove garlic*
3 *tomatoes, peeled, seeded and chopped (if available)*
teaspoon chopped parsley

½ *cup Tomato Sauce* (page 31) *(or 1 cup canned tomatoes)*
1 *cup chicken or veal stock (or water)*
½ *teaspoon salt*
a little pepper
1 *faggot of 3 sprigs of parsley, 2 stalks celery, 1 bay leaf and ½ teaspoon thyme*

Cook onions in butter in saucepan until golden. Add garlic, chopped tomatoes, Tomato Sauce (or canned tomatoes) tripe, stock, seasoning and faggot. Bring to a boil, cover and cook in a moderate oven of 350 degrees, or on top of stove over a very low heat for about 3 hours. When meat is well done, remove faggot. Skim off the fat, add a little water if sauce is too thick, correct the seasoning and add chopped parsley. Serve with baked or boiled potatoes, or rice. Serves 4.

TRIPE WITH CREAM SAUCE
(Tripe à la Crème)

1 *lb. tripe*
2 *tablespoons butter*
1 *onion, chopped*

1 *tablespoon flour*
½ *cup hot milk*
salt and pepper

Cook tripe in salted water 3 to 4 hours or until done. Cut in small pieces. Melt butter in saucepan, add onion and cook until soft, add flour and cook a few minutes. Add milk, and cook stirring constantly, until smooth. Continue cooking slowly about 15 minutes. Add tripe and correct seasoning. If sauce is too thick add a little more milk and, if desired, the onion may be strained out before combining the sauce with the tripe. To make a richer sauce add 1 or 2 tablespoons of cream. Serves 4.

TRIPE LYONNAISE

1 *lb. tripe, parboiled*	2 *tablespoons vinegar*
2 *tablespoons butter*	*a little salt and pepper*
2 *onions, minced*	1 *teaspoon chopped parsley*

Cook tripe, in enough water to cover, for 3 to 4 hours or until it is tender. Remove from the water, cut in small pieces and drain well. Melt 1 tablespoon butter in frying pan, add tripe and cook, moving the pieces around in the butter, until they are golden brown. In another pan melt the other tablespoon of butter and cook onions until golden. Add vinegar and then the tripe. Season with salt and pepper and add parsley. Serve with potatoes cooked as desired, sautéed, mashed, boiled or baked. Serves 3 to 4.

TRIPE A LA MODE DE CAEN

Ask any Frenchman how he prefers tripe—you don't need to ask if he likes it, they all do—and he will answer, "A la Mode de Caen." It is the most famous, the most popular, way of preparing tripe and a regular specialty of the great restaurants of Paris and other large cities. In fact, for many years this dish has been canned in France and shipped all over the world to homesick Frenchmen living in faraway lands.

The true dish is always made from beef tripe—plain, not honeycomb and always cooked with an ox-foot. And don't ever tell a real connoisseur that the ox-foot can be omitted—he would recognize the difference immediately. Some cooks, however, substitute a calf's-foot. A great deal of fat is required in the cooking, enough so that the top of the liquid is well covered, and this is very important because it keeps the tripe white.

In France a special earthenware casserole is used for the cooking, shaped somewhat like an old-fashioned tea kettle with sides curved over to form the top and only a small opening in the center for the cover. In making Tripe à la Mode de Caen, the cover is sealed in place with a roll of dough, and this, we think, is an essential part of the preparation because we have always felt the succulence of the dish depends upon this way of holding in the flavor and aroma.

Finally, Tripe à la Mode de Caen must be cooked at a very low temperature for many, many hours. For this reason French housewives, always fuel-thrifty, usually take it to the local *boulangerie* (bakery), or *pâtisserie* (pastry shop), to be cooked in one of the big brick ovens that is always hot.

4 lbs. plain tripe
4 onions, cut in small pieces
4 carrots, cut in small pieces
1 ox (or calf's) foot, split
4 leeks, tied together
1 faggot of 2 stalks celery, 4 sprigs
    parsley, 2 bay leaves and a little
    thyme
4 cloves garlic

1 teaspoon salt
a little pepper
1 glass white wine or cider
    (optional)
1 small glass applejack (optional)
a pinch of Parisian spice (optional)
½ lb. beef suet
water to cover

Spread onions and carrots in bottom of casserole. Lay ox-foot on top of onions and carrots. Cut tripe in 2 inch squares and add both, along with all the remaining ingredients, except suet, to the casserole. Cut suet in slices about ¼ inch thick and lay them on top so that the entire surface is covered. Add just enough water to come to the top of the ingredients. Cover casserole and seal with a roll of dough made by mixing 2 cups flour with enough water to make a stiff dough. Bring to a boil and put in an oven of 300 to 325 degrees and let cook for 8 to 10 hours. Remove dough and discard it. Uncover casserole and skim off all the fat. Remove tripe to another casserole. Remove ox-foot and cut meat from bone. Discard bone and cut meat in pieces like tripe. Strain liquid from vegetables and skim off any remaining fat. Return tripe and meat from ox-foot to casserole, then pour strained and skimmed liquid over it. Bring everything to a boil and serve very hot from the casserole. Serve with baked potatoes. Serves 8 to 10.

Veal

We ate more veal in France than beef, probably because it was plentiful, and very, very good, due to the way the young calves were raised, fed only on milk and the bran left from the flour which the miller ground in the local mill. They were never allowed out in the meadow to graze and were never more than three or four weeks old when slaughtered. As a result the meat was consistently white, firm and delicate with fine-textured, very white fat, all characteristics of good veal. Poor quality veal is easily recognized by its reddish color and soft flabby texture.

The leg of veal is considered the most desirable part. From it is cut

[94]

the meat for escalope, for cutlets and what we called *noix de veau*, a piece without any bone cut from the thick part at the top of the leg. *Noix de veau* is a choice cut which we liked larded with small pieces of fat pork—because veal is not very fat—and then braised. From lower down on the leg slices are cut to make the familiar veal cutlet with the small round bone in the center. In France a cutlet is called *rouelle de veau* and a chop *côte de veau*. I explain these French names merely because they appear so frequently on menus and many people find them confusing.

The loin and the rack of the veal may be either sliced for chops or left whole and roasted or braised; the shoulder and breast are best braised—often with a stuffing inside—or stewed; and the neck makes a very good stew. All the specialties—the liver, kidneys, heart, sweetbreads, brains, head and feet—have always been considered great delicacies in France. That some of them cost very little never made people spurn them, because what counts with gourmets is the flavor, the delicacy, or some particular characteristic of a food which distinguishes it from all others. This and the painstaking care of the French cook made these specialties as delicious as they were inexpensive.

BLANQUETTE OF VEAL
(Blanquette de Veau)

2 *lbs. breast or shoulder of veal*	¼ *lb. mushrooms*
1 *teaspoon salt*	2½ *tablespoons butter*
1 *quart water*	1½ *tablespoons flour*
1 *medium carrot, cut in pieces*	2 *egg yolks*
1 *onion, studded with* 1 *clove*	1 *cup cream or top milk*
1 *faggot* (page 294)	*juice of* ¼ *lemon*
10 *small onions*	½ *teaspoon chopped parsley*

Cut veal into 12 to 15 pieces, put in deep saucepan, cover with water, add salt and bring to a boil, skimming it well. Add carrot, clove-studded onion and faggot and cook slowly 1 to 1¼ hours or until the meat is tender. Add onions when meat is half done. Clean mushrooms and cook separately (page 186). In another saucepan make a blond roux (page 296) with butter and flour. Remove cooked meat, carrot and onions from cooking liquid to serving dish, cover and place where it will keep warm. Discard faggot and clove-studded onion. Add liquid from cooking mushrooms to meat liquor (there should be about 3 cups all together), and add all this slowly to roux, stirring

[95]

all the time and continue stirring until smooth and thickened. Cook 15 to 20 minutes longer, stirring occasionally. Correct the seasoning, add a little white pepper, if desired, and a few gratings of nutmeg. Mix egg yolks with cream and lemon juice, add a few spoonfuls of the hot sauce to it, then turn it into the sauce, stirring briskly to combine. Cook, stirring, just below boiling point until sauce is thickened. Do not let boil. Put mushrooms on top of meat, pour sauce over and sprinkle with parsley. Serve with boiled potatoes. Serves 5.

BRAISED LOIN OF VEAL
(Longe de Veau Braisée)

4 lbs. loin (or other cut of veal)	1 teaspoon salt
veal bone	a little pepper
1 large carrot, sliced	2 cups stock (or water)
2 onions, sliced	1 tablespoon veal (or beef fat)
1 faggot (page 294)	

Put carrot and onions, faggot and bone in bottom of saucepan. Season meat with salt and pepper and place on top. Spread fat over top of meat. Put in moderately hot oven of 425 degrees and cook 20 to 25 minutes or until top is brown. Add 1 cup stock (or water) and continue cooking, basting often. When the liquid is reduced about one-half add remaining stock (or water). Cover pan, reduce heat to 375 degrees and cook about 2 hours, basting often. Uncover and cook about 15 to 20 minutes longer, basting every few minutes in order to glaze the top with the gravy. Discard faggot and remove meat to serving dish. Gravy should have reduced to about one-half the original quantity during cooking—if not reduced enough, cook the gravy longer, then pour over meat. Serve with mashed potatoes and any desired vegetables. Serves 8.

ESCALOPE OF VEAL SAUTE CHASSEUR

Allow 5 to 6 ounces of leg of veal sliced less than ½ inch thick for each person. Have butcher flatten each piece with a wooden mallet, but not quite as thin as for Breaded Escalope of Veal. Rub each piece with flour seasoned with salt and pepper and sauté slowly in 2 tablespoons of butter until golden brown (about 6 to 7 minutes on each side). Put in serving dish. For 4 servings, clean and slice 4 to 5 mushrooms and add to butter remaining in pan after browning meat and cook very gently until they are soft. Add 2 finely chopped shallots and ⅛ glass white wine. Wine is optional and can be omitted. Cook until reduced to one-half the original quantity, add 1 cup canned tomatoes and cook until reduced to a third the original quantity. Cream together 1 tablespoon butter and 1 teaspoon flour, add to sauce and cook a few minutes, stirring constantly. Add ½ teaspoon chopped parsley mixed with a little chopped tarragon if that is available. Pour over the meat and serve.

VEAL BOURGEOISE
(Veau Braisé Bourgeoise)

Follow recipe for Braised Loin of Veal (page 96). In addition prepare equal amounts of onions and carrots, allowing enough for the number of people to be served. Parboil carrots. Brown onions, sprinkled with a little sugar, in hot fat. When the meat is half cooked add carrots and onions to pan and continue cooking until meat is done. Serve with small potatoes browned in butter.

BREADED ESCALOPE OF VEAL
(Escalope de Veau Panée)

Allow 4 to 5 ounces of leg of veal sliced less than ½ inch thick for each person. Have butcher flatten each piece very thin by pounding with a mallet. Rub each piece with flour seasoned with salt and pepper. Bread pieces of Veal à l'Anglaise (page 293), and sauté slowly in butter until golden brown (about 4 to 5 minutes on each side). Put in serving dish and pour butter over them. Serve with a piece of lemon and sautéed potatoes or noodles.

VEAL CHOPS
(Côte de Veau, Grand'mère)

4 veal chops, 1 inch thick   *12 small onions*
salt and pepper and flour   *2 potatoes, cut in large slices*
2 tablespoons butter   *½ cup stock or water*
¼ lb. fat salt pork

Season chops with salt and pepper and dip in flour. Melt butter in casserole, add pork dice and when brown remove them and reserve. Add chops and onions and sauté slowly on each side, moving onions in pan to brown them all over (about 20 to 25 minutes). After first 5 minutes of cooking add potatoes. Remove chops and vegetables, then add stock (or water) to casserole and stir it to make the gravy and scrape all the brown crust from the sides of casserole into gravy. Bring to a boil and return chops, vegetables, and pork dice. Cook

5 minutes longer to reheat meat and serve from casserole. Sautéed mushrooms may be added if desired. Serves 4.

VEAL CUTLET
(Rouelle de Veau)

3 lbs. veal cutlet about 1-1½ inches
   thick
1 teaspoon salt
a little pepper
2 tablespoons butter or veal fat

6 onions
6 carrots cut in pieces
1 faggot (page 294)
1½ cups fresh peas (optional)
½ glass white wine (if available)

Season veal with salt and pepper and sprinkle with a little flour. Melt butter in pan and when very hot put in veal and cook until golden brown on both sides. Add onions and carrots and brown a little. Add wine and cook until reduced to almost nothing (omitting this step if wine is not used). Add enough water to come about halfway to top of meat. Add faggot. Bring to a boil and cook very slowly 1¾ to 2 hours. After first hour of cooking, remove faggot, add peas and finish cooking all together. Serves 5 to 6.

GODIVEAU

1 tablespoon butter
⅔ cup boiling water
¼ cup flour
1 egg
¼ lb. lean veal (without sinews)

½ lb. beef kidney fat
1 teaspoon salt
a little pepper
a few gratings nutmeg

Make a panade as follows: add butter and pinch of salt to boiling water, then add flour and stir with a wooden spoon over fire until thoroughly mixed. There should be no lumps of flour and the mixture should not cling to the pan. Remove from fire and add egg.

Take out all membranes from suet, then run veal and suet through a meat grinder, using a fine knife. Add salt, pepper and nutmeg and run through meat grinder again to make a finer paste. Add panade and mix all together very thoroughly. Spread on a plate, cover with waxed paper and leave in refrigerator 3 to 4 hours. Divide into small portions and roll into pieces about the size and shape of sausages. Place on a flat baking dish and put in a slow oven of 300 degrees and cook until firm, about 10 to 15 minutes. (They should not be crusty on the outside.) Use for garnishing Vol-au-Vents or Bouchées, that is, foods that are served in Patty Shells.

VEAL BALLS
(Fricadelles de Veau)

1 *lb. veal*	2 *tablespoons butter*
⅛ *lb. fat salt pork*	½ *teaspoon salt*
1 *cup fresh bread crumbs*	*a little pepper*
1 *onion, finely chopped*	*nutmeg*
2 *shallots, finely chopped*	3 *tablespoons veal or beef fat*

Cut meat and salt pork into small dice and chop very fine. Put in a bowl and add bread crumbs which have been soaked in milk or water and squeezed dry. Cook onion and shallot slowly in butter about 5 minutes but do not let brown. Combine all these ingredients, add salt and pepper and mix thoroughly with a wooden spoon. Divide into small portions, shape into balls, roll in flour and flatten them to about ¾ inch thickness. These are the fricadelles. Put veal or beef fat in frying pan and when hot add fricadelles and sauté over a moderate fire until golden brown on both sides. Place in a moderate oven of 375 degrees and cook about 20 to 25 minutes. Serve with Tomato Sauce (page 31) or Mushroom Sauce (page 29) and mashed potatoes and any desired vegetable.

Veal Balls can also be made from leftover veal following recipe for Fricadelles of Beef (page 87). Serves 5 to 6.

VEAL SCALOPINI
(Scalopini de Veau)

When purchasing veal for scalopini, allow about 4 to 5 ounces for each person. The amount of wine, gravy and butter used in making the sauce will depend upon how much meat you have and may also depend upon what wine you use and also upon whether or not you have any meat gravy on hand. Your own taste can be your guide in making the sauce.

Have veal cut in very thin slices from the loin or any tender part. Then have butcher pound them with a mallet to make them thinner. Rub pieces with flour and sauté in butter until golden brown on both sides. Season with salt and pepper. Remove meat to serving dish. Add a few spoonfuls of sherry, Madeira or Marsala wine, a little leftover meat gravy (if any is available) and a spoonful of butter to the pan. Cook five minutes, stirring in the brown that clings to the pan and pour over the cooked meat. May be served with any desired sauce such as Mushroom, Portugaise, etc.

VEAL PIE
(Tourte de Veau)

2 *cups leftover cooked veal, chopped*   1 *teaspoon chopped parsley*
   as for hash   1 *medium onion, finely chopped*
½ *cup fresh bread crumbs, soaked in*   3-4 *tablespoons leftover veal gravy*
   water   ½ *teaspoon salt*
1 *egg, beaten*   *pepper*

Drain bread crumbs but do not squeeze them dry. Put in a bowl, add remaining ingredients and mix all together. The mixture should be about the consistency of hash. Prepare pâte dough (page 226) and line a deep pie plate or a shallow casserole with it. Put in the filling and cover with pastry. Brush top with a little milk and prick top to release steam which will form. Bake in a moderately hot oven of 375 to 400 degrees or until pastry is golden brown, about 40 minutes. Serve hot. Serves 4 to 6.

VEAL STEW
(Ragoût de Veau)
Follow recipe for Lamb Stew (page 111).

VEAL STEW BOURGUIGNONNE
(Ragoût de Veau Bourguignonne)

1 *tablespoon veal fat*   6 *medium carrots, cut in pieces*
¼ *lb. salt pork, diced and parboiled*   2 *shallots, chopped*
   5 *minutes*   1 *clove garlic, crushed*
2 *lbs. veal (shoulder, breast or neck)*   2 *tablespoons flour*
   cut in pieces   1 *pint red wine*
1 *tablespoon salt*   1 *faggot* (page 294)
a little pepper   ½ *lb. mushrooms, sautéed slowly in*
12 *small onions*   *butter*

Melt veal fat in saucepan. Drain pork dice, add to fat and cook until golden brown, remove from pan and reserve. Season veal with salt and pepper and fry in remaining fat in pan with onion and carrots until meat is golden brown. Drain off fat from pan, add shallots, garlic and sprinkle flour over top. Mix well and cook a few minutes or until flour is brown. Add wine (if it does not cover meat add water to it). Add faggot. Bring to a boil and simmer over low heat 1 to 1½ hours or until meat is tender. Remove meat, onions and carrots to serving dish, add pork dice and mushrooms. Reduce sauce if it is not thick enough, skim off all fat, correct the seasoning and pour over meat and vegetables. (The sauce may be strained if desired.) Serve with boiled potatoes or noodles. Serves 6.

VEAL STEW MARENGO
(Ragoût de Veau Marengo)

2 *tablespoons salad oil*
2 *lbs. veal (shoulder, breast or neck) cut in pieces*
1 *teaspoon salt*
a little pepper
2 *shallots, chopped (if available)*
1½ *tablespoons flour*
½ *glass white wine (optional)*
1½ *cups stock or water*

3 *tomatoes, peeled, seeded and chopped (or 1 cup canned tomatoes)*
1 *clove garlic, crushed*
1 *faggot (page 294)*
12 *small onions*
12 *small mushrooms*
1 *teaspoon coarsely chopped parsley*
6 *slices bread, fried in butter until brown on both sides*

Put oil in saucepan and heat until very hot. Season meat with salt and pepper and cook a few pieces at a time in the fat until all are golden brown. Add shallots and cook a few minutes. Add onions and cook until a little brown. Drain off the oil from pan and add flour to meat and onions. Mix it well and cook a few minutes or until flour is brown. Add wine and stock (or water), bring to a boil, add tomato, garlic and faggot. Cook about 45 minutes, add mushrooms and cook about 35 minutes longer or until meat is tender. Remove faggot, skim off fat and sprinkle top with parsley. Serve fried bread around meat. Other vegetables in season may be used. Sautéed Eggplant (page 177) added when the mushrooms and onions are combined with the meat is very tasty. Serves 5.

CALF'S BRAINS
(Cervelle de Veau)
Follow directions for Beef Brains (page 89).

CALF'S HEAD
(Tête de Veau)
Have butcher remove all bones from head. Soak in large quantity of water for 3 to 4 hours or until all blood has drained out. Parboil for 5 minutes in water to cover, drain and put in fresh cold water. Cut off the tongue, cut remainder of meat in pieces for serving. In another

pan put 2 tablespoons flour and mix with 3 tablespoons vinegar (or the juice of one lemon). Add 2 quarts water and 1 tablespoon salt. Add calf's-head and tongue, bring to a boil and cook about 1 to 1½ hours or until tender. Serve with the following Sauce Vinaigrette:

SAUCE VINAIGRETTE FOR CALF'S HEAD

1 cup Vinaigrette Sauce (page 35)
1 sour pickle, chopped
½ teaspoon chopped onion
a few capers

½ calf's brain, cooked (page 89)
  and chopped
a little chopped parsley

Mix together all ingredients. Serves 6 to 8.

VEAL HEART EN CASSEROLE BONNE FEMME

Open heart enough to remove arteries and blood. Season with salt and pepper, put in a bowl and sprinkle generously with oil and lemon juice. Let stand for about 30 minutes turning occasionally. Remove from this pickling liquid, fasten together with skewers and cover with thin slices of larding pork held on with skewers. Put in a casserole with 2 tablespoons veal fat (or butter) and cook in a moderate oven of 375 to 400 degrees 30 to 40 minutes. Remove heart, take out skewers and add ½ cup good gravy, if available, or lacking gravy, add ¼ cup hot water to juice in casserole. Mix up well and pour over heart. Garnish with small potatoes and small onions which have been parboiled and then browned in butter and with some sautéed salt pork dice. Use 2 hearts for 3 to 4 servings.

VEAL HEART SAUTE
(Coeur de Veau Sauté)

1 veal heart
2-3 tablespoons good fat
salt and pepper
2 tablespoons butter
3-4 mushrooms, minced
1 onion, finely chopped

1 shallot, finely chopped
1½ tablespoons flour
½ cup canned tomatoes
1 glass sherry
½ teaspoon chopped parsley

Cut heart in thin slices, remove arteries and blood, season with salt and pepper. Heat fat very hot and sauté slices of veal heart for a few minutes, then remove them from the pan. Drain off the fat and add butter, mushrooms and onion and cook until golden brown. Add shallot and flour, mix all together and cook until light brown. Add tomatoes, boil a few minutes, add sherry and parsley. Bring to a boil and add heart slices. Do not allow to boil after adding the meat. Serve in a rice ring. Serves 2.

VEAL KIDNEYS
(Rognons de Veau)

Veal kidneys are delicious when carefully prepared but can be tough and strong tasting if cooked too long over high heat. For sautéed kidneys, I think the way my mother prepared them is still the best. She cut the kidney in small dice and then sautéed them very quickly in fat that she trimmed from the kidney. The minute they were done she turned them into a strainer to drain. This seemed to drain away any objectionable strong flavor. Then when they were put into the sauce, she was careful to reheat the mixture only to boiling point, but never allowed it actually to boil. The result was as delicate in flavor as it was delectable.

BROILED VEAL KIDNEYS

Allow 1 kidney for each person. If layer of fat is very thick around the kidney, trim off some of it, but leave enough on to keep the kidney moist. Split in half to open it, but do not cut all the way through so that it is divided into two pieces. Pierce with a metal skewer so that the opened kidney lies flat. Season with salt and pepper, brush with melted butter and broil 8 to 10 minutes on each side—about 4 to 5 inches from the heat.

VEAL KIDNEY STEW
(Ragoût de Rognons)

4 *veal kidneys*	1 *onion, minced*
½ *teaspoon salt*	1 *tablespoon flour*
a little pepper	½ *glass white wine (optional)*
2 *tablespoons butter*	1 *cup canned tomatoes*
2 *tablespoons veal kidney fat*	½ *teaspoon chopped parsley*

Mince kidneys and season with salt and pepper. Melt veal fat and let become very hot in a saucepan. Add kidneys and cook for 5 to 7 minutes, then remove them and put in a colander to drain, discarding all fat from pan. Put butter in pan with onion and when onion is golden brown add flour and mix all together. Add wine (if used), tomatoes and parsley and cook all together until sauce has thickened.

Add kidneys and cook until they have reheated but do not allow the mixture to boil after the kidneys are in it. Serves 4.

VEAL KIDNEYS BONNE FEMME
(Rognons de Veau Bonne Femme)

Kidneys braised whole, should be cooked until they are tender, but the time required varies because kidneys themselves vary. An old French method for testing them is to pierce to the center of the kidney with a steel-tined kitchen fork and leave it there for a minute or two. Withdraw the fork and put the ends of the tines quickly to the tongue. If they are hot the kidney is done, if they are only warm, it needs longer cooking.

2 *veal kidneys*	1 *tablespoon flour*
1 *carrot, sliced*	1 *cup meat gravy or stock (or canned*
8 *small onions*	*tomatoes)*
2 *sprigs parsley*	½ *glass wine (optional)*
salt and pepper	

Trim off about half the fat from the kidney and melt in a casserole. Add carrot, onions and parsley. Season kidneys with salt and pepper and place on top of carrot and onions. Cook 45 minutes to one hour in a moderate oven of 375 degrees, basting often and covering the casserole as soon as the kidneys have browned. Remove kidneys and drain off fat from the casserole, add flour to casserole and mix well. Add gravy or stock (or canned tomatoes) and wine. Add kidneys. Let cook about 10 to 15 minutes or until sauce is thickened. Remove kidneys to serving platter, arrange carrot and onions around and pour sauce over. Garnish with diced potatoes sautéed in butter and sautéed mushrooms and sprinkle with chopped parsley. Serves 4.

CALF'S LIVER
(Foie de Veau)

Calf's liver is usually sliced and sautéed or broiled and served with bacon. First dip the slices in seasoned flour—and for broiled liver brush with salad oil—then cook quickly until brown on both sides.

A very delicious way of preparing liver, which is not very often done in America, is to braise the whole piece. It is particularly good for a large family, certainly easier and more practical than cooking slices of

[104]

liver for a large group. It is very delicious the second day served cold, either sliced in sandwiches, or served with salad.

BRAISED LIVER

1 *whole calf's liver*	1 *clove garlic*
3 *tablespoons butter or kidney suet*	1 *teaspoon salt*
2 *onions, sliced*	*a little pepper*
2 *carrots, sliced*	2 *tablespoons flour*
1 *faggot* (page 294)	1 *pt. red wine*

When purchasing the liver, have butcher lard it with strips of larding pork. Put 1 tablespoon butter (or suet) in saucepan and when hot add onions, carrots, faggot and garlic. Season liver with salt and pepper. Heat remaining 2 tablespoons fat in another pan until very hot, add liver and brown, turning it so it will be brown all over. Remove liver and place on top of onions and carrots. Put on a slow fire and cook until onions and carrots start to brown, then sprinkle flour over onions and carrots, mixing all together. Add wine and just enough extra water to cover liver. Cover pan and cook slowly in a moderate oven of 350 degrees for 2½ to 3 hours, turning liver several times to cook it evenly. Remove to serving dish. The sauce should have reduced to about half, if it has not, then cook it down. Strain sauce, skim off fat and serve with liver. Serves 8 to 10.

CALF'S LIVER BROILED

Dip slices of liver in flour and then brush with salad oil. Place on hot broiler about 4 to 5 inches from the heat and cook until brown on both sides. It should take only a few minutes on each side.

CALF'S LIVER SAUTE WITH BACON

Cook bacon in frying pan until done, then remove and set aside where it will keep hot. Season slices of liver with salt and dip in flour. Sauté quickly in hot bacon fat until brown on each side. (Long cooking will toughen liver.) Remove liver and put with bacon. Pour off fat from pan, add 1 or 2 tablespoons of butter and cook until hazelnut brown in color. Sprinkle liver with a few drops of lemon juice, if desired, and then pour browned butter over. Sprinkle with chopped parsley.

SWEETBREADS

Be sure that the sweetbreads you buy are very fresh. They are very delicate and deteriorate quickly. And remember, too, to handle them carefully all during the steps of preparation because they fall apart very easily.

There are two steps in preparing sweetbreads; the first a preliminary parboiling that should be done as soon as they are purchased. Then they may be kept in the refrigerator, but not longer than 24 hours, before they get their final cooking.

TO PREPARE SWEETBREADS

Soak sweetbreads in very cold water for several hours in refrigerator. Drain, cover with fresh cold water, bring slowly to a boil and cook gently 5 minutes. Drain again and plunge into fresh cold water. When cold remove from water, cut away and discard the "throat" (the tough tissue that connects them) and the sinews but do not remove the fine skin that covers them. Return to refrigerator with a plate laid on top to flatten and to give them a better appearance. Cook in any desired way and serve within 24 hours.

BRAISED SWEETBREADS

2 *pair sweetbreads*	*½ teaspoon thyme*
2 *tablespoons melted butter*	2 *sprigs parsley*
1 *teaspoon flour*	*salt and pepper*
1 *onion, sliced*	1 *cup water* (*or stock*)
1 *carrot, sliced*	2 *tablespoons dry sherry* (*optional*)
1 *bay leaf*	

Soak, parboil and trim sweetbreads as described above. Put butter in casserole, add flour and mix together. Add onion, carrot, bay leaf, thyme and parsley. Put in a hot oven of 450 degrees and cook until vegetables start to brown. Then season sweetbreads with salt and pepper, place on top of vegetables in casserole and add water (or stock). Bake, uncovered, 45 minutes or until brown on top and liquid is half cooked away, basting occasionally. Remove sweetbreads carefully to serving dish. Add sherry (if used) to casserole, correct seasoning and strain sauce over sweetbreads. Serves 4.

VEAL TONGUES
(Langues de Veau)

Although veal tongues are usually served with Calf's Head Vinaigrette they are just as delicious cooked by themselves and served with Sauce Piquante. To prepare them, follow directions for Calf's Head (page 101) and serve with Sauce Vinaigrette (page 35) or Sauce Piquante (page 29). Each tongue serves 2.

CREAMED SWEETBREADS AND CHICKEN

1 *or* 2 *pairs sweetbreads (depending*	2 *tablespoons butter*
on size)	2 *tablespoons flour*
1 *carrot, sliced*	1¾ *cups hot milk*
1 *onion, sliced*	¼ *cup cream or top milk*
a sprig of parsley	1 *cup diced cooked chicken*
½ *teaspoon salt*	½ *cup sliced cooked mushrooms*
3 *peppercorns*	*(page 186)*
2 *cups hot water*	2 *tablespoons dry sherry (optional)*

Soak, parboil and trim sweetbreads, as described above. Then put carrot, onion, parsley, salt and peppercorns in a saucepan and place sweetbreads on top. Add hot water and simmer very gently 20 minutes. Remove sweetbreads and cut carefully in large dice.

Meanwhile, melt butter, add flour and mix. Cook a few minutes, but do not allow to brown, then add milk and cook stirring constantly until it thickens. Cook gently ½ hour stirring often. Add cream. Combine this sauce with sweetbreads, chicken and mushrooms, mixing very carefully with a fork to keep sweetbreads from breaking apart. Keep hot by placing pan over boiling water. Serve in patty shells, on toast or with rice. Serves 6.

Lamb and Mutton

Our lamb was excellent and fairly plentiful, all of it locally raised and brought to market each week from outlying farms. It was especially fine in the spring while still very small at which time, too, the first peas were being picked and the tender young garden carrots just big enough to be pulled from the soil. Young lamb, new peas and carrots, all at their most succulent, were eaten together and made a treat worth remembering.

Good quality lamb has red meat and white fat, the flesh is firm and the fat thick. Its age can usually be judged by its size because obviously when the animal is large it has passed from the lamb stage to the adult, or mutton, stage. In either case if the flesh is plump as well as firm and the bones small in proportion to the meat it will be tender and juicy when cooked.

Leg and shoulder cuts are the most practical because of the number of servings they give. Here in America the chops are probably the most sought after, as they can be cooked so quickly. The leg is delicious either roasted, braised or boiled, its age and tenderness deciding which way to cook it. The shoulder is either roasted or braised, preferably braised, unless the meat is from very young lamb. If the butcher removes the bones, it makes carving easier and this cut is especially tasty if stuffed before it is rolled and tied. Other less tender parts, the shoulder end, end of rib section, neck and breast are best for stew which, when all is said and done, is the least expensive lamb dish and—when made well—as delicious as any.

Mint Sauce is a favorite accompaniment for roast lamb and equally good for a cold leftover roast. And don't scorn leftover lamb. Those who insist they never want to see the same piece of lamb served at a second meal have yet to taste it reheated in a piquante sauce or a really good hash.

ROAST LEG OF LAMB

If you like the flavor of garlic, use it generously on the outside of a leg of lamb that is to be roasted. We always cut small incisions in several places on the surface and inserted small pieces of garlic in them. The flavor works its way—not too strongly however—through the meat during the cooking. For a less pronounced flavor merely rub the outside of the leg with a cut piece of garlic.

In my home we usually roasted the leg with potatoes as described in the *"à la Boulangère"* recipe below, a method which we also liked for roast loin of pork. Lamb this way should be better known in America.

Rub leg with salt and put in roasting pan with some good fat, such as fresh beef drippings or a piece of suet, laid over the surface. Put a few spoonfuls of water in the pan, just enough to keep the fat from scorching. Roast in a moderately hot oven of 400 to 425 degrees, basting it often with the melting fat, allowing about 2 hours for a medium-sized leg. To make the gravy, pour off the fat from the pan and add one cup of stock or water. Cook over direct heat, stirring with a spoon, scraping in all the brown crust from the bottom and around the edges of the pan. Correct the seasoning and strain.

ROAST LEG OF LAMB A LA BOULANGERE

Roast the lamb as described above for about one hour or until it has acquired a good brown all over. Remove from pan, make gravy and set it aside. Have ready 6 to 8 potatoes (or more) pared and sliced about ¼ inch thick, 1 onion thinly sliced, 1 teaspoon chopped parsley, 1 teaspoon salt and a little pepper and put all together in the roasting pan. Add 2 cups boiling water or stock (or just about enough to reach the top of potatoes) and spread 1 tablespoon butter over the top. Bring to a boil on top of stove or in the oven, and then place the partially roasted lamb on top. Continue roasting about 45 minutes to 1 hour longer. If liquid cooks away, add a little more. Serve with the reheated gravy.

BOILED LEG OF LAMB

Boiled leg of lamb is not only a delicious way of preparing this cut but the liquid which is left makes a very fine soup. To make the soup reduce the amount of stock by boiling the liquid down, and add during the last hour of cooking some chopped vegetables and a little barley or rice.

leg of lamb, 4½-5 lbs.
3 carrots
3 white turnips (or 1 yellow)

*3 sprigs parsley, 1 stalk celery, 1 bay
leaf, a little thyme tied in a faggot*
4-5 potatoes
1½ cups Caper Sauce (page 25)

Have butcher cut shank bone short and remove the large irregular-shaped bone at the other end. Put in a pan with enough cold water to cover the meat, adding ½ teaspoon salt for each quart of water. Bring to a boil and add lamb, vegetables (except potatoes) and faggot. Boil gently, allowing 15 minutes for each pound of meat. Cook potatoes separately in salt water. Remove lamb from water and serve with vegetables around it. Serve Caper Sauce (page 25) separately. Serves 6.

BONED SHOULDER OF LAMB WITH BEANS BRETONNE

1 lamb shoulder
2 cups dried beans
1 carrot, cut in pieces
1 onion, studded with 1 clove
1 faggot (page 294)
1 teaspoon salt
a little pepper

3 tablespons fat (veal or beef or lard)
¼ lb. salt pork, half fat, half lean
2 onions, chopped
1 clove garlic, crushed
*2 tomatoes, peeled, seeded and
chopped (or ½ cup canned
tomatoes, strained)*

Soak beans for 2 hours. Drain and put in saucepan with 1 to 1½ quarts water and ½ teaspoon salt. Bring to a boil, add carrot, onion and faggot and cook 45 minutes to 1 hour or until beans are tender. Have butcher bone and roll the shoulder of lamb. When beans start cooking, also start to cook the meat as follows: rub it with salt and pepper, spread with fat and put in a moderately hot oven of 400 degrees. Cook, turning often to brown on all sides, for about 1 hour. In the meantime, cut pork in small dice, parboil, drain and then sauté until brown, add chopped onions and cook until they are golden brown, then add garlic and tomato. Remove carrot from beans and dice it. Drain beans, reserving the cooking liquor but discarding the clove-studded onion and faggot. Add carrot and drained beans to the pork, onions, etc. and mix all together, tossing them with a fork to avoid mashing beans. Place the mixture around the meat, add ½ cup of liquid in which beans were cooked, return to oven and cook 35-40 minutes longer. Baste often, adding more bean liquid if necessary. To serve, remove string from lamb and sprinkle with chopped parsley. Serves 4.

STUFFED SHOULDER OF LAMB

I remember watching my grandmother stuff a shoulder of lamb and rolling and tying it up neatly. As she said, *"Le plat fera plus de profit"* —"it will make the meat go farther." We thought it made it taste better, too. And the little garlic she rubbed on the outside before cooking added a nice flavor as well.

1 *lamb shoulder, boned*	1 *egg*
2-3 *tablespoons good fat*	1 *cup fresh bread crumbs*
1 *onion, finely chopped*	½ *teaspoon salt*
½ *lb. sausage meat or leftover cooked*	*a little pepper*
meat, chopped fine	1 *onion, sliced*
1 *teaspoon chopped parsley*	1 *carrot, sliced*
1 *tablespoon flour*	1 *faggot* (page 294)

Mix together sausage, cooked onion, parsley, bread crumbs, egg, salt and pepper and stuff the shoulder with this mixture. Roll up the shoulder and tie it with string. Spread the sliced onion and carrot in the bottom of a roasting pan and add the faggot. Rub stuffed shoulder with a little salt and pepper, spread with good fat and put on top of vegetables in roasting pan. Bake, uncovered, in a moderately hot oven of 425 degrees about 30 minutes, turning it often to brown it on all sides. Sprinkle flour on top of vegetables, add 1 cup hot water, cover pan and continue cooking at moderate heat of 375 to 400 degrees about 2 hours, basting often. If water cooks away, add more. Discard faggot. Remove meat and vegetables to serving dish. Strain gravy and skim off fat. Serves 6.

LAMB (OR MUTTON) STEW
(Ragoût d'Agneau ou Mouton)

Stews—the French name is "ragoût"—of all kinds are very popular in France. But of course stews have been popular at all times and in all places where people have had to be thrifty. The less expensive cuts of meat can be used, the addition of vegetables and the sauce—or gravy —make small amounts of meat stretch over more servings, and none of the good nourishment of meat and vegetables is lost in the cooking. Nor does it take much fuel to cook a stew, for the gentler the heat the better; rapid boiling makes the meat ragged and prevents the sauce from ever developing a full rich flavor.

In giving directions for making a stew it is always difficult to specify the exact length of time for cooking because that depends so much on the meat you are using. The age of the animal, its feeding and activity, and the part from which the meat is cut all affect the length of time required to make it tender. For example, in making the lamb stew given below, the cooking time can be shortened to ½ hour if the meat is from a tender spring lamb. Cooking meat too long is apt to make it ragged and tasteless, a fact which must never be forgotten.

Any stew tastes better if the onions, carrots and turnips are lightly browned in fat in a frying pan before adding them to the stew. I always sprinkle the carrots and turnips with a very little sugar while they are browning because this bit of carmelized sugar adds its special savor to the dish.

2 *lbs. breast, neck or shoulder of lamb, cut in pieces*	1 *faggot* (page 294)
2 *tablespoons fat*	3 *medium carrots cut in quarters*
1 *teaspoon salt*	2 *medium white turnips cut in pieces*
a little pepper	5 *medium potatoes, cut in quarters*
1 *clove garlic, crushed*	10 *small onions*
2 *tablespoons flour*	¼ *cup fresh peas (optional)*
2 *cups water*	¼ *cup string beans (optional)*
½ *cup canned tomatoes (or 3 fresh tomatoes, peeled, seeded and chopped)*	1 *teaspoon chopped parsley*

Put fat in saucepan and when very hot add pieces of meat, seasoned with salt and pepper. Sauté until well browned on all sides. Drain fat from meat, turn heat very low, add garlic to meat in pan and sprinkle the flour over it. Cook gently, moving the meat all the time, until the flour becomes golden. (If the oven is on, put the pan in the oven to brown the flour.) Add water and tomatoes. Bring to a boil, moving the meat around gently with a spatula to combine flour and liquid. Add faggot, salt (if necessary) and cook slowly for about 45 minutes to 1 hour. Remove meat and strain liquid into another pan. Clean pan in which meat was cooked and put meat back in it. Skim all fat from top of the strained liquid and correct the seasoning. Sauté carrots, turnips, and onions in a little fat until brown, then place with potatoes on top of meat, add strained liquid and bring to a boil. Cook gently for ½ hour, then add peas and beans and cook another ½ hour. Serve sprinkled with chopped parsley. Serves 5.

BONED SHOULDER OF LAMB A LA BOULANGERE
Follow recipe for Roast Leg of Lamb à la Boulangère (page 109).

LAMB STEW HOUSEWIFE STYLE
(Ragoût d'Agneau Ménagère)

2 lbs. breast, neck or shoulder of lamb, cut in pieces
3 onions, thinly sliced
4-5 potatoes, sliced
4 medium carrots, sliced

½ Savoy cabbage cut in pieces, parboiled 2 minutes and drained
1 faggot (page 294)
1 teaspoon salt
a little pepper
1 teaspoon chopped parsley

Parboil meat in enough water to cover for about 5 minutes. Drain meat and put one-half of it in a saucepan and cover with one-half the onions, carrots, potatoes, and cabbage. Add remaining meat, and cover with remaining onions, carrots, potatoes and cabbage. Season with salt and pepper, add faggot and enough water to cover the ingredients. Bring to a boil, cover pan and cook gently about 1½ hours or until meat is done and potatoes are soft enough to thicken the liquid. Remove faggot and serve sprinkled with parsley. Serves 4 to 5.

CASSOULET MENAGERE
Cassoulet originally was a specialty of the southwestern part of France, from Toulouse, which lies west of the Pyrenees, to Carcassone where the mountains start to go down to the shores of the Mediterranean. Toulouse, Castelnaudary, Carcassonne, and many other towns

have their own preferred combinations of ingredients and each, of course, considers its own the best. Thus there are various combinations of mutton, pork, goose, duck, sausage and white beans and in some places even the meat of an old partridge, when in season, is added. But, regardless of whatever else goes into the casserole, dried white beans and garlic sausages are always included.

Cassoulet is a hearty, inexpensive dish, perfect for a large family of hungry youngsters and grown-ups. But it takes a long time to cook and should have an oven with a steady even heat to bring it to its final tender succulence.

As people have moved to other parts of France from the Haute-Garonne department where cassoulet is a specialty, they have taken their recipes with them until now cassoulet is served in homes and restaurants everywhere. The following recipe is typical and generally popular. Instead of lamb, roast loin of pork cut in slices or sliced goose may be used. In some sections goose is a traditional ingredient.

2 lbs. breast, neck or shoulder of
    lamb, cut in pieces
2½-3 cups dried beans soaked in cold
    water for a few hours
½ lb. saucisson or pork sausage with
    garlic (if obtainable)
3 ozs. fat salt pork and rind, diced
½ tablespoon salt
3 tablespoons lard

a little pepper
2 onions, finely chopped
½ cup canned tomatoes (or 3 fresh
    tomatoes, peeled, seeded and
    chopped)
2 cloves garlic, crushed
1 faggot (page 294)
3 tablespoons bread crumbs
1 tablespoon chopped parsley

Drain beans, put in saucepan, cover with water, add ½ tablespoon salt and the saucisson. Bring to a boil and cook slowly about 1 hour, removing saucisson after it has cooked for 35 minutes. Parboil pork dice 5 minutes, drain and sauté in a little lard until golden brown. Remove them and set aside. Put lard in saucepan, heat very hot and add pieces of lamb seasoned with salt and pepper. Brown them on all sides. Drain off fat, add onions and cook with meat until they are golden brown. Add just enough water to cover meat, bring to a boil, add tomatoes, garlic, faggot, and pork dice and cook slowly for about half an hour, adding salt, if needed. Drain the beans and add. Cover pan and cook slowly 1½ to 2 hours longer or until meat and beans are done. Discard faggot. About 15 minutes before serving, rub the insides of individual casseroles (or one large one) with cut garlic. Cut saucisson in slices. Into each casserole put some meat with some beans, some slices of saucisson, some salt pork dice and pour sauce over. Sprinkle with bread crumbs and a little butter and put under broiler or in a hot oven until brown. Serve sprinkled with chopped parsley. Serves 5-6.

LAMB HASH

1 *lb. leftover cooked lamb from leg or shoulder*	1 *cup gravy (leftover from cooked meat)*
1 *onion, finely chopped*	½ *cup Tomato Sauce* (page 31)
1 *tablespoon butter*	½ *teaspoon salt*
1 *tablespoon chopped parsley*	*a little pepper*

Chop meat fairly fine. Brown onion in butter, add parsley, gravy, Tomato Sauce and meat. Braise 1 hour in a covered pan in the oven, stirring from time to time. Correct the seasoning. To serve, cover with creamy mashed potatoes, sprinkle with Parmesan cheese or bread crumbs or a mixture of cheese and bread crumbs and then with a little melted butter and brown slowly under a hot broiler. Serves 3 to 4.

BROILED LAMB KIDNEY MAITRE D'HOTEL

Many people in this country don't like lamb or mutton kidneys, insisting that they always have an odd, unpleasant flavor. The only reason I can give for that is that they have not been prepared correctly. Lamb fat has a definitely strong flavor and unless the kidneys are trimmed of all of it, they will hold some of this flavor after they are cooked. In addition, there is a thin skin covering each kidney which has to be pulled off before cooking.

Split kidneys and pierce each with a skewer to keep it flat. Place on a hot broiler about 3 inches from the heat and cook about 5 to 6 minutes on each side. Serve with Maître d'Hôtel butter made by mixing softened butter with a little lemon juice and chopped parsley. Allow 2 lamb kidneys for each serving.

LAMB KIDNEY STEW

8 *lamb kidneys*	1½ *tablespoons flour*
½ *teaspoon salt*	½ *cup canned tomatoes*
a little pepper	1 *glass sherry or Madeira, or*
2 *tablespoons fat*	¼ *cup stock*
2 *tablespoons butter*	½ *teaspoon chopped parsley*
1-2 *shallots (or ¼ onion) finely chopped*	

Remove fat from kidneys and peel off skin. Cut each in quarters and season with salt and pepper. Put fat in saucepan, heat very hot, add kidneys and sauté very quickly, about 2 or 3 minutes. Drain well in a colander. Put butter in saucepan, add shallots (or onion), cook a few minutes, add flour and continue cooking until flour is golden brown. Add tomato and stock (or water) and cook stirring constantly until thickened. Cook slowly 10 minutes longer, correct seasoning and add sherry or Madeira. Add kidneys, bring to a boil but do not allow to boil. Serve sprinkled with chopped parsley. If desired, the sauce may be strained before adding kidneys. Serves 4.

LAMB LIVER SAUTE

1 *lb. lamb liver cut in small pieces*	1 *tablespoon flour*
1 *tablespoon lard or good fat*	1 *clove garlic, crushed*
3 *oz. fat salt pork, diced*	½ *glass red or white wine (if available)*
½ *teaspoon salt*	*able)*
a little pepper	½ *cup meat stock (or water)*
2 *medium onions, minced*	½ *teaspoon chopped parsley*

Melt lard in saucepan, add diced salt pork and cook until dice are golden brown. Remove dice and set aside. Have remaining fat very hot and add liver which has been seasoned with salt and pepper. Sauté quickly about 2 or 3 minutes or until brown. Drain from the fat and keep in a dish in a warm place. Add onions to fat in pan and cook a few minutes stirring all the time. Add flour and garlic and cook a few minutes mixing all together. Add wine and stock, mix well, add salt pork dice and cook gently 15 to 20 minutes, stirring occasionally. Add cooked liver and reheat but be careful that sauce does not boil after liver has been added. Serve, sprinkled with chopped parsley. If wine is not used add a few drops of vinegar to the sauce. Serves 3 to 4.

FRESH LAMB'S TONGUE BRAISED

4-5 *lamb tongues (1 for each person)*	1 *tablespoon flour*
salt and pepper	1 *tablespoon chopped sour pickle*
1 *carrot, sliced*	½ *teaspoon chopped parsley*
1 *onion, sliced*	1 *faggot (page 294)*
1 *cup stock (or canned tomatoes)*	

Parboil tongues for 15 minutes. Drain, trim off skin and roots and season with salt and pepper. Put carrot, onion and faggot in saucepan, place tongues on top and add just enough stock, mixed with the flour (or tomatoes), to cover them. Cover pan. Cook slowly about 1½ to 2 hours or until tender. When ready to serve remove tongues, cut each in half lengthwise and arrange on serving dish. Cook the liquid until reduced to one half the original quantity, strain, add pickle and parsley and pour over tongues. Serves 4 to 5.

MOUSSAKA OF LAMB

Lamb Hash (page 114)   *Bread crumbs*
Sliced sautéed tomatoes   *Butter*
Sliced sautéed eggplant   *Cooked rice*

Use individual casseroles or one large casserole. Put a layer of Lamb Hash in the bottom of the casserole, then a layer of tomatoes and one of eggplant. Cover with remaining hash. Sprinkle with bread crumbs and a little butter and put in a hot oven until brown. Serve with cooked rice.

LAMB BRAINS

Clean, prepare and cook brains in court bouillon following directions for Veal or Beef Brains (page 89). To finish cooking, sauté Meunière (page 89), or make into fritters (page 90).

Pork

First quality pork is pinkish in color and firm to the touch and is generously layered with very firm, white fat. If the meat has a reddish color and the fat on it is scant, you can be almost sure that it is second grade, probably old pork that will lack the delicate texture and flavor that we expect in pork. Pork is a meat which lends itself beautifully to curing by salting, smoking and pickling, so what is not eaten fresh can be safely kept for future use. Every part of the animal from the head to the feet can be, and is, used.

The most common cuts of fresh pork are the loin which is roasted whole or else cut into chops to be sautéed or baked, and the shoulder which is roasted or made into a stew. Frequently, however, the shoulder is ground and used for stuffings and sausages. Hams are usually salted and smoked but many are also sold in the fresh state.

Ham is probably one of the most popular of the pork cuts but I never saw my mother fry or broil a slice of ham as is so frequently done here. Nor did she ever stud the top with cloves and put the sweet finish of brown sugar or molasses over the top, the very delicious manner of preparation that is usual in this country. Mother's way was to glaze a ham with Brown Sauce and to serve it with a Madeira Sauce made with the juice in the pan. And that was a dish for a special party. Most frequently our house-salted hams were boiled with cabbage or with either green or dry beans.

The fat parts of the hog are used in various ways. For example, the belly is salted and smoked for bacon. The fat near the skin is also salted and used for larding meat or cut into dice which, after being sautéed, are added to any number of meat dishes. The fat which lies around the kidneys is the well-known lard.

The head, feet, liver, blood and so on are made into many delicacies called *"charcuterie"* in France. Sausages, head-cheese and liver pâté are some of the better known ones. But these are seldom made at home; they are purchased all ready-made-up and cooked. Only people on farms far from town—people who slaughter their own hogs—would be apt to make them.

ROAST LOIN OF PORK
(Longe de Porc Rôtie)

Of course you can serve Roast Pork with any vegetable you prefer but in France we almost always had red cabbage, Brussels sprouts, lentils or dried beans. Always potatoes, too, and apple sauce. The pork that was left over was served cold the next day usually with Potato Salad and Marinated Red Cabbage.

Season with salt and roast in a moderately hot oven of 375-400 degrees, allowing 30 minutes for each pound. To make the gravy, remove fat from pan and add ½ cup water. Cook a few minutes, scraping and stirring in all the brown from the sides and bottom of the pan.

LOIN OF PORK A LA BOULANGERE

4-4½ *lbs. loin of pork*	1 *tablespoon salt*
8 *potatoes, peeled and sliced*	*a little pepper*
1 *onion, chopped*	2 *tablespoons butter*
1 *teaspoon chopped parsley*	½ *cup or more water*

Use a large roasting pan. Season pork with salt, put in pan, roast in a moderately hot oven of 425 degrees for 1 hour, turning it several times to brown it all over. Remove pork from pan and pour off surplus fat, add a little water and make gravy, stirring in all the brown clinging to the pan. Remove gravy from pan and set aside. Mix potatoes with onions, parsley and remaining salt and pepper and put in the pan, spread with butter and lay the meat on top. Add enough water to come almost to the top of the potatoes. Bring to a boil, then return to oven, now turned to 400 degrees, and cook about 1½ hours longer or until done. Reheat gravy to serve with the meat. Serves 8.

PORK CHOPS SAUTEED
(Côtelette de Porc Sautée)

Season chops with salt and pepper and rub with flour. Try out some of the fat which has been cut from the chops and sauté slowly on both sides. Pork must be well done and for a medium thick chop at least 10 to 12 minutes should be allowed for each side. Serve with Tomato Sauce (page 31) or Piquante Sauce (page 29).

PORK CHOPS BREADED
(Côtelette de Porc Panée)

Coat chops à l'Anglaise (page 293) and follow directions for Pork Chops Sautéed (above).

RISOTTO WITH SAUSAGES
(Saucisses en Risotto)

1 cup rice	½ teaspoon salt
3 tablespoons butter	2 tablespoons grated Parmesan or
1 medium onion, finely chopped	Swiss cheese
2 cups boiling stock, white preferred (or water)	1 lb. sausage

Melt 2 tablespoons butter in saucepan, add onion and cook until it starts to turn golden. Add rice and shake pan until grains are covered with fat. Add stock (or water) and salt, cover pan and cook in moderately hot oven of 400 degrees or over a very low fire 20 minutes. Add remaining butter and cheese, carefully mixing it through the rice with a fork without breaking or mashing the grains. Cook sausage and serve on top of the rice a little Tomato Sauce (page 31) or Brown Sauce (page 24). Serves 4.

CROUTE WITH PUREE OF PORK BRAINS
(Croûte de Cervelle de Porc)

5-6 thick slices of bread	1 teaspoon chopped chives
melted butter	2 tablespoons butter
2 pork brains	½ teaspoon salt
1 onion, finely chopped	a little pepper
1 clove garlic, crushed	

Cut bread in rounds and then hollow out the center of each one by cutting away the center part with a sharp knife. The hollow in center should be about half as thick as the edges. Brush all over with butter, put on a pan in a hot oven and bake until golden brown.

Melt two tablespoons butter in saucepan, add onions and cook over a slow fire until soft but not brown. Clean brains well, removing skin, blood, etc. Add to onion, crush all together with a fork, add salt and pepper and cook about 8 to 10 minutes. Add garlic and chives and correct the seasoning. To serve, spread on top of the toasted bread, making the surface smooth and level. Sprinkle with chopped parsley and serve very hot. Serves 5 to 6.

STEW OF PORK, COUNTRY STYLE
(Ragoût de Porc, Fermière)

2 lbs. shoulder or neck of pork (cut in 10 to 12 pieces)	2 tablespoons flour
	1 clove garlic, crushed
1 teaspoon salt	1 teaspoon chopped parsley
a little pepper	water to cover meat
2 tablespoons lard	1½ cups chopped celery
1 onion, chopped	1 faggot (page 294)
3 leeks, minced	6 potatoes, peeled and cut in pieces
1 carrot, diced	

Season meat with salt and pepper. Put lard in saucepan and when very hot add meat a few pieces at a time, cooking until they are golden brown all over. Add onion, leeks and carrots and cook until they start to turn brown. Pour off surplus fat. Add flour and garlic, mix well and cook a few minutes to brown flour. Add just enough water to cover meat, mix all together, bring to a boil, add faggot and celery, cover and cook slowly about 25 minutes. Add potatoes and continue cooking 40 to 45 minutes longer or until meat is tender and potatoes are done. Remove faggot, skim off fat from top, put in serving dish and sprinkle with parsley. Serves 5 to 6.

PORK LIVER WITH ONIONS
(Foie de Porc aux Oignons)

6 slices of pork liver, cut thin	a little salt
2 tablespoons butter or pork fat	a little pepper
2 onions, sliced	2 tablespoons vinegar

Put butter (or fat) in frying pan and when hot add onions and cook until golden brown. Season them with salt and pepper. Season liver with salt and pepper, rub with flour, and sauté in pork fat in another pan over a quick fire until done on both sides. Remove liver to serving dish and pour fat from pan. Put vinegar and cooked onions in pan, mix together and bring to a boil. Pour over liver and sprinkle with chopped parsley. Serves 2 to 3.

FRESSURE DE PORC

This dish combines the heart, liver and lungs in a wine sauce. It was a very common dish at home and well liked. Sometimes it was served as a hot hors d'oeuvre.

2 lbs. heart, lungs and liver of pork, cut in small pieces	2 onions, chopped
	2 leeks, chopped
2 tablespoons lard	2 tablespoons flour
1 teaspoon salt	2 glasses red wine
a little pepper	1 faggot (page 294)

Put lard in saucepan and when very hot add meat, seasoned with salt and pepper. Move and turn pieces to brown them all over. Add onions and leeks, then flour and mix well. Cook about 5 minutes or until flour is slightly browned. Add wine to cover meat or add water to make enough liquid and add faggot. Bring to a boil, shaking pan to mix everything well, cover and cook slowly about 1 hour. 6 potatoes cut in pieces may be added and cooked during the last 40 minutes. Serves 4 to 6.

SMOKED HAM
(Jambon Fumé)

Although a ham is a large cut of meat, it is not the extravagance it appears to be because it provides many generous servings. It is as delicious served cold as hot and every bit that is left can be used— even to the bone in soup. Leftover ham, in fact, can be used in more ways than almost any other meat. Ham is always a good choice for a large family and also for a small one that is preparing for guests.

Hams vary according to the way they are cured and for this reason the cooking of differently cured hams varies. The main difference is that those with a heavy salting and smoking require a longer soaking and cooking. Hams that are specially cured, particularly those which can be baked without soaking or boiling, are usually accompanied by special directions for cooking. The directions below are for the average ham which is bought in markets all over the country.

[120]

Try to have a large utensil in which to boil a ham. It is important because unless the meat is well surrounded with water, too much of the salt will be left in it and the result will not be as delicately succulent as it could be.

BAKED HAM WITH MADEIRA SAUCE
(Jambon Braisé au Madère)

Soak ham for 24 hours well covered with water. Drain, put in a large kettle, cover with plenty of water and bring slowly to a boil. Let simmer, allowing 15 minutes to the pound, counting from the time it starts to boil. Remove from the water, cut off skin and surplus fat, leaving, however, a good layer of fat covering the meat. Place in a baking pan, pour over it one cup of Madeira or sherry, cover pan and bake in a moderate oven of 350 to 375 degrees, 30 minutes. Uncover and pour over it 1 cup Brown Sauce (page 24). Return to oven and bake, uncovered, basting often, allowing 5 minutes to the pound. At the end of that time it should be well browned and done. Serve with Madeira Sauce (page 27) or sauce from the pan.

Poultry

CHICKEN
(Poulet)

We always bought live chickens, then killed and plucked them ourselves. And, oddly enough, we never bought single birds, always a pair, selecting birds about 4 to 6 months old and weighing about 2½ to 3½ pounds. Chickens of that age and weight are young enough to be tender and plump enough to make them a profitable buy. For home cooking we seldom purchased small broilers feeling that because there is so little eating on them they were a bit extravagant when feeding a family.

Chickens raised in pens with special feeding and not allowed to run have flesh which is very white and fine textured. But I prefer those that run in the fields and are later penned up for fattening. The meat has a special tasty quality with much more flavor.

In judging a chicken, notice the bony lower legs and the feet which in a young bird are thick and heavy looking. As a bird ages these parts, and also the neck, become thinner and dry looking. Also the end of the spur, on the back of the foot, changes from round to sharp and pointed.

The breastbone of a young chicken is soft enough to break easily when pressed with the fingers and a young bird will not have the long hairs that grow out of the skin and under the feathers of older fowl.

Chickens are usually trussed for roasting. This is done to hold the legs and wings close to the body to keep them from drying out during cooking. If they are not tied to the body the heat spreads them out and they are apt to become dry and tough. Using a long needle, a string can be passed straight through the second joints and body, then back through the legs and body and then passed through the wings and body and tied, and another string run through the folded-back wing tips. Or a metal skewer can be run through the legs and another through the wings with the two protruding ends tied so that the legs and wings are held close to the body. The string is always crossed and tied on the back so that no mark will be left on the breast.

ROAST CHICKEN

Clean and singe a 2½ to 3 lb. chicken and truss so that the wings and legs are close to the body. Spread with 2 tablespoons butter and put in roasting pan. Add ¼ cup water to pan and cook in a moderately hot oven of 400 to 425 degrees. Baste often with the melted fat. If water cooks away, add a little more so that the gravy won't scorch, stirring in the brown crust that forms around the pan when adding the water. Allow about 1 hour for a 2½ to 3½ lb. chicken and longer for a larger bird. To test when done, pierce the thick part of the second joint with a sharp kitchen fork and if the juice which follows the fork when it is withdrawn is clear the chicken is done. If it is pink, more cooking is required. Serve with the gravy from the pan. A 3 lb. chicken serves 4.

ROAST CAPON

Follow directions for roasting turkey (page 144).

BROILED CHICKEN

Select a small broiler of about 2 lbs. and have the butcher split it down the back. Season each half with salt and spread with chicken or bacon fat. Heat both broiling oven and broiling grill until hot and broil on both sides, first on the skin side and then on the inside until golden brown. Turn down heat and continue cooking until chicken is done or finish the cooking in the oven. Baste often. Allow about 30 to 35 minutes for the entire cooking. Test by piercing with a fork as described in Roast Chicken. Make gravy, if desired, from juice in pan or serve with Devil Sauce (page 25). Serves 2 to 3.

DEVILLED BROILED CHICKEN

Follow directions for Broiled Chicken (above). When chicken is done brush with prepared mustard, sprinkle with bread crumbs and then with melted butter or bacon drippings. Return to broiler to brown the crumbs. Serve with Devil Sauce (page 25).

CHICKEN EN CASSEROLE WITH VEGETABLES

3-3½ lb. chicken	6 small onions
1 tablespoon butter	2 potatoes, diced
⅓ cup diced bacon or fat salt pork	¼ cup water
1 teaspoon salt	1 cup peas
¼ cup diced carrots (if old, parboil)	

Clean, singe and truss chicken. Melt butter in casserole or saucepan and add bacon or pork dice. Cook until dice become golden brown, then remove them and set aside. Season chicken with salt and put hot fat in pan and brown it by cooking about ten minutes on each side. Put chicken on its back, add carrots and onions to casserole and cook about ten minutes or until they become golden brown. Add water, turn chicken on its side and cover pan. After cooking ten minutes, turn chicken on its other side and cook another ten minutes. Add peas, turn chicken on its back and continue cooking until peas are done, about 20 minutes. Sauté potatoes in butter or other good fat, season with salt and serve with the chicken. Serves 4.

CHICKEN EN CASSEROLE GRAND'MERE

2½-3 lb. chicken	¼ lb. mushrooms
1 clove garlic	12 small onions
2 tablespoons lard (or bacon fat)	2 tablespoons butter (or fat)
a little salt	2-3 medium potatoes, diced
¼ cup water	chopped parsley
¼ lb. fat salt pork, diced	

Clean and singe chicken, truss as for roasting and put garlic inside. Place in a casserole with lard (or bacon fat) and a little salt. Put in a moderately hot oven of 400 to 425 degrees and cook, uncovered, about ½ hour or until it is a good brown all over, turning it occasionally and basting with the fat. Pour off the fat from the casserole and reserve. Add water to casserole and stir in all the brown crust from sides of casserole. In the meantime parboil salt pork and drain, then sauté in fat drained from casserole. When golden brown remove and set aside. Cook mushrooms in fat left in pan and season with salt and pepper. Put onions in a pan with 2 tablespoons water, a sprinkling of sugar and ½ tablespoon butter, then cook slowly until water cooks away and onions take on a good brown color from cooking in the butter. Add pork dice, mushrooms and onions to chicken and if gravy has reduced too much add a little more water. Cover casserole, reduce oven heat to 350 to 375 degrees and cook ½ hour longer or until chicken is done, basting often. Cook potatoes in remaining butter or in fat until brown and done, and put them on top of other vegetables in casserole. Sprinkle with chopped parsley and serve all from the casserole. Other vegetables like peas and asparagus can be added if desired. Serves 4.

CHICKEN WITH RED WINE SAUCE
(Coq au Vin)

3-3½ lb. chicken or 2 spring chickens	12 small mushrooms
(2-2½ lb. broilers)	2-3 shallots, minced
½ cup diced fat salt pork or bacon	1 clove garlic, crushed
2 tablespoons butter	2 tablespoons flour
1 teaspoon salt	1 pint red wine
a little pepper	1 faggot (page 294)
12 small onions	chopped parsley

Clean and singe chicken. If one large chicken is used cut in 8 pieces, but if two small ones, cut each in 4 pieces. Parboil pork (or bacon) dice about 5 minutes and drain them. Put butter in saucepan, add pork dice and cook until they are golden brown. Remove dice and reserve. Season pieces of chicken with salt and pepper, put in hot fat and cook until golden brown on all sides. Add onions and mushrooms, cover pan and continue cooking over a slow fire until onions are a little soft and are starting to brown. Pour off half the fat. Add shallots and garlic to fat remaining in pan and sprinkle the flour over. If oven is hot put the pan in it and leave a few minutes to brown flour. Otherwise, cook a few minutes over low heat on top of stove stirring to prevent scorching. Add wine and if it does not cover chicken add a little water; there should be just enough liquid to cover chicken. Add faggot, bring to a boil, add pork dice, cover pan, and cook in a moderately hot oven of 400 degrees or simmer on top of stove about 35 to 45 minutes or until chicken is tender. If sauce needs it, skim fat from surface. Remove faggot and correct seasoning. Arrange chicken, mushrooms, onions and pork dice in serving dish and pour the sauce over. Sprinkle with chopped parsley. Serves 3 to 4.

CHICKEN FRICASSEE OLD STYLE
(Poulet à l'Ancienne)

3-3½ *lb. chicken*
1 *teaspoon salt*
white pepper
3 *tablespoons butter*
2 *tablespoons flour*
1 *shallot, chopped or ½ onion*
2 *cups hot water*

1 *faggot* (page 294)
12 *small white onions*
12 *small mushrooms, cooked* (page 186)
1 *egg yolk*
¼ *cup cream (or top milk)*

Clean and singe chicken and cut as for Chicken Sauté (below). Season pieces with salt and pepper. Put butter in saucepan and when melted, but not hot, add chicken. Cook over very low heat about 7 to 8 minutes moving chicken all the time to prevent it taking on any color. Mix flour and shallots (or onion), add them and cook a few minutes longer. Add water, bring to a boil, stirring carefully to dissolve flour. Add faggot and onions and cook 35 to 50 minutes or until chicken is done. Remove faggot, add mushrooms. Just before serving, mix together egg yolks and cream (or top milk) and add to liquid in pan, cooking all together just long enough to thoroughly combine the ingredients. Do not allow to boil. If sauce is too thick add a little of the liquor from the cooked mushrooms. A few drops of lemon juice may be added if desired. Serve with rice or boiled potatoes. Serves 4.

CHICKEN SAUTE
(Poulet Sauté)

Clean and singe a 2½ to 3 lb. chicken and cut in pieces as follows: cut off leg and second joint in 1 piece from each side, cut off wings, cut breast in 3 pieces (1 center piece and the 2 sides); leave back in 1 or 2 pieces depending upon size of chicken. Season all pieces with salt and pepper. Spread 3 tablespoons butter in a frying pan and arrange pieces of chicken on it, skin side down. Place on a medium fire and cook slowly until they are golden brown on skin side, then turn them over. Place cover on pan to partly cover it and continue the cooking about 25 or 30 minutes. Remove breast pieces and cook remaining pieces 5 minutes longer or until done. Test for doneness by piercing with a fork and if no pink juice follows the fork when it is withdrawn, the chicken is done. Remove from pan. Add 2 chopped shallots and ½ tablespoon flour to butter in pan. Mix all together and add ½ cup canned tomatoes (or ¼ cup white wine and ¼ cup water). Let boil a few minutes stirring in all the butter and browned juice in the pan. Correct the seasoning. Return chicken to sauce and simmer a few minutes or until ready to serve. Sprinkle with chopped parsley.

If chicken is not a tender one, it should stay in the sauce for an extra half hour. In this case more sauce will be needed which requires adding an extra tablespoon flour and 1 cup of canned tomatoes at the time they were added to butter in pan. Serves 4.

CHICKEN SAUTE CHASSEUR
(Poulet Sauté Chasseur)

2½-3 *lb. chicken*	2 *shallots, minced*
1 *teaspoon salt*	1 *tablespoon flour*
a little pepper	½ *glass white wine*
2 *tablespoons oil*	¾ *cup canned tomatoes*
¼ *lb. mushrooms, sliced*	1 *teaspoon chopped tarragon, chervil*
2 *tablespoons butter*	*and parsley*

Clean and singe chicken and cut as for Sautéed Chicken (page 125). Season pieces with salt and pepper. Put oil in frying pan and when hot arrange pieces of chicken in it and cook, turning them as needed, until golden brown on all sides. Add mushrooms and continue cooking until mushrooms are soft. Remove pieces of chicken from pan and pour off all the oil from pan. Melt butter in pan, add shallots, sprinkle flour over all and cook until golden brown. Add wine and continue cooking until wine is reduced to half. Add tomatoes, mix all together well and boil 5 to 6 minutes. Return pieces of chicken to sauce and simmer about 10 minutes or until chicken is done. Remove chicken to serving dish, correct seasoning of sauce, add chopped herbs and serve. Serves 4.

CHICKEN SAUTE LOUISETTE

2½-3 *lb. chicken*	½ *cup stock (or leftover gravy or*
2 *tablespoons butter or salad oil*	*canned tomatoes)*
1 *small onion, chopped*	4 *tomatoes, peeled, seeded and*
½ *glass white wine*	*chopped*
1 *tablespoon flour*	*cooked rice*
1 *clove garlic, crushed*	*chopped cooked ham*
	1 *teaspoon chopped parsley*

Clean and singe chicken and cut in 8 pieces (each leg and second joint in one piece, the two wings, the breast in 3 pieces, and the back). Put butter (or oil) in saucepan and when hot arrange pieces of chicken in it and cook until brown on both sides. Add onion and continue cooking until onion is golden brown. Sprinkle in the flour, add garlic. Add wine and stock (or tomatoes), cover and cook 25 to 30 minutes. Remove pieces of chicken to another pan, place fresh chopped tomatoes on top and strain the sauce over. Cook about 10 minutes longer, then arrange in center of a ring of cooked rice in which a little chopped ham has been mixed. Sprinkle with chopped parsley. Serves 4.

CHICKEN SAUTE WITH MUSHROOMS
(Poulet Sauté aux Champignons)

3-3½ *lb. spring chicken*	1 *tablespoon flour*
½ *teaspoon salt*	1 *glass white wine (or water and*
a little pepper	*juice of ¼ lemon)*
2 *tablespoons butter*	1 *faggot* (page 294)
8-12 *medium mushrooms*	1 *egg yolk*
2 *shallots (or ½ onion) finely chopped*	¼ *cup cream (or top milk)*

Cut chicken in pieces as for Sautéed Chicken (page 125) and season with salt and pepper. Melt butter in saucepan, when hot add chicken and cook until it just begins to turn golden. Add mushrooms which have been cleaned and peeled and cook 4 to 5 minutes, then add shallots (or onion) and sprinkle in the flour. Mix all together and cook for a few minutes. Add wine (or water) and faggot and cook slowly 35 to 45 minutes or until chicken is done. Discard faggot. Mix together egg yolk and cream and add, little by little, some of the sauce from the pan to this mixture. Turn off heat under chicken and carefully add egg-cream-sauce mixture to pan, shaking and moving the pan around to blend all together. Correct the seasoning and if water was used instead of wine add lemon juice. Serves 4.

CHICKEN SAUTE WITH TOMATOES

2½-3 *lb. chicken*	½ *cup stock or leftover gravy*
2 *tablespoons butter or oil*	(*or canned tomatoes*)
1 *small onion, chopped*	4 *tomatoes, peeled, seeded and*
½ *glass white wine*	*chopped*
1 *tablespoon flour*	4 *baked stuffed tomatoes* (page 204)
1 *clove garlic, crushed*	*for garnishing (optional)*
	1 *teaspoon chopped parsley*

Clean and singe chicken and cut as for Sautéed Chicken (page 125). Season pieces with salt and pepper. Put butter or oil in saucepan and when hot arrange pieces of chicken in pan and cook until golden brown on all sides. Add chopped onion and continue cooking slowly until golden brown. Sprinkle in the flour, add garlic. Add wine, stock (or canned tomatoes) cover pan and cook 25 to 30 minutes. Remove chicken to another pan and then strain sauce over it. Add fresh chopped tomatoes and cook about 15 minutes longer. Put in serving dish, garnish with stuffed tomatoes and sprinkle with parsley. Serves 3 to 4.

CHICKEN SAUTE LILLY
(Poulet Sauté Lilly)

Follow recipe for Chicken Sauté with Mushrooms, then just before serving add 4 tomatoes which have been peeled, cut in half crosswise, seeded and sautéed in butter.

CHICKEN SAUTE MARENGO

2½-3 *lb. chicken*	⅓ *cup canned tomatoes*
3 *tablespoons salad oil*	3 *fresh tomatoes, peeled, seeded*
1 *tablespoon butter*	*and chopped*
1 *tablespoon flour*	½ *lb. mushrooms, cleaned*
1 *teaspoon salt*	4 *slices bread, toasted or fried in*
pepper	*butter*
1 *clove garlic, crushed*	4 *eggs fried French style* (page 68)
½ *glass white wine*	*cooked crawfish or shrimps (optional)*

Clean and singe chicken, cut in pieces as for Chicken Sauté (page 125) and season with salt and pepper. Put salad oil in pan and heat very hot. Arrange chicken in the oil and cook until golden brown on all sides. Turn down heat, half cover pan and cook 25 to 30 minutes. Remove chicken and pour off oil from pan. Add butter to pan, sprinkle in flour and add garlic and wine. Cook until liquid is reduced to one-half the original quantity. Add canned tomatoes, bring to a boil, then add fresh tomatoes and mushrooms. Put chicken back in pan and cook slowly 15 to 18 minutes longer. Correct the seasoning of the sauce. Place chicken in serving dish with mushrooms on top and pour the sauce over. Arrange bread around chicken with an egg on top of each piece of bread. Garnish with crawfish or shrimp and sprinkle with parsley. Serves 3 to 4.

FOWL WITH RICE
(Poule au Riz)

4-4½ lb. fowl, water to cover	1 faggot (page 294)
1-2 carrots	1-2 leeks (if available)
1-2 onions, studded with a clove	1 tablespoon salt

Clean and singe fowl and leave whole. Put everything in a deep pan, bring to a boil, skim and cook slowly about 2 hours or until fowl is tender.

Prepare rice as follows:

2 tablespoons butter	2 cups chicken stock
½ onion, chopped	(from cooking fowl)
1 cup rice	1 tablespoon melted butter

Melt butter in saucepan, add onion and cook until it is golden brown. Add rice and shake over fire for a minute or two until grains are coated with butter. Add hot chicken stock, cover closely and cook in a medium hot oven of 375 degrees or on top of stove over low heat 20 to 25 minutes, or until liquid is cooked away. When done, add melted butter tossing all together carefully with a fork to avoid mashing the grains.

Prepare sauce as follows:

2 tablespoons butter	1 egg yolk
1½ tablespoons flour	3-4 tablespoons cream (or top milk)
1½ cups chicken stock	few drops lemon juice
(from cooking fowl)	

Melt butter, add flour and cook until mixed together. Add stock, mix all together well and cook, stirring, until the sauce is smooth and thickened. Correct the seasoning, adding a little nutmeg if desired, and continue cooking very slowly about 10 minutes. Mix egg yolk with cream (or top milk) and combine with sauce by adding a little hot sauce to egg and cream mixture and then stirring it all carefully into the sauce. Add lemon juice and cook just long enough to combine ingredients but do not allow to boil. Make a bed of the rice in serving dish, carve fowl and place on top of rice. Pour half the sauce over it and serve remaining sauce separately. Serves 5 to 6.

CAPILOTADE OF CHICKEN

Capilotade means all kinds of leftover chicken reheated in a sauce. Generally it is a mushroom sauce, unless of course it is made in a season when mushrooms are unobtainable. It makes a nice change from cold chicken or chicken salad.

2 *tablespoons butter*	1 *cup white stock* (*or canned*
1 *medium onion, chopped*	*tomatoes*)
1 *shallot, minced*	1 *tomato, peeled, seeded and*
1 *clove garlic, crushed*	*chopped*
½ *cup chopped mushrooms*	1-2 *lbs. leftover cooked chicken*
1 *tablespoon flour*	(*not necessary to bone it*)
¼ *glass white wine* (*optional*)	1 *teaspoon chopped parsley*

Put butter in saucepan, add onion and cook until golden brown. Add shallots, garlic and mushrooms and cook slowly until mushrooms are soft. Sprinkle in the flour, mix well, add wine, stock and tomato. Cook, stirring, until smooth and continue cooking about 10 minutes. Cut chicken in pieces, not too small, and put in the sauce a few minutes before serving, cooking it gently, just to reheat it. Do not allow mixture to boil. Place in a serving dish and sprinkle with chopped parsley. If desired, garnish with bread fried in butter. Serves 4 to 5.

CHICKEN CROQUETTES

2 *tablespoons butter*	2 *cups cooked chicken, diced*
3 *tablespoons flour*	6 *mushrooms, cooked* (page 186)
1 *cup hot milk*	*drained and finely diced* (*optional*)
½ *teaspoon salt*	2 *tablespoons chopped, cooked ham*
a little pepper	(*if available*)
2 *eggs, slightly beaten*	

Melt butter, add flour, mix well and cook until it starts to turn golden. Add milk and cook 15 minutes stirring occasionally with a whip to have a very thick, smooth sauce. Add salt and pepper and combine with eggs. Add chickens, ham and mushrooms, mix all together and bring to a boil, stirring constantly until mixture doesn't stick to sides of pan. Correct the seasoning, spread on a flat buttered dish and let cool. When cold, shape the croquettes as desired in cylinders, cones or balls. Coat à l'Anglaise (page 293) and fry in deep hot fat or sauté in butter. Serve with Cream Sauce (page 25) or Tomato Sauce (page 31). Serves 4 to 6.

CHICKEN GALANTINE AND FARCE OF CHICKEN

Galantine is a cold chicken dish, one that is particularly nice for a cold buffet, so popular at summer parties. Of course it is delicious any time of the year but in our country houses, not too well heated, we never thought of serving cold main dishes in wintertime. Galantine was one of our great picnic favorites, too. My mother usually made her own galantine but when there were too many other things to do she bought it from the neighborhood *charcutier.*

Quenelles are light delicate balls that are made from Farce of Chicken. They are added to the chicken, mushrooms and Suprême Sauce which make up the filling for a Vol-au-Vent. A Vol-au-Vent is merely an over-sized patty shell, about the size of a large hollow pie with a big flaky cover for the top. Some French housewives make their own Vol-au-Vents but many prefer to buy them at the pastry shop. Here in this country they can usually be ordered from any French bakery.

These two recipes may seem complicated to some, but I know there are many people, who would be disappointed in a French cook book which left them out. And I can assure those who take the trouble to make either of these dishes that they will be well rewarded for their work.

CHICKEN GALANTINE

1 *fowl, 3½-4 lbs.*	3 *sprigs parsley*
½ *lb. lean veal (leg)*	2 *shallots, finely chopped*
½ *lb. lean pork (tenderloin)*	*(or 1 small onion)*
1½ *lbs. fat pork*	4 *tablespoons cognac (or sherry)*
¼ *lb. cooked ham*	2 *eggs, beaten*
¼ *lb. cooked ox tongue*	3 *quarts chicken stock made from*
1 *tablespoon salt with a little*	*chicken bones, carrot, onion,*
Parisian spice (optional)	*parsley and leeks*
1 *bay leaf*	

Split chicken down the back, open it up flat and lay it skin-side-up on a cutting board. Remove the skin very carefully by cutting it away from the flesh so that it comes off in one piece. Remove breasts and tenderloin under breasts and cut in lengthwise strips, making about six from each side. Cut one-half the veal and lean pork, and all the tongue and ham into strips similar in size to the chicken strips. Also cut enough from the fat pork to make 12 strips similar to the chicken. Put all these strips into a bowl with one half the salt and the shallots, thyme, parsley and cognac (or sherry). Cover and leave in refrigerator to marinate several hours or overnight. Cut 4 thin strips from the remaining fat pork and set them aside. Take all the remaining meat from the fowl (leg, wings, etc.), remove the sinews, combine with remaining lean veal, lean pork and fat pork and run through food chopper using finest knife. Season with remaining salt and add eggs. Drain the marinade from meat strips and add this liquid to the ground meat. Lay a clean cloth or towel on the table, cover it with the 4 slices of fat pork and then spread over this the skin of the fowl with the outside of the skin against the fat pork. Spread one-fourth of the ground meat evenly over the skin, then place on this one-third of the strips of each kind of meat alternating them so that a mosaic will be formed when the galantine is finally cut. Cover with another layer of one-fourth the ground meat, a layer of meat strips and repeat until there are 4 layers of ground meat and 3 of the meat strips. Form all together into a roll and enclose firmly in the skin. Then roll up securely in the towel. Tie ends tightly, tying in both skin and towel in order to keep filling firmly packed. Bring broth to a boil, drop in the roll and cook slowly 1 hour and 45 minutes (or allow 25 minutes per pound). Remove from broth, let stand until cool enough to handle, take off towel and roll galantine up in a clean towel, tightening it up again and tying ends securely. Lay on a platter and place a board on top, weighing the board down with 5 or 6 plates, just enough to press the galantine a little but not enough to squeeze out the juice. When cold, remove towel and keep galantine in refrigerator until ready to serve. (It may be kept for a week or more.) To serve, cut in slices. The stock in which it was cooked may be strained and jellied and served as a garnish for the sliced galantine. (See Aspic, page 293.)

FARCE OF CHICKEN FOR QUENELLES

2 breasts from 3½-4 lb. fowl	a little Parisian spice (optional)
½ cup milk	3 tablespoons butter
3 tablespoons flour	2 small eggs
¼ teaspoon salt	4 tablespoons cream
a little pepper	

Bring milk to a boil and add flour, little by little, mixing vigorously to keep it from becoming lumpy. Cook over a hot fire, stirring all the time until it is thick and smooth. Spread on a plate to cool. Put chicken through food chopper using finest knife, add seasoning and combine with cold flour and milk mixture, pounding it to mix together well. Add butter, also pounding it in. Add eggs, little by little, and combine them thoroughly. Force this mixture through a fine sieve into a very cold bowl. Add cream which should be very cold, little by little, working it in with a spatula. To make quenelles break off small pieces—about a rounded teaspoon—and form into balls or small sausages. Poach about 8 to 10 minutes in a shallow pan of salted water, having water only deep enough to cover them. Drain well and serve with Chicken Patty filling or Vol-au-Vent filling or in consommé.

FILLING FOR VOL-AU-VENT

2 *tablespoons reduced mushroom* *liquor*
2 *cups Cream Sauce* (page 25)
1 *egg yolk*
2 *tablespoons cream*
½ *lb. cooked chicken* (*without* *bone*), *cut in pieces*
¼ *lb. cooked mushrooms* (page 186)

½ *lb. cooked sweetbreads* (page 106) *cut in pieces similar to chicken* (*optional*)
¼ *lb. Quenelles of Chicken* (above) *or Godiveau* (page 98)
¼ *glass dry sherry* (*or 2 tablespoons chicken stock*)
1 *Vol-au-Vent* (page 226)

Add reduced liquor, from cooking mushrooms, to hot Cream Sauce. Beat egg yolk slightly, mix with cream and combine with sauce. Put chicken, cooked mushrooms, sweetbreads and quenelles in saucepan, pour sherry over and cook very slowly 5 to 6 minutes, then pour the hot Cream Sauce and egg mixture over. Do not boil after adding sauce. To keep hot, place pan where it will keep warm or in another pan of hot water. Just before serving place Vol-au-Vent crust on serving dish, fill with meat and sauce mixture and place Vol-au-Vent cover on top. It is important to have plenty of sauce. Serves 5 to 6.

CHICKEN SALAD

Mix together equal parts of cold, cooked chicken (removed from the bones and cut in small pieces) and shredded lettuce. Moisten with Vinaigrette Sauce (page 35) to taste. Sprinkle with a little chopped parsley and chives mixed together and garnish with sliced tomatoes and hard-boiled eggs.

CHICKEN MAYONNAISE

4-5 *lb. fowl, boiled and chilled*
1 *cup chopped celery*
1 *cup outside green lettuce leaves* *cut in julienne*
1 *cup mayonnaise*

salt
1 *tablespoon capers*
2 *hard-boiled eggs*
1 *tomato, sliced*

Remove meat from bones and cut in small pieces. Combine celery and lettuce julienne with a few spoonfuls of mayonnaise and place in bottom of salad bowl. Mix chicken with remaining mayonnaise, season with salt to taste and place on top of celery and lettuce. Sprinkle capers on top of chicken. Garnish with lettuce leaves and quarters of hard-boiled eggs alternated with eighths of tomatoes. Serves 4 to 6.

PATTY A LA REINE

2 *tablespoons cream*
1 *egg yolk* (*optional*)
1½ *cups Cream Sauce* (page 25)
1 *cup leftover cooked chicken, cut in dice*

½ *cup cooked mushrooms* (page 186) *cut in dice*
½ *cup cooked sweetbreads* (page 106), *cut in dice*
1 *glass sherry* (*optional*)
Puff Paste Patties (page 226)

Mix together cream and egg yolk. Combine with hot cream sauce, bring to the boil, stirring all the time, removing from heat before it actually boils. Mix together chicken, mushrooms and sweetbreads. Add sherry, if used. Pour sauce over this mixture and cook a minute or two just to heat up the mixture. Serve in puff-paste patties (page 226). (Patties ready to serve can be purchased.) Serves 5.

RISSOLES OF CHICKEN

¾ *lb. Tart Pastry* (page 228) *or Puff Pastry* (page 227)

1 *recipe of Chicken Croquette mixture* (page 130)
milk

Roll out pastry about ⅛ inch thick and cut into 4-inch rounds. Put a spoonful of croquette mixture in center of each, moisten edges with water and fold over to enclose filling, making half circles. Pinch edges to hold them together and prick top to let out the steam that will form. Place on a greased baking sheet, brush with a little milk and cook in a hot oven of 425 to 450 degrees until brown. If preferred, these rissoles can be fried in deep fat like fritters; or leftover-cooked fish may be used instead of chicken. Makes 12 rissoles.

DUCK AND GOOSE
(Canard et Oie)

Almost every farm in France has a small pond with a flock of ducks and geese, but only in sections where there is plenty of water are they raised in any great number. Those who do raise ducks for the market find them very profitable because they mature so quickly. In only four months after hatching they are at their best and large enough for roasting, which means of course that feed and care do not have to be supplied for as long as in larger birds such as turkeys and geese or even chickens.

The way to tell a young duck, one that is sure to be tender, is to examine its beak. It should be soft and flexible and bend when pressed with the fingers. As ducks increase in age their beaks become hard and firm. How the bird should be cooked will depend upon its age. Young and tender ducks are best roasted but older birds whose tenderness is doubtful should be braised or cooked in wine like *Coq au Vin* or else made into a terrine.

Geese are used pretty generally in France for special occasions, Christmas, New Year's and the holidays on which turkey reigns in this country. At home we had turkey only if the group was very large; at other times goose was always served.

Geese over a year old are hardly worth cooking. An old French culinary adage says, *"Une vieille oye* (old form for oie) *est nourriture de diable,"* meaning *"an old goose is only good for the devil to eat."* The test for a young goose is the same as for duck, the beak is soft and flexible.

Goose fat is generally acknowledged to be the best of all meat and poultry fats, the most delicate of any kind of fat except butter. Many people like it spread on bread like butter and all continental people prefer goose fat to any other for vegetables and for basting all meat and poultry. There is always a great deal of fat inside the goose and around the gizzard which should be put aside when the goose is cleaned. Then after melting it over very low heat, taking great care to keep it from scorching, it can be strained into a jar and kept in the refrigerator to be used for cooking in place of butter.

DUCKLING CHIPOLATA MENAGERE

1 *duckling, 5-6 lbs.*
½ *cup diced salt pork*
1 *tablespoon butter*
8 *small onions*
2 *medium carrots, diced*
1 *tablespoon flour*
1 *clove garlic, crushed*
½ *glass white wine (optional)*
1 *cup stock (or water)*
½ *cup canned tomatoes (or 2 fresh tomatoes, peeled, seeded and chopped)*

a little pepper
1 *faggot (page 294)*
12 *chestnuts, shelled and parboiled in a little stock*
½ *lb. mushrooms, sautéed in a little butter or oil*
12 *small sausages, broiled*
1 *teaspoon sugar*
1 *tablespoon salt*

Clean and singe duck and truss legs and wings close to body. Season with salt and roast in a hot oven of 450 degrees about 15 minutes or until golden brown. Parboil salt pork dice a few minutes to remove salt and drain them. Melt butter in saucepan, add salt pork dice and cook until golden. Remove dice and set aside. Put onions in fat left in pan and cook until almost brown, then add carrots, sprinkle sugar over them and continue cooking until carrots are brown. Remove onions and carrots and set aside with pork dice. Add flour and garlic to fat in pan and stir until all are combined. Add wine, stock (or water) and tomatoes and cook, stirring until sauce is smooth and thickened. Correct seasoning, add pepper and faggot, lay partly roasted duckling on top. Cover, cook slowly 20 to 25 minutes. Add carrots, onions, pork dice, . chestnuts and mushrooms. Cook slowly 40 to 50 minutes longer. Remove duckling, carve and arrange on serving dish. Discard faggot. Arrange vegetables and sausages around duckling and pour sauce over all. Serves 4 to 5.

DUCKLING WITH OLIVES

1 *duckling, 5-6 lbs.*	1 *faggot of 2 sprigs parsley,* 1 *stalk*
1 *tablespoon flour*	*celery, a bit of bay leaf and a*
½-1 *cup water (or stock)*	*pinch of thyme*
½ *cup white wine*	24 *olives, pitted*

Clean and singe duck and truss to hold legs and wings close to body. Put in a moderately hot oven of 425 degrees and roast ½ hour or until a good brown all over. Remove from pan and pour off all the fat except about 2 tablespoons which should be left in pan. Add flour and cook until flour is golden brown. Add water (or stock) and wine and cook, stirring briskly until smooth and thickened. Season with salt and pepper, add faggot, return duck to pan, cover it and cook 45 minutes to 1 hour. Meanwhile, parboil olives in a little water about 5 minutes to remove salt. Drain. Remove duckling, carve and arrange on hot platter. Add olives to sauce and pour over duckling. Serves 4 to 5.

DUCKLING WITH ORANGES
(Canard à l'Orange)

1 *duckling, 5-6 lbs.*	3 *oranges*
1 *tablespoon butter or good fat*	1 *tablespoon sugar*
1 *tablespoon flour*	1 *tablespoon water*
1 *cup stock (or water)*	½ *lemon (the juice)*
½ *glass white wine (optional)*	

Clean and singe duck and truss to hold legs and wings close to body.

[136]

Season with salt and roast in a hot oven of 450 degrees 15 to 20 minutes or until golden brown. Remove from pan. Pour off fat from pan, leaving about 1 tablespoon. Add butter (or other good fat) and flour, mix all together and cook until flour is golden brown. Add stock and wine and cook, stirring briskly, until combined. Return duckling to pan, cover and roast in moderate oven 1 to 1½ hours or until duck is done. Meanwhile, peel the zest (that is the outside orange part of the skin without any of the white) from 2 oranges and cut in very fine strips, boil in water to cover 2 or 3 minutes and drain. Pare away all the white covering from the 2 oranges, pare remaining orange and separate into segments or cut in slices. Place duck in serving dish, then cook down sauce remaining in pan until it is reduced to about 1 cup. Cook sugar and water in a small saucepan until it becomes a light caramel color, strain reduced sauce into it and cook until combined. Add strips of orange peel, all juice that has drained from orange segments and lemon juice. Correct seasoning. Carve duck, arrange on hot platter with orange segments around it and pour sauce over duck. Serves 4 to 5.

DUCKLING WITH TURNIPS

1 *duckling*, 5-6 *lbs.*	1 *faggot* (page 294)
1 *tablespoon flour*	8 *small onions*
1 *cup stock* (*or water*)	2 *cups diced white turnips*
½ *glass white wine*	2 *tablespoons butter*

Clean and singe duck and truss legs and wings close to body. Season with salt, put in a moderately hot oven of 425 to 450 degrees and roast for 15 to 20 minutes or until a good brown. Remove duckling from pan and pour off all the fat except about 2 tablespoons which should be left in pan. Add flour to this fat and cook until golden brown. Add stock (or water) and wine and cook, stirring constantly, until smooth and thickened. Add faggot, and return duck to sauce, cover and cook 25 to 30 minutes longer but with heat reduced to 400 degrees. In the meantime prepare onions and turnips as follows: melt butter in saucepan, add onions and brown them slightly. Add turnips (if they are old, parboil first for 5 minutes) and let brown, sprinkling a little sugar over both onions and turnips to aid the browning. Put onions and turnips in pan with duckling and continue cooking in a moderate oven of 375 degrees about 40 to 45 minutes. Remove duckling, carve and place in serving dish with onions and turnips around it. Correct the seasoning of the sauce and pour over all. Serves 4 to 5.

DUCKLING WITH PEAS
(Canard aux Petits Pois Bonne Femme)

1 *duckling, 5-6 lbs.*	6-8 *small onions*
2 *cups shelled peas*	½ *cup water*
½ *cup diced fat salt pork, sautéed*	1 *faggot* (page 294)
until crisp	1 *tablespoon butter*
2 *to 4 leaves green lettuce*	1 *teaspoon flour*

Clean and singe duckling and truss legs and wings close to body. Season with salt, put in a casserole in a moderately hot oven of 425 degrees and roast ½ hour. Remove duck from casserole and pour off all the fat from the casserole. Mix together peas, pork dice, lettuce leaves, and onions and put in casserole. Add water and faggot, bring to a boil and lay duck on top. Cover casserole, return to oven, and continue cooking 45 minutes to 1 hour or until duckling is done. Remove duck to serving dish, correct seasoning of cooking liquid and thicken it with Manié Butter, made by creaming together butter and flour. Carve duck and serve surrounded with vegetables and sauce. Serves 4 to 5.

ROAST GOOSE, CHESTNUT STUFFING

1 *goose, 10-12 lbs.*	3 *tablespoons cognac (or small glass*
5 *tablespoons goose fat*	*sherry or Madeira)*
2 *medium onions, chopped*	1 *egg, well beaten*
½ *lb. fresh lean pork*	12-15 *cooked chestnuts for stuffing*
½ *lb. fresh fat pork (or 1 lb. sausage*	1 *teaspoon chopped parsley*
meat instead of the lean and fat	10-12 *mushrooms*
pork)	10-12 *chipolata sausages*
1 *teaspoon salt, with a little Parisian*	15 *whole cooked chestnuts for*
spice (optional)	*garnish*

Clean the goose and singe if necessary. Melt 3 tablespoons goose fat in saucepan, add onions and cook until onions are golden brown. Add chopped goose liver, and mix it well with the hot fat and onions but do not cook it. Season with salt and pepper. Run lean and fat pork through meat grinder, season with salt and Parisian spice. Add cognac, the onion and liver mixture, egg, stuffing chestnuts and chopped parsley and mix all together well. Stuff the goose, sew up vent and truss bird to hold legs and wings close to body. Rub outside with a little salt, put in roasting pan, laying it on its side and brush with 2 tablespoons goose fat. Pour ½ cup hot water in roasting pan. Roast in a moderately hot oven of 425 degrees, allowing 15 to 16 minutes for each pound and basting it often with the fat. If water evaporates and juice which comes out of bird gets too brown, add a little hot water to roasting pan. Skim off some of surplus fat from time to time. After 1 hour turn bird on other side, then turn it about every half hour. Bird will be done when juice which follows the withdrawn fork when testing second joint is clear, not pink. Put on back for last 15 minutes to brown the breast. Remove bird to serving dish. Skim all fat from pan, add ½ cup water and cook to make the gravy, stirring in all the brown crustiness that has formed around the pan. Strain if desired. During last half hour of roasting prepare garnish: clean mushrooms (if large cut in pieces) and sauté in 2 tablespoons goose fat, broil or sauté chipolata sausages and arrange around bird with whole chestnuts. Serves 8 to 10.

GOOSE WITH RICE, RAIFORD SAUCE

1 *goose, 10-12 lbs.*
4 *tablespoons goose fat*
1 *onion, finely chopped*
1 *teaspoon chopped shallots (if available)*
1 *clove garlic, crushed*
1 *cup fresh bread crumbs soaked in milk or water*
2 *tablespoons chopped cooked ham (optional)*
1 *teaspoon parsley*

1 *egg, well beaten*
1 *tablespoon salt*
a little pepper
2 *tablespoons fat*
½ *onion, chopped*
1 *cup rice*
2 *cups stock (or water)*
1 *faggot* (page 294)
2 *tablespoons butter*
6-8 *sausages; sautéed or broiled*
2 *cups Raiford Sauce* (page 30)

Clean goose and singe if necessary. Chop liver very fine. Melt 2 tablespoons goose fat, add onion and cook until golden. Add shallots, liver and garlic. Press all moisture out of crumbs and add them along with ham, parsley and egg. Season with salt and pepper and mix all together. Stuff goose with this mixture, sew up vent and truss bird. Rub it with salt, spread about 2 tablespoons fat over it, and lay on its side in a roasting pan. Add 1 cup water to the pan and roast in a moderately hot oven of 425 degrees, allowing 15 to 16 minutes per pound (weight of cleaned goose before stuffing). After about 1 hour turn onto other side, then turn about every half hour, placing on back for last 15 minutes to brown the breast. Baste often during entire cooking with the fat, skimming it from the top of the water.

About ½ hour before goose will be done prepare rice as follows: put 2 tablespoons goose fat in a saucepan, add chopped onion and cook until golden brown. Add rice and shake pan well so that all grains are coated with fat. Add boiling stock (or water), faggot and 1 teaspoon salt. Cover and cook over very low heat 25 to 30 minutes or until liquid is cooked away. Remove faggot and add 2 tablespoons butter tossing it in with a fork to separate grains without mashing them.

Remove goose to serving dish. Skim off fat from pan and add ½ cup water to make gravy. Cook, stirring in all the brown crustiness from around sides of pan. Arrange rice and cooked sausages around goose and serve gravy separately. Serve with Raiford Sauce (page 30).

STEW OF GOSLING, MENAGERE

1 *goose, 8-10 lbs., cut in pieces for*	1 *faggot* (page 294)
stew	2 *cups chopped celery* (*or knob*
1 *tablespoon salt*	*celery*)
a little pepper	10 *small onions*
2 *tablespoons lard*	3 *carrots, cut in pieces*
1 *onion, chopped*	1 *teaspoon chopped parsley*
1 *clove garlic, crushed*	*water* (*or stock*) *to cover*
2 *tablespoons flour*	

Season pieces of goose with salt and pepper. Melt lard in large pan, add pieces of goose and cook until golden brown all over. Drain fat from pan, add chopped onion, garlic and flour. Mix all together and cook until flour is golden brown. (If convenient, brown in the oven, about 6 to 7 minutes.) Add enough water (or stock) to cover pieces of goose. Bring to a boil, mix all together, add faggot and cook slowly 15 to 20 minutes. In another pan, parboil celery 7 to 8 minutes and drain it. Sauté onions in goose fat until golden brown. Parboil carrots. Add celery, carrots and onions to goose and cook 1 hour longer or until goose is tender. Remove faggot. Correct seasoning, put meat and vegetables in serving dish and sprinkle with chopped parsley. If desired, the gizzard may be cleaned and cooked with stew from the beginning; then the liver may be sautéed in a little goose fat and added to stew just before serving. Serves 8 to 10.

CONFIT D'OIE

Of all the list of dishes that are as French as France itself, Confit d'Oie is certainly one that should not be omitted. It is a specialty of the Midi, especially Toulouse, and also of Alsace where they raise geese for the sake of the liver and then have the remainder of the geese for eating. Even though they have learned how to cook geese there in many, many ways, they always seem to have more than they can eat. And so they have worked out a method which can be used to preserve a tough old goose as well as a tender one. This way the cooked meat if stored in a cold place can be kept for many months.

Confit d'Oie is sliced and served cold on the hors d'oeuvres tray or it is heated in the oven—or on top of the stove—after which it is sliced and served with vegetables or used in Cassoulet.

1 goose   3 *cloves garlic,* 2 *cloves,* 12 *pepper-*
coarse salt   *corns,* 1 *bay leaf, a little thyme*
½ *cup water*

Clean goose. Remove fat from inside and from around gizzard and melt it. There should be at least 1 quart; if not, add melted fresh pork fat. Add water and heat together over a gentle fire. In the meantime cut goose in four pieces making 2 breast pieces and 2 leg and second joint pieces. Rub generously with coarse salt. Leave in a bowl with seasonings for 24 hours, moving the pieces occasionally so that every piece is covered with salt. After 24 hours wipe off the salt and dry with a towel and put to cook in the fat for 1 hour or until done, simmering slowly and never allowing the fat to get hot enough to fry the meat. To test when done pierce with a metal skewer. If the juice which follows the skewer when it is withdrawn is clear and shows no pink color, the goose is cooked enough. Remove goose from fat, drain and separate meat from bones. Strain fat and separate it from gravy. Pour about 1 inch of the clear melted fat into a large jar and let harden. Place the pieces of meat on this, then pour in remaining fat making sure that it covers every part of the meat, that none of the meat is uncovered and that none touches the sides of the jar. It is very important that no gravy at all be left in the fat. Let stand about 2 days then pour in more fat to fill any interstices formed by the cooling fat. Cover closely with waxed paper and keep in refrigerator or other cold place until ready to use.

SQUAB
(Pigeon)

Squabs are very young pigeons, in France called "pigeonneaux." Actually these are only half-grown birds that have not yet left the nest; their muscles have not been toughened up with flying and are extremely tender and succulent. These young squabs are usually roasted or sautéed. Sometimes the squabs you purchase are 4 to 6 months old, which means they have left the nest and are suitable only for braising or making into a terrine or a pie. Gourmets are of two schools when it comes to eating squab. They either want them very rare or else so well done that the meat falls from the bones.

ROAST SQUAB

Clean squabs, singe and truss to hold legs close to body. Season with salt and cover with slices of fat pork. Place on their sides in roasting pan and cook in a moderately hot oven of 425 degrees. For a well-done bird cook about 35 to 45 minutes, turning after the first 10 minutes of cooking and placing breast side up during the last 10 minutes. Baste often during the entire time. For a rare bird cut this time in half. One squab serves one person.

SQUAB SAUTE AU BEURRE

Clean and split squabs and season with salt. Melt enough butter in frying pan to generously cover bottom of pan. When hot place squabs in pan, skin side down, and sauté until golden, turn and continue cooking, skin side up, until done, about 15 to 20 minutes in all. Test by piercing second joint with kitchen fork and if juice comes out clear with no pink tinge the birds are done. One squab serves 1.

SQUAB EN COMPOTE

Follow recipe for Squab with Peas substituting for the peas 1 cup of mushrooms which have been sautéed in a little butter.

SQUAB WITH NEW PEAS

3 *squabs*	½ *tablespoon flour*
½ *teaspoon salt*	½ *cup stock (or water)*
2 *tablespoons butter*	2 *cups shelled new peas*
½ *cup diced fat salt pork, parboiled*	*a little pepper*
8-10 *small onions*	

Clean squabs, singe and truss to hold legs close to body. Season with salt. Put butter in saucepan with pork dice and cook until they are golden. Remove dice and set aside. Add onion to fat in pan and cook until golden brown, remove and set aside with pork dice. Put squabs in hot fat in pan and cook, turning frequently, until all sides are evenly browned. Remove squabs and set aside. Remove all the fat except 2 tablespoons. Add flour to fat in pan, mix well, cook until golden brown, then add stock (or water), peas, salt and pepper and bring to a boil, stirring constantly. Put squabs, onions, pork dice and faggot in pan, bring to a boil, cover and cook over a hot fire for about

50 to 55 minutes. Correct the seasoning. Remove squabs to serving dish and pour sauce along with onions and peas around squabs. If desired, a half cup of finely shredded lettuce may be added and cooked with the peas. Serves 3.

SQUAB WITH OLIVES

Follow recipe for Squab with Peas omitting the peas and adding ½ cup pitted olives to the sauce about 10 to 15 minutes before the squabs will be done.

SQUAB PIE
(Pâté de Pigeons)

3 *squabs*
salt
2-3 *tablespoons good fat*
Pastry for Meat Pâté (page 226)
1½ *cups Madeira Sauce* (page 27)
2 *cups Farce au Gratin* (page 145)

6 *mushrooms, sliced and cooked*
(page 186)
a little parsley
a little thyme
a little crushed bay leaf

Clean squabs, season with salt and cook 15 minutes in a hot oven of 450 degrees, basting with fat.

Grease a mold or deep baking dish. Roll out pastry and line mold with it. Prick bottom with a fork. Cut each squab in 10 pieces (after removing from the bones), as follows: 2 slices from each leg and 3 from each breast. Mix 2 tablespoons Madeira Sauce with Farce au Gratin and spread a layer over the pastry, add a layer of sliced squab, a few mushrooms and sprinkle with a little chopped parsley. Add a layer of Farce au Gratin, one of squab and repeat until there are three layers of squab and four of Farce au Gratin with the top one Farce au Gratin. Sprinkle top with a little thyme and crushed bay leaf. Cover with remaining pastry, moistening edges to seal them. Brush top with beaten egg and cut a small hole in center for steam vent. Decorate the top if desired. Bake in a moderately hot oven of 400 degrees about 1 hour. Remove from baking dish and place on serving dish. Cut off the top crust, then cut it in small pieces and place it around the dish as a garnish. Spread 3 tablespoons Madeira Sauce over the top of the pie. Serve a piece of crust and a slice of pie with some of the remaining sauce. Serves 6 to 8.

TURKEY
(Dinde)

In the section of France from which I came, turkey was not a very common bird. Goose was more usually chosen for a holiday feast. But sometimes turkey did appear at Christmastime, especially if the family was large. Occasionally, it was roasted plain, that is without stuffing, but as a rule it was stuffed and always with a chestnut stuffing. Turkeys are at their best when 6 to 10 months old. After they are a year old, they begin to get tough and then the only thing to do is to boil them and use the meat for something like hash.

Whenever we were going to have turkey at my home, we knew it a day ahead because our dinner on the day preceding was always Abattis. This was a kind of stew made with the neck, wing tips, liver and gizzard, sometimes combined with turnips and sometimes with chestnuts.

ROAST TURKEY

Clean bird well inside and out, singe if necessary and truss legs and wings close to body. Season with salt and lay on its side in roasting pan. Put slices of fat salt pork or bacon over breast and spread bird generously with good fat. Place in an oven of about 425 degrees, cook 15 minutes, then turn onto other side and cook 15 minutes longer. Turn heat to moderately hot, 375 degrees, and continue cooking, turning bird from side to side and basting frequently with fat from pan. If fat in pan tends to scorch add a few tablespoons water. Allow 15 minutes per lb. for roasting, weight after bird is cleaned, placing it on its back for last 15 minutes' cooking. If it is stuffed allow an extra 5 minutes per lb. To test, pierce second joint with a two-tined kitchen fork or metal skewer and if juice which comes out is clear with no tinge of pink, the bird is done. To make gravy, skim off most of the fat from pan, add a little boiling water and cook, stirring in all the brown crustiness from around the pan. Correct seasoning and serve separately. A 10 to 12 lb. turkey serves 8 to 10.

ABATTIS OF TURKEY WITH TURNIPS

2 tablespoons lard or other good fat	a little pepper
½ cup diced fat salt pork, parboiled and drained	1 tablespoon flour
	1 cup canned tomatoes
8 small onions	1 clove garlic, crushed
neck, wing tips, gizzard and liver of turkey	1 faggot (page 294)
	2 cups diced turnips
1 teaspoon salt	1 teaspoon chopped parsley
	3 potatoes, cut in pieces

Melt fat in saucepan, add pork dice and cook until they are golden brown. Remove dice and set aside. Add onions to fat remaining in pan and cook until they are brown, remove from fat and set aside with pork dice. Season all turkey parts, except liver, with salt and pepper, add to fat in pan and cook until they are brown. Pour off fat. Sprinkle in the flour, add garlic and mix all together. Add tomatoes and just enough water to cover the ingredients. Add faggot and cook all together slowly, about 35 to 40 minutes. Add onions, pork dice and potatoes. Parboil turnips a few minutes, drain and sauté in a little butter, sprinkling them as they cook with a little sugar and then add them to the meat, onions and pork dice. Correct the seasoning and cook about 1 hour longer. Add liver and continue cooking 8 to 10 minutes more. Serve, sprinkled with chopped parsley. Serves 3 to 4.

ABATTIS OF TURKEY CHIPOLATA

Follow recipe for Abattis with Turnips, substituting for the turnips 1 cup diced carrots (sprinkled with a little sugar and sautéed in butter), 24 shelled and peeled chestnuts and 2 stalks celery cut in pieces. Serve garnished with small broiled chipolata sausages.

CHESTNUT STUFFING FOR TURKEY

1 *lb. fresh lean pork*	1 *lb. fresh chestnuts, shelled and*
1 *lb. fresh fat pork*	*cooked* (page 174)
1 *teaspoon salt*	1 *cup fresh bread crumbs*
a little poultry seasoning	1 *teaspoon salt*
	1 *glass sherry* (*optional*)

Run lean and fat pork through meat grinder using finest knife. Add seasoning, chestnuts, wine and bread crumbs, tossing all together lightly. Use to stuff turkey, capon or chicken. Sufficient for 10 to 12 lb. bird.

LIVER STUFFING
(Farce au Gratin)

3 *tablespoons butter or good fat*	3 *shallots, minced* (*or ½ a medium*
½ *cup finely diced fat salt pork*	*onion*)
½ *cup diced, uncooked lean veal*	*a little thyme*
1 *teaspoon salt*	1 *small bay leaf*
a little pepper	*a small glass Madeira or sherry*
¾ *cup diced, uncooked liver*	2 *egg yolks*
(*chicken, duck or calf*)	

Melt 1½ tablespoons butter in saucepan, add pork dice and cook over a hot fire until golden brown. Remove dice and reserve. Add veal dice to fat in pan and sauté lightly. Season with salt and pepper, then remove and set aside with pork dice. Add liver to fat and sauté quickly for just a few minutes. Return pork and veal dice to pan, add shallots, spices and sherry (or Madeira) and cook slowly about 5 to 6 minutes, stirring occasionally. Drain through a coarse strainer and set aside until the fat drains out. Save this fat. Force the solid part through the strainer to obtain a fine mixture. Add remaining butter and egg yolks, then combine it with the fat that was drained off. Pack in a bowl or jar and keep in refrigerator until ready to use. To keep for several days pour some melted fat over top to form a seal. Use for stuffing birds; may also be used for making pâté or for hors d'oeuvres.

Feathered Game

We usually divide game into two classes, game with feathers and furred game. At home, whenever a hunter had especially good luck, a few friends would be invited in for a party two or three days later. That gave sufficient time for the game to hang, to prepare the terrines and to marinate the meat in spiced wine for the civet. A big bowl of salad and fruit in season would complete the meal. The main attraction was the game and there was always plenty of that.

MALLARD DUCK

Mallard, or any other wild ducks, are cooked very quickly in a hot oven and served very rare. Long cooking toughens them, but even more important is the fact that sportsmen like the flavor of the undercooked bird. A mallard duck is roasted for only 8 to 12 minutes in an oven of 450 to 500 degrees. The breast is removed and sliced thin and the remainder of the meat and carcass is crushed to remove all the blood which is then added to the Sauce au Sang (below) that is served over the sliced breast meat. The dish is usually garnished with small pieces of bread cut in any desired shapes and fried in butter. Fried hominy or wild rice and red currant jelly are served with it.

SAUCE AU SANG

1 *glass red wine*	2 *shallots, chopped*
5 *peppercorns, crushed*	1 *tablespoon Brown Sauce* (page 24)
1 *bay leaf*	*blood from crushed duck carcass*
½ *teaspoon thyme*	

Cook wine, peppercorns, bay leaf, thyme and shallots in a saucepan until reduced to about ⅓ the original quantity. Add Brown Sauce—if none is available use Manié Butter, made by creaming together 1 tablespoon butter and ½ teaspoon flour—mix all together, bring to a boil and then rub mixture through a fine sieve. Just before serving, add duck blood and season to taste.

LIVER PASTE
(Rouennaise)

Rouennaise is a rich mixture of poultry liver and seasonings used for spreading on the toast which is served with game. It is used also in making the Rouennaise Sauce that is often served with duck. In making it you must pound the mixture together to combine it and then in order to have a fine, smooth paste it must be rubbed through a sieve.

Melt 2 tablespoons salt pork fat and heat until it is very, very hot. Add 1 cup chicken or duck livers, a little thyme, 1 bay leaf, 1 teaspoon salt and a little pepper. Cook 3 to 4 minutes over a hot fire. Add a small pony of cognac or sherry, mix all together, pounding it well, then rub through a sieve to make a paste.

GUINEA HEN
(Pintade)

Except for being more "gamey" in taste, guinea hen is very much like pheasant and is prepared in the same ways as pheasant. The small baby guinea hen called a *"pintadeau"* is delicious when roasted. The breast of guinea hen makes a good salmis following the directions for Salmis of Pheasant but the legs are often tough and so are better if cooked with the bones in the sauce to give it flavor. Older birds are good braised and served with sauerkraut.

PARTRIDGE
(Perdreau)

The French partridge is a smaller bird than the American partridge, not much larger than a quail, and the meat is much darker. But like the American variety they are at their best when about 4 to 5 months old, that is in September and October, immediately after the harvest.

The age of a partridge determines the best way to cook it. Young birds, called in French *"perdreaux,"* are best roasted. Serving it on toast which has been spread with Rouennaise or liver paste adds to the deliciousness of the dish. Most sportsmen like their roast partridge served with sauerkraut or cabbage. If the bird is over a year old, it is better braised and the favorite French way is to do it with cabbage. Or it can be made into a terrine and served cold. A small partridge serves one, a large one can be stretched to two servings.

ROAST YOUNG PARTRIDGE

Clean birds and truss to hold legs close to body. Cover breast with slices of fat salt pork or bacon and tie in place. Season with salt. Place birds on their sides in roasting pan and spread with butter or good fat. Put in a hot oven of 450 to 475 degrees and roast, basting frequently for 35 to 40 minutes, then turn them on their backs and continue cooking about 5 minutes longer or until they are done. To test when bird is done, remove it from pan and hold over plate to let juice run out from inside. If it is clear and has no pink tinge it is done. When done, remove trussing strings, take off pieces of browned salt pork and reserve. Pour off most of fat from pan, add a little water or stock and make gravy, stirring in all the brown crustiness around pan as it cooks. Serve whole or half partridge (according to size) on toast which has been spread with a little Rouennaise or Liver Paste (page 147) and garnish with the pieces of brown fat pork. Serve gravy separately.

PARTRIDGE WITH CREAM SAUCE

Follow directions for roast partridge. When done, remove bird from pan and pour off fat from pan. Add to the pan ½ cup cream or top milk and cook, stirring in the brown crustiness from around the pan, until reduced to about one half the original quantity. Thicken with Manié Butter, made by creaming together 1 tablespoon butter with 1 teaspoon flour. Bring to a boil, correct the seasoning and strain through a fine strainer over the partridge. If desired a little lemon juice may be added to the sauce.

BRAISED PARTRIDGE WITH CABBAGE

1 *partridge*	1 *faggot* (page 294)
1 *cabbage* (*Savoy preferred*)	½ *lb. fat pork in one piece* (*parboiled*)
1 *teaspoon salt*	1 *raw sausage* (*garlic type preferred*)
a little pepper	1 *qt. stock* (*or water*)
1 *carrot*	6 *chipolata sausages* (*optional*)
1 *onion, studded with a clove*	

Clean partridge and truss to hold legs close to body and roast in a hot oven of 450 degrees about 10 minutes on each side. Clean cabbage, cut in quarters and parboil about 5 minutes. Drain, put in cold water, drain again very thoroughly and season with salt and pepper. Grease a deep saucepan or place 2 slices of salt pork or bacon in the bottom. Spread leaves from one-third the cabbage in the pan, lay the partly roasted partridge on the cabbage. Add carrot, onion and faggot. Place another third of cabbage over the bird, add salt pork and garlic sausage and add remaining cabbage. Add salt and pepper and stock (or water), having just enough to cover the cabbage. Bring to a boil, cover with a piece of greased paper and then put on the cover of the pan. Place in a moderate oven of 375 degrees and cook 35 to 40 minutes. Remove sausage. Test pork, and if tender remove, if not tender cook longer. Continue cooking 45 minutes to 1 hour or until bird is so tender that the meat is soft and leg is separating from the body. Remove partridge and carrot. Discard faggot. Take out the cabbage with a skimmer to drain it and place in serving dish. Carve partridge and place on top of cabbage. Slice the pork, carrot and garlic sausage and garnish the dish with them. If chipolata sausages are used, fry them until done and arrange them around bird. Serves 3 to 4 depending on size of bird.

SALMIS OF PARTRIDGE

Follow recipe for Salmis of Pheasant (page 151).

PHEASANT
(Faisan)

Pheasant is one of the most popular game birds, probably because it is larger than partridge or quail and so serves more people. There are several good ways of preparing it but it is best to wait to decide on how you are going to cook a pheasant until you have seen the bird. If it turns out to be an old bird, it is apt to be tough and will not be good roasted. Then it is better to braise it with cabbage or make a salmis.

When a pheasant is young and tender, it can be roasted just like a chicken, remembering, however, that it is a dry bird and so requires extra fat in the cooking. It should always have salt pork tied around it and plenty of good fat spread over it also, and should be basted with the fat all the time it is cooking. Some people think that in addition a pheasant should always be larded with strips of fat salt pork. It is most important that a roast pheasant be served the minute it is done because it does not hold well. Let the guests wait for the pheasant but never let the pheasant wait for the guests.

A terrine, or pâté, made of pheasant is a delicious cold pheasant dish and a good way to use a bird that you suspect will not be too tender.

ROAST PHEASANT

Clean pheasant and truss to hold legs and wings close to body. Cover breast with slices of fat salt pork or bacon, tying it on with a string. Season with salt and pepper, place on its side in roasting pan and spread generously with good fat. Put in a hot oven of 450 degrees and roast, basting frequently, about 15 minutes. Turn onto other side and cook 15 minutes longer. Turn it on its back and cook 10 to 15 minutes or until done, basting all the time. To test if done, lift bird and let juice run out. If it is clear and has no pink tinge, the bird is done. Remove to serving dish, pour off fat from pan and make gravy by adding a little water or stock and stirring in all the brown crustiness around the pan as it cooks. Serve garnished, or not, with toast spread with Rouennaise or Liver Paste (page 147).

TERRINE OF PHEASANT
(Terrine de Faisan)

1 *pheasant*	1 *bay leaf*
½ *teaspoon salt*	1 *small onion, sliced*
a little Parisian spice (*optional*)	2-3 *slices of carrot*
1 *pony cognac* (*optional*)	*a pinch of thyme*
1 *glass dry sherry or Madeira*	2 *sprigs parsley*

Clean pheasant, remove skin in one piece and save it. Cut off breasts and cut each one in six slices and put in a bowl. Combine remaining ingredients and pour over sliced breasts. Let stand to marinate for a few hours. Then prepare the following stuffing mixture:

¾ *lb. fresh lean pork*	*a little Parisian spice* (*optional*)
1 *lb. fresh fat pork*	1 *egg, beaten*
legs and remaining parts of pheasant	1 *bay leaf*
½ *teaspoon salt*	

Remove bones and sinews from pheasant, combine with lean pork and one-half the fat pork and chop all very, very fine or run through food chopper. Put in a bowl with remaining ingredients and add the marinade which has been drained from the breasts. Mix all together well. Line a small terrine (or casserole) with the skin from the pheas-

[150]

ant. Slice the remaining half of the fat pork thinly and place slices on skin, covering bottom and sides. Pack in ⅓ of stuffing mixture, then lay 6 slices of the breasts on it. Put in another ⅓ of stuffing mixture and lay remaining slices of breasts on top. Finish with remaining stuffing mixture. Cover with remaining fat pork slices, place bay leaf on top and cover dish closely. Place in a pan of water and bake in a hot oven of 425 to 450 degrees about 1½ hours (or allow 20 minutes per lb.). To tell when terrine is done, remove cover and if fat on top is clear, the terrine is done; if fat is cloudy in appearance, more cooking is required. When done, remove cover and put a plate with a small weight on it to press and pack it down. When cold remove from casserole, scrape away fat from the outside. Wash casserole and replace the Terrine of Pheasant with the skin side up. Cover with Aspic made from the pheasant carcass (page 293). Serve in slices cutting them right from the casserole. May be kept in refrigerator several days.

BRAISED PHEASANT WITH CABBAGE
Follow recipe for Braised Partridge with Cabbage (page 148).

SALMIS OF PHEASANT
(Faisan en Salmis)
Roast the pheasant. Remove breast and legs. Put breasts on warm plate and spread with butter or fat from roasting pan to keep the meat from drying out. Put legs aside. Chop up carcass, bones, skin, etc. Then make the following sauce:

2 tablespoons oil
1 medium onion, chopped
1 shallot, chopped
1 clove garlic
1½ tablespoons flour
1 glass red (or white) wine
1 cup stock (or canned tomatoes)

½ teaspoon salt
3 peppercorns
1 faggot (page 294)
legs and chopped carcass of pheasant
10-12 cooked mushrooms (page 186)

Heat oil, add onion and cook until it is golden brown. Add shallot, garlic and flour and cook a few minutes. Add wine and mix well, then cook until thick, stirring constantly. Add stock (or tomatoes), salt, peppercorns, faggot, legs and chopped carcass of the pheasant. Simmer about 1 hour. Remove legs from sauce, cut meat away from bones and skin, then cut leg meat in 3 or 4 slices. Cut each breast in 3 or 4 slices. Put sliced meat in serving dish, place mushrooms on top. Strain sauce, correct the seasoning and pour over meat and mushrooms. Garnish with toast spread with Rouennaise (page 147). Serves 3 to 4.

QUAIL
(Caìlle)

The best ways to cook quail are the simplest ones, that is by broiling or roasting. Roasting is probably the most popular. Since quail are usually brought in by hunters in the fall when grapes are also in season, it is customary in France to wrap the birds in grape leaves before roasting them. One quail will serve only one person.

ROAST QUAIL

Clean the birds, roll them in grape leaves, then wrap a thin slice of fresh fat pork around each one, tying it in place. Spread with a little butter and roast in a very hot oven of 450 to 475 degrees, 12 to 15 minutes, basting frequently. After removing from pan, make gravy in pan by adding a little water, cooking and stirring in all the brown crustiness around the pan. Serve each bird on toast which has been spread with Rouennaise or Liver Paste (page 147). Little white seeded grapes and a little sherry are a delicious addition when cooked in the gravy. Wild rice or Risotto (page 216) to which a little chopped cooked ham has been added, are two favorite accompaniments for quail.

BROILED QUAIL

Split quail, spread with fat and broil, following directions for broiling chicken, allowing 10 to 12 minutes for the entire cooking. Serve on toast spread with Rouennaise or Liver Paste (page 147).

Furred Game

HARE AND RABBIT
(Lièvre et Lapìn)

Hare and rabbit are two delicious kinds of game that are always very plentiful when the season is on. And if one of your huntsman friends comes home with more than he can use, don't refuse a gift of either a hare or a rabbit. Learn how to cook them and you will find out what good eating they make.

Hare is the wilder of the two animals, is a little larger and has a more gamey taste. Hunters usually prefer its gamey flavor although many other people would rather have rabbit. The same rules of preparation can be applied to both. They are best when about 7 to 8 months old, which is the age when they have reached their full weight, but are still young and tender. They make a good stew or civet or, if desired, the back can be roasted and served with Cream Sauce. When the animals are older, and consequently less tender, they are best used for pâté or terrine.

The age of a hare or a rabbit can be most easily told by examining the ears. They should be tender and tear easily. When they are thick and tough the animal is not a young one.

A rabbit or hare, after it is skinned and cleaned is cut up in 16 or 18 pieces, as follows: legs in 3 pieces, forelegs in 1 or 2 pieces, neck in 2 pieces, saddle and filet in about 6 pieces. The head can be used or not but, if used, must be cleaned—and left whole—before putting it in the civet. All the blood should be saved for thickening the sauce.

Both hare and rabbit are best if eaten within two or three days after killing, and not be allowed to get too "gamey." And it must be remembered the meat of these animals is heavy and not too easily digested.

STEW OF HARE WITH WINE
(Civet de Lièvre)

1 *hare, cut in pieces*	2 *tablespoons flour*
1 *pt. red wine*	1 *clove garlic, crushed*
1½ *tablespoons vinegar*	1 *cup (or more) stock or water*
1 *cup diced fat salt pork*	1 *faggot* (page 294)
4 *tablespoons butter (or good fat)*	2 *bread slices quartered and fried in*
12 *small onions*	*butter or toasted*
½ *lb. mushrooms (if large cut in*	*chopped parsley*
pieces)	

Clean hare and reserve blood, if there is any. Mix blood with 2 tablespoons wine and 1½ tablespoons vinegar and keep in refrigerator. Put hare in a bowl and mix thoroughly with the following marinade: 1 tablespoon salt, a little pepper, 1 slice of onion, 2 minced shallots, 3 sprigs parsley, a little thyme, 1 bay leaf, 3 tablespoons salad oil and 1 glass wine (red or white). Let stand overnight in a cold place.

Parboil diced pork, drain and sauté in 2 tablespoons butter (or fat). When golden brown remove from fat and reserve. Put onions in same fat, sprinkle with a pinch of sugar and cook until they are brown all over. Remove and put with pork dice. Sauté mushrooms in remaining butter until they are soft and their moisture is cooked away and put with pork dice and onions. Remove hare from marinade, dry each piece and cook in fat (left from pork dice and onions), heated very hot, until they are brown all over. Drain fat from pan, sprinkle hare with flour, add garlic, mix well and cook in oven or over low heat until flour is golden brown. Add wine and enough stock (or water) to cover meat. Stir with a wooden spoon or spatula as it comes to a boil and cook until sauce is smooth. Add faggot, cover pan and cook slowly 40 to 45 minutes. Remove meat from pan to another and add pork dice, onions and mushrooms to it. Correct seasoning of sauce, strain over meat and vegetables, bring to a boil and cook slowly 30 to 35 minutes longer or until meat is tender.

Clean liver of hare, cutting away bitter end near the gall. Cut in small pieces, add to stew and cook 8 to 10 minutes longer. Stir 3 tablespoons of sauce from stew gradually into the blood. Remove stew from heat and pour blood and sauce slowly into the stew. Move pan in a circular motion to combine blood and thicken sauce because stirring with a spoon will break up meat and vegetables and make them unattractive. Do not allow to boil. Serve garnished with fried bread and sprinkled with parsley. Serves 6 to 8.

RABBIT STEW
(Lapin en Gibelotte)

1 *rabbit, about* 3 *lbs. when cleaned,*	1 *tablespoon salt*
cut in pieces	*a little pepper*
3 *tablespoons lard* (*or good fat*)	2 *tablespoons flour*
1 *cup diced fat salt pork*	1 *clove garlic, crushed*
8-10 *small onions*	1 *glass white wine*
½ *lb. mushrooms*	1 *faggot* (*page 294*)
2 *tablespoons butter*	1 *teaspoon finely chopped parsley*

Put lard (or fat) in saucepan and when hot add pork dice and cook until they are golden brown. Remove cooked dice and reserve. Add onions to fat in pan and cook them until they are brown all over, then remove and set aside with pork dice. Clean mushrooms and sauté in butter until they are soft and their moisture is cooked away and put with pork dice and onions. Clean pieces of rabbit, season them with salt and pepper and cook until brown all over in the fat left from pork dice and onions. Drain off fat from pan, add flour and garlic, mix well and cook until flour is golden brown. Add wine and enough water to cover meat. Bring to a boil, add faggot, cover pan and cook slowly 25 to 30 minutes. Add mushrooms, onions and pork dice and cook 30 to 40 minutes longer or until meat is tender. Remove faggot and correct seasoning. Serve sprinkled with parsley. Serves 6 to 8.

RABBIT STEW COUNTRY STYLE
(Lapin Sauté Fermière)

Follow recipe for Rabbit Stew (above) using either red or white wine and replacing mushrooms with potatoes cut in pieces.

TERRINE OF HARE
(Terrine de Lièvre)

Terrines are always a part of a French party or picnic and a favorite for lunch or supper, too. Certainly there is nothing more tasty. We thought them very practical because they can be made up several days ahead and put away in a cold place until wanted. Although at first glance the recipe may seem long and complicated, the actual making of a terrine is not particularly difficult, not nearly as difficult as trying to describe in a few words the way it is prepared, layered up and so on.

Usually people who hunt in the fall and bring in a lot of game look for more and different ways of cooking it. A terrine is one good answer. And because it can be made and kept in a refrigerator for a week or ten days this is a way of storing some of the surplus. People who live in the country and have more game than they can use in the fall hunting season could hardly find a more acceptable food gift for their city friends than a terrine made of hare or pheasant.

1 *hind saddle of hare*	1 *pony cognac (or* 1 *glass white*
½ *lb. filet of fresh pork*	*wine)*
½ *lb. lean veal*	1 *onion, sliced*
2 *lbs. fat salt pork*	1 *bay leaf*
½ *lb. cooked ham*	2-3 *sprigs parsley*
1 *tablespoon salt*	*a little thyme*
pinch of Parisian spice (optional)	2 *eggs*
	2-3 *tablespoons blood of hare (if any)*

Remove bones and sinews from filet and tender part of the leg of hare leaving the meat whole. Cut ½ the fresh pork, ½ the veal, ½ the fat pork and all the ham in slices ⅛ inch thick and then cut the slices

[155]

in strips ⅛ inch wide. Put all in a bowl and add ½ the salt, the Parisian spice, ½ the cognac (or wine), onion, bay leaf, parsley, thyme and salad oil. Let stand a few hours or overnight to marinate. Cut 4 thin slices from the remaining pound of fat pork and reserve. Remove all the remaining meat from the bones of the hare, and combine with remaining fresh pork and fat salt pork and veal. Mince all this meat very, very fine or run through a food chopper, add remaining ½ tablespoon salt. Add eggs one at a time mixing well, add remaining cognac (or wine) and blood, if any and mix all together well. Lay 3 of the reserved thin slices of fat pork on the bottom and sides of a terrine (or casserole), pack in about 1 inch of the ground-meat mixture, then a layer of the spiced-meat strips alternating the different ones, add another layer of meat mixture and a layer of meat strips. Continue until there are 4 layers of meat mixture and 3 of meat strips with the hare filet and leg meat in the center of each layer and with meat mixture on top of all. Cover with a thin slice fat pork. Put a pinch of thyme and a bay leaf on top of all. Cover dish and seal with a roll of dough made by mixing together flour and water to make a stiff dough. Set in a pan of boiling water and bake in a moderately hot oven of 400 to 425 degrees about 1¾ to 2 hours. When the fat which cooks out of the steam vent in the cover is clear, without any cloudy appearance, the terrine is done.

While the terrine is baking, prepare the following Aspic: mix together bones from hare, veal or chicken bones (if available), 1 sliced onion, 1 sliced carrot and a few sprigs parsley. Put in a hot oven and let brown. Turn into a saucepan, add 1 quart water, 1 teaspoon salt and cook very slowly, to keep stock clear, 1 to 1½ hours when it should be reduced to 2 cups. Add 2 teaspoons gelatin which has been softened in a little cold water. Strain through a muslin cloth. If desired add ½ glass of sherry or Madeira. When terrine is done, remove from oven and let stand 15 minutes before removing dough. Uncover and place the plate with a weight of about 6 lbs. on top to compress and pack the meat into a pâté and to squeeze out the fat which will rise to the top. When cold, remove plate and weight, scrape off fat and pour in Aspic, pricking with a metal skewer so that the Aspic will go all through the terrine as well as around the outside. Chill thoroughly. Serve in slices, cutting them right from the casserole. This can be kept in the refrigerator for a week or ten days.

WILD BOAR

Prepare wild boar the same as venison.

RABBIT EN CIVET

Follow recipe for Stew of Hare with Wine (page 153), substituting rabbit for hare.

VENISON

Venison is good only in the fall and winter but since this is the only time that it is legal to hunt deer there is not much opportunity of eating venison when it is not good. I was rather surprised when I first cooked deer in this country because the animal is so much larger here than in France. But the meat, I find, is about the same.

The best parts of venison are the leg and saddle which can be cut into steaks and cutlets or cooked whole. The loin is very tender and delectable if cut in thick slices similar to beef filet and sautéed in oil. This is called a *"noisette"* or *"grenadin."* The shoulder and neck are not as tender as the other parts and are best in a stew or civet, the latter being a game stew made with a wine sauce.

These are a few points to remember in preparing game which will insure good results. First it should hang for at least 24 hours before eating and will be improved still more if it hangs for several days. Then before it is cooked it should be larded with strips of fat pork because venison has so little fat in it. And last, it should be marinated in spiced wine or vinegar for a few hours or a few days, the length of time depending upon the age of the animal. The purpose of this pickling liquor is not only to make the meat more tasty but also to make it more tender, therefore the meat from older animals should be left in it longer than that from young deer.

VENISON STEAK

Venison steaks are cut from the leg of the deer, usually about ¾ inch thick, and served quite rare. Chops and steaks cut from the loin are prepared and served in the same way as the leg steaks. The customary accompaniment is Purée of Chestnuts but some like Braised Celery with venison. Wild rice and currant jelly are two other favorite accompaniments.

Put the steaks in a bowl with the following marinade: 1 teaspoon salt, 3 to 4 peppercorns, 1 sliced onion, 1 sliced carrot, 4 sprigs parsley, a little thyme, 1 bay leaf, 1 glass white wine (or 4 tablespoons vinegar) and 3 tablespoons salad oil. Let stand in a cold place from 12 to 24 hours turning the meat in the marinade from time to time. Remove from marinade and dry thoroughly. Heat about 3 tablespoons salad oil

[157]

in a frying pan and when very hot add the steaks. Cook about 3 minutes on each side—or a little longer if you want it less rare. Serve with Poivrade Sauce (page 32) or the following sour cream sauce:

SOUR CREAM SAUCE

1 *tablespoon butter*	*½ cup boiling top milk or cream*
1 *tablespoon flour*	*a little salt*
2 *tablespoons vinegar*	*a little pepper*

Drain off fat from pan in which venison steaks were cooked and put butter in pan. When melted add flour and mix together stirring in all the brown from around the edges of the pan. Cook a few minutes. Add vinegar and top milk or cream, salt and pepper. Cook a few minutes stirring constantly or until thickened. Correct the seasoning and pour over the meat.

This sauce is also very good if made in the pan after braising veal or chicken.

CIVET OF VENISON

3 *lbs. vension, shoulder, neck or*	*½ lb. mushrooms*
other parts not tender enough to	2 *tablespoons flour*
roast or cut in steaks	1 *clove garlic, crushed*
½ cup fat (or oil)	1 *glass red wine*
1 *cup diced fat salt pork*	1 *faggot (page 294)*
12-15 *small onions*	*chopped parsley*
2 *carrots, sliced*	

Remove sinews from meat and cut in pieces as for stew. Cover with same marinade used for hare (page 153) and let stand in a cold place 1 day or overnight. Put fat (or oil) in frying pan, when hot add pork dice and cook until golden brown. Remove dice and reserve. Add onions to same fat and when they have started to brown add carrots, sprinkle with a little sugar and continue cooking about 5 to 6 minutes or until golden brown. Remove and put with pork dice. Sauté mushrooms in same fat until they are soft and their moisture is cooked away. Remove meat from marinade and dry each piece, then cook in same fat until brown all over. Remove from fat and put in a saucepan, sprinkle with flour, mix together and cook until flour is brown. Add wine, faggot, garlic, the marinade liquor and enough water to cover meat. Bring to a boil and cook 1 hour. Add onions, carrots, mushrooms and pork dice and cook 40 minutes longer or until meat is tender. Remove faggot and correct the seasoning. Serve sprinkled with chopped parsley. Serves 6 to 8.

Vegetables

⟨⊐ ✤ ⊏⟩

VEGETABLES are very important in French homes. But we ate vegetables only in season or ate the kinds that can be stored for the winter. From spring's first tender peas to fall's last Brussels sprouts we enjoyed each at its best, then were satisfied to wait until the calendar brought it around again. In winter the root vegetables—carrots, onions, potatoes and so on—and those of the cabbage family, were used as long as they would keep. I never saw vegetables canned in my home, except tomatoes and occasionally peas, but we did preserve green beans in salt and the many varieties of shelled beans that we dried were a real stand-by all winter.

It seems to me we cooked vegetables in more ways than is usual in this country, probably because they were often our main dish and also because we seldom ate vegetables on our plate with meat but only after we had finished eating the meat. Mother frequently combined two vegetables and cooked them with bacon or salt pork—potatoes and green beans, for example—seasoning the bacon-flavored liquor in which they were cooked and serving it first as a bouillon, then perhaps dressing up the vegetables themselves with a sauce. And, of course, she wasted nothing, from the green parts of leeks and celery leaves which went into the soup kettle to the finely shredded outside leaves of lettuce which added their nourishment and flavor to peas.

ARTICHOKES
(Artichauts)

The artichokes which can be purchased in American markets are, for the most part, the large ones. The tiny ones which we thought so delectable at home in France don't seem to be obtainable in many sections of this country. Those were the ones which we always used for the hors d'oeuvres dish.

The length of time required to cook artichokes will depend upon their size, but the average large artichokes which are found in the markets here need about 1 hour's cooking. The heart—or bottom—must be done and the pulp at the base of the leaves succulent. After they are cooked and drained they can be served either hot or cold. For those who are very fond of this vegetable a convenient and time-saving way is to cook enough for two meals at one time. Then one-half can be served hot, the others saved to serve cold another day. The prickly choke in the center must be removed before serving an artichoke. To do this, separate the center leaves and pull out the fine prickly ones all in one bunch. Then scrape away with a spoon any remaining. One artichoke is usually allowed for one person, although it can be split in half, cutting straight down through the center, and made into two servings.

To Prepare Artichokes

Break off, instead of cutting off, the stem and then all the stringy fibres will pull out. Then trim the bottom of the stem with a knife. Trim the tops of the leaves, cutting away about a half inch, then tie a string around the artichoke to hold the leaves in place. To keep the base white, a thin slice of lemon may be tied to the bottom of each one. Cook slowly in boiling salted water about 1 hour. To test when done, pull out a leaf and if it comes away easily the artichoke is cooked enough. Remove prickly choke from the center. Serve hot with melted butter or Hollandaise (page 26), or cold with Vinaigrette Sauce (page 35) or Mayonnaise (page 34), serving the sauce on the side.

STUFFED ARTICHOKES

3 *artichokes*	1 *tablespoon chopped ham*
2 *tablespoons butter*	1 *teaspoon chopped parsley*
1 *shallot, chopped (or 1 tablespoon chopped onion)*	½ *teaspoon salt*
	a little pepper
3 *tablespoons finely chopped mushrooms*	3 *slices fat pork*

Cut off ⅓ the tops of the artichokes and trim off tops of lower leaves. Put in boiling salted water and cook 15 minutes. Put in cold water and when cold drain them. Remove prickly chokes from the centers. Melt butter in saucepan, add shallots (or onion) and mushrooms and cook a few minutes or until the moisture is cooked out of the mushrooms. Add ham, parsley, salt and pepper. Fill artichoke centers with this mixture. Wrap a slice of fresh fat pork around each one and tie with a string to keep artichokes in shape. Then prepare the following:

[160]

1 *carrot, sliced*
1 *onion, sliced*
1 *sprig parsley*
1 *bay leaf*

a little thyme
½ glass white wine (or stock or water
with juice of ½ lemon)

Mix all ingredients together in the bottom of a casserole. Place artichokes on top of vegetables and wine in casserole, bring to a boil, cover and cook in a moderate oven of 350 to 375 degrees about 1 hour. 15 minutes before they are done, remove cover to brown the slices of fat pork. Remove artichokes to serving dish and cut away strings. Strain liquid from casserole into another pan and cook until reduced to ½ the original quantity (adding meat gravy if any is on hand) and serve as a sauce for the artichokes.

ASPARAGUS
(Asperges)

Asparagus, one of the most delicate of vegetables, has a characteristic flavor and texture that is different from all others. But the fresher it is, the better the flavor.

Always remember in preparing asparagus that it is grown in sandy soil and must be cleaned extra carefully because the grains of sand are hard to dislodge from the scales of the tips. Also remember that a vegetable as delicate as asparagus requires careful handling during preparation. The water in which it is cooked must boil very gently to keep the tips from breaking apart, and after cooking the stalks must be very thoroughly drained otherwise the butter or any sauce that is served will pick up so much water that it will be tasteless. I find that laying the stalks on a towel will absorb all this moisture. But the towel used, however, must not have been washed or bleached with chemicals —that will impart an unpleasant flavor to the asparagus.

To Cook Asparagus

Peel or scrape stems and wash stalks well in cold water. Tie in small bunches of 6 to 12 stalks to make it easier to remove them from the pan after cooking. Cut off tough ends. Cook gently in boiling salted water, adding 1 teaspoon salt to each quart of water, about 15 to 20 minutes or longer, depending upon the thickness of the stalks and their freshness. If the point of a small knife slips easily into the tips they are done. Drain thoroughly. Serve hot with melted butter, Hollandaise Sauce (page 26), Sauce Blanche (page 36), or with slices of hard-

[161]

cooked eggs placed on top of the tips and Brown Butter (page 32) poured over.

ASPARAGUS TIPS

Follow directions for cooking asparagus and serve hot with meat, fish or chicken dishes or serve cold in salad or as a garnish for salads or cold meats. Or serve cold with Vinaigrette (page 35) or a light Mayonnaise (page 34) made by mixing Mayonnaise with half as much whipped cream and a few drops of lemon juice.

ASPARAGUS MILANAISE

Cook asparagus and drain well. Put in serving dish, sprinkle top with grated cheese, Parmesan preferred, and pour Brown Butter (page 32) over it.

ASPARAGUS POLONAISE

Cook asparagus and drain well. Put coarsely chopped hard-cooked eggs on top of tips and sprinkle with chopped parsley. Cook fine fresh bread crumbs in butter until they are brown, then pour butter and crumbs over eggs, using 2 tablespoons crumbs and 4 tablespoons butter for each bunch of 18 to 24 asparagus stalks.

COLD ASPARAGUS

Cook, drain and chill asparagus. Serve with Vinaigrette Sauce (page 35) or Mayonnaise (page 34).

ASPARAGUS TIEDE, SAUCE VINAIGRETTE

Cook and drain asparagus and when lukewarm serve with Vinaigrette Sauce (page 35).

BEETS
(Betteraves)

Beets are not served as a hot vegetable very often in France. Usually they appear as an hors d'oeuvre made into the kind of beet salad given in the Hors D'oeuvres section of this book. For this we used the large winter beets and, as a rule, baked them.

BUTTERED BEETS

Young garden beets, plentiful in this country in the summer season, do not require baking when they are young and tender. They can be boiled in 30 to 50 minutes, the length of time required depending upon their age. In preparing them, do not trim off the tails too closely because this causes the beet to bleed leaving a white, or at best a pinkish, vegetable to serve. When done, peel them and then reheat—either sliced or whole—in butter and season with salt and pepper.

STRING BEANS
(Haricots Verts)

Occasionally green beans were cooked plain and served with butter as is usual in this country but more often they were combined with other foods like onions or salt pork and made into a heartier dish. My mother generally prepared them with a piece of salt pork—striped lean and fat like a piece of bacon—put an onion and carrot in for flavor and added some potatoes to provide more nourishment. This, then, would be the main dish of our meal—and very good and satisfying it was, too. The water in which all these ingredients were cooked made a bouillon which was well flavored with the pork, onion, carrots, and of course the beans, while some of the starch from the potato thickened it a little. This bouillon was served first with toasted crusts of bread, then the beans and other ingredients were eaten as the main dish. All this makes a meal in country places where vegetables and salt pork are much more plentiful than fresh meat.

We also liked the string beans sautéed Lyonnaise style, especially the young tender ones that were the first picking off the plants. They were cooked plain and then finished in butter in which finely chopped onion had been browned and which gave the beans a delicious brown butter and onion flavor. But the beans which were put down in salt in crocks for the winter came to the table *à la Crème*, that is creamed, or were prepared Bourbonnaise style.

PLAIN STRING BEANS

Clean and remove ends from 1 lb. string beans. If large, cut in 2 or 3 pieces or cut lengthwise through the center. Small ones can be left whole. Cook about 20 minutes or until tender over hot fire in 1 quart of water to which 1 teaspoon salt has been added. Drain thoroughly and serve plain with butter and season to taste with salt and pepper. Or put in a serving dish with a lump of butter and sprinkle with finely chopped parsley. Serves 4 to 5.

STRING BEANS, LYONNAISE
(Haricots Verts, Lyonnaise)

Chop 1 onion finely and put in saucepan with 2 tablespoons butter

[163]

and cook until onion becomes golden brown. Cook 1 lb. string beans as for Plain String Beans (page 163), drain well and add to butter and onion. Sauté a few minutes shaking the pan so they will mix with the onion. Correct the seasoning and sprinkle top with finely chopped parsley. Serves 4 to 5.

CREAMED STRING BEANS
(Haricots Verts à la Crème)

1st method. Mix 1 lb. well-drained, cooked string beans (following directions for Plain String Beans) with 1 cup Béchamel Sauce (page 24) made light by adding a little top milk or cream.

2nd method. Chop ½ onion finely and cook in 2 tablespoons butter until it starts to turn golden. Add 1 teaspoon flour and cook a few minutes longer. Add ½ cup milk or top milk, mix well and cook, stirring, until smooth and a little thick. Add 1 lb. string beans which have been cooked and drained following directions for Plain String Beans. Cook a few minutes shaking pan to combine sauce and beans and to cook liquid down a little. Correct the seasoning and serve sprinkled with finely chopped parsley. Serves 4 to 5.

STRING BEANS PAYSANNE

1 *lb. string beans*	3 *tomatoes, peeled, seeded and*
1 *tablespoon butter*	*coarsely chopped*
⅓ *cup diced salt pork or bacon,*	2 *potatoes, cut in pieces*
parboiled and drained	½ *teaspoon salt*
1 *onion, finely chopped*	*a little pepper*
	½ *cup water*

Clean and remove ends from beans. If large, cut in 2 or 3 pieces. Put butter and bacon in saucepan and cook until bacon dice are golden brown. Remove dice and reserve. Add onions to fat in pan and cook until golden. Add beans, tomatoes, potatoes, seasoning, water and browned bacon dice. Bring to a boil, cover pan and cook slowly until beans are cooked, about 40 minutes. Serve with the liquid in which they were cooked and which should be about half cooked away. Serves 4 to 5.

CREAMED LIMA BEANS AND MUSHROOMS

1 *cup cooked lima beans*	½ *teaspoon flour*
½ *cup mushrooms, diced*	*a little pepper*
1 *shallot (or ½ small onion, chopped)*	½ *cup top milk (or cream)*
1 *tablespoon butter*	

[164]

Melt 1 tablespoon butter in saucepan, add mushrooms and cook until they are soft, about 5 minutes. Add shallot (or onion), cook a few minutes, add top milk (or cream) and cook until reduced to ½ the original quantity. Add lima beans. Cream together remaining tablespoon butter and flour, add to mixture in pan and bring to a boil. Serves 3.

BEANS BOURBONNAISE

3 *cups shelled beans, cooked*
½ *teaspoon salt*
1 *onion, finely chopped*
3 *tablespoons butter*
1 *cup milk*

½ *teaspoon salt*
a little pepper
½ *teaspoon flour*
2-3 *tablespoons cream (optional)*
½ *teaspoon chopped parsley*

Use those beans that are on the vine at the end of the season which are too old and dry to cook unless they are shelled. Cook them in boiling salted water, the same as any dry beans. Drain. Brown onion in 2 tablespoons butter until it starts to turn golden. Add beans and milk and cook until milk is reduced to ½ the original quantity. Add salt and pepper. Thicken sauce with Manié Butter, made by creaming together remaining tablespoon butter and the flour. For a richer sauce add 2 to 3 tablespoons cream. Bring to a boil, correct the seasoning and serve sprinkled with parsley. Serves 6.

BROCCOLI

Broccoli should be washed in a large quantity of water to which a little vinegar or salt has been added and left in the water for about an hour. This is to draw out any insects hidden in the stalks, and is exceedingly important.

To Cook Broccoli

After washing put the broccoli in boiling salted water and turn down the heat so that the water simmers but does not boil. Cook for about 20 minutes or until the broccoli sinks to the bottom of the pan which indicates that it is done. Drain very thoroughly. Serve hot with melted butter, Polonaise Sauce (page 33), or Hollandaise Sauce (page 26). Or chill and serve with Vinaigrette Sauce (page 35).

BRUSSELS SPROUTS
(Choux de Bruxelles)
To Prepare Brussels Sprouts

Trim and wash sprouts well. Cook in salted water about 25 to 30 minutes or until they are soft. Drain well, sauté in butter or good fat and season with salt and pepper.

BRUSSELS SPROUTS MENAGERE

Follow directions for preparing Brussels sprouts. Instead of sautéing in butter or fat, cut a few slices of bacon or salt pork into small dice and sauté until golden brown in some good fat (goose or pork fat preferred). After draining the sprouts well, add them to the cooked pork dice and mix all together well. Season with salt and pepper and serve sprinkled with finely chopped parsley.

BRUSSELS SPROUTS WITH CHESTNUTS

Follow directions for preparing Brussels sprouts and add some whole cooked chestnuts while the sprouts are sautéing in the butter.

BRUSSELS SPROUTS AU GRATIN

Follow directions for preparing Brussels sprouts. Drain well. Make a ring of Duchess Potato (page 194) on a heatproof serving platter and spread a little Mornay Sauce (page 28) on the dish inside the ring. Fill the center of the ring with the cooked sprouts, cover them with more Mornay Sauce, sprinkle tops of sprouts and potato ring with grated cheese and a little melted butter. Place in a hot oven of 450 degrees or under a broiler and cook until the top is golden brown. If desired the Duchess Potato may be replaced with sliced boiled potatoes arranged in a ring on the platter.

CABBAGE
(Chou)

In all countries, France included, cabbage is considered a food for poor people. It is usually the most plentiful and cheapest of year-round vegetables. But those who like good food never scorn cabbage. It is a vegetable with its own distinctive flavor, which can be cooked in many delicious ways, made into cold hors d'oeuvres and salads, and fermented to make the ever-popular sauerkraut.

There are two schools of thought as to the time for cooking cabbage, but the quick way which is fairly common in this country was never used in France. We always liked cabbage well cooked. The tender green varieties like Savoy cabbage are best for braising and boiling. The hard firm heads with white centers are best for making cole slaw or other salads, and the red kind can be used for both cold and hot dishes.

[166]

BRAISED CABBAGE
(Chou Braisé)

1 or 2 cabbages
½ lb. bacon or salt pork
1 onion, sliced
1 carrot, sliced
2 leeks
2 stalks celery
1 garlic sausage
1 bay leaf

3 sprigs parsley
a little thyme
1 clove garlic
6 peppercorns
bones of roasted veal, poultry or
    game (if available)
water (or white stock)

Cut cabbage in quarters and remove hard core. Parboil 10 minutes. Drain and season with salt and pepper. Parboil bacon (or pork) and drain. Put all ingredients except water in saucepan, lay cabbage on top and add enough water (or stock) to just cover it. Bring to a boil and cook slowly for 1½ to 2 hours. Remove cabbage and serve with bacon and sausage which have been sliced and with the vegetables from the pan. Serves 5 to 6.

STUFFED CABBAGE

1 cabbage, preferably Savoy
¼ lb. pork sausage meat
¼ lb. leftover meat
2 tablespoons fresh bread crumbs
1 cup cooked rice
1 clove garlic, crushed
Stock (or canned tomatoes)

1 onion, finely chopped and cooked
    until soft in butter
½ teaspoon salt
a little pepper
a pinch of Parisian spice (optional)
1 egg, beaten
2-3 slices fat fresh or salt pork

Wash cabbage, remove stem, put in boiling water and parboil 10 minutes. Drain and plunge into cold water. Drain again in a colander with stem end up so that all the water will run out. Prepare stuffing by mixing together all the remaining ingredients except the slices of pork. Place cabbage stem end down in a bowl and carefully cut out the hard center core leaving, however, a base at the bottom to hold in the stuffing. Sprinkle salt and pepper through the leaves. Fill the cavity with the stuffing and also fill in the spaces between the leaves. Wrap the pork fat slices around the cabbage and tie all together securely with a string.

Spread 1 sliced carrot and 1 sliced onion in the bottom of a casserole, place cabbage on top and add stock (or canned tomatoes) to about ⅓ the height of the cabbage. Bring to a boil, cover and cook in a moderate oven of 350 to 375 degrees about 2 hours, basting from time to time.

Remove cabbage to serving dish. Strain liquid into a saucepan, skim off fat and cook until reduced to about 1 cup. Add any leftover-meat gravy that may be on hand. Pour sauce around cabbage. Serves 6 to 8.

STUFFED CABBAGE LEAVES

The following recipe is just another way of preparing stuffed cabbage but you can make as many cabbage rolls or as few as you wish, a decided advantage if you have only a little filling or need to serve only two or three people. When served for the main dish of a meal it is best to allow 2 or even 3 for a person. If any are left over, let them chill in the refrigerator overnight and the next day cut them in thick slices and serve as an hors d'oeuvre either plain or with Vinaigrette Sauce (page 35).

Lay 2 to 3 leaves of cabbage together on the table and spread them flat. Cover with a few spoonfuls of stuffing (follow recipe for stuffing Stuffed Cabbage), roll up the leaves and tie with a string. Place on heatproof serving dish and add boiling stock (or canned tomatoes) to come about halfway up the rolls. Bake in a moderate oven of 350 to 375 degrees 45 minutes to 1 hour. To make sauce, follow directions for Stuffed Cabbage.

RED CABBAGE

Red cabbage is another member of the cabbage family that doesn't seem to appear on American tables as often as I saw it at home. It is good both hot and cold. It was always a popular hors d'oeuvre because it was so inexpensive and at the same time so tasty. I liked the way my mother cooked it with apples, especially when she served it with pork dishes. Pork, red cabbage and apples—three foods that go together perfectly. But if you make this Red Cabbage and apple dish remember that you must use very tart apples. The mild sweet kinds won't give enough flavor and zest to the dish.

RED CABBAGE FOR HORS D'OEUVRES

Clean 1 large head of red cabbage and cut in julienne. Place in a bowl and season with 1 tablespoon salt. Let stand in a cold place for 24 hours stirring it from time to time. Drain well, squeezing out as much water as possible. Return to bowl and add 1 clove garlic, 1 bay leaf, 8 to 10 peppercorns, 2 tablespoons vinegar. Let stand to pickle a few hours before serving.

COOKED RED CABBAGE

1 *large red cabbage*	1 *onion, finely chopped*
1 *teaspoon salt*	1 *tablespoon vinegar*
a little pepper	1 *cup water*
a little nutmeg	2 *green apples, peeled, cored and*
2 *tablespoons butter or fat (goose or*	*sliced*
pork preferred)	

Clean cabbage and cut in julienne. Drain well. Season with salt, pepper and nutmeg. Melt butter (or fat) in saucepan, add onion and cook until it is golden brown. Add vinegar, cabbage and water and cook over medium heat 30 minutes. Add apples and continue cooking 30 to 35 minutes longer, adding more water if it cooks away. Serves 4 to 6.

SAUERKRAUT
(Choucroute)

Sauerkraut was imported from Alsace-Lorraine, but most of it went to the big cities. When we did have sauerkraut, it was always prepared with smoked fat pork or bacon and smoked lean pork, a piece of each. When ready for the table this meat was sliced and was the meat of the meal. During the hunting season we were always pretty sure of having sauerkraut. Any real huntsman from my country would have felt cheated if he did not have sauerkraut to go with his partridge or pheasant.

For those who want to cook something ahead for the sake of convenience or who like to prepare at one time enough for two days' meals, the following recipe is perfect. It is just as good, if not better, when reheated the second day as it is when freshly prepared.

SAUERKRAUT

4 *lbs. sauerkraut*	2 *lbs. smoked bacon*
2-3 *slices fat salt pork (or skin of*	2 *lbs. smoked pork*
larding pork)	1 *tablespoon lard*
2 *onions, each studded with 4 cloves*	2 *glasses white wine (if available)*
10 *peppercorns*	3 *cups white stock (or water)*
6 *juniper berries*	2 *carrots*
½ *teaspoon salt*	

Wash sauerkraut in several changes of water. Drain well, squeezing out as much water as possible. Place salt pork slices (or skin of larding pork) in bottom of a deep saucepan and add onions, carrots, peppercorns and juniper berries. Place bacon, smoked pork and lard on it. Add remaining sauerkraut, wine and stock (or water). Bring to a boil and cook slowly 4 hours. Remove bacon and pork and cut in slices. Serve sauerkraut garnished with sliced bacon and pork. Serves 6 to 8.

CARDOONS
(Cardons)

Cardoons are very common in France, where they are grown in much the same way as celery. They look like celery, too, except that they grow about three times as tall. The heart which is the most delicate part has a delicate flavor somewhat like that of an artichoke bottom.

Separate the stalks of the cardoons, discarding the outside tough ones. Clean, scrape off the strings and cut in 3 to 4 inch pieces but leave the heart whole. Put all together in boiling water to which has been added 1 tablespoon flour mixed until smooth with the juice of ½ lemon (or 3 tablespoons vinegar) for each 2 quarts water. Cook, covered about 2 hours. Drain and serve with Cream (page 25) or Mornay (page 28) or Bordelaise Sauce (page 24). Garnish the top with the heart cut in ½ inch slices or with these slices alternated with pieces of marrow poached for 5 minutes in warm water.

CARROTS
(Carottes)

French carrots, because they are raised in such rich soil, mature very quickly and as a result are unusually tender and succulent. The ones I remember were so delicate that the first crop of little spring carrots —a short and round variety called "jardinière," which looked like a very large radish—could be sautéed without first cooking them in water. Carrots Vichy were prepared from the larger, older carrots but when thinly sliced were always tender enough to need no parboiling. If carrots are home grown in the good soil of a kitchen garden, they should mature quickly and require a very short time for cooking. Most of the carrots that are sold in the markets in this country, however, are less tender and should be parboiled for 10 to 15 minutes before putting into other dishes. In cooking carrots, only a little water and very little salt are required. With too much water and salt they lose their sweetness and delicate flavor.

To Prepare Carrots

Scrape 1 lb. carrots and put in saucepan with water to barely cover. Add ¼ teaspoon salt, 1 tablespoon sugar and 2 tablespoons butter. Bring to a boil, cover pan and cook until the liquid is reduced to a syrup. Continue cooking slowly, shaking them in the pan until the liquid cooks away and the carrots are a little brown and glazed all over. Serves 4 to 5.

CREAMED CARROTS
(Carottes à la Crème)

Follow directions (page 170) for preparing carrots. Add ½ cup Béchamel Sauce (page 24) to which has been added enough top milk or cream to bring it to the desired consistency. Serves 4 to 5.

CARROTS VICHY

2 *cups sliced carrots*	½ *cup water*
1 *tablespoon sugar*	¼ *teaspoon salt*
2 *tablespoons butter*	*chopped parsley*

Mix together all ingredients except parsley in saucepan, cover closely and cook until all the water has cooked away. Let carrots sauté in the butter that remains in the pan until they are golden brown. Sprinkle with parsley. Serves 4 to 5.

CAULIFLOWER
(Choufleur)

Cauliflowers were plentiful in France and from late summer when the first were picked until well into the winter when we had used up the last of those that had been put away, cauliflower was one of the very popular vegetables. Probably one reason was that it seemed to us a hearty vegetable. Served à la Crème or Au Gratin, a large firm head gave big generous servings to our family of five, and with one of my mother's good omelets would be the main course of a meal. Two dishes, in fact, often constituted a meal because, although the French housewife will spend much time and thought on what she does cook, she seldom prepares many dishes at a time, preferring to serve larger portions of the one or two she does make.

In choosing cauliflower, be sure the head is very white, very firm and has small compact flowers that are squeezed tightly together. A yellow cauliflower is strong tasting and one in which the flowers are loosely separated from each other is usually too mature to taste any-

[171]

thing but strong. Of course sometimes you are unable to find a head that is as white as desired and in this case the best way to serve it is with Polonaise Sauce because the browned butter and crumbs offset to an extent the fact that the vegetable is not young and white. A large cauliflower will serve 4 to 5 persons generously.

To Prepare Cauliflower

Remove green leaves and stem and separate the flowers. Wash in cold water that contains either a little salt or a little vinegar so that any hidden insects will be forced out. Put into boiling, salted water using 1 teaspoon salt to 1 quart water and cook 20 to 25 minutes. To tell when it is done, pierce with a fork; it should be soft but should not be cooked until it is mushy. Drain well and arrange the flowers in their original shape in the serving dish. Serve with melted butter, Cream Sauce (page 25), Polonaise Sauce (page 33), Sauce Blanche (page 36) or Hollandaise Sauce (page 26).

CAULIFLOWER AU GRATIN

Follow directions for preparing cauliflower (above). Drain very thoroughly. Prepare 2 cups Mornay Sauce (page 28) and spread a little on the bottom of a heatproof dish. Arrange cauliflower in its original shape on this and cover with remaining Mornay Sauce. Sprinkle with grated cheese, a few fine bread crumbs and a little melted butter. Cook in a hot oven of 450 degrees or under broiler until brown. Serves 4 to 5.

CREAMED CAULIFLOWER

Follow directions for preparing cauliflower (above). Drain very thoroughly. Combine Cream Sauce (page 25) and cauliflower and simmer all together about 5 to 6 minutes. Serves 4 to 5.

SAUTEED CAULIFLOWER

Follow directions for preparing cauliflower (above). Drain very thoroughly. Heat 2 tablespoons butter until hazelnut brown, add cauliflower and sauté on all sides until brown, taking care not to crush or mash the flowers in turning them. Serve sprinkled with chopped parsley. Serves 4 to 5.

CELERY
(Céleri)

Many people who have served celery for eating raw or have used it raw in salads have never cooked it. Thus in many homes the outside stalks that are too coarse to be eaten raw are wasted. With a relatively expensive vegetable like celery, wasting any part of it is doubly extravagant. The tough outside stalks are full of flavor and are perfect for faggots, or can be diced for soups or added to the vegetable base that is to be puréed for cream soups. Like onions, celery enhances every dish to which it is added, whether it is used raw in salads or cooked in soups or stews.

Knob or root celery—the French call it *céleri-rave*—has a stronger flavor and quite a different texture from the stalk celery that grows above ground. It darkens, however, as soon as it is peeled and if it is to be used in salads or hors d'oeuvres must be boiled a few minutes to keep it white. This also makes its flavor more delicate. It is cooked until tender when it is to be served as a vegetable.

BRAISED CELERY

Cut through the celery, making 2 pieces, and clean well. Parboil 5 to 6 minutes and remove to cold water to take out all the sand. Drain, place in saucepan in which has been placed a few slices of onion and carrot. Add just enough stock (or water) to cover the celery, a little piece of beef suet and a little salt. Bring to a boil, cover, place in a moderately hot oven of 375 to 400 degrees and cook until celery is tender, about 1 to 1½ hours. Remove celery to serving dish and serve with veal or chicken gravy or with a sauce made by cooking the strained cooking liquid (from which the fat has been removed) until reduced to about ½ cup and then thickening it with Manié Butter, made by creaming together 1 tablespoon butter and ½ teaspoon flour. Serve 1 or 2 pieces for each person.

KNOB CELERY COUNTRY STYLE
(Céleri-rave Fermière)

2 tablespoons lard
1 onion, chopped
¼ cup diced fat salt pork, parboiled
   and drained
2 leeks, white part, minced
1 tablespoon flour

1 cup stock (or water)
3 stalks celery, diced
1 faggot (page 294)
1 lb. knob celery, peeled and cut in
   large dice
chopped parsley

Melt lard in saucepan, add onion and pork dice and cook over hot fire until they are golden brown. Add leeks and flour, mix together and cook a few minutes. Add stock (or water), celery, faggot and knob celery. Bring to a boil, cover and cook slowly 50 minutes to 1 hour or

[173]

until knob celery is done. Discard faggot. Serve sprinkled with chopped parsley. Serves 4 to 6.

CREAMED CELERY

Use outside stalks of celery and cut in 2 inch lengths, clean well and cook as for Braised Celery (page 173). Make a white roux by melting 1 tablespoon butter, adding 1 tablespoon flour and cooking together until well mixed but not brown. Strain the cooking liquid from the celery, remove the fat and cook until reduced to about 1 cup. Combine liquid and roux and cook, stirring until smooth and thickened. Add ¼ cup top milk (or cream), bring back to a boil and pour over the celery.

PUREE OF CELERY
(Céleri-rave)

1 *lb. knob celery, peeled and cut in*   1 *teaspoon salt*
   pieces   2 *tablespoons butter*
2-3 *stalks celery*   *milk or top milk*
2 *medium potatoes, cut in pieces*

Put celery knob and stalk celery in saucepan, cover with water, add salt and boil 15 minutes. Add potatoes and celery stalks and cook 30 minutes longer or until well done. Drain well, then rub through a sieve. Return to saucepan and cook, mixing with a wooden spoon until it is dried out a little. Add butter and enough milk or top milk to make it like mashed potatoes. Correct the seasoning. Serves 4 to 5.

CHESTNUTS

There are several varieties of chestnuts, of which the best known and the most generally used are the marrons and the châtaignes. The marrons are the very large chestnuts which grow in the southern part of France, particularly in the *Departement du Var,* and in Italy. These are the ones that are made into the delectable and famous *marrons glacées.* Châtaignes grow farther north in the central part of France and are used for general cooking. It is also from the châtaignes that chestnut flour is made, which is packaged and exported to all parts of the world where chestnuts are unobtainable for gourmets who crave a good chestnut purée.

To Cook Chestnuts

Cut a small incision through the shell of each chestnut, using a very sharp knife. Put them in a very hot oven or under the broiler for 5 to 6 minutes. Remove from the heat and take off the shells. If they are well roasted (or broiled) the skins underneath the shells should come off along with the shells. Put the shelled nuts in a saucepan with enough water (or white stock) to cover them and add 2 to 3 stalks of celery. Bring to a boil and cook slowly 20 to 25 minutes. Leave chestnuts in the stock to cool removing them when ready to use.

CHESTNUTS FOR GARNISHING

Follow directions for cooking chestnuts (above), selecting the whole chestnuts for garnishing.

CHESTNUT PUREE

Chestnut purée may be made from chestnut flour or from cooked chestnuts. When using chestnut flour bring about 2 cups of milk to the boiling point for each cup of chestnut flour. Gradually stir the chestnut flour into the milk stirring briskly all the time and cooking it only until the mixture is completely combined. The mixture should be about the same consistency as mashed potatoes. If not as thick as mashed potatoes, add a little more chestnut flour. Finish by adding a tablespoon (or more if desired) of butter.

To make Chestnut Purée from cooked chestnuts, rub them through a sieve and reheat with a little butter or top milk.

CHICKORY
(Chicorée)

We ate a lot of chickory in France, it was plentiful and well liked. Only the white center part was used for salad; the outside green leaves were cooked and served hot. As a matter of fact, all salad plants were handled this way so that the recipes given for cooked chickory can also be used for lettuce, romaine and escarole.

CHICKORY WITH GRAVY

3-4 *bunches chickory*	1 *teaspoon sugar*
2 *tablespoons butter*	*a little grated nutmeg*
1 *tablespoon flour*	*½ cup stock*
½ teaspoon salt	*meat gravy*
a little pepper	

Remove center white parts from chickory and use for salad. Clean outside green leaves, put into boiling salted water and parboil 10 to 12 minutes. Drain and plunge into cold water. Drain again, pressing out all the water, chop very fine and drain again on a towel to remove

[175]

all remaining moisture. Melt butter in saucepan, add flour, mix well and cook until it starts to turn golden. Add chickory, seasonings and stock, mix well and bring to a boil. Place a piece of buttered paper over top of chickory, cover pan and cook slowly on top of stove or in a moderate oven of 350 degrees 45 minutes to 1 hour. Add 1 tablespoon butter, correct the seasoning and serve with some meat gravy on top.

CREAMED CHICKORY

Follow recipe for Chickory with Gravy, substituting milk for the stock. Just before serving add 2 tablespoons cream or top milk.

CUCUMBERS
(Concombres)

We usually think of cucumbers in the raw state, sliced or chopped and marinated in Sauce Vinaigre or added to a salad. Very few people seem to think of cooking them. But those who grow cucumbers in their own gardens are apt to suddenly come upon a time when every vine in the garden is putting forth too many ripe cucumbers. Then is the time to serve them hot as a vegetable. They are unusually tasty and add something new and different to the vegetable repertory.

In preparing cucumbers, it is best to remove the center seedy part particularly if the seeds are large and tough. For eating raw, cucumbers should be sprinkled with salt and allowed to stand a couple of hours after which all the salt and moisture should be squeezed out.

CREAMED CUCUMBERS

Peel 3 cucumbers and cut in two lengthwise. Remove seeds and cut in pieces about an inch long, about 8 to 10 pieces to a cucumber. Put in boiling salted water and parboil 5 to 8 minutes. Drain well. Return to pan and add ½ cup milk and continue cooking 8 to 10 minutes. Thicken with Manié Butter, made by creaming together 1 tablespoon butter with ½ teaspoon flour, adding it to the milk and cooking until it is thickened. Correct the seasoning and add a little sugar. Serves 3 to 4.

SAUTEED CUCUMBERS

Peel large cucumbers and cut in two lengthwise. Remove seeds and cut in pieces about an inch long, about 8 to 10 pieces to a cucumber. Put in boiling salted water and parboil 10 to 15 minutes. Drain well. Melt a little butter in a frying pan and when hot add cucumbers and cook slowly, sprinkling them with a little salt and sugar, until they take on a brown color.

STUFFED CUCUMBERS

Peel a large cucumber and slice it in pieces about 2 inches long. Put in boiling salted water and parboil 8 to 10 minutes. Drain well. Remove seeds leaving a thick ring of cucumber. Set the pieces, cut side down on a heatproof platter and stuff them with Mushroom Duxelles (page 185), or with finely chopped leftover cooked meat seasoned and mixed with chopped onion and parsley, or with cooked rice that has been mixed with Duxelles or with the chopped meat mixture or with seasoned leftover cooked fish.

Sprinkle tops with fine bread crumbs and a little melted butter. Pour a little stock (about ½ inch) in pan around cucumbers and put in a hot oven of 450 degrees or under the broiler and cook until tops are brown. If preferred, the cucumbers can be cut in half lengthwise, seeds removed and after parboiling them, the centers can be filled with one of the above mixtures. Serves 2.

EGGPLANT
(Aubergine)

Eggplant grown in France are very much smaller than the ones in this country, and are different in shape, too, growing about the size and shape of a cucumber. This makes them easier to stuff because the shell, which becomes soft when baked, is more apt to hold its shape.

The simplest and easiest ways to cook eggplant are to sauté them or fry them in deep fat. But when prepared with tomatoes and garlic they are particularly tasty because these are flavors that go well with eggplant.

SAUTEED EGGPLANT

Peel eggplant and cut in ¼ to ½ inch slices. Season with salt, dip in milk and then in flour. Sauté in hot oil until golden brown, about 2 to 3 minutes on each side.

EGGPLANT MENAGERE

This was one of the very common and popular ways of preparing eggplant in my mother's home. She prepared it in a rather shallow earthenware casserole, and brought the cooking dish to the table for serving. The water from the tomato provides enough liquid to cook the eggplant, but as the moisture cooks away it becomes about as thick as a purée and makes a sauce for the diced eggplant. Take care not to cook the eggplant dice so long that they become mushy and lose their shape.

1 *medium eggplant*
flour
3 *tablespoons salad oil*
1 *medium onion, chopped*
2 *cloves garlic, crushed*

3 *tomatoes, peeled, seeded and*
   chopped (or ½ cup canned)
1 *faggot* (page 294)
½ *teaspoon salt*
a little pepper
1 *tablespoon chopped parsley*

Peel eggplant, cut in large dice and sprinkle with flour. Heat oil very hot and sauté eggplant quickly in it. Add onion to pan, garlic, tomatoes, faggot, salt and pepper. Cook slowly until tomatoes are cooked down to a sauce-like consistency, about 20 to 25 minutes. Discard faggot and serve sprinkled with chopped parsley.

FRIED EGGPLANT

Peel eggplant and cut in ¼ to ½ inch slices. Coat à l'Anglaise (page 293) and fry in deep, hot fat or oil until golden brown, about 3 to 4 minutes. Drain well and season with a little salt.

EGGPLANT AU GRATIN

Cut eggplant lengthwise, in half or quarters, depending upon the size. Score the inside with cuts about ½ inch deep. Fry in deep hot fat 5 to 7 minutes. Drain well. Scrape the inside away from the skins and arrange skins on a heatproof oven platter. Chop inside part fine and mix with one-half as much mushroom Duxelles (page 185). Season with salt and pepper and fill skins with this mixture. Sprinkle tops with fine bread crumbs and a little melted butter. Brown in a hot oven or under broiler. Serve plain or with meat gravy. Serves 4.

EGGPLANT A L'ALGERIENNE

8 *mushrooms*
1 *tablespoon butter*
1 *shallot, chopped*
1 *teaspoon flour*
½ *cup cream* (*or top milk*)
12 *slices eggplant,* ½ *inch thick*

salt
pepper
8 *slices tomato,* ¼ *inch thick*
¾ *cup Rice Pilau* (page 216)
   or Risotto (page 216)

Clean and peel mushrooms, drain and sauté in butter a few minutes. Add shallot and flour, mix well, then add cream (or top milk) and

[178]

blend. Cook, stirring, until thickened and continue cooking, stirring occasionally, until the sauce is reduced to about one half the original quantity. Season sliced eggplant with salt and pepper, dip in milk and then in flour and fry in deep, hot fat or oil until golden brown, or sauté them in oil. Dip sliced tomatoes in flour and sauté in hot oil. Spread rice mixture over bottom of hot serving dish, place eggplant and tomato on rice, alternating and overlapping the two vegetables. Pour creamed mushrooms over all. Serves 4.

EGGPLANT WITH TOMATOES

3-4 *tomatoes*
1 *tablespoon butter* (*or oil*)
½ *onion, chopped*
1 *clove garlic, crushed*
1 *teaspoon flour*
12 *slices eggplant,* ½ *inch thick*

flour
salt
pepper
deep fat or oil for frying
chopped parsley

Prepare Tomato Sauce as follows: peel and seed tomatoes and chop coarsely. Melt butter, add onion and cook until golden brown. Add garlic, sprinkle in the flour and mix all together. Add tomatoes and cook until mixture is reduced to sauce-like thickness. Peel and slice eggplant, season with salt and pepper and dip in milk, then in flour.

Cook in deep hot fat or oil until golden brown, about 4 to 5 minutes, or sauté in oil. Drain well. Place in a heatproof serving dish, overlapping the slices and pour the sauce over. Heat over a very low fire about 5 minutes. Sprinkle with chopped parsley. Serves 4.

EGGPLANT PROVENCALE

1 *medium eggplant*
½ *teaspoon salt*
a little pepper
flour
4 *tablespoons salad oil*

4 *tomatoes, peeled, seeded and cut*
in quarters
2 *cloves garlic, crushed*
1 *teaspoon chopped parsley*

Peel eggplant and cut in large dice. Season with salt and sprinkle with flour. Heat 2 tablespoons oil very hot and sauté eggplant dice until golden brown. Heat remaining oil very hot in another pan and sauté tomatoes in it. Combine the two vegetables, add garlic, and continue cooking a few minutes longer. Serve sprinkled with chopped parsley. Serves 4.

ENDIVE

Endive is a winter-salad plant more common in the northern sections of France and Belgium than in the central or southern parts. Although in this country it is almost always served raw in salad, in France it is just as often cooked and is very popular when prepared that way.

To Cook Endive

Wash 1 to 1½ lbs. endive in cold water, drain well. Arrange in saucepan so that all are lying in the same direction and none on top of the others. Add ½ teaspoon salt, 1 tablespoon sugar, juice of ½ lemon, 2 tablespoons butter and ½ cup water. Bring to a boil, cover endive with a piece of buttered paper, then cover pan. Cook in a moderate oven of 350 degrees or very slowly on top of stove 40 to 45 minutes. Remove endive to serving dish. Cook liquid remaining in pan until reduced to about ¼ cup. Add 1 tablespoon butter and pour over endive. Serves 6.

ENDIVE FLAMANDE

8 *stalks endive*	*a little sugar*
2 *tablespoons butter*	*juice 1 lemon*
a little salt	*¼ cup water*

Wash endive well and drain. Put butter in a pan large enough so that endive can be arranged side by side with none on top of the others, then arrange endive so that all are lying in the same direction. Add salt, sugar, lemon juice and water. Cover endive with buttered paper, cover pan and cook in a moderate oven of 350 degrees 40 minutes or until the moisture is cooked away and endive has started to take on a golden brown color. Serve with the butter from the pan poured over it. A little good meat gravy added to the butter improves the dish. Serves 3 to 4.

CREAMED ENDIVE
(Endive à la Crème)

Follow recipe for Endive Flamande. Remove from oven and add 1 cup Cream Sauce (page 25). Cook slowly on top of stove 10 to 15 minutes, remove endive to serving dish, correct seasoning of sauce and pour over endive. Serves 3 to 4.

FENNEL
(Fenouil)

Fennel is very much like celery and is usually served raw for hors d'oeuvre. But it can also be braised following directions for Braised

Celery (page 173). Some people use it in soup and it is particularly well liked in Bortsch.

ENDIVE AU GRATIN

Follow recipe for Endive Flamande. Before serving sprinkle top with grated cheese and brown under broiler.

LEEKS
(Poireaux)

In France leeks are called "the asparagus of the poor." They are very plentiful and very good. In this country, they are used primarily for soup, and are indispensable for such soups as the pot-au-feu. Although the leek is one of the onion family and the flavor is very similar, the flavor of the leek is much more delicate and blends in more perfectly with other soup flavors. When making the purée for any cream soup it is always desirable to include a leek in cooking the vegetable.

But leeks can also be cooked as a vegetable and are especially delicious when cooked and served cold with a well-seasoned Vinaigrette Sauce and eaten as an Hors D'oeuvre (page 7). I remember seeing them often on the hors d'oeuvre plate with cooked celery and marinated fish.

When using leeks they must be very well cleaned because as they grow the soil works its way in between the leaves. The best method is to cut each one in half lengthwise, opening up the interstices so all the dirt and sand can be thoroughly washed out. Although leeks can be cooked in boiling salted water like any other vegetable it is usual to cook them in soup (in France it would be in the pot-au-feu), remove them when done and serve hot or cold as desired.

To Cook Leeks

Follow directions for cooking leeks as for Hors D'oeuvres (page 7).

LETTUCE
(Laitue)

BRAISED LETTUCE

Clean and wash well, leaving heads whole. Do not remove outside green leaves except those that are bruised or damaged. Put in boiling salted water to cover, using 1 teaspoon salt to a quart of water. Parboil 10 minutes. Plunge into a large quantity of cold water, then drain well, squeezing out as much of the water as possible. Put some sliced fat pork (or skin of larding pork), a few slices of onion and carrot and

[181]

a faggot (page 294) in bottom of a saucepan. Put lettuce on this, add enough stock (or water) just to cover lettuce and put a piece of beef suet on top. Bring to a boil and cover with a piece of buttered paper and place cover on pan. Put in a moderate oven of 350 to 375 degrees for 45 minutes to 1 hour or until the center core is soft. Remove lettuce from pan and place in serving dish. Skim all fat from the cooking liquid, strain liquid and cook until reduced to a third the original quantity. Add a few spoonfuls of meat gravy or brown sauce (if available), correct seasoning and pour over lettuce.

BRAISED LETTUCE WITH CREAM SAUCE

Follow recipe for Braised Lettuce (page 181) and cut heads in half after removing from cooking liquid. Then pour over them a light Béchamel or Cream Sauce (pages 24 and 25).

CREAMED LETTUCE

Separate and wash green leaves of lettuce. Put in boiling salted water and cook about 40 to 45 minutes. Drain well and chop fine. For 2 cups cooked lettuce put 2 tablespoons butter in saucepan, add 1 tablespoon flour and cook until it starts to turn golden. Add lettuce, mix all together thoroughly and add ½ cup top milk. Cook, stirring all together until mixture starts to boil. Correct seasoning and serve. Serves 3 to 4.

STUFFED LETTUCE

This is a good way to use the outside green leaves of the lettuce when only the center delicate white ones are to be used in a salad. If the head is small to medium in size allow one stuffed head for two servings.

Remove center part of head of lettuce leaving enough outside green leaves and thick base to hold in the stuffing. Parboil a few minutes in boiling salted water and drain well inverting it in a colander to remove as much water as possible. Stuff, tie and cook following directions for Stuffed Cabbage (page 167), allowing 45 minutes to 1 hour for cooking.

MUSHROOMS

Mushrooms are very important in French cooking. Of course, at home they were only plentiful in their season because those that were raised commercially and sold out of season were pretty expensive. We did, however, use many canned mushrooms which are very common in France.

Mushrooms appeal to French tastes because of their unusual flavor and because they are so versatile and go with so many foods. We like ingredients which turn ordinary foods into something extra special. Mushrooms we know go equally well with robust foods like beef stew or with delicate mixtures like sweetbread and mushroom patties, with full-flavored brown and tomato sauces or with a subtly flavored white wine sauce on a fine piece of fish.

There are several kinds of mushrooms beside the usual wild and cultivated ones. The *cèpes,* for example, are a type of wild mushroom that grow in the woods, preferring the soil under oak trees. They have their own special flavor, are very soft and tender and are the joy of gourmets. They are so craved by lovers of good eating that they are canned in France and sold all over the world. The *girolles* and *mousserons* were two other varieties fairly common in some sections and very well liked. And in the section near Alsace-Lorraine are found *morilles,* famous for the savour they give to fish dishes. But a word of advice if morilles ever cross your path—they are always full of sand and must be carefully washed in many waters in order to get it all out. In preparing morilles use the same recipes used in preparing mushrooms.

People disagree as to whether or not mushrooms should be peeled. I think it depends upon the mushrooms. Wild ones often have such fine, tender skins that peeling is obviously entirely unnecessary but I have seen wild ones with tough skins that should be removed. Some of the cultivated ones brought in the market have tender skins that need not be removed especially when they are to be broiled or stuffed. On the other hand mushrooms do appear on the market with thick, tough skins and then I prefer to peel them. The skins, however, are full of flavor and should be used. Cook them in a little water which when strained gives a mushroom stock that may be added to mushroom soup and to many kinds of sauces.

BROILED MUSHROOMS

Remove stems from large mushrooms, wash them and dry well. Sprinkle with salt and pepper and brush with salad oil. Put on a hot broiler about 4 inches from the heat and broil 8 to 10 minutes. Serve on buttered toast or as a garnish for broiled meat.

CREAMED MUSHROOMS

Remove the stems, peel (if necessary) and wash ½ lb. of mushrooms.

[183]

Season with salt and pepper. Melt 2 tablespoons butter in a saucepan and sauté mushrooms in it until golden brown. Add 1 teaspoon flour, mixing it in well. Add ½ cup cream or top milk, cover and cook slowly 10 minutes. Remove mushrooms and reserve. Cook sauce until thick and smooth, correct seasoning and add 2 to 3 drops lemon juice. Place mushrooms on toast and pour sauce over. Serves 3.

CROUTES WITH MUSHROOMS MENAGERE

6 *thick slices of bread*
3 *tablespoons butter*
2 *tablespoons flour*
1½ *cups white stock*
1 *faggot* (page 294)
¼ *teaspoon salt*

a little pepper
a little nutmeg
1 *lb. mushrooms*
½ *lemon (juice)*
1 *egg yolk*
2 *tablespoons cream (or top milk)*

Make a hollow in each slice of bread by cutting out a little of the center part with a sharp knife. Brush all over with butter and bake in a hot oven until golden brown. Melt butter in saucepan, add flour and cook gently until golden brown. Add stock and mix well. Add faggot, salt, pepper and nutmeg and cook, stirring constantly until sauce is thickened. Continue cooking slowly about 20 minutes. Clean mushrooms, peel and add peelings to sauce as it cooks. Cook mushrooms in ½ cup salted water with the lemon juice for 5 to 6 minutes. Mix egg yolk with cream, combine with sauce and bring back to boiling point but do not allow to boil after the yolk has been added. If sauce is too thick add some liquor from the cooked mushrooms. Correct the seasoning. Drain mushrooms, divide in six parts and place on the toasted bread slices, strain the sauce and pour over the mushrooms. Serves 6.

MUSHROOMS SAUTE PROVENCALE

Follow recipe for Sautéed Mushrooms (page 185). Remove mushrooms from pan and reserve. Add to the butter 1 chopped shallot, 1 clove crushed garlic and ½ teaspoon finely chopped parsley. Cook, shaking the pan, about 2 minutes but do not let them brown. Return mushrooms to pan and reheat them mixing all together. Serves 3.

DUXELLES OF MUSHROOMS

Duxelles of Mushrooms are used to combine with other ingredients, such as rice, vegetables, bread crumbs for stuffing fowl, fish or vegetables. Making Duxelles is a good way of using up the stems of mushrooms that have been served broiled or stuffed. The Duxelle mixture can be put in a jar and kept in the refrigerator for several days. It adds such a fine flavor to any mixture that an ordinary dish is changed into something really distinguished in flavor.

DUXELLES OF MUSHROOMS

½ *lb. mushrooms*
2 *tablespoons butter (or salad oil)*
½ *teaspoon salt*

1 *shallot, chopped (or ½ onion)*
1 *teaspoon chopped parsley*

Clean mushrooms and dry them thoroughly. Chop very fine. Heat butter (or oil), add shallot (or onion) and mushrooms. Cook until all the moisture is cooked away and add salt and parsley. If desired 2 tablespoons tomato purée may be added just before they are done.

MUSHROOM SOUFFLE

Follow recipe for Purée of Mushrooms (below), using ½ cup mushrooms and ½ cup Béchamel Sauce. Cook until the mixture is quite thick. Add 4 beaten egg yolks and cook stirring briskly all the time but removing from the fire as soon as it reaches boiling point. Fold in 4 stiffly beaten egg whites. Pour into soufflé mold (or deep casserole) that has been buttered and floured and bake in a hot oven of 450 degrees about 15 to 20 minutes. Serves 4 to 6.

PUREE OF MUSHROOMS

Wash mushrooms and chop very fine. (If mushroom stems left from broiled or stuffed mushrooms are on hand, they can be added and chopped.) Squeeze out all surplus moisture. For 1 cup finely chopped mushrooms put 2 tablespoons butter in saucepan, heat it until it just starts to turn brown, add mushrooms and cook until moisture is cooked away. Add 1 cup thick Béchamel Sauce (page 24), mix all together and correct the seasoning. Serve with meat or poultry.

SAUTEED MUSHROOMS

Remove stems, peel (if necessary) and wash ½ pound mushrooms. Season them with salt and pepper. Melt 2 tablespoons butter in a saucepan and sauté mushrooms in it until golden brown on both sides. Serve with butter from pan and sprinkle with finely chopped parsley.

STUFFED MUSHROOMS

Remove stems from large mushrooms and wash. Sprinkle with salt and pepper, brush with salad oil, place on hot broiler and cook 8 to

[185]

10 minutes. Remove from heat, stuff with Mushroom Duxelle (page 185), spread tops with fine bread crumbs and sprinkle with butter. Arrange on a heatproof platter and cook in a hot oven of 450 degrees about 8 to 10 minutes or until crumbs are brown. Serve with the gravy of the meat which the mushrooms will accompany.

CEPES A LA BORDELAISE

Leave small cèpes whole and cut large ones in pieces. Sauté in very hot salad oil until they are golden brown. Turn out of pan and drain. Put some butter in pan and when it is hot return drained cèpes to it. Season with salt and pepper and add some chopped shallots, a little crushed garlic, some chopped parsley and a few fine, fresh bread crumbs. Cook all together a few minutes until crumbs are golden, shaking the pan all the time to combine all the ingredients.

MUSHROOMS FOR GARNISHING

Remove stems, peel and wash mushrooms. For 1 pound mushrooms use ½ cup water to which has been added 1 tablespoon butter and the juice of 1 lemon. Boil mushrooms actively in this liquid 3 to 5 minutes. Let cool in the liquid. The cooking liquid should be saved and used as part of the liquid in sauces.

MORILLES

Wash well and cook, following directions for cooking mushrooms for garnishing (above), but continue cooking until the liquid is almost all cooked away, then add 1 tablespoon butter and sauté the morilles in it. Correct seasoning and serve sprinkled with parsley.

ONIONS
(Oignons)

Of all the vegetables that we use in cooking, onions, to me, are about the most important. French cooks in general consider them indispensable. They are of course good in themselves when served as a vegetable, but their greatest value lies in the contribution they make to all the hundreds of dishes in which they are cooked or to which a small bit of onion produces a flavor nothing else can equal. As a flavoring ingredient onions are generally combined with carrots because their flavors seem to complement each other, but celery, parsley and all the many herbs used in cooking also go well with the flavor of onions.

There are many varieties of onions and they come in all sizes. Some countries like Bermuda, for example, make a specialty of growing one type that is world famous. In France we grew both large and small onions, using the large ones for stuffed onions, for frying and Purée Soubise. But to eat with meat and poultry or as one of the vegetables in a casserole or stew we always selected the very tiny ones. These little, young onions—no larger than walnuts—are very plentiful and very popular, are very white and very delicate in flavor. In the spring the first tiny onions were as delicate a vegetable as you can imagine, always cooked with fresh green peas and always served with the tender spring lamb.

FRIED ONIONS

Cut large onions in ¼ inch slices and separate the rings formed. Dip in milk, then in flour and fry in deep hot fat or oil until golden brown. Drain well and season with salt.

GLAZED ONIONS FOR GARNISHING

Peel 1 cup small onions and put in a saucepan with just enough water to cover. Add ½ teaspoon salt, 1 teaspoon sugar and 1 tablespoon butter. Cook over a moderate fire until the water is cooked away, then continue cooking in the butter that remains in the pan until they become golden, shaking the pan gently so they will brown all over.

STUFFED ONIONS
(Oignons Farcis)

Parboil large onions about 10 minutes. Drain well, remove centers leaving about a half inch of shell all around and being careful not to cut through the bottom so there will be a base intact which will hold in the stuffing. Chop center part that was removed and mix with chopped leftover meat, or cooked rice or Duxelles of Mushrooms (page 185) or a mixture of all or any two of them. Season with salt and pepper. Fill onions with this mixture, sprinkle tops with fine bread crumbs and a little melted butter and arrange on a heatproof serving dish. Add stock (or strained canned tomatoes) to the dish so that it comes about halfway up the onions. Cook in a hot oven of 450 degrees about 20 to 25 minutes or until the tops are browned. Serve 1 onion to each person.

PUREE OF ONIONS
(Purée Soubise)

Purée of Onions is a typically French recipe, one of those combinations with dozens of uses. It should be better known and more generally used in this country because it is so very inexpensive and easy to make and yet, at the same time, has a flavor and texture which puts it in the fine cookery class. In many French restaurants you will find "Soubise" in the names of dishes on the menus and it means that this particular mixture of onions and rice is combined in some way with the meat or other ingredients.

Purée Soubise is always very popular with lamb and veal. For example, slices of leftover lamb or veal can be spread with the mixture arranged in overlapping slices, sprinkled with bread crumbs and then baked in the oven 20 to 30 minutes. At home my mother often served Purée Soubise as a vegetable in winter when fresh green vegetables were unobtainable and she had to use her ingenuity to make as tasty and unusual as she could the few kinds that lasted all winter.

4 *large onions, minced*	½ *cup boiling water*
2 *tablespoons butter*	½ *teaspoon salt*
4 *tablespoons uncooked rice*	½ *cup Béchamel Sauce* (*very thick*)

Melt butter in saucepan, add onions and cook until they are soft. Add rice, water and salt. Cover closely and cook over low heat about 35 to 40 minutes or until the water is entirely cooked away. Rub through a fine sieve, return to fire and cook out any surplus moisture, stirring briskly all the time to avoid scorching. Add very thick Béchamel Sauce and continue cooking and stirring until smooth and well combined. Serves 4 to 5.

OYSTERPLANT
(Salsifis)

Oysterplant is a late fall vegetable which did not appear in our markets until the summer vegetables were no longer available. Then they lasted for quite some time, like turnips and parsnips. We liked them especially well when they were served cold for hors d'oeuvre or in salad. But we also ate them hot, usually creamed or fried (after first boiling them) in much the same way that we prepared parsnips. The most popular oysterplant dish that I remember was oysterplant fritters.

In preparing oysterplant, it is important to know that after they are peeled and the inside is exposed to the air they darken quicker than almost any other food. Therefore, it is necessary to plunge them the minute the skin is scraped off into water to which a little vinegar or lemon juice has been added.

To Cook Oysterplant

Cut off the tops of oysterplant, scrape them and plunge into water to which vinegar has been added, using 2 tablespoons vinegar to each quart water. Cut the larger ones in half so that all pieces are about 3 to 4 inches long. Mix 1 tablespoon flour with a little water, add 1 quart water, 1 teaspoon salt and 1 tablespoon vinegar. Bring to a boil, add oysterplant, cover pan and cook 1 to 1½ hours or until tender. Drain. Finish preparation as desired—creamed, sautéed, with meat gravy and so on.

CREAMED OYSTERPLANT

After draining cooked oysterplant combine with Cream Sauce (page 25) and cook all together slowly about 5 minutes.

SAUTEED OYSTERPLANT

After draining cooked oysterplant sauté in butter until golden brown. Serve sprinkled with finely chopped parsley.

OYSTERPLANT AU JUS

After draining cooked oysterplant combine with meat gravy, preferably chicken or veal, and cook slowly about 5 minutes.

OYSTERPLANT FRITTERS

Drain cooked oysterplant, making sure that they are thoroughly dry. Roll each piece in finely chopped parsley and sprinkle with a mixture of lemon juice and salad oil, using twice as much oil as lemon juice. Let stand 15 to 20 minutes. Remove one by one from the oil and lemon-juice mixture and dip in fritter batter (below), covering each piece completely with it. Fry in deep hot fat until golden brown. Drain well, season with salt and serve.

FRITTER BATTER

3 *tablespoons flour*	5 *tablespoons lukewarm water*
a little salt	1 *egg white, beaten stiff*
1 *teaspoon salad oil*	

Combine all ingredients except egg white and mix until batter is smooth. Fold in egg white.

FRIED PARSLEY
(Persil Frit)

Wash parsley thoroughly and dry well. Drop in very hot deep fat and cook a few minutes or until parsley comes to the surface of the fat and has become crisp. Drain well and sprinkle with a little salt.

PARSNIPS
(Panais)

Most of the parsnips we ate were those that were cooked in the pot-au-feu. But when they were very plentiful we did have them creamed and fried and also made into parsnip cakes.

It is difficult to specify an exact length of time for cooking parsnips. When young and fresh they will be tender in 30 minutes but when they are older or have been stored for some time it may take 45 minutes.

CREAMED PARSNIPS

Clean and peel parsnips and cut in small stick-like pieces. Cook until tender in boiling salted water to cover. Drain. For 2 cups parsnips, melt 1 tablespoon butter in a saucepan, add 1 teaspoon flour and cook until it starts to turn golden. Add ¾ cup top milk and cook, stirring until it thickens. Continue cooking slowly about 10 minutes, stirring occasionally. Correct the seasoning, add parsnips and cook a few minutes longer. For a richer sauce add 2 tablespoons cream. Serves 4 to 5.

FRIED PARSNIPS

Follow directions for cooking parsnips for Creamed Parsnips (above). Drain. Dip in Fritter Batter (page 189), covering each piece completely with it. Fry in deep hot fat or oil until golden brown. Drain well, season with salt and serve.

PARSNIP CAKES

Clean and peel parsnips and boil in salted water to cover until soft. Drain and mash. Put in a saucepan and place over the heat to dry them, shaking the pan all the time to prevent scorching. For 2 cups mashed parsnips, add 2 tablespoons butter, 2 tablespoons cream, 1 teaspoon salt and 2 egg yolks. Mix all together thoroughly and spread on a plate to cool. Form into small square or round croquettes, coat à l'Anglaise (page 293), and fry in deep hot fat or oil or sauté on both sides in butter until golden brown. Serves 4 to 5.

PEAS

Peas are served with almost every meat and fish in France. They are so delicate and sweet that we feel they enhance any dish with which they are combined. But we preferred and generally used the small, young tender ones, and did not particularly like the large varieties or those that were large because they had been left on the vines until well developed, which we used for making purée or soups like Potage St. Germain. The tiny, young peas are the ones that are canned in France and sold all over the world under the name of *"petits pois."*

We seldom ate plain buttered peas—to us that was the English method of preparing them. Our French way was to cook them with such vegetables as the young, delicate spring onions or tiny sweet carrots that were just maturing when the peas were also at their best. We always included a few leaves of finely shredded lettuce also; it practically disappears in the cooking but provides flavor and moisture.

In cooking peas very little water should be used. Some water always cooks out of the vegetable itself and if there is shredded lettuce in the pan it adds more moisture. A half cup of water will be enough if the peas are so young and fresh that they require only a short time for cooking them. How long peas should be cooked depends entirely of course upon their size and freshness.

PEAS, ENGLISH STYLE
(Petits Pois à l'Anglaise)

2 *cups shelled peas*   sugar
2 *cups boiling water*   ½ *teaspoon salt*
1 *tablespoon butter*

Add peas to boiling salted water and cook slowly until done, about 20 to 25 minutes. Drain them, add butter and a sprinkling of sugar, correct seasoning and mix all together. Serves 4 to 5.

PEAS, FRENCH STYLE
(Petits Pois à la Française)

2 *cups shelled peas*   ½ *teaspoon salt*
6 *small onions*   3 *tablespoons butter*
5-6 *green lettuce leaves, shredded*   ¼ *cup water*
3 *sprigs parsley and 2 sprigs chervil*   ½ *teaspoon flour*
   tied in a faggot

Put peas, onions, lettuce, faggot, salt, sugar and 2 tablespoons butter in saucepan. Mix all together and add water. Cover closely and cook over a good fire about 25 to 30 minutes, when the water should be cooked away leaving only about 2-3 tablespoons liquid in the pan.

[191]

Discard faggot. Cream together remaining tablespoon butter with the flour and add, shaking the pan in a circular motion (stirring with a spoon crushes the tender peas) to combine it and thicken the liquid. As soon as it comes back to a boil remove from fire and serve. Serves 4 to 5.

NEW PEAS, COUNTRY STYLE

2 cups shelled peas
¼ cup diced fat salt pork
1 tablespoon butter
8 small onions
½ cup diced carrots
½ teaspoon flour
½-¾ cup water

3-4 green lettuce leaves, shredded
3 sprigs parsley and 2 of chervil tied
   in a faggot
1 tablespoon sugar
a little pepper
½ teaspoon salt

Parboil salt pork dice and drain. Put butter in saucepan, add pork dice, onions and carrots and cook until all are golden brown. Remove pork dice, onions and carrots and reserve. Add flour to fat in pan, mix well and cook until it starts to turn golden. Add water, bring to a boil, add peas, pork dice, onions, faggot, sugar and seasoning. Cover pan and cook over a good fire 30 to 35 minutes or until vegetables are done. Discard faggot. If the liquid has not reduced to about ¼ cup remove vegetables and cook it down. Serves 4 to 5.

PEAS AND CARROTS IN CREAM
(Petits Pois et Carottes à la Crème)

12 tiny spring carrots (or ½ cup diced
   carrots)
½ teaspoon salt
1 tablespoon sugar

1 tablespoon butter
2 cups peas, cooked à l'Anglaise
   (page 191)
1 cup Cream Sauce (page 25)

Put carrots, salt, sugar and butter in a saucepan and add just enough water to cover them. Cover pan and cook over a good fire until the liquid is cooked away. Add cooked peas and Cream Sauce, shaking all together until well combined. Serves 5 to 6.

POTATOES

Potatoes are a basic food in France, as important as bread to the average Frenchman. Yet, potatoes were comparatively rare up to the beginning of the nineteenth century when Parmentier first grew them successfully in France and discovered ways of preparing them. The many French potato dishes which have "Parmentier" in their names are in honor of his work.

The soil and climate of France is excellent for raising potatoes, the potatoes being fine flavored, fine textured, cheap and plentiful. Potatoes are served daily, often as the main dish of a meal, perhaps cooked with a little salt pork or bacon—called *Pommes au Lard*—or in Potato and Leek Soup. Plenty of such a main dish with a generous bowl of green salad and a fruit tart to finish it off would satisfy a Frenchman very nicely.

Probably the best known French way of cooking potatoes is to fry them in deep hot fat, called in this country, "French Fried Potatoes," but in France, "Pommes de Terre Frites." Americans love them done as every French cook knows how to do them, golden and crispy outside, white and mealy within.

BAKED POTATOES

Wash potatoes and bake in a hot oven of 400 to 425 degrees, allowing 1 hour for large potatoes or a little less time for smaller ones. To tell when done press gently between thumb and forefinger and if the potatoes have lost their firmness they are done. Prick with a fork or cut a small incision in the top as soon as they are taken from the oven to let the steam escape instead of condensing inside. To serve cut a small cross in the top, open up the corners and place a piece of butter in the opening and salt as desired.

BOILED POTATOES

Boil or steam small potatoes in salted water to cover for 25 minutes. Drain well and then dry them by putting them in the oven for a few minutes or on top of the fire shaking the pan to keep them from scorching.

CREAMED POTATOES
(Pommes de terre à la Crème)

Follow recipe for Potatoes Maître d'Hôtel (page 197) omitting the parsley.

FRENCH FRIED POTATOES
(Pommes de terre Frites)

Peel potatoes and cut in pieces about the length and thickness of the little finger or as large or small as desired. Cook in deep hot fat or oil about 7 or 8 minutes or until potatoes are soft but not very brown. Remove from fat and drain. When ready to serve, return to the fat which has been heated very hot and cook 1 to 2 minutes or until crispy and golden brown. Remove from fat and drain well on a paper towel to remove all surplus fat. Season with salt and serve immediately. Never cover French Fried Potatoes after they are done because then they will lose all their crispness.

DUCHESS POTATOES
(Pommes de terre Duchesse)

Duchess Potatoes have a rich smoothness that differs a little from mashed potatoes because there is no milk in the mixture. They have many uses but probably the most popular one is as a border for any meat or fish that has been minced for hash or chopped for combining with a sauce. We also use them to make potato croquettes; or shape them in individual servings preferably with a pastry tube to make a rose shape and brown on a baking sheet, then garnish a meat dish with them. It is possible to use leftover mashed potatoes for Duchess potatoes but there is always a chance that they may be a little too soft.

1 *lb. potatoes*	*a little white pepper*
1 *tablespoon butter*	*a little nutmeg*
½ *teaspoon salt*	1 *egg and* 1 *yolk, slightly beaten*

Peel potatoes, cut in pieces and cook until soft in boiling salted water to cover. Drain and dry out well in oven or on top of stove. Rub through a sieve and put in hot saucepan, then work up the mixture with a wooden spatula or spoon until it is very smooth. Add butter, seasonings, egg and egg yolk and mix all together thoroughly. These potatoes may be made up ahead of time and kept until ready to use by brushing a little butter over the top to prevent a crust from forming. Reheat over a very gentle fire, stirring constantly. Makes 2 to 3 cups.

HASHED BROWN POTATOES MENAGERE
(Pommes de terre au Gratin Ménagère)

4-5 *large potatoes*	1 *teaspoon salt*
1 *medium onion, chopped*	*a little pepper*
3 *tablespoons butter*	3 *tablespoons grated cheese*

Peel potatoes, cut in large pieces and cook with onion until done in boiling salted water to cover. Drain well. Put on a platter and crush with a fork, mixing in 2 tablespoons butter, salt and pepper. Spread remaining tablespoon butter on a heatproof platter and spread potato mixture over it. Sprinkle top with cheese and a little melted butter.

Put in a moderately hot oven of 400 degrees and cook until golden brown. Serves 3 to 4.

HASHED CREAMED POTATOES

Follow recipe for Potatoes Maître d'Hôtel (page 197), chopping potatoes or cutting them into fine dice and omitting parsley.

MASHED POTATOES

My mother always put half an onion in the pan when she cooked the potatoes for mashing to give them a little better flavor. This also is a trick of mine. While mashed potatoes seem a simple enough dish to prepare, there are two points that, to me, make all the difference between good and not-so-good mashed potatoes. The first is to be careful not to boil the potatoes too long. They should be soft but never cooked until mushy because then they become watery and do not have a good flavor. Then when the milk is added the pan should be over a fire that is just hot enough to keep the potatoes hot without boiling. If they cook too much the flavor is spoiled.

Peel 1 lb. potatoes and cut in pieces. If desired add ½ onion. Cook in boiling salted water to cover 25 to 30 minutes or until potatoes are done. When tested, they should break under the pressure of a fork but should not be mushy. Drain and dry by shaking pan over the fire or putting in a slow oven for a few minutes. Run through a sieve, return to pan and work up with a wooden spatula or spoon until the potatoes are smooth and elastic. Add a little salt and, if desired, a little nutmeg and 2 tablespoons butter, then add ½ to 1 cup boiling milk, little by little, mixing over a very low heat and using enough to give the desired consistency. Serves 3 to 4.

PARSLEY POTATOES

12 *small new potatoes (or 3 large,*	1 *teaspoon chopped parsley*
cut in quarters)	1 *tablespoon butter*
½ *teaspoon salt*	*water (or white stock)*
a little pepper	

Peel potatoes and put in saucepan with remaining ingredients using enough water (or stock) to come to about half the height of the potatoes. Cover with buttered paper, cover pan, bring to a boil and cook in a moderately hot oven of 375 to 400 degrees or on top of stove about 30 minutes or until potatoes are done. If liquid has not cooked away to about ¼ cup, cook it down quickly to this amount. Serve the potatoes with the liquid from the pan poured over them and a little parsley sprinkled over the top. Serves 4.

SAUTEED POTATOES

Slice leftover-plain-boiled potatoes and sauté slowly in butter until golden brown on both sides. Care must be taken not to have the fat too hot because they should never be cooked quickly like potatoes fried in deep fat. Serve sprinkled with finely chopped parsley.

SAUTEED POTATOES LYONNAISE

Slice 2 cups plain-boiled potatoes and sauté slowly in butter until golden brown on both sides. Remove potatoes from pan, leaving the butter in the pan. Mince ½ onion fine, put in the pan and cook until golden brown. Return potatoes to pan and mix all together. Serve sprinkled with finely chopped parsley. Serves 3 to 4.

POTATOES ANNA
(Pommes de terre Anna)

Peel 4 potatoes and slice as thinly as possible. Drain and dry well in a clean towel. Season with ½ teaspoon salt and a little pepper. Butter a round mold or small baking dish and arrange potatoes in it in layers, putting about ⅕ the potatoes in each layer, and spreading 1 tablespoon butter over each layer and one tablespoon butter on top of all. Bake in a hot oven of 425 to 450 degrees 40 to 50 minutes or until potatoes are done. To test them, insert a small knife and make sure that potatoes are soft. To serve, invert the baking dish on serving dish so that potatoes slip out in a molded form that is golden brown all around and on top. Save the butter which comes out on the serving dish for sautéing other foods. Serves 4.

POTATOES BOULANGERE
(Pommes de terre Boulangère)

1 *lb. potatoes*	1 *teaspoon chopped parsley*
1 *medium onion in thin slices*	2 *tablespoons butter*
½ *teaspoon salt*	¾ *cup boiling water*
a little pepper	

Peel and slice potatoes and mix with onion, salt, pepper and parsley. Spread about ½ inch deep in heatproof platter. Spread butter over the top and add boiling water. Cook in a hot oven of 425 to 450 degrees about 30 to 40 minutes or until potatoes are soft and brown and crusty on top. If desired, a leg of lamb or loin of pork may be roasted on top of the potatoes following directions on pages 109 and 117. Serves 3 to 4.

POTATO CROQUETTES

Use Duchess Potato (page 194) mixture. When cold, form into small oblong, cylinder or cone shapes and coat à l'Anglaise (page 293). Fry in deep hot fat or oil or sauté in butter until brown.

POTATO AU GRATIN

Although the recipe for Potato au Gratin calls for mashed potatoes, when my mother made this dish she almost always used freshly boiled potatoes which she crushed with a fork and mixed with a little butter and milk. She spread this mixture on an earthenware platter and cooked it as in the recipe below. This is a quicker, easier way, of course, but we liked it because the potatoes were not so smooth and there were always tiny pieces of crushed potatoes through the mixture, crisp on the bottom or brown on top.

Prepare mashed potatoes and spread about 2 inches thick on an earthenware platter. Sprinkle top with grated cheese and a little melted butter. Put in a hot oven of 450 degrees or under broiler and cook until golden brown.

POTATO PANCAKES
(Beignets de Pommes de terre)

2 *large potatoes (peeled and grated)*	*a little nutmeg*
1 *medium onion, grated*	½ *teaspoon chopped parsley*
2 *tablespoons flour*	2 *egg yolks, slightly beaten*
¼ *teaspoon salt*	2 *egg whites, stiffly beaten*
a little pepper	

Put potatoes and onion in a bowl, add flour and seasonings and mix all together well. Add egg yolks and when they are well combined fold in the egg whites. Put a little butter in a skillet and when hot add 2 tablespoons of this mixture for each cake. Fry over a medium hot fire until golden brown on both sides. Serves 4 to 5.

POTATOES MAITRE D'HOTEL
(Pommes de terre Maître d'Hôtel)

Cook, without peeling, 8 to 10 small potatoes until done, in boiling salted water to cover. Drain and dry over the fire. Remove skins and cut in ¼ inch slices. Put in saucepan with just enough boiling milk to cover. Add ¼ teaspoon salt, a little white pepper and, if desired, a little nutmeg. Bring to a boil and cook until the milk is reduced to about ½ the original quantity. Add 2 tablespoons butter and swirl the pan around to combine. This butter should thicken the sauce just enough. Correct the seasoning and serve sprinkled with finely chopped parsley. Instead of milk, chicken stock may be used, if preferred. Serves 4.

POTATOES PAYSANNE
(Pommes de terre au Lard)

1½ *lbs. potatoes*	1½ *cups water*
¾ *cup* (¼ *lb.*) *diced fat salt pork*	2 *tablespoons tomato purée*
(*or bacon*)	(*optional*)
1 *tablespoon butter* (*or lard*)	1 *faggot* (page 294)
2 *medium onions, diced*	½ *teaspoon salt*
1 *tablespoon flour*	*a little pepper*
1 *clove garlic, crushed*	1 *teaspoon chopped parsley*

Peel and cut potatoes in pieces, about 4 pieces from a medium potato. Parboil pork dice about 5 minutes and drain. Melt butter or lard in pan, add pork dice and when they start to cook add onions and cook until they are golden brown. Add flour and cook a few minutes longer. Add garlic, water, tomato purée and faggot. Bring to a boil, add potatoes and salt and pepper, cover and cook slowly 35 to 40 minutes or until potatoes are well done. If cooking liquid has not reduced to about one-third the original quantity, cook it down quickly. Remove faggot and discard. Put potatoes in serving dish with the liquid and sprinkle top with chopped parsley. If cooked in an earthenware casserole serve them from that. Serves 6.

POTATO PIE
(Pâté aux Pommes de terre)

Potato Pie is one of those typical Bourbonnaise dishes so common in the country from which I came that we had it about once every week or at least every other week. But I do not think it is familiar at all to Americans. It is delicious and rather unusual.

6 *medium potatoes*	1 *teaspoon chopped parsley*
1½ *teaspoons salt*	2 *tablespoons butter*
a little pepper	1 *lb. tart pastry* (page 228)
1 *large onion, chopped*	1½ *cups cream*

Peel potatoes and cut in thin slices, season with salt and pepper and mix with onion and parsley. Roll out ½ the pastry about ¼ inch thick in either a round or oblong shape and place on a baking sheet. Drain potatoes and arrange about 1½ inches thick on the pastry, leaving an edge of pastry at least an inch wide. Roll out remaining pastry and place on the potatoes. Moisten lower edge to hold top and bottom crusts together and then roll the two edges together so that no juice can escape. Prick or cut a few tiny gashes in the top. Brush top with an egg mixed with a little milk. Bake 1 to 1¼ hours in a moderately hot oven of 375 to 400 degrees. Cut a small round opening in the top and test with a knife to make sure potatoes are done. If they are done pour the cream into the hot pie through the opening. Let cool a little and serve either warm or cold. Serves 6.

POTATO RISSOLEE

Potatoes can be varied in three different ways when prepared by the following recipe. For Pommes de terre Rissolée, small potatoes, especially the very little ones are used. If they come large from the market, cut into balls about the size of the little new ones. Pommes de terre Parisienne are cooked the same way but are first cut into much smaller, tiny balls. Pommes de terre Parmentier are the same except that they are cut in small dice. If desired, the potatoes can be cooked from the beginning in butter, in which case they are not removed from the pan and drained but are finished in the same butter in which they were cooked.

Peel potatoes and cut into balls and parboil in enough salted water to cover, about 5 minutes. Drain well. For each cup of potatoes allow 2 tablespoons good fat. Heat fat quite hot, add potatoes and cook until golden brown all over. Remove from pan, drain off all the fat from them, and pour off all the fat from the pan. Return potatoes to pan and add 1 tablespoon butter for each cup of potatoes. Roll potatoes in butter as it melts until all pieces are coated with butter. Season with salt and sprinkle with finely chopped parsley.

POTATOES SAVOYARDE

4-5 *large potatoes*	2 *tablespoons butter*
1 *medium onion, sliced*	½ *teaspoon salt*
5-6 *thin slices Swiss cheese*	*stock (or water)*

Peel and cut potatoes in very thin slices, wash and drain them. Cook onion in butter until soft but not brown. Combine onion and salt with potato and put in a baking dish with layers of cheese between layers of potatoes. Add stock (or water) to come just to the top of potatoes. Bake in a moderately hot oven of 400 degrees about 45 minutes or until potatoes are done and top is brown. Serves 3 to 4.

POTATOES SUZETTE

Wash and bake large potatoes until done. Make a small opening in the top of each one and remove pulp from inside. Rub this through a sieve or mash with a fork and add 1 tablespoon butter and 1 tablespoon cream (or top milk) for each potato. Thicken mixture by adding 1 egg yolk and season with salt. Replace mixture in skins, sprinkle tops with Parmesan cheese and brown in a hot oven or under a broiler.

POTATOES WITH CHEESE COUNTRY STYLE
(Pommes de terre Fermière)

6-8 *medium potatoes*	2 *cups boiled milk*
½ *teaspoon salt*	1 *egg, beaten*
a little pepper	2 *tablespoons butter*
½ *cup grated Swiss cheese*	*garlic*

Peel potatoes and slice ¼ inch thick. Put in a bowl with salt, pepper and cheese, reserving a couple of spoonfuls of cheese for the top. Mix together egg and milk and add. Rub a heatproof platter with a cut piece of garlic and spread potato mixture in the dish. Sprinkle top with remaining cheese and dot top with butter broken into small pieces. Cook in a moderately hot oven of 375 to 400 degrees about 45 minutes to 1 hour or until potatoes are done and top is browned. Serves 5 to 6.

SORREL

Sorrel is most often used for soup and the soup section of this book contains recipes for soups made with sorrel. Its fresh delicious flavor is particularly good in cream-type soups. But sometimes sorrel is braised and when cooked this way is an excellent accompaniment for meat, especially for veal.

PRESERVING SORREL

We liked sorrel in soup so well that when it was in season we used to put it down in jars for use in the winter. To do this the sorrel is first cleaned well and finely shredded. Then it is cooked in its own juice until the juice is practically all cooked away and the sorrel has melted down into a thick purée. This purée can be put into sterilized jars and covered with wax or melted pork fat and kept in a cool place until ready to use. We added it to leek and potato or any cream soup.

BRAISED SORREL
(Oseille)

Clean and wash 3 pounds sorrel. Drain and put in a saucepan and cook in the water which clings to the leaves over a hot fire about 15 to 20 minutes or until it is very soft. (We speak of it as "melted.") Drain thoroughly in a sieve and when all the water is drained out, rub the sorrel through the sieve. For about 2 cups of this purée of sorrel make a roux in a saucepan by combining 2 tablespoons melted butter and 1½ tablespoons flour and cooking until it just starts to turn golden. Add sorrel purée, mix all together thoroughly and add ½ cup stock. Season with ½ teaspoon salt and 1 tablespoon sugar, mix well and bring to boiling point. Cover with a piece of buttered paper, cover pan and put in a moderately hot oven of 375 to 400 degrees and cook about 1 hour. After removing from oven, combine with 2 beaten eggs and mix well. Bring back to boiling point, remove from fire, correct seasoning and add 1 tablespoon butter (or 2 tablespoons cream), or add 2 tablespoons gravy from the meat it is to accompany. Serves 3 to 4.

SPINACH
(Epinards)

Spinach, one of our inexpensive and plentiful vegetables, makes an excellent vegetable accompaniment to many other foods. It is served with eggs, chicken, meat and poultry in various ways. Often it is a base on which to put the other foods. Sometimes a Mornay or Supreme Sauce is poured over and the whole thing put under the broiler to brown. Foods prepared this way are called "Florentine."

Spinach is very deceiving in that it cooks away so much that it takes about 3 lbs. fresh spinach to make 1 lb. when cooked and drained. This is enough for 3 to 4 servings. Because spinach grows close to the ground its leaves are filled with soil and it takes many waters to wash out all this sand. Unless it is carefully and thoroughly done the finished dish will be gritty in the mouth.

At home we served the tender fresh young spinach that came in the spring differently from the larger and less tender leaves which came later in the season. The tender spring spinach were served "en branche," that is without being chopped or puréed, usually with some

[201]

meat gravy poured over each serving. But when it became older and less tender it was puréed and combined with a little cream sauce.

To Cook Spinach

Clean thoroughly 3 lbs. spinach, cutting away any very coarse stems. Cook about 6 to 8 minutes over a quick fire in a quart of water to which has been added ½ teaspoon salt. Drain well, pressing out as much of the water as possible and serve with a little melted butter or the gravy from the meat with which the spinach will be served. Serves 4.

CREAMED SPINACH

Clean and cook 3 lbs. spinach. After draining and pressing out the water chop very fine or rub through a sieve. Put 1 or 2 tablespoons butter in a saucepan and when hot add 1 teaspoon flour and cook until it starts to turn golden. Add spinach, mix well and cook a few minutes or until all the moisture is cooked away. Season with salt and a sprinkling of nutmeg if desired. Add ½ cup hot milk (or top milk). Mix well, bring to a boil and cook a few minutes longer. If served with meat, put a spoonful of gravy on top of each serving. Garnish with small triangles of bread fried in butter until golden brown, or with quartered hard-boiled eggs. Serves 4.

SPINACH AU JUS

Follow recipe for Creamed Spinach, substituting stock for the milk. Put a spoonful of gravy on top of each serving.

BAKED SWEET POTATOES

Select fairly large potatoes and wash them well. Put in a moderately hot oven of 400 degrees about 45 minutes to 1 hour. To test when done press gently between thumb and forefinger and if they have lost their firmness they are ready to eat.

BOILED SWEET POTATOES

Select medium size potatoes and wash but do not peel them. Cook in boiling salted water to cover or steam about 30 minutes. Peel and serve plain.

FRIED SWEET POTATOES

Follow directions for Boiled Sweet Potatoes (above) and after peeling them cut in pieces about the width and length of the little finger or in ¼ inch slices. Fry in deep hot fat or oil until brown, drain well and season with salt.

MASHED SWEET POTATOES

Follow directions for Boiled Sweet Potatoes (above) and after peeling them rub through a sieve and then dry them out a little in a saucepan over the fire. Add butter and cream (or top milk) to make them creamy but not too thin. Season with salt.

SWEET POTATOES WITH MAPLE SYRUP

Follow directions for Boiled Sweet Potatoes (above) and after peeling cut in ¼ inch slices. Arrange in overlapping circles in a round earthenware dish and pour maple syrup over them. Put in a moderately hot oven of 400 to 425 degrees and cook about 10 to 15 minutes or until top is brown.

TOMATOES
(Tomates)

Tomatoes, like onions and potatoes, are used so much in our cooking today it almost seems impossible that there was a time when people did not eat them. We look to their flavor and acidity to enhance dishes of all kinds and depend upon their bright red color to put a spot of interest in many an otherwise colorless plate.

One of the problems, however, in using fresh tomatoes in salads and in cooked dishes is that they are full of seeds and extremely watery. There is a trick that careful cooks use to take care of this. To remove seeds—and surplus liquid at the same time—cut in half crosswise and then, grasping the half in the palm of the hand, squeeze very gently so that seeds and juice run out. If handled gently the pulpy dividing parts and shell will remain intact. This juice need not be wasted but can be used in soups or sauces that will be strained anyway. In using canned tomatoes in sauces that are to be cooked quickly, the canned purée is usually preferable to canned whole tomatoes because quick cooking will not reduce the volume of liquid.

Tomatoes in season are always so plentiful that using them up is a problem. In France we not only ate them raw but we cooked the nice firm ones in many ways—sautéed, creamed, stuffed and so on. Stuffed Tomatoes—we called them "Tomates Farcies"—are a favorite of mine. I think you could hardly find a more delicious way of using those bits of leftover meats that at first glance seem almost useless.

TOMATO PORTUGAISE

Peel 3 tomatoes, cut in half and press gently to remove seeds and water. Cut each piece in half again. Sauté in hot salad oil until soft and browned. Add to the pan 1 shallot, finely chopped, and 1 clove of garlic, crushed. Season with salt and pepper, add a few spoonfuls of meat gravy (if any is available) and serve sprinkled with finely chopped parsley. Serves 2 to 3.

CREAMED TOMATOES

6-8 *medium tomatoes*　　　　　　1 *teaspoon butter*
2 *tablespoons butter*　　　　　　½ *teaspoon flour*
½ *cup top milk (or cream)*　　　　½ *teaspoon sugar*

Peel tomatoes, cut in half and gently press out seeds and water. Season with salt. Melt 2 tablespoons butter in frying pan and when quite hot add tomatoes. Sauté on both sides. Add milk (or cream), bring to a boil and cook slowly about 8 to 10 minutes. Remove tomato slices to serving dish. Cook liquid in pan until reduced to about one-half the original quantity, then thicken with Manié Butter, made by creaming together the teaspoon butter with the flour and adding to the liquid in the pan. Correct the seasoning, add sugar and pour over tomato slices. Serves 3 to 4.

TOMATOES PROVENCALE

3 *tomatoes*　　　　　　　　　　　1 *clove garlic, crushed*
½ *cup fine fresh bread crumbs*　　1 *teaspoon chopped parsley*

Cut tomatoes in half and press gently to remove seeds and water. Season with salt and pepper. Mix together remaining ingredients and spread cut sides of tomatoes with this mixture. Sprinkle tops with a little melted butter or salad oil. Arrange on a heatproof serving dish and cook in a hot oven of 450 degrees or under a broiler 10 to 15 minutes or until tomatoes are soft and tops are browned. Serves 2 to 3.

TOMATO SAUTE

Cut tomatoes in thick slices. Season with salt. Roll in flour and sauté in hot oil or butter until brown on both sides.

STUFFED TOMATOES
(Tomates Farcies)

Select firm tomatoes not over ripe. Cut a hole in the top about 1½ inches in diameter. Turn upside down and press very gently to remove seeds and water. Season with salt and pepper. Stuff with finely chopped meat (leftover cooked lamb, veal, beef or poultry) which has been seasoned with finely chopped onion or stuff with cooked rice or with mushroom Duxelles or with a mixture of all or any two of them, pressing the stuffing down into the tomatoes and rounding it over the tops. Sprinkle with fine bread crumbs and a little melted butter. Arrange on a heatproof dish and pour a little stock or water around them. Bake in a moderately hot oven of 400 to 425 degrees about 15 to 20 minutes or until the tomatoes are soft and the crumbs on top are brown.

TURNIPS
(Navets)

Just as in this country we had both white and yellow turnips in France. The white were usually eaten when they were freshly harvested, the yellow were stored and used all winter. In addition we also had a very delicate variety called "les raves" that I never have seen here. These grew so quickly in the rich soil of my country, that they matured in about 4 or 5 weeks and were as soft and tender as good mealy potatoes. Those we used for making into a cream soup. The yellow ones were almost always mashed and finished with butter and cream or top milk. They were also a favorite vegetable for the Pot-au-Feu. The white turnips we prepared in several ways such as creaming and stuffing.

To Prepare Yellow Turnips

Peel turnips, cut in pieces and cook in enough boiling salted water to cover about 30 minutes or until soft. Drain well and mash or rub through a sieve. Return to pan and dry out surplus water over heat, stirring all the time to avoid scorching them. Add butter, top milk or cream to make them about the consistency of mashed potatoes and season with salt and with pepper if desired.

To Prepare White Turnips

Peel young white turnips and cut in slices or large dice. If young ones are unobtainable and old ones that tend to be tough must be cooked, slice them very thin. Cook in enough boiling salted water to cover about 30 minutes or until soft. Drain well and sauté in butter, sprinkling them with a little parsley.

CREAMED TURNIPS

Follow receipe for preparing white turnips (above). After draining them add just enough Cream Sauce (page 25) to cover them and let simmer a few minutes.

STUFFED TURNIPS

Select well-shaped, round, young, white turnips. Peel and remove centers, leaving an outside shell and base about a half inch thick. Parboil 8 to 10 minutes. Drain. Stuff centers with a hash made of leftover meat. Arrange on a heatproof dish and pour enough stock around them so that it comes halfway to the tops of them. Sprinkle tops with fine bread crumbs and a little melted butter. Bake in a hot oven about 20-25 minutes or until crumbs are brown.

VEGETABLE MARROW
(Courgette)

We always prepared vegetable marrow when it was still so young and tender that it was not much larger than a cucumber. The same recipes used for cucumbers can also be used for vegetable marrow.

SAUTEED VEGETABLE MARROW

Peel and cut vegetable marrow in very thin slices and sauté in butter. Season with salt and serve with the butter from the pan poured over. Allow 1 vegetable marrow for each serving.

STUFFED VEGETABLE MARROW

8-12 *small vegetable marrow*	*meat gravy (or tomato sauce)*
1 *cup finely minced leftover cooked*	*salt*
meat	*a little pepper*
1 *onion, finely chopped*	1 *carrot, sliced*
1 *tablespoon butter*	1 *onion, sliced*
1 *cup cooked rice*	2-3 *slices fat salt pork (or bacon)*
1 *teaspoon chopped parsley*	

Peel vegetable marrow, cut off ends and scoop out seeds from centers, leaving the vegetable whole. Put in boiling salted water and parboil 5 minutes. Drain well. Cook chopped onion in butter until it starts to turn golden and combine with meat, rice and parsley. Add gravy or tomato sauce to make it the consistency of hash and season with salt and pepper to taste. Place sliced carrot, sliced onion and sliced pork (or bacon) in a pan. Stuff marrows and place side by side on top and add enough water to come not quite halfway to the top of the marrow. Bring to a boil, cover pan and place in a moderately hot oven of 400 to 425 degrees and cook 30 to 35 minutes or until marrow is done. Serve with roast meat and its gravy. Or serve as a main dish, in which case cook liquid in pan until reduced to about 1 cup and pour over the marrow. Serves 4 to 6.

DRIED BEANS, PEAS AND LENTILS

Dried beans were more common and plentiful at home than either peas or lentils, probably because we grew the beans locally and had to purchase peas and lentils. We used dried legumes in soups and with meats and vegetables, and cooked and served them in a sauce, such as Bourbonnaise style. We liked them especially with pork—they can stand more fat in cooking than many foods—and thought a loin of pork prepared with dried beans a great treat. And without dried beans what would we do for our Cassoulet, that famous specialty of certain sections of France?

DRIED WHITE BEANS, BRETONNE STYLE
(Haricots Blancs Bretonne)

1 *lb. dried white beans*	1 *clove garlic*
1 *teaspoon salt*	1 *onion, chopped*
¼ *lb. salt pork, parboiled*	2 *tablespoons butter*
1 *onion*	1 *clove garlic, crushed*
2-3 *cloves*	2 *tomatoes, peeled, seeded and*
1 *carrot*	*chopped* (¼ *cup tomato purée*)
1 *faggot* (page 294)	1 *teaspoon chopped parsley*

Soak beans a few hours in cold water to cover well. Drain, wash them and cook in salted water, to which has been added the salt pork, onion, cloves, carrot, faggot and garlic, about 1 hour or until soft. Melt butter in saucepan, add chopped onion and cook until brown. Add garlic and tomatoes (or purée). Remove salt pork from beans, cut in small dice and add. Drain beans and add them, add parsley, correct the seasoning, add pepper and if sauce is too thick add a little of the liquid in which the beans were cooked. Serves 6 to 8.

LENTILS BRETONNE STYLE
(Lentilles Bretonne)

Follow recipe for Dried White Beans Bretonne Style (above), substituting lentils for the beans. After soaking the lentils, however, wash them in several changes of water and make sure that there are no little brown stones left. Serve cooked lentils with sausages, roast pork or with game.

SPLIT PEAS

We used split peas primarily for soup but we also made a dish of puréed split peas which was very good. It was a dish for cold weather and I remember how good it tasted with little French sausages, sautéed and placed on top of the purée.

PUREE OF SPLIT PEAS

1 *lb. split peas*
1 *teaspoon salt*
1 *onion, chopped*
1 *carrot, chopped*
¼ *cup diced salt pork parboiled*
  (*or bacon*)

2-3 *leaves lettuce* (*or green part of leeks*) *finely chopped*
2 *tablespoons butter*
1 *teaspoon sugar*

Soak peas a few hours, wash well and put in a saucepan with just enough cold water to cover. Bring to a boil and skim well. Cook pork or bacon dice in saucepan until fat cooks out, add onion and carrot and cook until they start to turn golden. Add lettuce and cook a few minutes longer, then add all this to the split peas. Cook slowly 1 to 1½ hours or until peas have become soft and mushy and water is pretty well cooked away. Rub through a fine sieve. The purée should be very thick. Reheat with butter and sugar, but do not let it boil; correct the seasoning. Serves 6 to 8.

RED KIDNEY BEANS, COUNTRY STYLE

All varieties of beans are common in France but dried red kidney beans are used very extensively. They must be cleaned very carefully because little stones and sand are apt to be mixed with them. Use plenty of water and lift them out of it with your hands so that the sand is left in the bottom of the pan.

2 *cups kidney beans*
1 *glass red wine* (*or water*)
1 *large onion, chopped*
2 *tablespoons butter*
1 *faggot* (page 294)

2 *cloves garlic, crushed*
¼-½ *lb. salt pork or bacon, parboiled*
1 *teaspoon flour*
1 *teaspoon salt*
a little pepper

After cleaning beans soak for 1 hour in lukewarm water to cover. Drain and put in pan with wine and just enough water to cover them. Bring to a boil, skim well. In the meantime, sauté onion in 1 tablespoon butter until soft but not brown and add to beans. Add faggot, garlic and salt pork or bacon and cook slowly about 1½ hours. If the liquid cooks down too much add a little boiling water. When done there should be between ½ and 1 cup of liquid. Discard faggot. Remove pork.

Thicken liquid on beans with Manié Butter, made by creaming together 1 tablespoon butter with 1 teaspoon flour. Correct the seasoning and add pepper to taste. Put beans and their sauce in a serving dish, slice pork and arrange around the edge and sprinkle chopped parsley over top of beans. Serves 6.

Salads

⟨⚹⟩

ALTHOUGH the most popular French salad is, without a doubt, the tossed green one when in season, we did serve many other kinds in our home, using cooked vegetables, meat or fish, or combinations of them. Sometimes the vegetables were cooked especially for the salad— potatoes, for example—but more often this was a way of using up leftovers. A big salad would be the main course of the meal, but small amounts came to the table on the hors d'oeuvres plate. Always the ingredients had been left to marinate in the dressing long enough to absorb its flavor.

As an accompaniment to dinner, the only salad I remember seeing served was the tossed green salad; greens in season put together with a well seasoned French dressing and a little *fines herbes*—that is, chopped parsley, chives, chervil, and tarragon—if any were available. In making the tossed green salad, a French cook uses all the leaves that are tender, the outside green ones as well as the inside white ones. They are very carefully washed and just as carefully dried because a good salad allows no moisture on the leaves to dilute the dressing. The greens were dried in a special basket called a *panier a salade,* or, lacking that, in a clean napkin or towel, which was swirled so as to toss out the water without bruising the leaves.

The dressing for a tossed green salad is always a French dressing well seasoned and flavored with garlic. Either the bowl is rubbed with a cut piece of garlic or *chapons* are tossed with the greens, *chapons* being small pieces of crusty bread rubbed with garlic. When they have picked up some of the dressing these chapons are delicious tid-bits for those who like the flavor of garlic. Greens, chapons, and dressing are turned and tossed over and over with a wooden fork and spoon until every bit of green is coated with dressing and no liquid remains in the bottom of the bowl.

SALAD COUNTRY STYLE

This salad is very provincial, using pork fat in place of salad oil.

Country people as a rule prefer this dressing on field salad, which consists of all the edible young greens that grow wild in the fields and can be picked before the lettuce, romaine, and other salads planted in kitchen gardens are ready.

½ cup fat salt pork (or bacon) diced
  very small
1 lb. field salad (or green salad)
salt and pepper

⅔ tablespoon vinegar
½ teaspoon fines herbes (if available)
fresh pork fat

Sauté pork (or bacon) dice in a little fresh pork fat until golden brown. Wash salad, drain, and dry thoroughly. Sprinkle pork dice and the fat in which it cooked over salad. Add salt and pepper to taste, vinegar, and fines herbes. Mix all together well. Serves 6.

CHESTNUT SALAD

1 lb. chestnuts, shelled and cooked
  (page 174)
¼ lb. field salad
1 boiled onion, chopped
1 cup cooked beets, sliced or diced

2 hard-boiled eggs, sliced or diced
½ teaspoon fines herbes
½ cup Vinaigrette Sauce (page 35)
salt

Mix together all ingredients, adding salt to taste. Serves 5 to 6.

SALADE HELEN

Peel celery knobs and cut in julienne. Cook about two minutes in boiling salt water to cover, drain, and cool. Combine with Mayonnaise (page 34) to which a little prepared mustard has been added. Garnish with sliced cooked beets and chopped walnuts.

HERRING AND POTATO SALAD

2 marinated (or sour) herrings
milk
½ teaspoon salt
a little pepper
½ teaspoon dry mustard
3 tablespoons vinegar

5 tablespoons salad oil
3 cooked potatoes, sliced
2 small apples, sliced
2 hard-boiled eggs, diced
½ teaspoon fines herbes

Drain herrings, remove bones, and soak for one hour in just enough milk to cover them. Mix together salt, pepper, mustard, vinegar, and oil. If there is any roe, force it through a sieve and add to this dressing. Add potato, apple and eggs to dressing. Drain herring and cut in large dice, add to other ingredients and toss all together. Serves 3 to 4.

SALADE MAISON

1 *cup cooked cauliflower*	⅜ *tablespoon vinegar*
1 *cup cooked string beans*	6 *tablespoons salad oil*
2 *tomatoes, peeled, seeded, and*	½ *teaspoon dry mustard*
chopped	½ *teaspoon salt*
1 *cup sliced leftover cooked chicken*	*pepper*
2 *hard-boiled eggs*	½ *teaspoon fines herbes*

Put cauliflower, string beans, tomatoes, and chicken in salad bowl. Separate eggs, cut whites in julienne, and add to bowl. Crush the yolks to a smooth paste and combine with seasoning, vinegar and oil, then add this dressing to the ingredients in the bowl. Sprinkle top with fines herbes. Serves 6.

SALADE NORMANDE

2 *tablespoons Mayonnaise* (page 34)	1 *cup diced celery*
1 *teaspoon prepared mustard*	1 *cup diced apple*
2 *tablespoons whipped cream*	*sliced cooked beets*
salt	

Combine Mayonnaise with mustard, fold in cream, and correct the seasoning. Mix with celery and apple and garnish with sliced cooked beets. Serves 4.

SALADE NICOISE

Mix cooked sliced potatoes and string beans with Vinaigrette Sauce (page 35) to taste and garnish with sliced tomatoes, olives, and cucumbers.

SALADE PARISIENNE

Mix cooked vegetables, such as cooked carrots and turnips cut in small dice, string beans and peas, with Mayonnaise (page 34). Arrange in bowl with pieces of cooked lobster coated with Mayonnaise and placed on top of the vegetables.

POTATO SALAD

Potato Salad is so often poorly made that many people avoid it as a dry, unpalatable affair. But well made Potato Salad actually provides one of the most delicious dishes when something hearty, but cold, is desired. The following few tips on making it date back to my mother's kitchen, and they are rules I still follow in making Potato Salad.

First, the potatoes. Use old ones if possible—they absorb the dressing better than the new ones and so make a tastier salad. Next, add the dressing to the potatoes while they are still warm because this way they absorb more flavor from the dressing. And finally, never make Potato Salad a day ahead or keep it in the refrigerator to get too cold. Both staleness and extreme cold are bad actors, and can usually be depended upon to make an unpalatable Potato Salad. I myself prefer it, like red wine, at room temperature, as do many gourmets also. Hot water in Potato Salad may surprise you, but it makes for creamy succulence. I remember at home we used white wine instead of water —for better flavor—cutting down at the same time the amount of vinegar in the dressing. In this case the amount of vinegar used depends upon your taste.

5-6 *medium potatoes*
1 *teaspoon salt*
pepper
2-3 *tablespoons vinegar*
6-7 *tablespoons salad oil*

4 *tablespoons hot water*
chopped spring onions (if desired)
chopped parsley, chives, chervil, and tarragon (if available)

Boil potatoes until done in salted water to cover. Drain, peel and cut in thin slices. While still warm season with salt and pepper and add vinegar and oil. Add water and mix all together, tossing with a fork to avoid mashing the potatoes. Add chopped onion and herbs to taste. Serves 4.

SPRING SALAD

½ *cup cooked asparagus tips*
½ *cup cooked string beans*
½ *cup cooked peas*
½ *cup sliced radishes*
2 *artichoke bottoms, cooked and sliced*
2 *hard-boiled eggs, chopped*

½ *teaspoon salt*
½ *teaspoon dry mustard*
2 *tablespoons vinegar*
6 *tablespoons oil*
¼ *cup Mayonnaise* (page 34)
a little pepper
1 *teaspoon fines herbes*

Mix together salt, pepper, mustard, vinegar and oil in the salad bowl. Add vegetables, toss all together, and let marinate one-half to one hour. Just before serving add Mayonnaise. Serves 5 to 6.

SALADE RUSSE

It is almost impossible to describe Salade Russe because it is a mixture of practically anything and everything that you want to put into it. It is well known in every French household. Of course it is always possible to combine in a Salade Russe many ingredients that don't go particularly well together. And so in French slang when anyone wishes to describe a hodge-podge of anything, whether it be an over-furnished room, a queer assortment of wearing apparel, or even a confusion of ideas or conversation, he says it is a "Salade Russe."

Mix together any desired vegetables, julienne of cooked meats, hard-boiled eggs, etc., that go well together, and combine with Mayonnaise (page 34) to taste. Garnish top with capers.

SALADE ST. JEAN

2 *hard-boiled eggs*	½ *cup cooked asparagus tips*
salt and pepper	½ *cup cooked string beans*
½ *teaspoon prepared mustard*	½ *cup cooked peas*
1 *tablespoon vinegar*	2 *artichoke bottoms, cooked and*
3 *tablespoons salad oil*	*sliced*
1 *cucumber*	½ *teaspoon fines herbes*

To make dressing remove yolks from eggs and mash to a paste. Season with salt, pepper and mustard, and add vinegar. Add oil gradually as in making mayonnaise. Peel and slice cucumber, sprinkle with salt, and let stand about half an hour, then press to remove as much of the water as possible. Combine cucumber with remaining vegetables and fines herbes, add chopped egg white, and toss together with the dressing. Serves 4 to 5.

TOSSED GREEN SALAD

Select salads that are in season such as lettuce, romaine, chicory, and escarole—any combination will be good. Separate the leaves, removing the bruised and damaged ones, and wash in a large quantity of water, making sure that all sand is removed. Drain, dry thoroughly, and chill a little. Rub bowl with a cut piece of garlic or put Chapons (page 294) in the bowl with the greens, allowing one or two for each person. Add Vinaigrette Sauce (page 35) when ready to serve, allowing one tablespoon for each serving, and toss all together until all the dressing has coated the leaves.

Rice, Spaghetti and Other Pastes

⬅✷➡

We SERVED rice often with poultry, always with Poule-au-Pot—Boiled Chicken—and with many other meats, and almost always with shellfish dishes. But we used plenty, too, in various kinds of milk puddings, for a hearty rice dessert made a substantial ending to a simple meal when the main dish was merely soup or a light entrée.

Opinion differs as to the length of time that rice should be cooked, because some prefer it softer than others, the French for the most part liking rice a little softer than the Italians do. A good general rule is to cook rice for desserts thoroughly so that it is quite soft but for main dishes to stop the cooking at the point where it just starts to get soft. Most important is the extra care required in handling cooked rice. The grains mash very, very easily and so they must never be stirred with a spoon, but always tossed lightly with a fork. Even in serving rice, it pays to handle it carefully and lightly. And many people don't realize that hot rice dishes, with the exception of Rice Pilau, should be served as soon as they are done because the rice becomes mashed and sticky on standing.

Macaroni, spaghetti, noodles and the other pastes are as well liked, it seems to me, by the French as by the Italians. We didn't actually eat these foods as often as the Italians because we are a potato-loving country while they depend more upon the pastes for the starchy part of their meals. But in cooking them we preferred a slightly softer product than the Italians like; some Italians will hardly touch their macaroni and spaghetti unless it is taken from the fire while still quite firm.

We ate the pastes dressed rather simply, seldom with heavy, rich tomato and meat sauces. We liked, for example, to partly cook spaghetti or macaroni—about 10 minutes—then drain and turn it into the pan in which veal or beef was being braised and let it cook in the gravy for 5 minutes or until done. Or we would melt some butter in a pan and

[215]

shake and roll the spaghetti in it until all the pieces were well coated. This was eaten merely with whatever meat gravy was on our plates.

It must be remembered that overcooking ruins any of the pastes because they take on a gummy consistency. Also they can never be left in the water after they are done, but must be drained immediately and thoroughly the minute they are cooked enough. The time of cooking varies with the paste but about 12 to 18 minutes is usual. The way to test for doneness is to taste a piece or, if you are accustomed to their feel, to pinch a piece between the thumb and forefinger.

RICE PILAU

2 tablespoons butter
½ onion, finely chopped
1 cup rice

2 cups boiling water or white stock
1 teaspoon salt

Select a pan that can be tightly covered, melt 1 tablespoon butter in it, add onion and cook until onion is soft but not brown. Add rice and mix all together well. Add boiling water or stock and salt, bring to a boil and cook, tightly covered, 18 to 20 minutes in the oven or over a very low heat on top of stove. Turn out into a hot serving dish, separate grains with a fork and mix in remaining tablespoon butter. Let stand a few minutes to get rid of steam, then put in a warm place until ready to serve. Serves 3 to 4.

RISOTTO

2 tablespoons butter
1 medium onion, chopped
1 cup rice

2 cups chicken broth
1 tablespoon grated Parmesan cheese

Melt 1 tablespoon butter, add onion and cook until it is golden. Add rice, mix well and gradually add chicken broth, stirring with a wooden spoon. Let boil slowly 18 to 20 minutes, depending upon whether it is desired well done or underdone. Add remaining tablespoon butter and cheese and serve immediately. The rice should be moist and creamy. Serve Parmesan cheese separately. Serves 3 to 4.

RICE WITH BROTH AND CHEESE
(Riz au Fromage)

2 tablespoons butter
1 medium onion, finely chopped
1 cup rice
2 cups chicken broth

½ teaspoon salt (omit if broth is seasoned)
½ cup grated Parmesan cheese
2 tablespoons meat gravy

Melt butter, add onion and cook until soft but not brown. Add rice and mix all together. Add boiling chicken broth and salt, cover pan and cook over very low heat about 18 to 20 minutes. If too dry add a little more broth. Mix in the Parmesan cheese, reserving a little for the top. Put gravy on top and sprinkle with Parmesan cheese.

GNOCCHI

Gnocchi are made from a paste very much like Cream Puff paste but using milk instead of water. They are dropped in boiling water and cooked, after which they must be well drained and dried on a towel. At this point they can be left for a few hours covered with a towel until ready to use them. Then the gnocchi are baked in a sauce but after the baking they must be served immediately because they puff up in the oven and if allowed to stand after that they will collapse and become heavy. The sauce must not be too thick, but light and creamy. Gnocchi à la Parisienne are hearty and rich and with a salad or fruit will make an adequate lunch or supper.

GNOCCHI A LA PARISIENNE

2 cups milk	1 cup flour
2 tablespoons butter	4 eggs
1 teaspoon salt	3 tablespoons grated Parmesan
a pinch of nutmeg	cheese

Heat milk, butter and seasoning, then gradually add flour mixing with a wooden spoon. When smooth remove from heat and add eggs one at a time mixing well after each addition. Add 1 tablespoon cheese. Meanwhile, have a pan of boiling water ready. Put dough in a pastry bag having a tube with a ¼ to ⅜ inch opening and force through the tube letting it drop into the boiling water as you cut it off in half inch pieces with a knife. Let boil slowly until Gnocchi are firm, about 5 to 8 minutes, drain and dry well on towel.

Spread a shallow baking dish with some thin Cream Sauce (page 25) or Mornay Sauce (page 28), place the Gnocchi on it and cover it with the sauce. Sprinkle remaining grated Parmesan cheese over the top, spread with a little melted butter and bake in a moderate oven about 15 to 20 minutes or until well browned. Serves 3 to 4.

SPAGHETTI, MACARONI OR NOODLES IN CREAM

Cook spaghetti, macaroni or noodles in boiling salted water 12 to 18 minutes or until done. Drain well. Melt a little butter in a saucepan, add spaghetti and toss and shake until well mixed. Add enough cream or top milk to come halfway to the top of the spaghetti and cook until reduced to one-half the original quantity. Add a little more butter and some grated cheese (Parmesan preferred) and shake, tossing the mixture over and over until the sauce is creamy.

NOODLES

3 *cups flour*
½ *teaspoon salt*
2 *eggs*

2 *egg yolks*
1-2 *tablespoons water (amount*
depends on size of eggs)

Sift flour and salt onto bread board and make a well in center. Drop in the eggs, egg yolks and water and mix with the hands, gradually working in the flour until all is thoroughly combined. Knead until dough is smooth. Place on a clean towel, sprinkle with a little flour to keep a crust from forming, wrap the towel around it and let stand for two hours. Divide in small pieces about the size of an egg and roll out until about as thick as a 10 cent piece. Hang these pieces on a cord to dry. When dry, lay each piece on the board, rub with a little flour and roll up to form a tube. Then cut off in ⅛ inch slices which will make ribbons and pile up loosely on a flat dish to dry. Cook in boiling salted water 15 to 18 minutes, drain well and sauté in butter or prepare according to any spaghetti or macaroni recipe.

MACARONI OR SPAGHETTI POLONAISE

1½ *lbs. spaghetti or macaroni*
2 *tablespoons butter*
2 *tablespoons heavy cream*
2 *teaspoons salt*
a little pepper
2 *chopped hard-boiled eggs*

1 *teaspoon chopped parsley*
2 *tablespoons grated Parmesan*
cheese
2 *tablespoons browned butter*
(page 32)
1 *tablespoon fresh bread crumbs*

Cook macaroni or spaghetti in boiling salted water 12 to 18 minutes or until done. Drain well. Melt butter in saucepan, add spaghetti and toss and shake until well mixed. Add cream, salt and pepper and mix well. Place in serving dish and sprinkle with hard-boiled eggs and with parsley and grated cheese. Add bread crumbs to brown butter, spread over the top, and place dish under broiler to brown the top. Serves 6·

SPAGHETTI OR MACARONI WITH
TOMATO SAUCE AND CHEESE

Cook spaghetti or macaroni in boiling salted water 12 to 18 minutes or until done. Drain well. Melt a little butter in a saucepan, add spaghetti and shake and toss until well mixed. Serve with Tomato Sauce (page 31) to which has been added several fresh tomatoes, skinned, seeded and chopped and sprinkled with grated Parmesan cheese.

SPAGHETTI OR MACARONI AU GRATIN

1 *lb. spaghetti or macaroni*	*½ cup cream (or top milk)*
3 *tablespoons butter*	4 *tablespoons grated Parmesan*
1 *teaspoon salt*	*cheese*

Cook spaghetti or macaroni in boiling salted water 12 to 18 minutes or until done. Drain well. Melt butter in saucepan, add spaghetti and shake and toss until well mixed. Add salt, pepper and cream (or top milk), bring to a boil and cook until reduced to one-third the original quantity. Add 2 tablespoons cheese, mix well and place in baking dish. Sprinkle with other 2 tablespoons cheese, a little melted butter and place under broiler to brown the top. Serves 4 to 5.

SPAGHETTI A LA BORDELAISE

1 *lb. spaghetti*	*a little pepper*
4 *tablespoons butter*	1 *teaspoon salt*
2 *shallots*	*½ teaspoon parsley*
½ glass white wine (optional)	4 *tablespoons grated Parmesan or*
6 *tomatoes, peeled, seeded, and*	*Swiss cheese*
chopped	*½ cup tomato purée*

Cook spaghetti in boiling salted water 12 to 18 minutes or until done. Drain well. Melt 2 tablespoons butter in a saucepan and sauté the spaghetti in it. In another pan melt 2 tablespoons butter, add shallots, wine, and tomatoes, tomato purée, salt and pepper. Cook until reduced to one-half the original quantity. Place spaghetti in serving dish, pour the sauce over and sprinkle with parsley and one-half the grated cheese. Serve remaining cheese separately. Serves 4 to 5.

VERMICELLI A LA BOURBONNAISE

2 *tablespoons butter*	2 *cups vermicelli*
4 *medium mushrooms, thinly sliced*	3 *cups chicken broth*

Melt butter, add mushrooms and let mushrooms cook in it over a low heat for a few minutes. Add vermicelli, mix well with the butter and cook until it turns golden. Add boiling chicken broth and cook 6 to 8 minutes. Correct the seasoning and serve plain or with chicken dishes.

Bread, Rolls and Pastry

 ⟨⫿ ✳ ⫿⟩

Bread and Rolls

THE French are certainly the world's greatest bread lovers, but except in the farming sections far removed from any town very few people make their own bread. Our bread, the typical, crispy, crusted type known here as "French" bread, was baked in very long loaves or large rings and the baker cut off as much as we wanted or sold the whole loaf. A darker bread made of mixed white and rye flour was baked in big round loaves. It was very flavorful and kept soft longer than white bread. All the flour was ground and refined in local flour mills and the leavening was a piece of dough saved from the previous baking to be the raiser for the next one.

Handling yeast doughs, the combined process of mixing, kneading and baking them is, I think, a special kind of skill. Success does not always follow first attempts but perfection invariably comes after continued practice. It is one of the cookery skills that you do well only after you have acquired the "feel" of it. For example, flours vary considerably so you have to know the "feel" of the dough when the right amount has been added, just as you must learn the smooth and elastic "feel" of a dough that is kneaded sufficiently, and as you must recognize the "feel" of lightness when it has risen enough. But to be able to make really good bread, rolls and sweet doughs is, to my way of thinking, not only a great satisfaction but a feat to be proud of as well.

FRENCH BREAD

½ cup milk	1½ teaspoons salt
1¼ cups water	1½ yeast cakes
1 tablespoon sugar	¼ cup lukewarm water
1 tablespoon butter (or other shortening)	5 cups flour

Mix yeast with lukewarm water. Heat milk and water until lukewarm and add butter (or shortening), sugar and salt. When butter is melted add yeast and water mixture, then mix in the flour. Knead until dough is smooth and does not stick to the hands. Place in a bowl, cover and let rise in a warm place until double in bulk, about 2 hours. If the dough falls when touched lightly with the fingers it has risen enough. Punch down, let rise another 45 minutes, then knead again. Divide in 3 parts and shape into loaves (long cylinders about 1½ inches in diameter) or make into 24 rolls and place on greased baking sheet. Cover and let rise until double in bulk. Cut small diagonal slits about ¼ inch deep in top of loaves when half risen. Before baking brush with a little milk. Bake in a hot oven of 450 degrees until done.

ROLLS

To make rolls, follow recipe above and after the second kneading divide dough into 2 even portions and then cut each into 12 pieces. Roll each piece into a round ball and then shape into a cylinder with pointed ends. Place on a greased baking sheet, cover with a towel and set in a warm (not hot) place to rise until double in bulk, about 25 to 45 minutes depending on the temperature of the room. When half risen make 2 or 3 slits about ¼ inch deep on top of each one. Before baking brush with a little milk. Bake in a hot oven of 450 degrees about 12 minutes or until brown.

BRIOCHE

Brioche is one of the favorite breadstuffs of France, eaten everywhere and by everyone. Some housewives make their own brioche at home, others buy it either at the *boulangerie*—the bakery, or at the *pâtisserie*—pastry shop, where a richer kind is sold.

As compared with bread dough, brioche is very light and very rich, containing much butter and many eggs. It is never kneaded as much as bread dough, only until it has a good elastic consistency. Brioche is best if mixed the night before and allowed to stand 8 to 10 hours before it is baked. Brioche is baked in a very hot oven because it must rise quickly and take on a good brown color and crusty exterior while the center remains soft.

4 *cups flour*	½ *cup milk*
1 *cake yeast*	6 *eggs, slightly beaten*
1 *teaspoon salt*	1 *cup butter*
1 *tablespoon sugar*	¼ *cup warm water*

Sift flour into a bowl or in a mound on a pastry board. Remove 1 cup. Soften yeast in warm water and mix with the cup of flour. Form in a ball, put in a bowl, cut a cross on the top, cover and put in a warm place to rise. Meanwhile add salt and sugar to remaining flour. Work the butter to remove all water. Make a well in center of flour and put in eggs and butter. Using the hands work the flour gradually into the eggs and butter until all is well combined. Add milk, little by little. (It may take less than ½ cup to make a dough that should be a little softer than bread dough.) Add the raiser (that is the yeast and flour) and mix all together well. Form into a ball, place in a large bowl, sprinkle lightly with flour, cover with a towel and leave at room temperature about 1 to 2 hours. Punch down the dough and leave in refrigerator or cold place overnight or until ready to use. When ready to use shape as desired—in a mold, or a ring, or a loaf—and leave in a warm place 15 to 30 minutes or until raised about ⅓ more in bulk. Brush with beaten egg mixed with a little milk. Bake in a hot oven of 450 degrees 10 to 20 minutes, depending upon the size, or until brown. When done, a small pointed knife inserted in center will come out clean. Makes 2 rings or loaves or 18 to 24 individual brioche.

PLAIN BRIOCHE
(Brioche Ordinaire)

For a simple brioche follow brioche recipe using 4 eggs and ⅔ cup butter and replace milk with water.

RICH BRIOCHE
(Brioche Riche)

For a rich brioche follow brioche recipe using 8 eggs and 1½ cups butter.

BABA
(Pâte à Baba)

2 cups flour
⅔ cup butter
1 cake yeast
½ teaspoon salt
1 tablespoon sugar

½ cup lukewarm milk
4 eggs, slightly beaten
1 tablespoon sultana raisins
1 tablespoon currants

Sift flour. Dissolve yeast in lukewarm milk and add to flour. Add eggs and work all together until dough is elastic. Work butter to remove all water and divide in small pieces, then mix with dough. The dough should be a little softer than brioche dough. Cover and put in a warm place to rise until it has doubled in bulk. Work dough again adding salt, sugar, raisins and currants. Put in well-buttered molds but do not fill more than ⅔ full. Put in a warm place (not hot) and let rise until it just fills the mold. Bake in a moderately hot oven of 400 to 425 degrees about 12 to 15 minutes or until brown. Invert mold and turn out Baba. While still warm pour a light syrup (page 297) over and sprinkle with rum or Kirsch. Makes 12 individual Babas.

SAVARIN

Follow recipe (above) for Baba, omitting raisins and currants and baking it in a ring mold. Serve with a macedoine of cooked fruit thickened with Apricot Sauce (page 276) in the center of the ring of Baba.

CROISSANTS

Croissants—like a few other recipes in this book—are not distinctly French home cooking. They are fussy to make and so in French homes it was usually more convenient, more practical and not unduly expensive to purchase them at the *pâtisserie* where every pastry cook made them beautifully. But I know there will be many disappointed readers if I don't include in this book the recipe for these light, flaky rolls. As you will see, they are made in the same way that Puff Paste is made and have that same delicate flakiness. The difference is that Croissants are raised with yeast.

4 *cups flour*	1 *tablespoon sugar*
2 *yeast cakes*	1½ *cups milk*
½ *teaspoon salt*	¾ *lb. butter*
¼ *cup lukewarm water*	

Sift flour in a mound on the board. Remove 1 cup. Dissolve yeast in lukewarm water and mix with the cup of flour. Form into a ball, cut a cross in the top, cover and put in a warm (not hot) place to rise. Meanwhile add salt and sugar to remaining flour and mix in the milk, stirring and working it on the board to make a smooth dough. Add the raiser (that is the flour and yeast). Cover with a towel and let stand 15 minutes. Roll out in a sheet about ½ inch thick. Work the butter to remove all water that is in it. Spread butter on top of dough. Fold ⅓ of the dough over the center third and then fold the remaining third on top to make three layers. Turn folded dough so that open end faces you. Roll out and fold over again as before. This is called 2 turns. Put in a cold place for several hours or overnight. When ready to use, roll out and fold, then repeat this operation, that is, make 2 more turns. Return to cold place for ½ to 1 hour. Cut dough in 24 pieces and roll out each piece to make a triangle about ⅛ to ¼ inch thick. Starting with the broad side of the triangle roll up each piece and turn the ends toward each other to form a crescent with the pointed end of the triangle on top. Place on a baking sheet, cover and let rise in a warm place about ½ hour or until double in bulk. Brush with milk and bake in a moderate oven of 350 to 375 degrees until brown. Makes 24 croissants.

PATE A GOUGLOFF

Pâte à Gougloff is a sweet yeast cake that is between a Brioche and a Baba in richness and flavor. It is of Alsatian origin and very popular in France for afternoon tea. Pâte à Gougloff always has raisins in it, is always baked in a round pan with a tube in the center similar to the one used here for baking sponge and angel food cakes and we always liked to eat this cake the same day it was made.

2 cups flour	¼ lb. large raisins
⅓ cup butter	½ teaspoon salt
1½ tablespoons powdered sugar	2 eggs
1 cake yeast	1 cup milk
¼ cup lukewarm water	chopped almonds

Mix yeast and lukewarm water in a warm bowl. Add ½ cup of the flour to the yeast mixture to make the raiser. Sift remaining flour over the top. Put in a warm place until the raiser rises up through the dry flour. Then mix all together well. Add eggs one at a time, then the milk and mix all together. Work dough until it is elastic. Cream butter, add salt and sugar and combine with the dough. Add raisins. Put in a tube pan 8 to 9 inches in diameter which has been buttered and sprinkled with chopped almonds and with the bottom decorated with half almonds. Leave in a warm place to rise until pan is almost full. Bake in a hot oven 400 to 425 degrees about 40 to 45 minutes.

Pastry

The French speak of the various kinds of pastries as *"pâtes"* and include not only pie and tart pastry but also cream puff—or éclair—paste, fritter batter and so on. The word *"pâte,"* incidentally is a one syllable word—rhymes with "cat"—and should not be confused with "pâté," the two-syllable word that rhymes with "Cathay" and which refers to a finely minced meat mixture cooked in a loaf. The expression *"Pâte a pâté,"* therefore, means the pastry crust used around a pâté mixture.

Different *pâtes*—or pastries—are used for different fillings, not the same pastry for all pies and tarts as is usual in this country. For example, a tart with apple sauce, or other very wet fruit, like Gâteau Normand was made with "sweet pastry" which does not absorb as much moisture as the other kind; open tarts were usually made with regular tart pastry. But double crust fruit pies, called *"tourtes,"* had a special pastry, and meat pie still another kind.

Puff Paste, the pride of every French pastry cook, the pastry which puffs up to an unbelievably delicate, flaky lightness, has almost as many uses as it has flaky layers. Puff paste patties—*bouchées* in French—and oversized patties called *Vol-au-Vents* are filled with richly sauced meats and fish and served as an entrée, especially at parties; tarts and many fancy petits fours made with puff paste are for dessert. In addition, puff paste trimmings are always carefully saved and rerolled to make the edges of tarts and gâteaux that have thick, moist fillings, the bases of which are made of tart pastry that will not crush and become heavy under the weight of the filling.

The small individual round tarts so familiar here were not as common in my home as large oblong ones. Mother's tarts were about 12 to 15 inches long and 4 to 5 inches wide and for serving she cut them across into 2 or 3 inch pieces, a very practical way of making the open fruit tarts that we liked so well.

CREAM PUFFS OR ECLAIRS
(Pâte à Choux)

1 *cup water*	1 *teaspoon sugar*
½ *cup butter*	1 *cup flour*
¼ *teaspoon salt*	4 *eggs*

[225]

Put water, butter, salt and sugar in saucepan and bring to a boil. Remove from heat and add flour. Return to fire and cook, stirring briskly, until mixture rolls away from sides of pan without sticking. Add eggs one at a time, mixing well after each addition. Drop by spoonfuls (or through a pastry bag) on a greased baking sheet to make either large or small puffs or to shape for éclairs of any desired size. Bake in a moderately hot oven of 400 degrees about 15 minutes or until very light and golden brown. The time required will depend upon the size of the puff or éclair.

FRITTER BATTER FOR ENTREES
(Pâte à Frire)

1 *cup flour*	¾ *cup warm water*
pinch of salt	1 *egg yolk*
1 *tablespoon olive* (*or salad*) *oil*	1 *egg white, stiffly beaten*

Sift flour into a warm bowl, make a well in the center and add salt, oil and water. Mix all together quickly and thoroughly. Do not overmix or it will make a tough fritter. The batter should be rather thick. Cover and leave in a warm place 3 to 4 hours. When ready to use fold in the beaten egg white.

PASTRY FOR FRUIT PIES
(Pâte à Tourte)

2 *cups flour*	1 *teaspoon salt*
4 *tablespoons butter*	*cold water* (*about* 6 *tablespoons*)
6 *tablespoons lard*	

Mix butter and lard with flour using the hand, a pastry blender or a fork. Add water gradually, using just enough to make a dough that is quite firm. Do not work the dough. Use for fruit pies with two crusts.

PASTRY FOR MEAT PIES
(Pâte à Pâté)

2 *cups flour*	1 *egg*
4 *tablespoons butter*	½ *teaspoon salt*
4 *tablespoons lard*	*cold water* (*about* 6 *tablespoons*)

Mix as for Tart Pastry (page 228). Use for meat pies and pâtés that are enclosed in a crust.

CRUST FOR PATTIES OR VOL-AU-VENT
Roll Puff Paste (below) about ⅛ inch thick and using a sharp knife cut a circle the desired size. A plate placed on top of the pastry can

be a guide in cutting. Place top side down on a baking sheet moistened with water. Cut another circle of pastry and then cut out the center of it with a smaller plate as a guide in order to make a ring about 1 inch wide. Moisten the edge of the first circle with water and lay the ring, top side down, on it. Press gently to make sure the ring adheres to the base. Make tiny cuts ½ inch apart around the edge to form little scallops all around the edge. Leave in refrigerator about 10 minutes. Brush top of ring (but never the outside edge) with a little beaten egg and milk. Bake in a hot oven of 425 to 450 degrees 15 to 25 minutes, depending on the size or until it rises and is golden brown. Using a sharp knife cut around the inside of the rim and remove the top crusty part for the cover. At this time remove from the center any dough that is not thoroughly cooked. Place on serving dish. Fill with any desired Vol-au-Vent mixture and place cover on top. Usually the Vol-au-Vent crust is made ahead of time and then reheated just before it is filled and served.

For small patties roll the pastry ⅓ inch thick and cut in small circles with a scalloped cookie cutter. Place top side down on a baking sheet moistened with water. Brush tops with a little beaten egg mixed with milk. Using a sharp knife cut a circle at least half way into the dough and about ½ inch from the edge or press half way down with a sharp cookie cutter that is ½ inch smaller than the patty. Leave in refrigerator 10 minutes. Bake in a hot oven of 425 to 450 degrees 10 to 12 minutes or until they rise and are golden brown. Cut out the center section which had been previously scored with knife or cookie cutter and reserve for the covers. Remove any dough from the center that is not thoroughly cooked. Fill with any desired sauced mixture and place covers on top. Usually the patties are made ahead of time and then reheated just before filling and serving.

PUFF PASTE
(Feuilletage)

4 *cups flour*	1¼ *cups water*
1 *teaspoon salt*	1 *lb. butter*

Sift flour in a bowl or in a mound on a board. Add salt and water ⁓ixing as little as possible in combining it. It must never be worked. ₔf dough is stiff, add a little more water. Roll out about 1 inch thick. Work butter to remove all water, and then place the piece of butter in the center of the dough. Fold ⅓ the dough over the center third, covering the butter. Then fold the other third on top to make 3 layers. Now fold ⅓ of the oblong that has been formed over the center third and the remaining third on top, making 3 more layers and forming a square. Leave in a cold place about 20 to 25 minutes. Roll out in an oblong about ½ inch thick and 20 inches long. Fold in thirds as already described and turn dough around so that end faces you. Rolling, folding and turning in this manner is called a "turn." Make another turn and put in a cold place for 20 to 25 minutes. Make 2 more turns and chill again. Repeat, making 6 turns in all. Keep in a refrigerator 15 minutes or until ready to use. This pastry may be kept several days in the refrigerator if desired but in this case the last two turns are not made until the time of using.

PASTRY FOR TARTS
(Pâte à Flan)

2 *cups flour*	½ *teaspoon salt*
½ *cup butter*	1 *tablespoon sugar*
1 *small egg*	*cold water* (*about 4 to 5 tablespoons*)

Cream butter and add salt, sugar and egg. Mix in the flour, using the hands or a pastry blender or a fork. Add water gradually, using just enough to make a dough that is quite firm. Do not work the dough, just mix it well. Use for the lower crust of fruit tarts.

SWEET PASTRY
(Pâte Sucrée)

This has an entirely different texture from any of the flaky types of pastry. It contains an egg but no water—or very little—and this makes it extra short, while the sugar in the mixture adds a bit of sweetness. It is used for Petits Fours, usually with jelly or marmalade and for tarts or gâteaux using apple sauce or other moist fruits because it doesn't absorb moisture from the fruit and become soggy as quickly as some other types of pastry do.

1 *cup flour*	*pinch salt*
¼ *cup butter, creamed*	1 *egg*
¼ *cup sugar*	

Sift flour and make a well in the center of it. Put in the remaining ingredients and mix them all together, gradually adding the flour until all is thoroughly combined. A few drops of water may be added if mixture is too stiff to roll. Let stand 2 to 3 hours in a cool place. When ready to use roll out about ⅛ inch thick.

GALETTES

A galette is a kind of pastry seldom seen in this country. It is actually a plain sheet of pastry, not quite as flaky as Puff Paste, not quite as plain as tart paste. It might be called a simple sort of Puff Paste in that it has a light, delicate flakiness but at the same time has its own special crispness. It is rich with butter or other shortening, is baked to an appetizing golden brown but is not sweet because it has no filling like a tart or a gâteau. It is always baked in a large shallow round or square pan and cut in squares or pie-shaped wedges and served warm or cold. Then we spread it with one of our favorite confitures such as Apricot Marmalade or Currant Jelly.

GALETTE DE PLOMB MENAGERE

2 *cups flour*	½ *cup butter*
pinch salt	1 *egg*
1 *teaspoon sugar*	1 *egg yolk*
2 *tablespoons milk*	

Sift flour on a board, make a well in the center and put salt, sugar, butter, egg, egg yolk and milk in it. Using the hands, work these ingredients together and gradually mix in the flour until well combined and dough is smooth. Form into ball and wrap in a towel. Let stand 2 hours in a cold place. Roll out about ¾ to 1 inch thick in a round, oblong or square shape. Place on a buttered baking sheet. Brush with beaten egg mixed with a little milk. Prick top with a fork or small pointed knife to form a design. Bake in a medium hot oven of 400 to 425 degrees 20 to 25 minutes or until brown. Serve warm or cold and cut in serving pieces at the table.

GALETTE DES ROIS

A special galette was called "*Galette des Rois.*" In it a tiny metal doll—or almond or other symbol of the Infant—was hidden. The one at the table who found this symbol in his piece of galette was the king (or queen) of the festivities and could choose his own queen (or king) to lead the games at any Twelfth Night Party.

2 *cups flour*	*pinch of salt*
¾ *cup butter*	¾ *cup water*

Sift flour into a bowl or in a mound on a board. Make a well in the center and put salt, butter and water in it. Using the hands, work butter and water together and gradually, yet quickly, mix in the flour. Work it as little as possible. Make into a ball and let stand 1 hour in a cold place. Roll out like Puff Paste (page 227), making 4 turns in all and letting it stand 20 minutes in a cold place between each turn. Let stand 15 minutes. Press doll or almond into the dough and roll about ½ inch thick in a round, oblong or square shape. Place on a buttered baking sheet and brush top with beaten egg mixed with a little milk. Prick top with a fork or small pointed knife to form a design. Let stand 10 minutes, then bake in a hot oven of 450 degrees 20 to 25 minutes or until brown. Serve either warm or cold and cut in serving pieces at the table.

GALETTE DE MENAGE AUX POMMES

3 *cups flour*	1 *cup water*
½ *teaspoon salt*	1 *cup diced raw, peeled apples*
1 *cup butter (or half butter and half other shortening)*	

Sift flour on board. Make a well in the center and put salt, butter and water in it. Using the hands, work these ingredients together, mixing in the flour gradually. Continue mixing until the dough is smooth, then mix in the apples. Form in a ball, put in a bowl covered with a towel and let stand in a cool place about 1 hour. Roll about ½ inch thick, then fold and roll out, making 2 turns as in making Puff Paste (page 227), letting it stand 15 minutes between each turn. Roll out about ½ inch thick in a round, oblong or square shape. Or roll the dough out into a long strip, roll up from the long side to form a long, thin cylinder and join the ends to form a ring. Place on buttered baking sheet and brush top with beaten egg mixed with a little milk. Mark the top with a fork or small pointed knife to form a design (or cut openings in the top of the ring with scissors). Bake in a moderately hot oven of 400 degrees about 45 minutes or until brown and apple is cooked. Serve warm or cold.

LITTLE SALTY GALETTES
(Petites Galettes Salées)

2 *cups flour*	1 *tablespoon sugar*
½ *cup butter*	1 *teaspoon salt*
½ *cup milk*	

Mix ingredients following directions for other galettes. Form into a ball, wrap in a towel and let stand in a cool place 1 hour. Roll about ⅜ inch thick and cut with a cookie cutter about 1½ inches in diameter. Place on a greased baking sheet, brush with salted milk and bake in a hot oven of 425 to 450 degrees about 8 to 10 minutes. Makes 40 to 50 galettes.

GALETTE MENAGERE AUX LARDONS

Follow the recipe for Galette aux Pommes omitting the apples and using only ½ cup butter. Add 1 cup fried lardons which are the little pieces of fat pork left in the kettle when making lard. Serve this galette while still warm.

Pastry Creams

Pastry creams include all the cream fillings used in making various kinds of pastry desserts. Some of these creamy mixtures such as *Crème Pâtissière* are also the foundations for many other desserts or, as we call them, *entremets*. Since most of these creams contain eggs it is important to know how to handle eggs when adding them to hot mixtures. You can't just stir them in as you do many other ingredients because when eggs are added directly to a hot liquid they will curdle. Nor can you allow the mixture to boil after eggs are added because that, too, will cause them to curdle. (If the mixture contains a thickening such as flour or cornstarch it can be boiled for a minute or two.) The following simple procedure will insure the desired smooth, delicate texture: add some of the hot liquid to the beaten eggs, stirring vigorously all the time, in order to thin them out a little and heat them up at the same time. Then turn this back into the hot mixture and stir constantly until boiling point is reached. Do not allow to boil. Remove from heat and pour immediately into a cold bowl and cool quickly. The quicker a pastry cream cools the better, and an occasional stirring will prevent a thin crust from forming on top.

CREME PATISSIERE

¾ cup sugar
5-6 egg yolks
⅓ cup flour

2 cups milk
1 piece vanilla bean (or extract)
pinch salt

Mix together sugar and egg yolks and work up with a spoon until the mixture is creamy and light colored. Add flour and mix just enough to combine it but don't work it up. Scald milk and vanilla bean. Add to egg yolk mixture, little by little, and stir until well combined. Turn mixture back into saucepan and cook, stirring vigorously, until it comes back to boiling point. Boil about 2 minutes. Remove vanilla bean (or add extract to taste). Strain and let cool, stirring occasionally, to prevent a crust from forming on top.

MOCHA CREAM
(Crème Cuite au Café)

Follow directions for Crème Pâtissière (page 231), flavoring the milk by following the directions for Mocha Crème au Beurre (below).

CHOCOLATE CREAM
(Crème Cuite au Chocolat)

Follow directions for Crème Pâtissière (page 231), adding 2 ounces unsweetened chocolate to the milk when it is scalded.

BUTTER CREAM
(Crème au Beurre)

Make one half the recipe for Crème Pâtissière (page 231). Work up ½ to ¾ cup sweet butter with a whip until it is creamy. Combine with cold Crème Pâtissière mixing it into the butter little by little. Add 1 tablespoon powdered sugar.

CHOCOLATE BUTTER CREAM
(Crème au Beurre au Chocolat)

Add melted chocolate to taste to Crème au Beurre (above).

MOCHA BUTTER CREAM
(Crème au Beurre au Café)

Prepare the milk for the Crème Pâtissière as follows: put 2 tablespoons coffee beans in a pan in a hot oven for a few minutes. When hot, crush coarsely and add to the milk, bring to a boil and strain it through cheesecloth. Using this coffee-flavored milk, follow Crème Pâtissière recipe (page 231). Or add coffee essence to taste to Crème au Beurre (above).

CREME ST. HONORE

This pastry cream is often called "Choux à la Crème" because it is the special cream that is used as a filling for Cream Puffs, as well as in making the famous Gâteau St. Honoré.

Combine Crème Pâtissière (page 231) and stiffly beaten egg whites, using twice as many whites as there are egg yolks in the Crème Pâtissière and folding them in when the crème is cold.

CREME BOURDALOUE

¾ *cup sugar*	2 *cups almond milk* (*below*)
1 *egg*	2 *tablespoons butter*
2 *egg yolks*	½ *pony kirsch* (*optional*)
3 *tablespoons rice flour*	

Mix together sugar, eggs and egg yolks. Add flour and combine. Scald almond milk, then add it little by little to egg mixture. Return to saucepan and cook stirring constantly until it boils. Boil about 2 minutes. Remove from fire, add butter and kirsch. Cool, stirring occasionally.

Almond Milk: blanch ⅓ lb. shelled almonds, remove skins and dry very thoroughly. Crush or run through food chopper. Add 1½ cups water very gradually, crushing almonds in the water until the liquid becomes milky colored and almond flavored. Strain through cheesecloth. Or almond milk can be made by using ¼ cup almond paste instead of the blanched almonds if that is more convenient, adding the water gradually to the paste as above. Almond milk made the latter way will not be as white as if made with blanched almonds.

WHIPPED CREAM
(Crème Fouettée)

When heavy cream is not obtainable a lighter cream can be used if done as follows: put cream in a well-chilled bowl and whip until it is light and foamy. Put in refrigerator and let stand for several hours. Skim off the top lighter whipped part from the milk that settles in the bottom of bowl and put in another well-chilled bowl. Whip this until it reaches the desired stiffness.

CREME FRANGIPANE

⅓ *cup flour*	1 *piece vanilla bean* (*or a little*
¾ *cup sugar*	*extract*)
pinch of salt	2 *tablespoons butter*
2 *eggs*	3-4 *crushed macaroons* (*or 2 table-*
2 *egg yolks*	*spoons almond paste*)
2 *cups milk*	

Mix together sugar, flour and salt. Add one egg and one yolk and when combined add remaining egg and yolk. Scald milk and vanilla

[233]

bean, then add, little by little, to egg mixture. Stir until combined, return to saucepan and cook, stirring vigorously, until it comes back to boiling point. Boil about 2 minutes. Remove from fire, take out vanilla bean (or add extract) and add butter and crushed macaroons (or almond paste). Cool, stirring occasionally to prevent crust from forming on top.

SWEETENED WHIPPED CREAM
(Crème Chantilly)

Add vanilla-flavored powdered sugar to taste to whipped cream, taking care not to mix it too much or it will fall and lose its lightness.

Gateaux

Gâteaux are large fancy cakes, or large fancy tarts, or cakes or tarts combined with pastry fillings, bavaroise mixtures and garnishings of whipped cream or fruit. Sometimes small cream puffs or an edge made of cream puff paste form the border of a gâteau.

We never thought of gâteaux as everyday desserts, or a casual sort of entremet but as a dish to serve on special occasions even though the gâteau itself might be one of the simpler, plainer ones. As a rule the French buy gâteaux at the neighborhood pastry shop. Every small town would have a pastry shop. Larger towns often boasted several and all with pastry cooks well trained in the arts of baking and fine decorating. You could put in your order for whatever you might like—no matter how elaborate your demands—and rest assured that it would taste as delectable as it always looked.

Smaller cakes, variously called *Petits Gâteaux, Petits Fours, Friandises* and *Gourmandises,* are as their name implies small editions of large gâteaux and include individual tarts and decorated cakes, the kind you see when you ask a waiter for French pastry. Petits Fours are the tiny tidbits that are served with entremets, with frozen desserts and with a cup of tea in the afternoon. Some of them are quite rich, very fancy and elaborately hand decorated, others are merely little dry sweet cookies. *Friandise* and *Gourmandise* are the fanciest kinds of *Petits Fours.*

The only kind of small cakes that the average French homemaker

[234]

bakes herself are simple little cookies and occasionally simple Petits Gâteaux such as individual tarts or one of the plainer cakes made into individual portions. Anything elaborate is purchased at the *pâtisserie.* Although I know they are not typical of French home cooking, I am including recipes for many of these because I think there are many Americans who do not have a French *pâtisserie* in the neighborhood, who like to try their hands at all kinds of baking and who would be disappointed if these small cakes were omitted.

ALMOND TART
(Dartois or Gâteaux d'Amande)

Roll Puff Paste (page 227) ⅛ inch thick and cut in a circle, using a plate for a guide. Place on a baking sheet that has been moistened with water. Prepare Almond Cream by mixing together ½ cup almond paste with 1 cup Crème Pâtissière (page 231). Spread ½ to ¾ inch thick on pastry. Cover with another layer of Puff Paste after first moistening lower edge with water to seal top and bottom together. Press firmly all around with the thumb and then make small cuts one half inch apart to make a scalloped edge. Brush top with beaten egg mixed with a little milk. Using a sharp pointed knife prick the top, making a design. Let stand 5 to 10 minutes in a cold place. Bake in a hot oven of 450 degrees until pastry has puffed and started to become crusty, then reduce heat to 400 degrees, baking 25 to 30 minutes in all or until tart is brown. A few minutes before done sprinkle a little powdered sugar over the top so that it will carmelize during the final cooking. May also be made in an oblong shape.

GATEAU ST. HONORE

Roll tart pastry (page 228) and cut in a circle about ¼ inch thick, using a plate as a guide. Then form an edge of Cream Puff paste (page 225) about the thickness of the thumb all around the circle. Brush top of Cream Puff Paste with beaten egg mixed with a little milk. Bake in a moderately hot oven of 400 to 425 degrees about 25 to 30 minutes or until this edge has puffed and the whole tart is brown. Meanwhile make some small puffs by dropping on a baking sheet Cream Puff paste in balls about the size of a large walnut; brush tops with the beaten egg and milk and bake in a moderately hot oven of 400 degrees until they are puffed and brown. When small puffs are cold, fill with Crème Pâtissière or whipped cream. Mix 1 cup sugar with water and cook until caramelized (page 297). Dip small filled puffs in this and arrange puffs on edge, adhering them with the caramel. Fill center of tart with either whipped cream or the following Crème St. Honoré:

CREME ST. HONORE

3 *cups Créme Pâtissière* (page 231)
6 *egg whites*
3 *tablespoons sugar*

1 *tablespoon gelatin*
2 *tablespoons cold water*

Soften gelatin in water and add to *Crème Pâtissière* while it is still hot. Beat egg whites until stiff, adding sugar during last few minutes of beating. Fold egg whites into crème. Decorate with some of the crème forced through a pastry bag with a fancy tube. If desired garnish the top of small puffs with candied cherries.

GENOISE CAKE
(Pâte à Génoise)

Génoise cake is the basis of many *Gâteaux* and *Petits Fours* which are cakes of the French type. The batter for Génoise cake is poured into a shallow pan usually to a thickness of about 1 inch. This makes a layer that can be split and filled with jam, jelly, or one of the various pastry creams, or the layer can be covered with a molded Bavaroise and decorated with whipped cream or fruit. For *Petits Fours* the layer is cut in small shapes and iced and decorated. Génoise cake is also the foundation for special anniversary and birthday cakes. In making them as many layers as desired are put together with jam or *Crème Pâtissière* or Butter Cream between the layers and then the top and sides finished with a fondant icing.

Génoise cake must be removed from the pan as soon as it is done and put on a cake rack to cool. It is too fine textured and close grained to cool in the pan which will make it sweat and develop a moist and heavy texture.

1 *cup sugar*
6 *eggs*
1 *cup flour*
¼ *cup melted butter*

flavoring optional, either the grated rind of ½ lemon, ½ teaspoon vanilla or seeds from vanilla bean

Beat sugar, flavoring and egg together with a whip in the top of a double boiler until mixture is lukewarm and light and fluffy. Remove from heat and beat until cold. Add the flour by sprinkling it lightly over the surface of the mixture and then folding it in gently with a

[236]

spatula. Continue folding the mixture very lightly until thoroughly combined. Add butter slowly, folding it in carefully. Butter a shallow pan and dust with flour. Pour in the batter to a thickness of about 1 inch. Bake in a moderate oven of 350 degrees 40 to 45 minutes. Remove from pan when done and cool on a wire rack. Makes 2 round 8 to 9 inch layers.

RAISIN CAKE
(Gâteau de Fruits)

1 *cup butter*	½ *cup currants*
1 *cup granulated sugar*	½ *cup sultana raisins*
2 *cups flour*	½ *cup candied cherries*
½ *teaspoon baking powder*	¼ *cup rum*
5 *eggs*	*grated rind* 1 *lemon*

Cream butter and sugar together. Add eggs one at a time, beating in well after each addition. Sift together flour and baking powder and fold into mixture lightly and carefully. Clean currants and raisins, mix with cherries and rum and fold into mixture. Line two loaf pans with paper, butter them and fill two thirds full. Bake in a slow oven of 300 degrees about 1¼ hours or until cakes are golden brown and shrink from the sides of the pan.

SPONGE CAKE RING
(Biscuit en Moule)

Follow recipe for Lady Fingers (page 242). Fill a ring mold that has been buttered and then dusted with flour two thirds full. Bake in a slow oven of 325 degrees, 40 to 45 minutes or until brown. Or bake in shallow round layer cake pans, and when layers are cold, put together with filling of any desired pastry cream.

SPONGE CAKE ROLL
(Biscuit Roulé)

½ *cup sugar*	3 *egg whites*
⅔ *cup flour*	2 *tablespoons melted butter*
4 *egg yolks*	

Combine egg yolks and sugar and work up with a wooden spoon until mixture is very light and "ribbons" when it runs off the spoon. Sift flour over the surface a little at a time and fold it carefully into the mixture. Beat whites until stiff but not dry and fold them in. Fold in melted butter slowly and carefully. Line a large shallow pan with paper, butter it and spread batter about ⅛ inch thick. Bake in a hot oven of 400 degrees, about 8 to 9 minutes. When done, invert on a table and remove paper. When cool spread with jelly or marmalade or a pastry cream and roll up. Makes 2 rolls.

May be cut in thirds and made into a layer cake with jelly, marmalade or pastry cream between the layers.

Gaufres

Trace French cookery through the years and you will find certain specialties such as Gaufres, appearing century after century. These thin crisp, waffle-like tidbits have been sold on the streets of French cities ever since the twelfth century. In those early days the *marchands de gaufres,* that is, the vendors who sold them, always set up business in the streets near the doors of cathedrals and churches on days of great religious festivals. There they made and sold their wares to the throngs of people coming from the mass, people whose devotions must surely have been interrupted by the drifting fragrance of gaufres sizzling outside. Gaufres are still sold in French cities but today you will find them more often in the parks where the youngsters congregate.

Gaufres are cooked in an iron called a *gaufrier* which has two flat iron plates clamped and held together by long handles. The iron plates are decorated with designs which become imprinted on the cakes and very old *gaufriers* have beautiful and interesting designs, many of which have some definite religious significance.

My mother baked a kind of gaufre on a baking sheet and rolled them on a small stick. When cold she filled them with a cream filling or whipped cream. They are called *gaufrettes,* sometimes *cigarettes.*

My favorites are Gaufres with Cream, sometimes called *Gaufres de Bruxelles,* made in an oblong iron which puts deep indentations on the cakes, much like an American waffle iron. I think an American waffle iron could be used. But for a real gaufrier, if you have nostalgia for one, seek out an importer of French cooking equipment to supply you.

GAUFRETTES OR CIGARETTES

In giving the proportions of ingredients for *gaufrettes* it is almost impossible to indicate exact measurements because the size of the egg whites and the kind of flour will affect the consistency. It is best to bake a trial one. If the finished *gaufrette* is so thin it breaks and cannot be handled, the mixture needs a little more flour. If on the other hand the *gaufrette* is thick and clumsy to roll, a little more melted butter should be added.

2 *egg whites*	3 *tablespoons butter, melted and*
½ *cup sugar*	*cooled*
vanilla extract (or seeds from bean)	⅓ *cup flour*

Beat egg whites until stiff. Sprinkle sugar over them a little at a time and fold into egg whites slowly and carefully. Add flour the same way. Add butter, also folding it in carefully. Butter and flour a baking sheet and put into a hot oven of 450 to 475 degrees until pan is hot. Drop batter by tablespoons on the hot pan, spreading it as thinly as possible. Bake in a hot oven of 450 to 475 degrees a few minutes until golden brown. When done, roll while still hot around a stick about the size of a thick pencil. When cold serve plain or filled with cream filling or whipped cream.

BATTER FOR GAUFRES
(Pâte à Gaufre)

1½ *cups flour*	1 *egg yolk*
⅔ *cup sugar*	milk (¾ *to* 1 *cup*)
4 *tablespoons butter, melted*	*vanilla extract (or seeds from bean)*
2 *eggs*	

Sift together flour and sugar. Mix together egg and egg yolk, add to flour mixture and mix until smooth. Add butter, vanilla and milk to make a thin batter. (Batter should be about the thickness of a crêpe batter.) Heat both sides of gaufrier on top of stove, then butter both sides. When butter is sizzling hot pour in a tablespoon of batter, spreading it thinly. Close the gaufrier and cook a few minutes on each side, or until golden brown. While still hot, roll around the handle of a wooden spoon or stick of similar size. Or if preferred leave them flat.

GAUFRETTES WITH CREAM
(Gaufres de Bruxelles)

These *gaufrettes* are baked in a special iron, one that is square in shape, and made with deep indentations, as contrasted with the usual flat, round gaufrier. It is in fact very much like a waffle iron. The finished *gaufrette* is both soft and crisp, is very light and exceedingly tender and delicate. The advantage of these gaufrettes over waffles is that they are served cold and so can be made up ahead of time. They are a very choice dainty for afternoon tea when something rich is desired.

1 *cup flour*	¼ *cup butter, melted and cooled*
6 *egg yolks*	*pinch of salt*
1 *tablespoon sugar*	6 *egg whites*
¼ *cup cream*	

Put all ingredients except egg whites in a bowl and mix together. Beat egg whites until stiff and carefully fold into batter. Pour into a square gaufrier with deep indentations (or a waffle iron) that has been heated and buttered. Cook on both sides until brown. Remove and cool. Fill each of the small holes with sweetened whipped cream or Crème Pâtissière (page 231). Makes 6.

Petits Fours

ALMOND COOKIES
(Milanais)

1 *cup flour*	*grated rind 1 orange (or lemon)*
⅓ *cup sugar*	1 *egg*
⅓ *cup finely ground almonds*	*pinch of salt*
⅓ *cup butter, creamed*	

Sift flour in bowl and make well in center. Put remaining ingredients in it and mix them together well with the hands or wooden spoon. Then gradually mix in flour until all is well combined. Form into a ball and wrap in a towel. Let stand 2 hours in a cool place. Roll about ¼ inch thick and cut with fancy cookie cutter. Roll out the scraps and continue cutting until all the dough is used. Place on buttered baking sheet, brush with beaten egg and decorate with almonds, candied fruit, etc. Bake in moderate oven of 375 degrees about 15 minutes or until brown.

LITTLE ALMOND COOKIES
(Amandines)

2 *cups flour*
⅔ *cup butter*
2 *eggs*
½ *cup sugar*

½ *teaspoon baking powder*
vanilla extract or grated orange rind
blanched almonds, finely chopped
beaten egg

Cream butter and sugar together, mix in flour and baking powder and then add eggs. Mix all together well and add flavoring. Form into a ball and let stand in a cold place about 1 hour. Roll out about ¼ inch thick, cut in strips 1½ inches wide and place on a greased baking sheet. Brush tops with beaten egg and sprinkle sugar and finely chopped blanched almonds, pressing them into the surface with a spatula. Score the strips every inch. Bake in a moderate oven of 375 degrees, 15 to 20 minutes. When cold break apart where they are scored, making little oblong cookies.

SMALL DRY COOKIES
(Gâteaux Secs)

2 *cups flour*
⅔ *cup sugar*
⅔ *cup butter, creamed*

2 *eggs* (*unbeaten*)
1 *tablespoon orange flower*
(*or vanilla*) *extract*

Sift flour into bowl and make a well in center. Put remaining ingredients in it and mix them together well with the hands or wooden spoon. Then gradually mix in flour until all is combined. Form into a ball and wrap in a towel. Leave in a cold place about 2 hours. Roll dough about ¼ inch thick and cut in fancy shapes with a cookie cutter. Place on baking sheet that has been moistened with a little water. Roll out the scraps and continue cutting until all the dough is used. Decorate with almonds, candied cherries, etc. Bake in a slow oven of 300 to 325 degrees about 15 minutes or until brown. Brush immediately with sweetened milk made by dissolving 2 tablespoons sugar in ½ cup hot milk. These cakes keep for several weeks.

CAT TONGUES
(Langues de Chat)

¼ *cup sugar*
¼ *cup butter*
¼ *cup flour*

2 *egg whites* (*unbeaten*)
vanilla extract

Cream butter, add sugar and a little vanilla extract and work up with

[241]

a wooden spoon until light. Add egg whites one at a time, mixing well after each addition. Sift flour, a little at a time, over the surface and carefully fold it in. Force through pastry bag with round tube on buttered and floured baking sheet, making tiny rolls about 2 inches long and as big around as a pencil. Bake in a hot oven of 450 to 475 degrees 4 to 5 minutes or until edges become golden brown. Remove from baking sheet immediately and place on unglazed paper to cool.

LADY FINGERS
(Biscuits à la Cuillère)

1 *cup sugar*	1 *cup flour*
6 *egg yolks*	1 *teaspoon orange flower*
6 *egg whites, stiffly beaten*	(*or vanilla*) *extract*

Combine sugar and egg yolks and beat with a wooden spoon until the mixture becomes white and creamy and "ribbons" when allowed to run off the spoon. Add flavoring. Sift flour over surface, a little at a time, and cut it in carefully and lightly. Fold in the stiffly beaten egg whites slowly and carefully. Force through a pastry bag, having a medium large round tube, in fingers about 2 to 3 inches long and ½ inch wide onto a piece of heavy white paper laid on a baking sheet. Sprinkle tops with a little powdered sugar. Bake in a slow oven of 325 degrees until light brown. Remove from paper while they are still warm, lifting them off with a sharp-edged spatula or knife. When cool put together in pairs.

CHOCOLATE LADY FINGERS
(Doigts de Dames au Chocolat)

Make Italian Meringue (page 244) and when done fold in 2 tablespoons cocoa mixed with 2 tablespoons sugar. Force through a pastry bag on a buttered and floured baking sheet following directions for shaping Cat Tongues (page 241). Bake in a slow oven of 250 to 300 degrees 10 to 12 minutes, leaving the oven door partly open. When done they will be a little crusty on top. Remove immediately from pan.

MACAROONS
(Massepain)

Macaroons, like many of the small cakes that the French call "*Petits Fours*," were usually purchased from a *patisserie*. I am including the recipes for macaroons and other petits fours because many people in this country may not know a place where they can be purchased and there is no reason why they cannot be made just as well at home.

½ lb. almond paste *3 to 4 egg whites*
1 cup sugar

Mix together almond paste and granulated sugar, working them until well combined. Add egg whites, one at a time, mixing well after each addition. The consistency should be such that the mixture goes easily through a pastry bag yet holds its shape without running when formed on the baking sheet and the number of egg whites used must be judged accordingly. Force through pastry bag, having a medium large round tube, onto paper laid on a baking sheet. Dampen tops with a wet towel, then sprinkle with a little confectioner's sugar. Bake in a slow oven of 300 to 325 degrees 12 to 15 minutes. To remove from paper, turn paper with macaroons clinging to it upside down immediately and brush the back of the hot paper with water. The macaroons will drop off.

MADELEINES

½ cup sugar *½ cup butter, melted*
4 eggs *½ cup flour*
vanilla (or orange flower) extract

Combine sugar and eggs and work up with a wooden spoon until mixture becomes white, has doubled in bulk and "ribbons" when it falls from the spoon. Add flavoring. Sift flour over the surface and carefully fold it in. Add butter, little by little, carefully folding it in. Fill well buttered and floured madeleine molds two-thirds full, place on baking sheet and bake in slow oven of 300 to 325 degrees 20 to 30 minutes or until golden brown. Remove from molds and invert on cake rack to cool. Makes 12.

MERINGUES

4 egg whites *1 cup powdered sugar*

Beat egg whites until stiff but not dry. Sprinkle sugar, a little at a time, over the surface and using a spatula fold slowly and carefully into the whites. Shape with a pastry bag, having a large round tube or with a spoon on a sheet of white paper laid on baking sheet, making them about the size and shape of an egg. Allow a little space between them. Sprinkle tops with a little powdered sugar. Bake in a very slow oven of 250 to 275 degrees 20 to 25 minutes or until they take on a little color. To remove from paper raise paper from baking sheet and sprinkle a little water underneath to moisten it, then lift off the meringues carefully with a spatula. Serve with ice cream or whipped cream. If stored in a box in a dry place they may be kept several weeks.

The meringue may be formed in one large ring on the paper and when ready to serve the center filled with ice cream.

ITALIAN MERINGUE

4 *egg whites*   ½ *cup water*
1 *cup sugar*   *vanilla*

Dissolve sugar in water and cook without stirring until it forms a soft ball when a little is dropped in cold water (238 degrees if the thermometer is used). Beat egg whites until stiff but not dry and pour sugar syrup in a thin thread into the whites, stirring briskly all the time. Shape in small fancy shapes with a pastry bag on white paper laid on a baking sheet, and bake in a very slow oven of 250 to 275 degrees. Remove from paper as described in Meringue recipe.

These meringues may also be made by combining all the ingredients except the water in the top of a double boiler and cooking them, beating meanwhile with an egg beater, until mixture becomes desired thickness.

PALETS DE DAMES

¼ *cup butter*   2 *tablespoons currants soaked in*
¼ *cup sugar*   1 *tablespoon rum*
⅓ *cup flour*   1 *egg*

Cream butter, add sugar and work up until light. Add egg. Beat a few minutes longer. Add flour and currants. Force through a pastry bag with a round tube onto a buttered and floured baking sheet in rounds about the size of a macaroon. Bake in hot oven of 450 to 475 degrees 5 minutes. Remove immediately from pan.

Tarts

APPLE TART
(Tartes aux Pommes)

Roll Tart Pastry (page 228) into a circle about ¼ inch thick. Place on a tart pan, shaping up the edge to make a rim about an inch high to hold in the fruit. Prick the bottom of the pastry. Spread generously with apple sauce and arrange thinly sliced raw apples on top, overlapping them in an orderly fashion. Sprinkle with powdered sugar and bake in a moderate oven of 350 to 375 degrees 35 to 40 minutes or until crust is golden brown. When done spread top with Apricot Sauce (page 276) which has been made very thin by cooking it with water or sugar syrup.

FRUIT TARTS

Follow directions for Apple Tart (above) using any desired fruit, and omitting the apple sauce. If fruit is very juicy such as plums or cherries, sprinkle the pastry with stale cake crumbs before putting in the fruit. Finish top with Apricot Sauce thinned with water or sugar syrup.

CHERRY TART, COUNTRY STYLE
(Millas aux Cerises Bourbonnaise)

3 *tablespoons flour*	1 *tablespoon sugar*
1 *egg, slightly beaten*	*pinch of salt*
½ *cup milk*	2 *cups sweet cherries*

Mix flour, egg, milk, sugar and salt to make a batter. Remove stems from cherries, wash and drain them. Put cherries in a baking dish and pour the batter over. Bake in a moderate oven of 375 degrees 40 to 45 minutes or until cherries are cooked and top is brown. Serve warm or cold. Or line a pie plate with tart pastry, forming an edge to hold in the filling. Fill with cherries, pour batter over and bake as above.

COUNTRY TART WITH MILK

Make a shell following directions for Apple Tart (above), but make edge higher. Mix together 3 tablespoons sugar, a pinch of salt with 1 tablespoon flour. Add 3 beaten eggs and flavor with orange flower extract (or vanilla) to taste. Add gradually 1½ cups milk. Pour

[245]

into tart shell and bake in a slow oven of 300 to 325 degrees until crust is brown and center is firm. When cold sprinkle top with powdered sugar.

STRAWBERRY OR RASPBERRY TART
(Uncooked fruit)

Roll Tart Pastry (page 228) into a circle about ¼ inch thick. Moisten the edge and lay all around it a strip of Puff Paste (page 227) about ½ inch wide using, if desired, leftover trimmings. Place on a baking sheet, prick the bottom, brush with milk and bake in a moderately hot oven of 375 degrees about 30 minutes or until golden brown. When cold·spread with Crème Pâtissière (page 231) or whipped cream. Arrange strawberries, raspberries or other fruit on top. Spread top with softened currant jelly.

GATEAU NORMAND

Roll out Sweet Pastry (page 228) about ⅛ inch thick and line a shallow oblong pan with it. Spread ½ to ¾ inch thick with thick applesauce. Cover top with same pastry, sealing the edges. Spread very thinly with Glace Royale (below) and sprinkle chopped almonds over the top. Bake in a hot oven of 400 degrees about 30 minutes or until top is crusty and starting to brown. Serve in slices.

GLACE ROYALE

Mix together ½ cup confectioner's sugar, 1 egg white and 2 to 3 drops of lemon juice. Work all up together until smooth and thick.

[246]

Entremets

<pre>⪦⪥ ❖ ⪦⪥</pre>

THE French *entremet* is the equivalent of the American dessert. In this country we have cold and hot desserts, in France we had cold and hot entremets. The choice of an entremet depended upon the meal it finished, something light when the meal was hearty, something heartier when the meal was light. Ice cream was seldom served except at very important parties and usually in the large pretentious *châteaux* where entertaining was done on a grand scale. Then the ice cream was purchased at the local *pâtisserie* where it was made especially for the occasion, elegantly molded and garnished.

In summer our entremets were more apt to be the fruits as they came into season. Often several were combined—with the larger ones cut in small pieces—to make a *macédoine* of fruit. Sometimes tarts or *tourtes* were made. Tarts are open-faced pies while *tourtes* have the fruit between two crusts like American two crust pies. The pastry we made was a little different from American pie crust, shorter and sweeter and not quite as flaky. If we wanted a flaky crust, we made French Puff Pastry which is as light and flaky as any crust can be. In winter our entremets were usually made with milk and eggs and cream because canned fruit was pretty expensive and our supply of home-dried and preserved fruit was always limited by the size of the preceding summer's crop.

Oeufs à la Neige, similar to the Floating Island served here, was the best liked of all the entremets, at least where I came from, and was served at many of our special dinners. The rich milk and many eggs that went into it produced a rich smooth custard which, when well chilled and served plain or with fruit, was as popular as ice cream is here. Other favorite cold entremets were *Bavaroise* Creams in various flavors and *Crème Caramel Renversée.* The popular hot ones were *Crème Frites, Crêpes, Soufflés* and *Beignets Soufflés.*

[247]

Cold Entremets

BAVAROISE

Bavaroise, or *Crème Bavaroise,* is the same dessert that is found in American cookbooks under the name of Bavarian Cream. It is either a custard or a fruit purée that has been thickened with gelatin and in which whipped cream has been folded. The flavorings range from vanilla, chocolate, coffee and so on through all the fruit flavors. Ordinarily at home one flavor will be used at a time but when something extra special is wanted two or more flavors can be used and molded in layers. In France where ice cream is not as generally served as in this country, the Bavaroise entremets play about the same rôle as ice cream in providing a cold, rich, flavorful—and at the same time delicate—finish to a meal.

Gelatin is one of the basic ingredients of all Bavarian Cream mixtures and the rules for handling unflavored gelatin must be followed. That is, the gelatin must first be softened in cold liquid and then dissolved in hot or boiling liquid. Sometimes it is not desirable to boil the liquid as in the case of fruits whose delicate flavor would be spoiled by heat. Then the bowl containing the gelatin and cold water is placed in a pan of boiling water and steamed for a few minutes or until the softened gelatin turns into a clear liquid.

The whipped cream is never added until the mixture has chilled to a point where it is just starting to thicken or has a syrupy consistency. If it has not reached this point the cream will not be evenly distributed throughout but will rise to the top. On the other hand, if the mixture is allowed to get too stiff it will have a lumpy appearance and texture.

When removing any of these gelatin mixtures from the mold, loosen the edges with a small, sharp-pointed knife and invert on the serving dish. If the pudding does not slip out, a cloth wrung out of hot water can be wrapped around the mold for a minute or two and this will loosen the contents from the mold.

VANILLA BAVARIAN CREAM
(Bavaroise Vanille)

1 *cup Crème à l'Anglaise Collée*   ¾ *cup whipping cream*
(page 255)

Prepare Crème à l'Anglaise Collée. Whip cream until stiff. When the Crème à l'Anglaise starts to become thick, fold in whipped cream and pour into a mold that has been oiled or rinsed in cold water. Chill until set. To serve, loosen edges and invert on serving dish. Serve with Chocolate Sauce (page 277) or any fruit sauce. Serves 5 to 6.

CHOCOLATE BAVARIAN CREAM
(Bavaroise au Chocolat)

Follow directions for Vanilla Bavarian Cream, adding 3 to 4 ounces grated sweet chocolate or 2 ounces bitter chocolate to the hot milk when making the Crème à l'Anglaise. Stir mixture during cooking until chocolate is thoroughly combined. If bitter chocolate is used add a little more sugar.

COFFEE BAVARIAN CREAM
(Bavaroise au Café)

Follow recipe for Vanilla Bavarian Cream flavoring the Crème à l'Anglaise with coffee essence or using coffee beans to flavor the milk as described in making Mocha Crème au Beurre (page 232).

ORANGE BAVARIAN CREAM
(Bavaroise à l'Orange)

2 *cups Crème à l'Anglaise Collée*	¼ *cup simple syrup* (page 297)
(*warm*) (page 255)	1 *cup whipping cream*
2 *tablespoons orange juice*	2 *tablespoons sugar*
finely grated rind 1 *orange*	*orange sections*

Cook orange rind in simple syrup until it is reduced to about 1 tablespoon and combine with orange juice. Add Crème à l'Anglaise Collée. When mixture starts to thicken fold in the cream which has been whipped until stiff. Pour into a mold that has been oiled or rinsed in cold water. Chill until set. When ready to serve loosen edges and invert on serving dish. Garnish with sections of orange. If desired English Custard (page 255) to which a little Curaçao has been added may be served with it. Serves 6 to 8.

STRAWBERRY BAVARIAN CREAM
(Bavaroise aux Fraises)

1 *qt. strawberries*	1½ *tablespoons gelatin*
¾ *cup powder sugar*	¼ *cup cold water*
juice 1 *lemon*	1 *cup whipping cream*
red coloring	

[249]

Wash and hull berries, drain well, then mash and strain through a fine sieve. Add lemon juice and sugar and stir until dissolved. Add 1 or 2 drops red color. Soften the gelatin in cold water, place over hot water, and steam until dissolved, then add to strawberries. When mixture starts to thicken fold in the cream which has been whipped until stiff. Pour into a mold that has been oiled or rinsed in cold water. Chill until set. When ready to serve loosen edges, invert on serving dish and garnish with strawberries. Serves 6 to 8.

BLANC MANGE

Blanc Mange—spelled in France *Blanc Manger* and meaning "white eating"—is one of the oldest of French entremets and very popular. But in France it is always a gelatin mixture and never made with cornstarch or arrowroot which are typical of American Blanc Mange recipes. And in France it is always flavored with almond which comes from almond milk, a preparation made by grinding fresh almonds in a mortar and then extracting the flavor with water. To make this an extra nice dessert a little rum or kirsch is added. The result, when chilled until firm and served very cold, is so delicious and delicate that it has been a dish for French gourmets during more than two centuries.

ALMOND MILK

To make the almond milk it is necessary to grind 1 cup blanched almonds, 2 or 3 of which are bitter almonds, in a mortar with a pestle until they are well crushed. Then add about 2 cups of water a very little at a time and continue grinding until it becomes milky. Strain through silk or fine muslin, squeezing it well to extract all the liquid and flavor.

BLANC MANGER

To make the French *Blanc Manger* combine 2 cups almond milk, 1 cup top milk, ½ cup sugar and 1½ tablespoons unflavored gelatin which has been softened in ¼ cup cold water. Bring slowly to boiling point, but do not boil, stirring to dissolve the sugar and gelatin in the liquid. Cool. (Add rum or kirsch to taste, if desired.) Pour into oiled mold and chill until firm. To serve, loosen edges and unmold by inverting on serving dish. Serve plain or with fresh or cooked fruit. Serves 6.

CHARLOTTE DE FRUITS

Prepare mold with lady fingers following directions for Charlotte Russe (page 251). Fill center with layers of Strawberry Bavarian

Cream (page 249), and sliced strawberries or peaches sprinkled with sugar and a little kirsch or maraschino, having three layers of Bavarian and two of fruit. Chill until set. When ready to serve invert on serving dish and pour very cold English Custard (page 255) or Fruit Sauce around. Serves 6 to 8.

CABINET PUDDING

2 cups milk
1 piece vanilla bean
½ cup sugar
2 eggs
4-5 lady fingers or macaroons
(broken up)

2 egg yolks
2 tablespoons raisins
2-3 diced candied fruits
1 tablespoon kirsch (or other
liqueur) or lemon juice

Soak raisins in a little warm water to make them plump. Drain. Mix with candied fruit and kirsch (or other liqueur). Scald milk and vanilla bean. Mix eggs and egg yolks with sugar and work them up together. Add milk gradually. Strain. Spread ½ the fruit in the bottom of a charlotte mold (or other deep mold), then ½ the lady fingers (or macaroons), then ½ the custard. Repeat, using all the ingredients. Cover mold and set in a pan of hot water. Bake in a moderate oven of 350 to 375 degrees about 40 to 50 minutes or until set like a custard. When done, a small knife inserted in the center will come out clean with no custard sticking to it. When ready to serve invert on serving dish and serve with English Custard (page 255) or Crème Sabayon (page 252). Serves 6.

CHARLOTTE RUSSE

Line a charlotte mold (or any deep mold) with lady fingers, fitting them in the bottom so they radiate from the center and are parallel on the sides. (They should not come above the edge of the mold.) Fill with Vanilla Bavarian Cream (page 248). Chill until set. When ready to serve invert on serving dish and decorate with sweetened whipped cream. Serves 6 to 8.

CITEAU AU KIRSCH

Bake a layer of Génoise cake (page 236) about ¾ inch thick or cut a ¾ inch slice from a thicker cake. Sprinkle the top with kirsch. Mold a Vanilla Bavaroise in an 8-inch layer cake pan, having it about ¾ inch thick. When it has set invert on top of the slice of cake and turn it out in the center, leaving a narrow edge of cake all around. (Or make a circular form with an inch-wide strip of glazed paper and set on top of the cake. Then fill with the Bavaroise and remove the paper circle when set and ready to serve.) When ready to serve decorate the edge with sweetened whipped cream. Serves 8.

CREME SABAYON

⅔ cup sugar
4 egg yolks
1 cup white wine

rum, kirsch or other liqueur or lemon juice

Whip sugar and egg yolks together until very light colored. Stir in wine and place in top of double boiler with cold water in the bottom. Cook, stirring vigorously, until the water in the bottom reaches the boiling point, at which time the mixture should have become very creamy. Add a little rum or kirsch to taste. Serve hot. If desired port, Madeira or Marsala wine may be used instead of white wine. Crème Sabayon can also be served cold but in this case, 2 more egg yolks should be added and the mixture must be stirred vigorously as it cools. Serves 4 to 6.

CUSTARD

Custard, nothing more or less than a combination of milk, eggs, sugar and flavoring, is either cooked on top of the stove until it attains a saucelike thickness or it is baked in the oven until it is firm enough to hold its shape when cool. Its texture will depend upon the number of eggs, and egg yolks, used in proportion to the milk, but at least three eggs are needed for each pint of milk to thicken it at all. Thereafter, more egg yolks can be added, each additional one producing a finer texture, a more satiny result. Some people prefer to use only egg yolks —no whites at all—because all yolks make a very rich, smooth custard.

There are a few warnings that everyone must heed in order to make perfect custard. One is that in combining the ingredients the hot milk must always be poured very gradually on the egg and sugar mixture stirring all the time. Then if it is cooked on top of the stove it must be brought to the boiling point only—never allowed actually to boil—and must be stirred every minute while it cooks. Let it boil or neglect to stir it and it will surely curdle. If it is baked, the dish must be set in a pan of water and the oven heat kept low enough so that the water does not boil. Otherwise the custard will be full of tiny holes and is very apt to water when a spoon is put into it.

The following recipes show how many variations there are of the same custard ingredients and some of the flavorings that are suitable.

For the best vanilla flavor nothing equals the vanilla bean itself. Wash it off, dry and save it and it can be used more than once. To bring out its flavor, a vanilla bean is always cooked in the milk. Vanilla extract, on the other hand, is always added after the milk is scalded because heat destroys the flavor of an extract.

VANILLA CUSTARD
(Crème Renversée à la Française)

3 *cups milk*	4 *eggs*
½ *cup sugar*	4 *egg yolks*
1 *piece vanilla bean* (*or a little*	
extract)	

Scald milk with vanilla bean, remove from fire and let stand 8 to 10 minutes to absorb vanilla flavor. Combine egg, egg yolks and sugar, working them up together until they are well mixed. Remove vanilla bean (or add extract if that is used) and add hot milk, little by little, to the egg mixture. When well combined, strain through a fine sieve into a buttered mold or into custard cups. Set in a pan of hot water and cook in a moderately slow oven of 325 to 350 degrees (or on top of stove in a covered pan) until custard is set. Allow about 45 to 50 minutes for a large dish or 20 to 25 minutes for individual ones. Do not allow the water to boil. When done, a small pointed knife inserted in the center should come out clean and have no custard sticking to it. Cool and when ready to serve invert on serving dish. Serve plain or with Fruit Sauce or Chocolate Sauce (page 277) or English Custard (page 255). Serves 6 to 8.

CHOCOLATE CUSTARD
(Crème Renversée au Chocolat)

Vanilla Custard recipe (above)	½ *cup water*
omitting ½ *cup milk*	¼ *lb. grated sweet chocolate*

Mix together chocolate and water and cook until smooth. Add to boiling milk when making Vanilla Custard mixture and proceed according to the custard directions.

COFFEE CUSTARD
(Crème Renversée au Café)

Follow recipe for Vanilla Custard (above) preparing coffee beans with milk as described in Mocha Crème au Beurre (page 232). Or use ½ cup very strong coffee and only 2 cups milk.

CREAM CARAMEL
(Crème Renversée Caramel)

2 *cups milk*
½ *cup sugar*
3 *eggs*
2 *egg yolks*

1 *piece vanilla bean* (*or a little extract*)
2-3 *tablespoons caramel* (page 297)

Scald milk with vanilla bean. Mix together eggs, egg yolks and sugar, working them up until well combined. Remove vanilla bean (or add extract) and pour hot milk gradually into egg mixture. Stir until combined. Line 6 custard cups or 1 large baking dish with caramelized sugar made by melting ½ cup sugar in ¼ cup water in a saucepan and cooking it until it turns golden color. When the caramel has set, pour the custard mixture on top of the caramel and place in a pan of hot water. Bake in a moderately slow oven of 325 to 350 degrees until custard is set. Allow 45 to 50 minutes for large dish or 20 to 25 for individual ones. When done, a small pointed knife inserted in the center should come out clean. Cool and unmold on serving dish. Serves 6.

CREME BRULEE

Follow recipe for Cream Caramel (above) but instead of lining the custard cups or mold with caramel, mix ¼ cup of caramel into the custard and reduce the amount of milk by ¼ cup.

SMALL VANILLA CUSTARDS
(Petits Pots de Crème Vanille)

2 *cups milk*
½ *cup granulated sugar*

6 *egg yolks, beaten*
1 *piece vanilla bean* (*or a little extract*)

Scald milk with vanilla bean and sugar, cool slightly and then combine with egg yolks, stirring constantly. Strain through a fine sieve and fill small custard cups. Set in pan of water, cover pan and bake in a moderately slow oven of 325 to 350 degrees about 15 minutes or until a small pointed knife inserted in the center comes out clean. Serves 6.

SMALL CHOCOLATE CUSTARDS
(Petits Pots de Crème Chocolat)

1 *pint milk*
6 *egg yolks*

½ *lb. sweet cooking chocolate, grated*

Scald milk, add chocolate and cook, stirring constantly, until it is

[254]

melted and has reached the boiling point. Beat egg yolks and pour hot mixture slowly onto them. Stir well for a few minutes. Strain through a fine sieve and fill small custard cups. Chill in refrigerator. Serve with heavy or whipped cream if desired. If chocolate is not very sweet, add sugar to taste while the mixture is still hot. These can be kept for 2 or 3 days in refrigerator. Serves 8.

ENGLISH CUSTARD
(Crème à l'Anglaise)

½ *cup sugar*   1½ *cups milk*
2-3 *egg yolks*   1 *piece vanilla bean*
1 *teaspoon flour*

Work up sugar and egg yolks with a wooden spoon until smooth and creamy. Add flour. Scald milk and vanilla bean together and then add egg yolk mixture to it, little by little. Return to saucepan and cook slowly, stirring constantly until it comes to the boiling point. Do not allow to boil. Remove vanilla bean. Cool, stirring vigorously at first and then from time to time to prevent crust from forming on top. Serve cold or a little warm. Other flavoring may be used. For coffee flavor use ½ top milk and ½ strong coffee, for chocolate flavor add grated chocolate to taste to hot milk. Serves 2 to 3.

MOLDED FLOATING ISLAND
(Ile Flottante)

8 *tablespoons roasted almonds*   ½ *cup sugar*
  (*or praline*)   ½ *teaspoon vanilla extract*
4 *egg whites*

Chop almonds (or praline) as fine as possible. (They should be powdered.) Beat whites stiff, adding sugar a little at a time as they start to stiffen, then add vanilla and almonds. Fill a buttered and sugared mold with this mixture or coat with caramel (page 297). Place in a pan of hot water and bake in a very slow oven of 250-275 degrees about 20 to 25 minutes or until mixture becomes firm. Let cool, unmold on deep serving dish and pour English Custard (above) around. Serves 6.

CREME A L'ANGLAISE COLLEE

This is a custard mixture combined with gelatin which is used for the foundation of many entremets. Whipped cream, fruit purées, macaroon and lady finger crumbs are some of the ingredients with which it is combined to make such dishes as Bavaroise and molded Charlottes. As the mixture sets or starts to become thickened it must be watched rather closely. If it becomes too stiff before folding in the cream or other ingredients the result will not be creamy and smooth throughout but instead will be streaky with gelatin and uneven in texture.

⅓ cup sugar
2-3 egg yolks
½ tablespoon unflavored gelatin
2 tablespoons water

1 cup milk
1 piece vanilla bean (or a little extract)

Add gelatin to water and let stand to soften. Work up sugar and egg yolks with a wooden spoon until smooth and creamy. Scald milk and vanilla bean together and then add yolk mixture little by little. Return to saucepan and cook slowly, stirring constantly until it comes to the boiling point. Do not allow to boil. Remove vanilla bean (or add extract). Add gelatin in water. Cool, stirring vigorously at first and then from time to time to prevent crust from forming on top.

FLOATING ISLAND
(Oeufs à la Neige)

3-4 eggs, separated
2 cups milk
½ cup sugar

1 teaspoon flour
1 piece vanilla bean

Beat egg whites until stiff, adding ¼ cup sugar, little by little, as they start to stiffen. Scald milk with vanilla bean, remove from fire and drop spoonfuls of egg white mixture formed like small eggs on top of milk. Cook over low heat 2 minutes, then turn them and cook 2 minutes on other side. Remove with skimmer to towel to drain. Mix together egg yolks and sugar, beating until smooth and creamy. Add flour. Pour the hot milk gradually over them, stirring constantly. Return to pan and cook, stirring constantly, until boiling point is reached and mixture has thickened. Do not boil. Strain through a fine sieve and chill. Serve with prepared egg whites floating on top. If desired, sprinkle floating egg whites with grated chocolate or caramelized sugar. Serves 3 to 4.

MACEDOINE OF FRUIT

Mix together fruits and berries in season, peeling when necessary and cutting large fruit into dice. Sprinkle with sugar to taste and add fruit juice such as orange or pineapple. Add a little kirsch (or other liqueur) if desired, or serve with fruit gelatin.

DIPLOMAT PUDDING

3-4 *lady fingers*
½ cup assorted candied fruits
1 *tablespoon kirsch (or other liqueur or lemon juice)*

2½ *cups Vanilla Bavarian Cream*
(page 248)

Cut lady fingers in pieces, mix with candied fruits, sprinkle with kirsch and let stand to absorb the liqueur. Prepare Bavarian Cream, and while still soft, spread ⅓ in the bottom of an oiled charlotte mold (or other mold). Put ½ the lady fingers and fruit mixture on the Bavarian. Add another layer of Bavarian, then the remaining lady finger mixture and finish with remaining Bavarian. Chill until set. When ready to serve, invert on serving dish and pour very cold English Custard (page 255) around. Serves 6 to 8.

FLAMRI DE SEMOULE

1 *quart milk*
1 *piece vanilla bean (or a little extract)*
¾ cup farina

½ cup sugar
1 *tablespoon gelatin*
2 *tablespoons cold water*
4 *egg whites, stiffly beaten*

Scald milk with vanilla bean. Remove vanilla bean and add farina gradually, stirring all the time to avoid lumps. Cook about 15 minutes, stirring occasionally. Add sugar (add vanilla extract if vanilla bean was not used). Soften gelatin in cold water and add. Stir all together well, then fold in the stiffly beaten egg whites. Pour into an oiled mold and chill until set. To serve, invert on serving dish, decorate with candied fruits and serve with any desired fruit sauce. Serves 6 to 8.

PLOMBIERE AUX MARRONS

½ cup purée of marrons glacés
2 *cups Crème à l'Anglaise Collée*
(page 255)

½ cup heavy whipping cream
4-5 *lady fingers (cut in pieces)*
1 *tablespoon rum*

Make purée of marrons glacés by forcing preserved marrons through a sieve. Mix Crème à l'Anglaise Collée while still warm with this purée, mix until thoroughly combined and smooth. When mixture starts to thicken, fold in the cream, which has been whipped stiff. Sprinkle rum on lady fingers. Put ⅓ of cream mixture in a lightly oiled charlotte (or other) mold, add ½ the lady fingers. Put in another third of the crème, then remaining lady fingers. Put in another third of crème, add remaining lady fingers and finish with remaining crème. Chill until firm. When ready to serve, loosen edges and invert mold on serving dish to remove pudding. Serve with cold Sabayon Sauce (page 252) to which a little rum has been added. Serves 6 to 8.

MELON SURPRISE

Cut a round opening, about 2 to 3 inches, in top of canteloupe or other desired melon. Remove seeds with a spoon. Cut out the melon pulp in small balls and mix with fresh fruits such as pineapple, orange, peach, etc. Add sugar to taste and either a tablespoon of kirsch (or curaçao or other liqueur) or a glass of port wine. Refill melon, put cover on top and chill in refrigerator 1 to 2 hours. Place on a serving dish and garnish dish with green leaves or ferns. One canteloupe serves 3 to 4, a larger melon will serve more.

PROFITEROLES AU CHOCOLAT

Form Cream Puff Paste (page 225) in balls about as large as a walnut on a lightly greased baking sheet and bake in a moderate oven of 350 to 375 degrees until puffed and light and brown all over. When cold, cut open and fill with sweetened whipped cream or Crème Pâtissière (page 231). Arrange in a pyramid on serving dish and pour hot Chocolate Sauce (page 277) over them.

PUDDING NESSELRODE

1 *cup Crème à l'Anglaise Collée*	¾ *cup whipping cream*
(page 255)	6 *marrons glacés, broken in pieces*
½ *cup marron glacés (puréed)*	

Prepare Crème à l'Anglaise and while still soft, add puréed marron glacé made by forcing preserved marrons through a sieve. When it starts to thicken, fold in the cream, which has been beaten until stiff. Put a layer of ⅓ this mixture in an oiled charlotte mold (or other mold). Sprinkle with half the broken marrons. Add another layer of crème, remaining marrons and finish with remaining crème. Chill until set. When ready to serve, invert on serving dish and decorate with sweetened whipped cream. Serves 6 to 8.

RICE FOR ENTREMETS

Rice for entremets is a kind of rice custard mixture which a French housewife makes as easily as she does a Cream Sauce and then uses in a dozen different ways. It is the base for Rice Croquettes, Rice

Soufflé and many other favorite rice desserts. If you have a pan with a heavy bottom and a burner that can be turned so low that the mixture will not scorch, it can be cooked more quickly by doing it directly over the heat. Otherwise it is better to use a double boiler.

1 *cup rice*	¼ *teaspoon salt*
2½ *cups milk, scalded*	*piece of vanilla bean* (*or a little*
6 *tablespoons sugar*	*vanilla extract*)
1 *tablespoon butter*	3 *egg yolks, slightly beaten*

Wash rice in cold water, put in a saucepan and cover well with water. Bring to a boil, turn off heat and let stand 5 minutes. Drain in a sieve and rinse by letting cold water run through the rice. Return to pan and add milk, sugar, salt and vanilla bean. Bring to a boil, add butter, cover pan and simmer very gently about ½ hour. (Or cook in top of double boiler about 45 minutes or until rice is done.) Toss with a fork to separate the grains, then combine with egg yolks. Spread on a platter to cool.

RICE PUDDING A L'ANGLAISE

2 *cups milk*	¼ *cup sugar*
½ *cup rice*	¼ *cup cream* (*or top milk*)
2 *egg yolks, beaten*	½ *teaspoon vanilla extract*

Cook milk and rice in double boiler about 45 minutes. stirring occasionally. Mix together egg yolks, sugar and cream and combine with rice and milk. Place in a baking dish and brown in a hot oven of 400 degrees or under broiler. Serves 3 to 4.

RICE CROQUETTES

Follow recipe for Rice for Entremets (page 258). When cold, divide into small portions and form in any desired shape, such as cylinders, cones or balls. Roll in flour and dip in beaten egg and then roll in fine fresh bread crumbs. Just before serving, fry in deep hot fat or oil until golden brown. Drain well and serve with English Custard (page 255), Sabayon Sauce (page 252) or Fruit Sauce (page 277).

RICE MOLD WITH CARAMEL
(Gâteau de Riz au Caramel)

⅔ *cup rice*	2 *cups milk*
½ *cup sugar*	1 *piece vanilla bean* (*or a little*
2 *tablespoons butter*	*extract*)
2 *egg yolks*	*caramelized sugar* (page 297)

Parboil rice 3 to 4 minutes in water to cover well. Drain and put in deep baking dish. Scald milk with vanilla bean and when it boils remove vanilla bean (or add vanilla extract) and pour over rice. Cover closely and cook in a moderate oven of 350 to 375 degrees or over very low heat on top of stove ½ hour. Do not stir or touch the rice. Meanwhile cream butter and sugar together, add egg yolks and work up all together well. Add rice, mixing it in carefully so that rice grains will not be crushed. Spread Caramel Syrup (page 297) over bottom and sides of baking dish. Fill with rice mixture and set in a pan of hot water. Bake in a moderately slow oven of 325 to 350 degrees 40 minutes. Do not let water in pan boil. Cool and serve either cold or lukewarm. To serve, invert on serving dish and pour a little caramel syrup around it. Serves 6 to 8.

RICE MOLD MARIE LOUISE

1 *cup rice cooked for entremet*
(page 258)
½ *cup Crème à l'Anglaise Collée*
(page 255)

¼ *cup mixed glazed fruits, finely diced*
1 *teaspoon kirsch* (*or maraschino*)
¾ *cup heavy whipping cream*

Combine rice while still warm with Crème à l'Anglaise Collée. Combine fruit and kirsch (or maraschino) and add to rice mixture. Whip cream until stiff and fold into the mixture. Fill oiled mold. Chill until firm. To serve, loosen edges and invert on serving dish with English Custard (page 255) or Fruit Sauce (page 277).

RICE PUDDING SOUFFLE
(Soufflé de Riz)

2 *cups rice cooked for entremet*
(page 258)

2 *egg yolks, beaten*
5 *egg whites, stiffly beaten*

Combine rice and egg yolks and fold in the beaten egg whites. Put into a buttered and sugared deep ring mold, filling it two thirds full. Set in pan of hot water and cook in a moderate oven of 350 to 375 degrees 45 to 50 minutes. After removing from oven, let stand 6 to 8 minutes, then invert on serving dish. Pour English Custard (page 255) or Crème Sabayon (page 252) around. Serves 6.

TIMBALE SUZANNE

Bake a Génoise cake (page 236) in a round 8-inch layer cake pan. Cut out the center part in a circle, leaving a ring about 1 inch wide all around the edge and a center part about ½ inch thick. Fill center with layers of Strawberry Bavarian (page 249) alternated with sliced peaches and strawberries sprinkled with kirsch or maraschino and having two layers of Bavarian with a layer of fruit between. Chill until set. When ready to serve, place on serving dish and decorate with sweetened whipped cream. Serves 8.

TURBAN D'AGEN

Agen is a town in the southern part of France about halfway between Bordeaux and Toulouse on the right bank of the Garonne River. It is famous for its dried prunes; in fact, the best prunes in France come from Agen. Hence dishes containing prunes often include "Agen" in their names. Turban means ring, so this particular dish is one of prunes in a ring.

½ *tablespoon gelatin*	1 *cup red wine*
1 *tablespoon cold water*	1 *cup water*
2 *cups Rice for Entremet* (page 258)	1 *slice lemon*
1 *cup heavy whipping cream*	3 *tablespoons Apricot jam*
½ *lb. prunes*	

Soften gelatin in tablespoon water and add to rice while it is still hot. Cool. Fold in cream which has been whipped stiff. Put in a ring mold that has been lightly oiled. Chill until firm. When ready to serve, loosen edges and invert on serving dish to remove pudding. Fill center with compote of prunes made as follows: soak prunes a few hours in water. Drain. Combine with wine and water and cook prunes in this liquid with lemon slice until prunes are soft and liquid is reduced to 1 cup. (Remove pits from prunes if desired.) Add Apricot jam. Cool. Put prunes in center of ring and pour sauce around the outside. Serves 6 to 8.

Hot Entremets

Hot fruit desserts were very popular in France, much more so than they seem to be in this country, probably because so many houses have no central heating system, and an ice cold dessert was not very attractive in cold wintry weather. But a hot dessert, and a substantial one, was very welcome indeed, especially if the meal itself had not been too hearty.

APRICOT EN SURPRISE

Cut apricots in half and remove pits. Cook in light syrup (page 297), (or use canned fruit) and drain well on a towel. Mix a little Rice for Entremet (page 258) with candied cherries or chopped pineapple. Fill the holes from which the pits were removed with rice mixture. Put the two halves together and dip in flour, then in beaten egg and then in fine fresh bread crumbs. Fry in deep hot fat or oil until golden brown. Drain. Sprinkle with powdered sugar and arrange in a circle in hot serving dish. Serve with Sabayon Sauce (page 252) or Fruit Sauce (page 277).

APRICOT HELEN

¼ lb. lady fingers (may be broken or stale)
1½ cups scalded milk
4 tablespoons sugar
Apricot Sauce (page 276)

4 eggs, beaten
12 apricots cooked in light syrup (or canned fruit)
glacéed marrons (or candied cherries)

Soak lady fingers in hot milk about 5 to 10 minutes. Press mixture through a fine sieve. Add sugar and combine with eggs. Pour into a mold that has been buttered and sugared, place in a pan of hot water and bake in a moderate oven of 350 degrees, 30 to 45 minutes or until set. Invert on serving dish. Cut apricots in half, remove pits and arrange cut side up around pudding. Fill each hole from which the pit was removed with a piece of glacéed marron or candied cherry and coat the fruit with Apricot Sauce. Serves 6.

APPLES BOURGEOISE

Peel apple, cut each in half and remove cores. Cook in light syrup until soft and place, cut side up, on a heatproof serving dish. Fill hole from which core was removed with mixed candied fruit. Coat top of each apple with Crème Pâtissière (page 231) sprinkle with chopped almonds or macaroon crumbs and then with sugar. Place in a hot oven of 425 degrees or under broiler and cook until top is browned.

BAKED APPLES
(Pommes Bonne Femme)

Remove core from large apples and make an incision straight around the center of each apple by slitting with a sharp knife to release steam without bursting skin. Place in a baking dish and put a small piece of butter and a tablespoon sugar in center of each apple. Add just enough water to pan to prevent scorching. Bake in a moderate oven of 350 to 375 degrees until soft and golden brown. Serve with juice from pan or cook down the juice a little and combine with Apricot Sauce (page 277).

APPLE CHARLOTTE
(Charlotte de Pommes)

Cut bread in thin slices, remove crusts and dip bread in melted butter. Cover bottom and sides of charlotte mold or deep casserole with the pieces of bread. Peel and core apples, cut in quarters and cook in a little butter until soft and thick, not watery. Add juice of ½ lemon. Fill center of mold with apples. Place mold on a baking sheet and bake in a hot oven of 425 degrees about 40 to 45 minutes, when it should be golden brown. Invert on serving dish and serve with Apricot Sauce (page 277).

CREAM-FILLED PINEAPPLE
(Ananas à la Crème)

Remove top from pineapple and cut out the pulp from the inside, leaving a shell about ½ inch thick. Cut the pulp in thin slices and cook in light syrup. Fill pineapple with alternating layers of Crème Pàtissière (page 231) and the cooked pineapple slices, starting and finishing with a layer of crème. Sprinkle top with macaroon crumbs and a little melted butter. Put in a hot oven of 425 degrees and cook until top is golden brown. Place on hot serving dish and arrange around it remaining slices of pineapple coated with Apricot Sauce (page 277). Serve hot. Serves 6 to 8.

CROUTES AUX FRUITS

Cut stale brioche or sweet buns or coffee cake in ¼-inch slices, place in baking pan, sprinkle with a little sugar and bake in hot oven of 400 to 425 degrees until golden brown. Prepare a macédoine of fruit, using pears, apples, peaches, oranges, cherries or any desired combination. If possible select fruits of different colors. Boil the fruit in a little sugar syrup and thicken it with enough Apricot Sauce (page 277) to give it a saucelike consistency. Flavor with rum or kirsch to taste. Make a ring of the browned brioche, bun or coffee cake slices and fill center with hot fruit. This is very attractive and delicious if served "flambé," done by pouring a little hot rum or other liquor on top of the fruit and igniting it at the table just before serving.

FRUITS A LA BOURDALOUE

Follow recipe for Pineapple with Almond Cream (page 266), substituting apples or pears for the pineapple. Peel and core apples or pears and cook in light syrup until soft. When these fruits are used the Crème Bourdaloue is always spread over the fruit instead of in the center, and chopped almonds or macaroon crumbs are sprinkled over it all.

FRUIT CONDE

Use pears, apricots or other fruit in season. Peel fruit and cook in light syrup until soft or use canned fruit. Drain well. Put a layer of Rice for Entremet (page 258) in bottom of serving bowl, place fruit on top and cover with Apricot Sauce (page 276). If desired, decorate with candied cherries. Serve hot or warm.

TIMBALE COUNTRY STYLE
(Timbale Paysanne)

Make an 8- or 9-inch tart shell with tart pastry (page 228). Fill the shell two thirds full with thick apple sauce and cook in a hot oven of 450 degrees about 20 minutes. In the meantime beat 2 egg whites stiff and fold into 2 cups Rice for Entremet (page 258). Spread this on the apple sauce and sprinkle top with sugar. Return to oven with heat reduced to 375 degrees and cook until top is browned. Serve hot or warm. Serves 6 to 8.

FRUIT TIMBALE
(Timbale de Fruits à la Parisienne)

Brioche dough (page 221)
2 cups mixed fruits, cooked or
   canned
2 cups syrup from fruit

1 tablespoon arrowroot (or corn-
   starch)
½ cup Apricot Sauce (page 276) *(or*
   jam)
kirsch or rum (optional)

Bake brioche dough in a charlotte mold or deep casserole, the previous day. It should not be too fresh. Cut a half-inch slice from the top. Cut out the inside with a sharp knife, making a shell at least an inch thick on the bottom and about half an inch thick on the sides. Spread thick Apricot Sauce (or jam) all over the outside of this shell, then sprinkle chopped almonds (and arrange candied fruits if desired) over the Apricot Sauce. Make a macédoine of the fruits, drain the syrup from them and cook it until reduced to one half the original quantity. Mix arrowroot (or cornstarch) with a little cold water, add to the hot fruit juice and cook, stirring all the time, until thick like a custard. Combine with the fruit and flavor with kirsch or rum if desired. Fill brioche with this and put the top in place for a cover. Serve while still warm, spooning out some of the fruit and cutting a piece of the brioche shell for each serving. Serves 6 to 8.

PEAR (OR PEACH) ANNETTE

Bake Génoise cake mixture (page 236) in a round 8- or 9-inch pan to make a layer about 1 inch thick. Or slice a baked layer to make an inch-thick slice. Place Rice for Entremet (page 258) on the center part, piling it up in a dome and leaving about a 2-inch border of cake all around. Peel, cut in half and remove cores (or pits) from pears (or peaches) and cook in light syrup or use canned fruit. Drain fruit well and arrange on the cake border. Cover rice with Meringue (page 243) and decorate between the pieces of fruit with it. Spread fruit with Apricot Sauce (page 276) and garnish with candied cherries. Put in a hot oven of 425 degrees and brown meringue quickly. Serve hot. Serves 6 to 8.

PEARS IN RED WINE
(Poires au Vin Rouge)

Prepare a syrup with ½ cup red wine, 1 cup sugar, a small piece of cinnamon stick and one piece of lemon rind. Bring to a boil. Peel 6 pears (if large, cut in half and remove cores) and cook in the syrup until soft. Remove pears to serving dish. Discard cinnamon stick and lemon rind and cook syrup until reduced to one-half the original quantity. Pour over pears. Serve hot or cold. Serves 6.

PEARS WITH RUM
(Poires Flambées)

Peel pears, and cook in light syrup (page 297) until soft. Put in a deep heatproof serving dish. Cook syrup until reduced to about half the original quantity and combine with a little Apricot Sauce (page 276) or currant jelly. Thicken with a little arrowroot or cornstarch (about 1 teaspoon mixed with a little cold water to each cup of sauce), so that the sauce will be thick enough to coat the pears. Pour sauce over pears and set dish where they will keep hot. Just before serving, heat some rum, cognac or kirsch, pour over all and ignite at the table.

PEARS DES VIGNERONS

4-6 *apples*
1¼ *cups sugar*
1 *tablespoon butter*
2 *small pieces stick cinnamon*
1½ *glasses red wine*

3 *tablespoons chopped walnuts*
6 *pears*
1 *piece lemon rind*
pony rum (*or cognac*)

Prepare apples as follows: peel, core and mince, then cook in butter with ¼ cup sugar and 1 piece stick cinnamon until apples are soft. When done, remove cinnamon stick and add walnuts. Make a syrup of wine, remaining cup sugar, lemon rind and other piece of stick cinnamon. Peel pears and cook in the syrup until soft. Put apple sauce in serving bowl and place cooked pears on top. Cook syrup until reduced to about half the original quantity and pour over pears. Just before serving heat rum or cognac and pour over all and ignite at the table. Serves 6.

PINEAPPLE WITH ALMOND CREAM
(Ananas à la Bourdaloue)

Bake Génoise cake mixture (page 236) in a ring mold. Remove from pan and cool. Cook slices of fresh pineapple in light syrup or use canned pineapple. Drain well and arrange overlapping slices on top of the ring. Fill center with Crème Bourdaloue (page 233), piling it up in the center. Sprinkle top of the crème with chopped almonds or macaroon crumbs, then with a little butter. Place under broiler and cook until golden brown. Spread Apricot Sauce (page 276) on pineapple and garnish with cherries.

BEIGNETS

Beignets are what Americans call fritters and the kinds that the French eat are almost innumerable. They are very often served as the main dish of meals made of such foods as fish, chicken, the meat specialties or vegetables. The beignets which follow, however, are sweet and are eaten as a dessert or entremet.

There are two or three hints which will help you in turning out a good beignet. For example, in making them with fruit, especially canned fruit, the surface of the fruit must always be well dried or the batter will not cling to it, as it does to fruits that are fairly dry like apples and bananas. Then there is the temperature of the fat to watch. It need not be quite as hot as for croquettes because they are made of already cooked food and only require heating up and browning, while

[266]

beignets are made with a raw batter which has to be cooked completely and browned, too. Of course it must be hot enough so the beignets will not become fat soaked before they brown. If you use a fat thermometer the temperature is around 370 degrees F. Or you can judge the temperature by the time it takes to cook them—they should be a nice golden brown in about 3 to 5 minutes. If it takes longer, then the fat is not hot enough, and if they brown more quickly, it is too hot. Sometimes the kind of food in the center will not be sufficiently cooked in 3 to 5 minutes; some varieties of apples, for example. But do not try to increase the cooking time by using cooler fat because this only makes a greasy beignet. Instead, brown them in the fat, drain as usual and then put them in the oven for a few minutes to finish cooking, sprinkling them with a little powdered sugar which glazes them attractively while the fruit .nside is cooking.

One of the most popular of the beignets, which is served everywhere, is the simple one made of Cream Puff Paste—Choux Paste and called Beignets Soufflés. They also are called Pets de Nonne or Soupir de Nonne so if you see any of these names on a menu you will know they all mean the same thing. When making Beignets Soufflés the best results are obtained if the fat is not quite as hot as for other beignets and the heat is increased as they cook. And incidentally Beignet Soufflés do not have to be turned. They do that of their own accord. They may turn over two or three times as they fry in the hot fat but when they have stopped turning and are golden brown all over they are done.

BEIGNET DE CARNAVAL

¼ *yeast cake*	*pinch of salt*
3 *tablespoons warm milk*	4 *eggs*
4 *cups flour*	2 *tablespoons rum*
½ *cup butter*	*vanilla extract*
⅓ *cup sugar*	*grated rind of* 1 *lemon*

Dissolve yeast in warm milk. Sift flour on board or in a bowl and make a well in the center. Put in the yeast mixture and then all remaining ingredients. Mix the ingredients with the hands or a wooden spoon, gradually adding the flour until all is thoroughly combined. Knead until smooth and elastic. Cover and let stand for a few hours (or make the day before and leave in a cold place overnight). Roll dough into a very thin sheet, as thin as for noodles. Using a pastry wheel or a knife cut in strips about ⅔ inch wide and 8 inches long.

Tie each strip in a loose knot. Let stand 15 to 20 minutes. Fry in deep hot fat or oil 7 to 8 minutes or until golden brown, having the fat the same temperature as for other beignets. Drain well and sprinkle with powdered sugar.

FRITTER BATTER FOR FRUIT
(Pâte à Frire)

½ cup flour
¼ teaspoon salt
1 tablespoon melted butter

1 egg, beaten
1 egg white, stiffly beaten
½ cup beer

Sift together flour and salt. Mix together butter and egg and add to flour. Add beer gradually, stirring only until mixture is smooth. Put in a warm place 1 to 2 hours to let the batter become light and foamy, then fold in the beaten egg white.

APPLE FRITTERS
(Beignets de Pommes)

Peel large apples, allowing one apple for two servings, and remove cores. Cut in ¼-inch slices and sprinkle with sugar (and a few drops of rum or kirsch, if desired) and a few drops lemon juice. Let stand about 1 hour, moving them around so all will absorb the liquid. Dry the slices a little, dip in Fritter Batter (above) and fry in deep hot fat or oil until golden brown all over. Drain well. Put in hot serving dish and sprinkle with powdered sugar. Or spread in a shallow pan and put under broiler until sugar glazes them.

BEIGNETS D'ORANGE

Peel an orange and cut in thick slices. Remove seeds. Dip in Fritter Batter (above) and fry in deep hot fat or oil until golden brown all over. Drain well. Put in a hot serving dish and sprinkle with powdered sugar. Serve with Apricot Sauce (page 276) to which orange juice has been added.

BEIGNETS SOUFFLES
(Pets de Nonne)

1 cup water (or milk and water)
½ cup butter
½ teaspoon salt
1 teaspoon sugar

1 cup flour
4 eggs
flavoring (lemon, vanilla or rum, as desired)

Put water, butter, salt and sugar in saucepan and bring to a boil. Remove from heat and add flour. Return to fire and cook, stirring briskly, until mixture rolls away from sides of pan without sticking to them. Add eggs one by one, mixing well after each addition. Add flavoring. To cook, fill a tablespoon full of the mixture and slip half of it off into deep hot fat or oil. Then slip off other half of mixture, making two beignets from each tablespoon. The fat should be moderately hot at first and gradually made hotter to brown the beignets. When brown on the underside they will turn themselves over. When they finish turning over and are golden brown they are done. Drain well. Put in hot serving dish and sprinkle with powdered sugar. Serve plain with English Custard (page 255) or Apricot Sauce (page 276).

BEIGNETS SUZETTE

2 *cups milk*	1 *tablespoon butter*
½ *cup farina*	2 *egg yolks, beaten*
½ *cup sugar*	

Heat milk, add farina gradually, stirring all the time to prevent lumps. Cook, stirring occasionally, about 10 to 15 minutes or until the mixture becomes very thick. Add sugar, butter and egg yolks, mix all together and cook 2 minutes longer. Spread about ¾ inch thick on a buttered shallow pan. Chill. Turn pan upside down on lightly floured board to remove the sheet of pudding. Cut with a doughnut cutter to make rings about 2 inches in diameter with a small hole in the center. Dip in flour, then in beaten egg and then in fine fresh bread crumbs. Sauté in hot butter until golden brown on both sides. To serve, form into an overlapping ring on a serving dish with a candied cherry in center of each beignet. Sprinkle with powdered sugar and serve with Apricot Sauce (page 276). Serves 6 to 8.

CREME FRITE

4 *tablespoons sugar*	2 *cups scalded milk*
5 *tablespoons flour (rice or wheat)*	1 *piece vanilla bean (scalded with*
pinch of salt	*the milk) or a little extract*
3 *eggs*	1 *tablespoon butter*
3 *egg yolks*	

Mix together sugar, flour and salt. Add 1 egg and 1 egg yolk at a time, mixing thoroughly after each addition. Work up with a spoon until mixture is well combined and smooth. Remove vanilla bean from milk (or add extract) and pour hot milk slowly into this mixture, mixing with a whip. Add butter, return to saucepan and bring back to the boil, stirring vigorously all the time. Boil about 2 minutes. Pour into a shallow buttered pan, having mixture ¾ inch thick. Chill. Turn pan upside down on a lightly floured board to remove the contents. Cut in 1½-inch squares or other desired shapes. Dust each piece with flour, dip in beaten egg and then in fresh bread crumbs. Just before serving, drop into deep hot fat or oil and fry until golden brown. Remove from fat, drain thoroughly and serve sprinkled with powdered sugar. Serves 6 to 8.

CREPES

Crêpes, the thin, delicate pancakes that the French love so well, are eaten as the main course of the meal and also as the dessert. It all depends upon how and with what they are served. But they are seldom, if ever, eaten for breakfast as pancakes are in this country.

⅔ *cup flour*	2 *egg yolks*
1 *tablespoon sugar*	1¾ *cups milk*
pinch of salt	2 *tablespoons melted butter*
2 *whole eggs*	1 *teaspoon cognac or rum* (*optional*)

Mix together flour, sugar and salt. Beat eggs and egg yolks together and mix with dry ingredients. Add milk and stir until smooth. Add butter and liqueur. Strain through a fine sieve. This batter should be made up about 2 hours before using. To make the crêpes, put a little butter in a very hot skillet, just enough to grease it. Pour in a very thin layer of crêpe batter. When set and brown on the underside (which takes about a minute), turn on the other side and cook until golden brown. The pan must be very hot because the quicker they cook the better they are. Long cooking toughens them. Put in hot serving dish and sprinkle with powdered sugar. Makes 12 crêpes.

CREPES WITH PINEAPPLE
(Crêpes à l'Ananas)

Cut sliced canned pineapple to make 3 thin slices from each piece. Dry them well. Put a very thin layer of Crêpe batter (above) in a very hot buttered skillet. When it is set and brown on the underside, put one of the pieces of pineapple on it. Pour another very thin layer of Crêpe batter on it, turn over and cook until golden brown. Put in a hot serving dish and sprinkle with powdered sugar.

CREPES WITH APPLES
(Crêpes aux Pommes)

Peel 1 large apple, remove core and mince pulp very fine, and sauté quickly in a little butter. Put a very thin layer of Crêpe batter (page 270) in a very hot buttered skillet. When it is set and brown on the underside, spread it with a layer of minced apple. Pour another very thin layer of Crêpe batter on it, turn over and cook until golden brown. Put in a hot serving dish and sprinkle with powdered sugar.

CREPES SUZETTE CHEZ SOI

Follow directions for making Crêpes (page 270). Cream ½ cup butter with ½ cup powdered (or sifted granulated) sugar. Remove the zest of 2 oranges with a very fine grater and add to the creamed butter and sugar. Add a few drops lemon and orange juice and a pony of curaçao (or any desired liqueur). Spread this on the cooked crêpes, then fold or roll them up. Put in a very hot heatproof serving dish and sprinkle with sugar. Pour a pony of brandy over them and ignite.

CREPES WITH CONFITURE

Follow directions for making Crêpes (page 270), having them slightly larger than ordinary crêpes. When done, spread with any desired jam or marmalade and roll them up. Put on a hot heatproof serving dish, sprinkle with sugar and put under broiler or in a very hot oven until sugar is caramelized.

PANCAKES
(Crêpes Menagère)

½ cup flour
2 tablespoons sugar
¼ teaspoon salt
3 eggs

1¾ cup milk
flavoring (orange, vanilla or rum as desired)

Mix together flour, sugar and salt. Add eggs and mix well with a whip. Add milk and flavoring. Mix all together until smooth. Strain through a fine sieve. Put butter in a hot skillet, using just enough to grease it. When very hot, pour in just enough batter to cover the bottom of the skillet thinly. When set and brown on the underside, turn over and cook until golden brown. Put in a hot serving dish and sprinkle with powdered sugar. Or serve with maple syrup or honey. Or spread with marmalade or jelly and roll up. Makes 15 pancakes.

SOUFFLES

Soufflés are typically French. There are two general kinds, savory soufflés that are eaten as an hors d'oeuvre or an entrée and the sweet soufflés that are eaten for dessert. Cheese and Fish Soufflés are examples of the first group while the recipes which follow are examples of the second.

Basically a soufflé is a purée thickened with egg yolks and lightened with enough stiffly beaten egg white to make them puff up to delicate heights when baked. The yolks are beaten until light and foamy and added to the purée base. The whites are then beaten until stiff and folded in. They must not be dry, however, and to prevent this a little sugar is added when they are starting to form in delicate peaks and the beating is continued only until they are still in the "glistening" stage. "Folding" means cutting through the mixture, raising and folding it over and over so that none of the lightness so carefully beaten in will be lost. Stirring crushes and breaks down the tiny air cells upon which the light delicacy of a soufflé depends.

The mold for a sweet soufflé is always buttered and sprinkled with sugar. This forms a thin sweet crust and prevents the soufflé from sticking to the mold. Then 15 to 20 minutes in a hot oven will puff it up several inches above the top of the mold and the resulting pudding will have a nicely browned crust surrounding a light, creamy center.

There are three ways of making a soufflé. The conventional one starts with a butter and flour roux; the second—and this requires a little less butter—cooks the flour in hot milk; and the third way— usually followed in restaurants—is to start with Crème Pâtissière as the base. Since Crème Pâtissière can be kept for a couple of days in the refrigerator this last method is also practical at home. For example, whenever this crème is made up for éclairs or any other purpose a little extra can be made and put aside for a soufflé a day or two later. Any soufflé must be served immediately, because only a few minutes' standing will cause it to fall and be a heavy, disappointing and unattractive dessert. In other words, a soufflé must go in the oven just twenty minutes before it is to be eaten and will wait for no one. And after it is done, it can never be transferred to another serving dish but must be served from the mold or casserole in which it was baked.

There is a soufflé variation called a Pudding Soufflé which has the advantage that it can be held and reheated if dinner must be delayed. It will fall down while it stands but can be returned to the oven to be reheated and will puff up again. It is usually made in a mold with a tube center and for serving is inverted on the serving dish and a sauce poured over and around it.

VANILLA SOUFFLE NO. 1

2 *tablespoons butter*
1 *tablespoon flour*
½ *cup scalded milk*
1 *piece vanilla bean (or a little
   extract)*

4-5 *egg yolks*
6 *egg whites*
¼ *cup sugar*

Melt butter, add flour and cook until it starts to turn golden. Add milk and vanilla bean and cook, stirring constantly, until it thickens and then continue cooking, stirring occasionally, about 5 minutes. Beat egg yolks and 3 tablespoons sugar together and combine with the milk mixture. Remove vanilla bean (or add extract). Beat egg whites stiff, adding remaining tablespoon sugar during last few minutes of beating. Fold carefully into the mixture, cutting through the mixture, raising and folding it over and over until the whites are completely but lightly incorporated. Pour in a buttered and sugared baking dish and bake in a hot oven of 425 degrees 15 to 20 minutes. Serve immediately. Serves 3 to 4.

VANILLA SOUFFLE NO. 2

½ *cup milk*
¼ *cup sugar*
1 *piece of vanilla bean (or a little
   extract)*
1 *tablespoon flour*

3 *tablespoons cold milk*
1 *tablespoon butter*
4 *egg yolks*
5 *egg whites*

Scald milk with vanilla bean. Mix flour and 3 tablespoons sugar, and add cold milk, then add this to hot milk. Cook, stirring constantly, until thick. Remove vanilla bean (or add extract) and add butter. Remove from heat. Beat egg yolks and combine with milk mixture. Beat egg whites stiff, adding remaining tablespoon sugar during last few minutes. Fold whites carefully into mixture, cutting through the mixture, raising and folding it over and over until whites are completely but lightly incorporated. Pour into a buttered and sugared mold and bake in a hot oven of 425 to 450 degrees 15 to 20 minutes. Serves 3 to 4.

VANILLA SOUFFLE NO. 3

¼ *cup Crème Pâtissière* (page 231)
4 *egg yolks*
5 *egg whites*

1 *tablespoon sugar*
1 *piece vanilla bean (or a little
   extract)*

Beat yolks with ½ tablespoon sugar and combine with Crème Pâtissière. Scrape out the seeds from the vanilla bean and add (or add extract). Beat egg whites until stiff, adding remaining ½ tablespoon sugar during last few minutes of beating. Fold carefully into the mixture, cutting through the mixture, raising and folding it over and over until whites are completely but lightly incorporated. Pour into a buttered and sugared mold and bake in a hot oven of 425 to 450 degrees 15 to 20 minutes. Serves 3 to 4.

CHOCOLATE SOUFFLE

Follow recipe for Vanilla Soufflé (page 273), adding 1½ ounces grated chocolate (sweetened or unsweetened) to the hot milk mixture, stirring until the chocolate is thoroughly combined. Add 2 tablespoons additional sugar when using unsweetened chocolate and 1 tablespoon when using sweetened chocolate.

COFFEE SOUFFLE

Follow recipe for Vanilla Soufflé (page 273), adding coffee essence to taste or coffee-flavored milk following directions for flavoring the milk given in Mocha Crème au Beurre (page 232).

LEMON SOUFFLE

Follow recipe for Vanilla Soufflé (page 273), omitting the vanilla and adding finely grated rind of ½ lemon and 1 tablespoon lemon juice to the mixture just before folding in the egg whites.

ORANGE SOUFFLE

Follow recipe for Vanilla Soufflé (page 273), omitting the vanilla and adding the finely grated rind of ½ orange and 2 tablespoons orange juice to the mixture just before folding in the egg whites.

LIQUEUR-FLAVORED SOUFFLE

Follow recipe for Vanilla Soufflé (page 273). Put ½ the mixture in the mold and spread on it a layer of lady fingers soaked in liqueur. Cover with remaining soufflé and bake as usual. Serve with English Custard (page 255) to which has been added a few spoonfuls of whipped cream and flavored with the same liqueur which was used for the lady fingers.

OTHER FLAVORED PUDDING SOUFFLE

Make chocolate, coffee, lemon, etc. Pudding Soufflé by following directions for varying soufflés (above) but using the Pudding Soufflé recipe (page 275) for the foundation.

PUDDING SOUFFLE

3 *tablespoons butter*   1 *piece vanilla bean* (*or extract*)
3 *tablespoons sugar*   4 *egg whites*
6 *tablespoons flour*   4 *egg yolks*
¾ *cup milk*   *pinch of salt*

Cream butter, add flour and cream together. Scald milk with vanilla bean (or add extract) and combine with butter and flour, then cook, stirring constantly, until the mixture no longer sticks to the pan but rolls away from the side of it. Remove from heat and add egg yolks and sugar which have been beaten together. Add salt and mix well. Beat whites until stiff and fold carefully into the mixture, cutting through the mixture, raising and folding it over and over until whites are completely but lightly incorporated. Pour into a buttered and sugared mold with a tube in the center. The mold should be only ¾ full. Set in a pan of hot water and bake in a moderate oven of 350 to 375 degrees 40 to 50 minutes. If soufflé browns too much, place a piece of buttered paper over the top. When done, remove from oven and let settle just a little bit. To serve, invert on serving dish and cover with English Custard (page 255) or Crème Sabayon (page 252). If desired to serve later leave in mold and return to oven in the pan of hot water and cook until it rises again. Serves 6.

OMELET SOUFFLE
(Omelette Soufflée)

In country places an Omelet Soufflé is much more often made than a conventional soufflé, probably because it is more quickly and more easily put together. An omelet soufflé is baked on a heatproof platter and looks very pretty when it comes to the table all puffed up and glistening from the sugar that was sprinkled all over the top of it. In spreading the omelet soufflé mixture on the platter it is mounded about four inches high and then a depression about two inches deep is drawn right through the center so that when it goes in the oven it looks very much like the top of a man's felt hat. This gives the heat a better chance to penetrate the soufflé evenly and makes an attractive top when it has finished baking.

5 *tablespoons sugar*   1 *piece vanilla bean* (*or a little*
4 *egg yolks*   *extract*)
5 *egg whites*

Mix together sugar and egg yolks with the seeds scraped from the vanilla bean (or extract). Work up well, beating until very light and pale colored. Beat whites until stiff and then fold them into the egg yolk and sugar mixture as in making other soufflés. Spread on a buttered heatproof serving platter, heaping the mixture in an oval-shaped mound, with a depression drawn through the center with a knife or spoon. Smooth over the top with a spatula and bake in a moderately hot oven of 375 to 400 degrees 18 to 20 minutes. It should be puffed and brown all over. A few minutes before it will be done, sprinkle the top with the sugar. Serves 3 to 4.

Sweet Sauces

Many of the best-liked entremets at my home were nothing more than various combinations of milk, cream and eggs with sometimes a thickening agent like farina, rice or gelatin. But, because these combinations are apt to be bland, we usually served sauces, most often made of fruit, with them. For example, an easy and inexpensive sauce was made from almost any fruit juice, flavored with a little lemon juice and thickened with arrowroot. (Cornstarch, if that is more easily obtained, gives about the same result as arrowroot.) Melted currant jelly was also very popular as a sauce but Apricot Sauce was used more than anything else. In fact, Apricot Sauce was an ingredient of many of our entremets as you can see by the recipes in this book. We made it from apricot jam or from dried apricots with equally good results and kept it in a jar in a cold place, using it as we needed it. If a little liqueur is poured on top, the sauce will not mold and can be kept a long time.

APRICOT SAUCE NO. 1

1½ cups apricot jam
½ cup water
2 tablespoons sugar

1-2 tablespoons kirsch (or other liqueur)

Mix together all ingredients except kirsch (or other liqueur). Bring to a boil, and cook 5 to 10 minutes, stirring to keep from scorching. Rub through a sieve and add kirsch (or other liqueur).

APRICOT SAUCE NO. 2

½ *lb. dried apricots*   ½ *cup sugar*
2 *cups water*

Wash apricots. Put to soak for several hours in the water. Bring to a boil and simmer until they are soft. Rub through a sieve and add sugar to the purée. Return to fire and cook until sugar is dissolved. If too thick, cook up with a little water to desired consistency.

CHOCOLATE SAUCE

Grate ½ lb. sweet cooking chocolate and mix with 1 cup water. Bring to a boil and cook until smooth. Rub through a fine strainer.

FRUIT SAUCE

Add a little lemon juice to any fruit juice and thicken with cornstarch, using 1 teaspoon cornstarch mixed with a little cold fruit juice to each cup of liquid. Boil until clear and thickened and add sugar to taste.

RED CURRANT SAUCE NO. 1

Heat red currant jelly slowly until melted.

RED CURRANT SAUCE NO. 2

Combine 1 cup strained, red currant juice with 1½ cups sugar and cook until dissolved. Boil, skim well until thick or to 238 degrees F. if a sugar thermometer is used.

P*reserves and* C*onfitures*

〜❄〜

THE amount of food preserving done at my home was small, never as extensive as is quite usual in country homes over here. Our preserving was a matter of preventing the waste of surplus vegetables and fruits from the home garden, which we couldn't consume as they ripened.

French jams, marmalades and jellies are grouped together under the name "*confiture*." I think the *confiture* which is best known as being typically French is Bar-le-Duc jelly, named for a town famous for very fine, large currants.

STRING BEANS IN SALT

Clean string beans, cut off ends and parboil in salted water 3 minutes. Drain and spread out on a towel to cool. Put in a crock in layers, sprinkling each layer generously with coarse salt. Finish with a layer of salt on top. Put a wooden cover with a heavy weight on top to keep the beans down in the brine as the liquid forms. When ready to use, remove as many beans as desired, and let stand in cold water, changing the water occasionally, for 24 hours to remove salt. Cook in unsalted water.

TOMATO PUREE

Cook tomatoes about 15 minutes. Place in colander and drain for a few hours. (Save the juice which drains out for soups or sauces.) Rub pulp through a sieve into a saucepan and cook until desired thickness. Fill sterilized jars, seal and put in water bath. Cook pint jars 45 minutes, half pints 35 minutes.

SOUR PICKLES
(Cornichons)

Place small pickling cucumbers on a heavy towel, sprinkle with coarse salt, roll up the towel and rub the cucumbers with it to remove all the roughness of the skin. When the towel becomes wet, tie up the four corners and hang where it can drip overnight. Remove cucumbers, dry them on a clean towel, put in a bowl, cover with boiling vinegar and let stand 24 hours. Drain off the vinegar, bring it to a boil, pour it over the cucumbers and let stand another 24 hours. Drain and pack in jars. Add an onion, a small red or green pepper, a clove of garlic and some tarragon to each jar. Measure enough vinegar to fill the jars, bring to the boiling point, pour over the pickles and seal.

SOUR PICKLES (COLD METHOD)

Prepare small pickling cucumbers in towel as in recipe above. When dry, pack in sterilized jars, putting a small onion, a clove of garlic, a small red pepper, a few branches of tarragon and a few peppercorns in each jar. Cover with vinegar, filling the jars to overflowing and seal jars.

APRICOT, PLUM OR PEACH JAM

For each pound of fruit use ¾ pound sugar. Place sugar in saucepan, add enough water to dissolve it, bring to a boil and cook until a little dropped in cold water forms a soft ball (238 degrees F. if a thermometer is used). Meanwhile, if peaches are used, peel and remove pits; if plums or apricots are used, remove pits but do not peel. Cut fruit in halves or quarters, depending upon size, add to syrup and cook about ½ hour. Remove fruit with a skimmer and put in sterilized glasses, filling them two thirds full. Break pits, blanch almonds from center, and put one in each glass. Cook syrup until a soft ball is formed when dropped in cold water (238 degrees F. if a thermometer is used) and pour over fruit, filling glasses completely, and seal.

CHERRY JAM
(Confiture de Cerises)

Follow directions for Strawberry Jam (page 282), using 1 pound sugar for each pound sour cherries or ¾ pound sugar for each pound sweet cherries.

BAR-LE-DUC JELLY
(Gelée de Groseilles de Bar-le-Duc)

Select the largest currants available, either red or white, and remove from the stems. Remove seeds as follows: Pierce the bottom of each berry with a sharp toothpick or darning needle and force seeds through the opening. For each pound of currants allow 1½ pounds

[279]

sugar and 1½ cups water. Dissolve sugar in water, bring to a boil and cook until it has not quite reached the stage where it forms a soft ball when a little is dropped in cold water (238 degrees if a thermometer is used). Skim if necessary. Add berries to sugar syrup, bring back to a boil and cook 1 minute. Pour into small sterilized jars. If berries tend to rise to the surface, press them down in the glass with the blunt end of a wooden skewer before the jelly sets.

CURRANT JELLY

For each 2 pounds of currants (all red currants or ⅔ red and ⅓ white) use 1 cup raspberries. Remove currants from stems and wash in cold water. Drain and place in a saucepan with raspberries and ½ cup water for each 2 pounds currants. Place over low heat and cook, stirring occasionally, until the juice is drawn out of the fruit, about 15 minutes. Turn into a jelly bag or muslin cloth to drain. Measure juice, add an equal quantity of sugar, bring to a boil and skim. Cook, skimming as needed, until it leaves the spoon in large clinging drops. (If a thermometer is used, cook to 220 degrees F.) Pour into sterilized glasses and seal.

UNCOOKED CURRANT JELLY

Crush currants (or ⅔ currants and ⅓ raspberries) well. Press through a sieve to remove all the juice. Weigh juice and for each pound of juice use 1½ pounds sugar. Stir sugar in juice until dissolved, fill small sterilized glasses and place them in very hot sunshine for 8 hours in the middle of the day for 2 days. Seal. This jelly does not keep as well as that cooked on the stove but it has a better flavor.

ORANGE MARMALADE

12 large oranges   sugar equal in weight to the oranges
2 large (or 3 medium) apples

Peel 6 of the oranges, removing only the yellow part, none of the white part. Cut this peel in very fine julienne, cover with boiling water and let stand 5 to 7 minutes. Strain, put peel in a bowl and cover with enough water containing a little sugar to prevent drying out and set aside. Add enough water to the sugar to dissolve it, bring to a boil, skim and cook until a little dropped in cold water forms a soft ball (238 degrees if a thermometer is used). Peel, seed and slice all the oranges, add to the sugar syrup and leave where the mixture will be hot, but not actually boiling, until the fruit juice is drawn out into the syrup. Bring to a boil, cook 8 to 10 minutes, pour into a bowl and let stand 24 hours. Return to the fire and boil 8 to 10 minutes, then replace in the bowl and let stand another 24 hours.

On the third day, remove the small black blossom from the end of each apple, chop the apples and put in a pan with enough water to cover them. Cook about 20 minutes and strain through a fine sieve or cheesecloth. Combine apple juice, the twice-cooked fruit and sugar syrup, and the finely cut peel which had been left in sugar and water. Bring all to a boil and cook until it drops from the side of the spoon in large clinging drops. Pour into sterilized glasses and seal. Unless orange marmalade is made by the three-day method, the sugar does not penetrate the skin and the pieces of fruit rind are apt to be tough.

QUINCE JELLY

Select good quinces with a nice golden color. Wash, dry and cut in quarters. Peel and seed and place everything in water with a little lemon juice to prevent the fruit from turning dark. Drain and put in a saucepan, adding 1 quart water for each pound of fruit. The seeds, cores and peelings improve the flavor and color of the jelly. Cover and cook until the pulp is very soft, about 30 to 40 minutes, depending upon the fruit. Strain through jelly bag or muslin cloth. Measure the juice and add to it an equal quantity of sugar. Bring to a boil, skim and cook until it leaves the side of the spoon in large clinging drops, about 45 minutes for 2 to 4 quarts of mixture. (If a thermometer is used, cook to 220 degrees F.)

QUINCE MARMALADE

Prepare quinces as for Quince Jelly (above). After cooking the pulp, peelings, cores and seeds, remove as many pieces of the pulp as possible and drain the remaining mixture through cheesecloth. Slice the reserved pieces of pulp as thinly as possible and add to the strained juice. Measure sliced pulp and juice, add an equal quantity of sugar and finish cooking as described in making Quince Jelly (above), taking care to prevent mixture from scorching.

QUINCE PASTE

Wash good, ripe quinces, cut in quarters, peel, seed and place in water with a little lemon juice to prevent the fruit from turning dark. Drain, place in a saucepan and add 1 quart water for each pound of fruit. Cover and cook until pulp is very soft, about 30 to 40 minutes, depending upon the fruit. Rub through a sieve. Measure the purée and add an equal quantity of sugar. Bring to a boil and cook until the mixture is very, very thick, stirring during the last of the cooking to prevent the mixture from scorching. (An asbestos or metal plate under the pan is a help in keeping it from scorching.) Pour into a shallow pan lined with heavy waxed paper having the paste about ½ to 1 inch thick. This sheet of paste can be wrapped in waxed paper and kept in a cold place almost indefinitely. When ready to use, cut in ½ to 1 inch squares and roll each one in granulated sugar. They are usually served on a plate with bonbons or with Petits Fours.

RHUBARB JAM
(Confiture de Rhubarbe)

Scrape strings from rhubarb stalks and cut in pieces about ½ inch long. Combine with an equal weight of sugar. Let stand 10 hours. Bring to a boil and cook until thick like marmalade. Pour into sterilized glasses and seal.

STRAWBERRY JAM
(Confiture de Fraises)

For each pound of strawberries use ½ pound sugar. Remove hulls, and wash and drain berries. Place sugar in saucepan and add enough water to dissolve it. Bring it to a boil, skim, and cook until a little dropped in cold water forms a ball (238 degrees F. if a thermometer is used). Add berries and put saucepan where it will remain hot, but not cook, in order to draw out the juice. Leave about 10 minutes and skim, if necessary. Remove berries with a skimmer and put in a bowl. Cook syrup down again to the same stage as above, replace the berries in it and let stand again in a hot place for 15 minutes. Remove berries again with skimmer and cook syrup down again to the same stage as before. Add berries and cook until the juice falls in thick clinging drops from the side of the spoon. Let cool for 24 hours. Fill sterilized glasses and seal.

TOMATO MARMALADE

Press ripe tomatoes through a coarse sieve or a colander, then put in a jelly bag or in muslin to drain. Weigh the pulp remaining in the cloth. For every 2 pounds tomato pulp add 1½ cups apple juice or red currant juice and 1½ cups sugar. Add a vanilla bean and cook all together until it becomes thick like marmalade. Pour into jars and seal.

French Eating Customs

⇦ ✻ ⇨

MOTHER at the kitchen table under the casement window, mincing and slicing, beating and stirring, and at the big, black stove deftly handling casseroles and skillets, was leading up to her final triumphs, the succulent dishes she set on the dining table.

We Bourbonnais love to eat. But then so do all the French. Every mother's son, peasant and workman as well as "those out of the top drawer," regards an appreciation of fine food as his cultural heritage. It isn't necessary to dine in the sophisticated elegance of the Ritz or Maxim's on caviar and *dinde truffés* to realize this.

We ate in the kitchen as did most families. Nor was this a makeshift arrangement until we might be more prosperous. We liked it that way. So our kitchens had enough room to accommodate the dining table with comfort. A faint wave of homesickness sweeps over me as I think of that pleasant, white-walled room; of the table with its checked cloth—bright blue squares against snowy white; of my father breaking off a piece of bread to ensnare the last drop of sauce on his plate, while mother waited to cut the fruit tart.

The blue-and-white cloth was universal, as symbolic of eating as the earthenware marmite was of cooking. Our dishes were fairly universal, too, at least near likenesses of them could be found in every French dish closet. Our clay casseroles and platters, a high round soup tureen called a *soupière*, our individual pottery bowls, the white china salad bowl with its pedestal base and the red-and-blue bordered china bowl for our beloved *Oeufs à la Neige* (Floating Island) were all traditional. My mother knew that some mysterious relationship existed between the spotless tablecloth, the nice accessories and her good food and the happy home her children will never forget. No psychologist had to tell her that.

Breakfast was called Petit Déjeuner and we usually ate soup, preferably potage or panade made with milk or else onion soup with chunky slices of dry French bread in it. This corresponds to the break-fast cereal of Britains and Americans. Father drank black coffee also and we children sometimes had chocolate or a light café au lait—coffee with milk, mostly milk. Each morning Madame Dujonc, the farm woman who delivered milk—*la laitière*—arrived on her daily round with her two milk pails on the ends of a wooden support rest-ing on her shoulders.

The midday meal, Déjeuner, was our main one. For city families it might be light, but even with them it was often the hearty meal. We might start with an hors d'oeuvres or with the main dish, a stew, hash, braised or roasted meat, except on fast days when we had an egg or cheese dish or perhaps fish. On Sundays, the traditional Pot-au-Feu was a "must." Our potatoes were good, cheap and plentiful and we ate them in some form almost every day, substituting rice, noodles or macaroni once in a while. Our custom was to serve the vegetable after the meat and potatoes had been eaten—unless, of course, it was cooked with the meat as in a stew. Salad was for warm weather meals because in wintertime we had no way of getting it. Déjeuner ended with fruit or cheese, often both, or a light *entremet*. Hearty desserts were only for very light meals.

Grown-ups drank wine, red or white, red preferred by most French-men. We children had a little spooned into our glasses of water, just enough to give the least bit of color and flavor. Every section had its own local wines, called *vins du pays*, usually so low in alcoholic con-tent that they can't be shipped away without spoiling. They are so inexpensive that everyone can have them.

The evening meal, called *diner* or *souper*, was very simple in country sections. Often a bowl of soup or merely bread and cheese with wine sufficed. But sometimes mother made an egg or cheese dish or gave us salad with cold cuts from the *charcuterie*. If pudding, galette or some sweet was left from the noonday meal we finished it at night or had fruit and cheese. Wine was the beverage, and milk for the children, but never hot tea or coffee. We didn't care for them in summer and we had soup in winter. In larger towns and cities where people stayed up later than in the country, this evening meal was hearty, like our noonday déjeuner.

The menus which follow are typical of the meals we ate every day for déjeuner and diner-souper.

DEJEUNER

Braised Calf's Liver with Red Wine

Mashed Potatoes   Creamed Spinach

Pancakes with Jam

———

Blanquette of Veal

Parsley Potatoes   String Beans Lyonnaise

Baked Apple

———

Beef à la Mode

Carrots   Onions   Noodles in Butter

Green Salad

Stewed Fruit

———

Fowl with Rice

Vegetables cooked with Fowl   Supreme Sauce

Fruit Tart

———

Loin of Pork à la Boulangère

Red Cabbage   Apple Sauce

DINER-SOUPER

Panade with Sorrel

Cold Cuts   Salad

Cheese

———

Potato Pie

String Bean Salad   Fruit

———

Leek and Potato Soup

Omelet with Chopped Herbs   Stewed Apples

———

Lamb Hash Lyonnaise

Salad   Cheese

———

Sorrel Soup

Headcheese   Tomato Salad

[285]

**MORE ELABORATE MENUS FOR DEJEUNER AND
DINER-SOUPER**

DEJEUNER

Marinated Mackerel or Herring

Pork Chop Sauté with Piquant Sauce   Mashed Potatoes

Apple Fritters

———

Rillettes de Porc

Partridge with Cabbage

English Custard   Lady Fingers

———

Onion Soup

Stewed Rabbit or Hare with Red Wine   Potatoes in their Jackets

Salad

French Pancakes with Apples

———

Gnocchi à la Parisienne

Breaded Escalope of Veal   Spinach with Gravy

Fruit Tart

———

Carbonnade de Boeuf Flamande

Eggplant Housewife Style   Boiled Potatoes

Vanilla Soufflé

———

DINER-SOUPER

Soup with Bread Crusts

Brook Trout Meunière

Chicken in Casserole Bonne Femme   Salad in Season

Caramel Custard

———

Cream of Watercress Soup

Matelote of Fish   Eggplant with Tomatoes

Rice Mold

———

Pot-au-Feu

Boiled Beef with Vegetables cooked with it

Cheese   Fruits

Cream of Potato and Sorrel Soup
Filet of Sole Bonne Femme
Roast Chicken with Watercress   Sautéed Green Beans
Vanilla Soufflé

————

Cream of Lentil Soup
Roast Rack of Lamb with Watercress
Creamed Spinach with Hard-Boiled Egg   Potatoes Parmentier
Blanc Mange

When party days came along, the quantities of food we French prepared would, I am sure, startle most Americans. In my early days —and they go back to the 1890's—family parties were a part of any event that could be an excuse for a celebration. Our fun, for the most part, was fun with our own families. A church holiday, a youngster's first communion, a marriage or a baptism was an occasion for a family reunion. Then aunts, uncles and cousins, and grandparents too, would come together for the festivities, no small part of which was the fine dinner at the long food-laden table. These were the times when every housewife put her best foot forward, never risking the aftermath of contemptuous gossip on the part of in-laws as regards her culinary skill.

In our house, the biggest room was cleared of superfluous furniture to make a place for the great long table, mother's bridal linens were brought out—some handed down to her from her mother—and extra china and tableware borrowed from near-by relatives. Usually some of the family arrived the day before the party and set to work to help with the cooking. In the meantime, extra bread was ordered from the *boulangerie* and Vol-au-Vents, brioches and gâteaux from the *pâtisserie*. Then, with a local girl or two hired to come in and wash dishes and be generally useful, everything was set to take care of the dinner.

The wedding party was always the finest. Scores of relatives would make the trip from far-off places, whereas only those living fairly close would come for a first communion, a baptism or a church holiday. Dinner started at about 2 o'clock when everyone had returned from church and the bridal couple had made the rounds of the village to receive the good wishes of the townfolk. The eating went on and on all day for great quantities of food had been lovingly and carefully prepared. Crawfish were in season and the familiar three-tiered dishes, bright pink against green parsley, known to all Frenchmen as Buisson d'Ecrevisses, were used as table decorations. In the center, of course,

[287]

was the cake, a Biscuit de Savoie beautifully frosted and decorated at our neighborhood *pâtisserie*.

The family talk lasted far into the night, but the young people danced to the tune of an accordion or other instrument played by someone from the village. Eating continued—mostly bread and cheese or brioches—and drinking wine went along with the talking. Next morning, after all who had stayed over night had a few hours' sleep, grand'mère served breakfast bowls of onion soup made with the leftover consommé. The wedding dinner leftovers were used for lunch along with a specially prepared game dish and freshly roasted chickens. After that, the party broke up, each one going his way, many not to meet again until a similar occasion brought them together.

COUNTRY WEDDING FEAST

Consommé Julienne	Bread Crusts with Marrow
Buisson of Crawfish	
Chicken in Red Wine	Parsleyed Potatoes
Roast Tenderloin of Beef	Small Peas Country Style
Salad in Season	

Citeau au Kirsch	Floating Island	Fruit Tart
Brioche	Lady Fingers	Macaroons
	Wedding Cake	

Local Wines	Old Wines
Coffee	Liqueurs

First communion was a smaller party, usually only grandparents and the near-by aunts and uncles coming for it. Two frosted and decorated cakes—each a Biscuit de Savoie—were ordered from the *pâtisserie*. One of these cakes was taken around the neighborhood by the youngster in whose honor they had been made, the mother going along to see that none of the neighborhood friends, the mayor, the doctor and so on were overlooked. Then came dinner at home and, as at all these family parties, it was more than ample, a fine Vol-au-Vent and a roast of beef, vegetables and all the usual array of entremets. If crawfish happened to be in season, the gay looking pink and green *Buisson d'Ecrevisses* was on the table to start the meal.

DINNER FOR A FIRST COMMUNION PARTY
Bouillon with Vermicelli
Vol-au-Vent of Chicken à la Reine
Roast Tenderloin of Beef

| String Beans with Butter | | Potato Rissolée |

Salad

| Oeufs à la Neige | Baked Caramel Custard | Fruit Tart |

Decorated Cake

| Lady Fingers | | Macaroons |
| Local Wines | Fruits | Old Wines |

Coffee

Baptism was a smaller and more intimate party because babies were baptized at such a tender age that the young mother might not have completely regained her strength. The grandmothers of the child on both sides of the house would come to help prepare the dinner—unless, of course, it was to be given in a restaurant.

One of the baptism customs, which all who have lived in France can hardly forget, is the throwing of Dragées—the Jordan almonds of the English—to the village children by the godparents as they leave the church, and the very fancy small boxes decorated in white, trimmed with pleated white paper and filled with the same Dragées that were given to all the members of the family and the close friends.

BAPTISM DINNER
Croûte-au-Pot

| Veal Cutlet with Peas and Carrots | | Mashed Potatoes |

Roast Chicken   Salad

| Baked Coffee Custard | | Lady Fingers |
| Local Wines | | Fruits |

Coffee

Christmas—*Noël*—in France is first of all a religious holiday. One's religious duties are taken care of, then the fun and the good Christmas dinner follows. Little children received gifts from the Christmas tree that was set up at school but family presents were given at New Year's. Instead of hanging up their stockings, they left their little wooden shoes—*sabots*—in front of the fireplace to be filled by *Le Père Janvier*—

Father January—who, like America's Santa Claus, was expected to come down the chimney. In the morning little boys found such simple toys as drums, horns and tin soldiers, while little girls crooned over new dolls or investigated the possibilities of sewing kits. Oranges and chocolates were there for all.

Everybody who possibly could went to midnight Mass on Christmas Eve. In the larger towns and cities it was followed by lively parties, many people going to restaurants as Americans do on New Year's Eve. This was called *Le Réveillon*. In country places the *réveillon* usually meant a little snack of charcuterie, brioche, galette or other favorite food and something to drink before going to bed. Then, on Christmas Day a fine dinner was served at noon with turkey or goose the *pièce de rèsistance*.

CHRISTMAS DINNER
Pork Hors D'oeuvres
Consommé Vermicelli
Roast Young Turkey or Goose

Potato Rissolée		Braised Celery
	String Bean Salad	
Crêpes with Apples		Plum Tart
Brioche		Galette
Local Wines	Coffee	Old Wines

Easter—*Pâques*—the other great day in the Christian calendar—also came in for its share of festivities. We always spent our Easter vacation days at our grandparents' farm in the country. On Easter Monday Grand'mère gave us eggs which she herself had colored and we rushed off to roll them on the newly sprouted grass in the meadow, making sure that we had baskets with us to fill with field salad and dandelions which were then at their tender best. When we returned with our baskets of greens and our eggs she would make a great bowl of salad of them both, for our supper.

The high spot of Easter-Sunday dinner was the tiny new spring lamb called *Agneau de Pâques*—Easter Lamb—that was served with the season's new peas and young fresh salad. *Andouillette* was also an Easter specialty. It was a kind of cooked sausage made with all kinds of seasoned pork specialties and was served either grilled or sautéed and then eaten with mustard.

EASTER DINNER

Pork Hors d'Oeuvres   Leek Salad

Pot-au-Feu Bouillon with Vegetables

Chicken Fricassée with Cream

Spring Lamb Boulangère   Small Peas à l'Etuvée

Salad

Brioches   Fruit Tarts   Ouefs à la Neige

Local Wines   Coffee

In summer we had picnics to celebrate feast days, merely walking to a pleasant spot in neighboring woods or meadow, or venturing farther away with our lunch hampers and ourselves packing the carriage. The lunch consisted of galantine and charcuterie or cold meat pies, potato salad, French bread and several kinds of cheese. There was always wine and we finished with tarts and little cakes either homemade or purchased from the *pâtisserie*.

Our special picnic was the one at Pentecost which came between late spring and summer, fifty days after Easter. We had a great family reunion at my Grandmother's because Pentecost also happened to be Feast Day of the village near which my grandparents' farm lay. Every village had its saint's or feast day to celebrate.

In the fall hunting picnics were frequent and then the lunch was, as a rule, either a meat or game pie and a salad of potatoes or other vegetables, with fruit and galette to top off the meal. And a good bottle of wine, of course.

Even at small railroad stations in France good food—as deliciously cooked and tasty as that found in any excellent inn—waited for hungry travelers. The call by the trainman "dix minutes d'ârret buffet," announced the ten-minute buffet stop. Then passengers would pile out of the train and go to the counter where plates—*plats du jour tout prêts* —were already fixed with *Ragoût de Mouton, Fricassée de Poulet, Coq au Vin* and *Civet de Lapin ou de Lièvre* for those who wanted something hot and didn't mind eating it quickly. Those who preferred to eat more leisurely could take little individual meat pies and small bottles of wine back to the train.

Yes, the French love good eating, a love so much a part of their daily lives that the French cuisine has become world famous. Their skill in combining simple raw materials to produce superlative dishes grows out of the *idée fixée* that anything eaten, even the daily potato, humble carrot and turnip and less tender cut of meat, must be well prepared. Gourmets are not made by eating occasional party fare or company meals or by infrequent excursions to famous restaurants. Good food must be eaten every day, every meal with each dish carefully prepared and suitably seasoned. Parties are merely the never-to-be-forgotten high spots. That is the French way and rare indeed is the Frenchman who does not believe that good living is an important part of a good life.

Glossary

Anglaise Coating. A coating which gives a crusty surface, a brown color and a good flavor to foods that are fried.

To Coat à l'Anglaise. Wipe dry any food that is moist. Dip in flour; then coat with a mixture made by combining 1 beaten egg with ¼ cup milk, 1 tablespoon salad oil and ½ teaspoon salt. Finally dip in fine dry bread crumbs and completely cover the surface. Each piece must be covered thoroughly with the egg and milk coating and then drained of surplus liquid so that it is just moist enough to hold crumbs.

To Cook à l'Anglaise. Boil food in salted water, drain and serve with plain butter.

Aspic. A jelly made from meat, poultry or fish stock or from fruit juice. If enough bones are used in making the stock (especially veal bones in meat and poultry stock) the mixture will stiffen or "jell" when cold. When bones are unobtainable, or when making a fruit-juice aspic, commercial gelatin is used in the proportion of 1 tablespoon granulated gelatin to each pint of liquid. The gelatin must be softened in 2 or 3 tablespoons cold liquid and then dissolved in the boiling stock or fruit juice.

Baste. To pour the cooking liquor or fat, or both, over food while it is cooking by ladling it over with a large spoon. Roasts are basted with the fat that collects in the roasting pan to keep the meat juicy and give it a nicely browned and glazed surface. Braised meats should be basted often with the cooking liquid to glaze the surface well. Baked fish is basted with the oil in which it cooks; braised fish is basted with the cooking liquid. Fruit poached in sugar syrup should be basted during cooking; baked apples should be basted with the juice in the pan.

Braise. To cook meat slowly in a little liquid in a covered utensil, basting it often, after first browning it in the uncovered utensil. Uncover last 10 minutes of cooking and baste with gravy. Braised fish is never browned.

Bread, Crusts for Soup. Small pieces of the outside crust of French bread without the soft crumb from the inside. Or slices of French bread cut about ¼ inch thick and dried in the oven. Usually served in Onion Soup or Petite Marmite.

Bread, Fried in Butter. Slices of bread, sometimes cut in fancy shapes, fried in butter. For Bouillabaisse they are fried in oil.

Bread Crumbs, Fresh. Soft crumbs from the inside of fresh bread, broken up very fine and strained through a coarse sieve.

Bread Crumbs, Dry. Crumbs from stale bread, strained through a coarse sieve.

Brochette. A long metal skewer—about 6 to 8 inches long—on which small pieces of meat or fish are put for broiling.

Bordelaise Mirepoix. A mixture of finely chopped vegetables, usually

[293]

carrots, onions, leeks and celery with a little thyme and bay leaf, put in the bottom of a pan and on which meat or fish is placed for cooking. Used to improve the flavor of meat or fish and also the flavor of the sauce made from the cooking liquid.

Bourbonnaise. As applied to foods and cooking this means the dishes prepared in the central part of France which borders on the Allier and Cher Rivers. This section is known for its good meat, poultry and game, its fine cheeses, rich milk and cream, and its succulent vegetables.

Capers. Flower buds from a shrub which are preserved in vinegar and used as a condiment. They are imported to this country in bottles.

Chapons. Rub pieces of bread crust well with garlic and toss in the bowl with a green salad.

Charcuterie. A store which sells all kinds of pork products. The products themselves are also called by this name. They include such dishes as pork chops cooked and taken home hot in their sauce; cold cuts, various kinds of sausages, head cheese, liver paste and so on. Many charcuterie specialties are used for hors d'oeuvres.

Chipolata Sausage. A variety of small spiced sausage used for garnishing.

Chervil. Garden herb of the parsley family. The young leaves are used in soups, sauces and salads.

Chives. A small herb with spear-shaped leaves similar in flavor to a leek or onion used in soups and salads. Always used raw and finely chopped.

To Clean Poultry. Singe off all hair and remove pin feathers. Cut slit in neck, cut out windpipe and discard. Cut slit around vent making it large enough to allow hand to pull out entrails and giblets. Discard entrails; save liver, gizzard and heart. Cut away gall sac from liver, split open gizzard and discard inner sac. Wash the inside of the bird with a moist cloth and wipe off the outside skin.

Coating Mold with Caramel. May be done in either of two ways as follows: 1. Sprinkle mold with sugar and cook in oven or on top of stove until golden brown. 2. Spread caramel syrup on inside of mold.

Caramel Syrup. 1. For coloring sauces or soups. Melt sugar (about ½ cup) in heavy, shallow pan and cook until brown and bubbling. Add 1 cup water and let sugar dissolve as it cools. 2. For desserts. Mix equal parts sugar and water and cook in heavy, shallow pan until water evaporates and syrup becomes golden. Use for coating molds or for flavoring dessert sauces.

Cocottes. Small, porcelain dishes, similar to ramekins, used for baking. Large cocottes are used for cooking chicken or entrées.

Croûtons. White bread cut in dice of any desired size and toasted in oven or broiler or sautéed in butter.

Faggot. 3 to 4 sprigs parsley, 1 to 2 stalks celery (sometimes 1 leek), ½ a bay leaf, and a pinch of dry (or 1 to 2 sprigs fresh) thyme tied together in a small bundle and cooked in a stew or sauce or with other foods to give it flavor.

Farce au Gratin. A stuffing made of liver, veal and pork that has been finely ground and well seasoned. Used for canapés and for various pâtés and usually accompanies feathered game. For recipe see LIVER STUFFING (page 145).

Fennel. A European herb of the parsley family, also grown in the United States. It has a mild anise-like flavor. Resembles celery in its overlapping stalks but has green feathery top.

Fines Herbes. A mixture of equal parts of finely chopped parsley, tarragon, chives and chervil.

Flambé. To sprinkle with brandy or a liqueur and ignite. The food takes on a special flavor after the alcohol is burned away.

To Fold in Whipped Egg Whites or Whipped Cream. Cut through the mixture with a spoon or spatula, folding the mixture up and over the egg whites or cream, continuing until they are thoroughly incorporated.

Garlic. A bulb with a pungent odor and flavor used in both raw and cooked mixtures. The bulb consists of a cluster of smaller ones, each called a clove.

Garnish. In French cooking, a garnish is any vegetable, sausage or other food served on the dish with the entrée. In American cooking, a garnish usually refers to something used to decorate a dish, such as parsley or watercress.

Hazelnut Brown. To melt butter and continue cooking it until it takes on a golden-brown color.

Julienne. Food cut in very fine strips.

Larding. Inserting, by means of a special needle, fine strips of fat salt or fresh pork through a piece of meat lacking in fat of its own. It adds fat and flavor to the inside of the meat muscle.

Larding Needle. Special needle used to insert fat salt or fresh pork in meat.

Lardons. Small pieces of fat salt or fresh pork inserted in meat which is lacking in fat of its own; or diced pork fat cooked until brown and used for garnishing.

Leeks. Long cylindrical bulbs with an onion-like flavor, but milder and sweeter. Used mainly in soups.

Macédoine. A mixture of fruit or vegetables. Larger kinds are usually cut in pieces.

Marinade. The spiced, acid liquid in which foods are allowed to stand and from which they obtain added flavor. Sometimes used to make tough meats tender.

To Marinate. To allow foods to stand in a spiced, acid liquid to improve their flavor and in the case of tough meats to make them more tender. The acid may be vinegar, wine or lemon juice.

Marmite. An earthenware cooking utensil usually taller than it is round. Used especially for cooking soups or stews.

Meunière. A food served "Meunière" is sautéed and then served with butter which has been melted and cooked to a light brown, poured over the top and sprinkled with a little chopped parsley and a little lemon juice. A slice of lemon is served on the side.

Mince. To cut up very, very finely. (The French word *émincé*, however, means to cut in slices.)

[295]

Mushroom Liquor. The cooking liquid remaining from cooking mushrooms for garnishing (page 186), which is strained and used for flavoring sauces.

Parisian Spice. A commercially blended spice which is purchased. To use, mix ½ teaspoon Parisian spice with 3 tablespoons salt.

Poach. To simmer very gently, basting during the cooking.

Parboil. To boil, in enough water to cover, for 5 to 10 minutes. Salt pork or bacon is parboiled to remove excess salt. Meat or poultry is parboiled to remove particles that may spoil clarity of soup.

Prepared Mustard. A commercial mixture of mustard and spice that is purchased in paste form.

Juniper Berries. Berries with a pungent flavor used in cooking such foods as sauerkraut.

Pastry Bag. A cornucopia made of heavy white cotton cloth, with the small end having an opening just large enough to hold a metal tube. Used in making decorations or shaping doughs for baking.

Purée. Vegetables, fruits or other foods forced through a fine sieve to remove skins, seeds, etc., and produce a fine-textured food. Puréed vegetables are usually finished with butter and a little cream.

Reduce. To cook a liquid in order to concentrate its flavor or make its consistency thicker.

To Ribbon. Applied to a sugar and egg mixture that is worked up with a whip or spoon until it ribbons as it flows from the spoon.

Roux, Blond. A mixture of fat and flour cooked until it just starts to turn golden. Must be stirred during cooking to insure an even color.

Roux, Brun. A mixture of fat and flour cooked until it is medium brown in color. Must be stirred during cooking to insure an even browning.

Saffron. A flavoring and coloring ingredient used in cooking. Is purchased in dry form.

Salt Pork Dice. Fat salt pork, preferably from the belly of the hog, and cut in dice of any desired size.

Saucisson. Varieties of long sausages made from pork and sold either raw or cooked. Used for hors d'oeuvres and garnishing.

Sauté. To cook in a shallow pan in a small amount of hot fat.

Scald. To bring to the boiling point, or to cook in the top of a double boiler until hottest temperature is reached.

Skewer. See BROCHETTE.

Shallot. Small bulb with an onion-like but milder flavor. When shallots are unobtainable onion may be used.

Score. To cut incisions about ¼ inch deep with a sharp knife. Usually done in a pattern of strips, diamonds or squares.

Spatula. 1. A flexible metal knife used to remove food from one dish to another. 2. A wooden spatula, similar to a wooden spoon but perfectly flat, used to work up flour mixtures or in mixing sauces.

Singe. To remove hairs from poultry by burning it off.

Simmer. To cook very, very gently so that the mixture bubbles but cooks at a temperature just under boiling.

Specialties. 1. Hors d'oeuvres specialties are meat mixtures, sausages, etc.

2. Meat specialties are the variety meats such as liver, sweetbreads, tongue, kidneys, heart, tripe, oxtails and brains.

Stock, Brown. Juice from beef that has been extracted by cooking in water. Bones, vegetables, and seasonings are usually added to the water.

Stock, White. Juice from poultry and veal extracted by cooking in water. Bones, vegetables and seasonings are usually added to the water.

Stock, Fish. Juice from fish extracted by cooking in water. Bones, vegetables and seasonings are usually added to the water.

Soufflé Mold. A deep mold or baking dish (made in several sizes).

Sugar Syrup. When sugar is dissolved in water it takes on different characteristics depending upon the concentration of the solution. There are about 6 stages important in home cooking, ranging from a light syrup to a dark caramel syrup. Each stage has its special uses. The mixture of sugar and water specified in a recipe is heated until the sugar is dissolved and then it is boiled until it reaches the desired concentration. As it becomes more concentrated through the evaporation of the water, the temperature on a thermometer placed in the mixture rises. This is a convenient way of determining syrup concentrations. During the boiling, impurities rise to the surface and should be skimmed off.

Light Syrup for Fruit Compotes. A light syrup to use for cooking fruit is made by boiling 2 cups water with ¾ cup sugar for 5 minutes. If desired, a slice of lemon or a piece of vanilla may be added to this syrup and cooked until soft. Berries, however, are put in the boiling syrup (after they have been well drained) and brought back just to the boiling point. They will become mushy if allowed to boil.

Simple Syrup for Baba and Savarin. Simple syrup is made by boiling equal quantities of sugar and water for 5 minutes or until a thermometer placed in it registers 218 degrees F.

Sugar and Fruit Juice for Jelly. In making jelly, the strained fruit juice and sugar are boiled until the mixture falls from the side of the spoon in heavy drops or a thin sheet, or until a thermometer placed in it registers 220 degrees F.

Sugar Syrup for Fondant, or the Soft Ball Stage. The sugar and water are boiled until a little of the syrup dropped in cold water forms a soft ball when rolled between the fingers, or until a thermometer placed in it registers 238 degrees F. This syrup is also used for making Italian meringue.

Light Caramel Syrup for Desserts. The sugar and water are boiled together until the syrup takes on a light golden color. This syrup is the one used for spun sugar, for dipping fruits and for coating dessert molds.

Dark Caramel. This is the last stage and the one at which the sugar and water are boiled until the syrup takes on a dark-brown color. At that point a little water—just enough to cover the surface of the sugar—is added and left to dissolve the browned sugar. This is used for coloring sauces and soups.

Tarragon. A plant with aromatic leaves used mainly for seasoning salads and sauces and for flavoring vinegar.

Tomalley. Fatty, soft, so-called liver of lobster, greenish gray in color when raw, turning to a bright green when cooked. The tomalley is used to thicken sauces for lobster, but the sauce cannot be boiled after the tomalley is added because the mixture will curdle.

Tomatoes, to Peel, Seed and Chop. Remove skins by scalding them for a minute, rinsing in cold water and then pulling off the skins. Seed them by cutting in half crosswise and pressing gently in palm of hand to squeeze out seeds and water. Chop coarsely or finely as desired.

Truss. To tie legs and wings of poultry to body to prevent them from spreading out and becoming overcooked and dry.

Try Out Fat. To heat meat fat or suet until fatty part melts away from the membranes. The heat should be low enough to prevent fat from burning.

Vanilla Beans, How to Use. To flavor a hot liquid with vanilla bean, split the bean and cook a piece of it in the liquid. To flavor a dish that does not contain a hot liquid, split vanilla bean, scrape out seeds and pulp and add to mixture. To flavor a recipe serving four, use as much as can be picked up on the end of a knife.

Vanilla Sugar. After using vanilla beans, they can be washed and thoroughly dried and put in a jar with sugar to which they will impart their flavor. For a stronger flavored sugar they can be crushed with sugar and then sieved to remove small particles. Use this vanilla sugar in cooking, for making custards and other desserts.

Yeast, to Soften It. For each ½ ounce cake of yeast, use about ¼ cup lukewarm water. Break up yeast in the water, stir and leave a few minutes to soften. The water must never be hot because that will destroy the leavening quality of yeast.

Index

[299]

INDEX

A CATALOGUE OF
SELECTED DOVER BOOKS
IN ALL FIELDS OF INTEREST

A CATALOGUE OF SELECTED DOVER BOOKS IN ALL FIELDS OF INTEREST

CELESTIAL OBJECTS FOR COMMON TELESCOPES, T. W. Webb. The most used book in amateur astronomy: inestimable aid for locating and identifying nearly 4,000 celestial objects. Edited, updated by Margaret W. Mayall. 77 illustrations. Total of 645pp. 5⅜ x 8½.
20917-2, 20918-0 Pa., Two-vol. set **$10.00**

HISTORICAL STUDIES IN THE LANGUAGE OF CHEMISTRY, M. P. Crosland. The important part language has played in the development of chemistry from the symbolism of alchemy to the adoption of systematic nomenclature in 1892. ". . . wholeheartedly recommended,"—Science. 15 illustrations. 416pp. of text. 5⅝ x 8¼. 63702-6 Pa. **$7.50**

BURNHAM'S CELESTIAL HANDBOOK, Robert Burnham, Jr. Thorough, readable guide to the stars beyond our solar system. Exhaustive treatment, fully illustrated. Breakdown is alphabetical by constellation: Andromeda to Cetus in Vol. 1; Chamaeleon to Orion in Vol. 2; and Pavo to Vulpecula in Vol. 3. Hundreds of illustrations. Total of about 2000pp. 6⅛ x 9¼.
23567-X, 23568-8, 23673-0 Pa., Three-vol. set **$32.85**

THEORY OF WING SECTIONS: INCLUDING A SUMMARY OF AIRFOIL DATA, Ira H. Abbott and A. E. von Doenhoff. Concise compilation of subatomic aerodynamic characteristics of modern NASA wing sections, plus description of theory. 350pp. of tables. 693pp. 5⅜ x 8½.
60586-8 Pa. **$9.95**

DE RE METALLICA, Georgius Agricola. Translated by Herbert C. Hoover and Lou H. Hoover. The famous Hoover translation of greatest treatise on technological chemistry, engineering, geology, mining of early modern times (1556). All 289 original woodcuts. 638pp. 6¾ x 11.
60006-8 Clothbd. **$19.95**

THE ORIGIN OF CONTINENTS AND OCEANS, Alfred Wegener. One of the most influential, most controversial books in science, the classic statement for continental drift. Full 1966 translation of Wegener's final (1929) version. 64 illustrations. 246pp. 5⅜ x 8½.(EBE)61708-4 Pa. **$5.00**

THE PRINCIPLES OF PSYCHOLOGY, William James. Famous long course complete, unabridged. Stream of thought, time perception, memory, experimental methods; great work decades ahead of its time. Still valid, useful; read in many classes. 94 figures. Total of 1391pp. 5⅜ x 8½.
20381-6, 20382-4 Pa., Two-vol. set **$19.90**

YUCATAN BEFORE AND AFTER THE CONQUEST, Diego de Landa. First English translation of basic book in Maya studies, the only significant account of Yucatan written in the early post-Conquest era. Translated by distinguished Maya scholar William Gates. Appendices, introduction, 4 maps and over 120 illustrations added by translator. 162pp. 5⅜ x 8½.
23622-6 Pa. $3.50

THE MALAY ARCHIPELAGO, Alfred R. Wallace. Spirited travel account by one of founders of modern biology. Touches on zoology, botany, ethnography, geography, and geology. 62 illustrations, maps. 515pp. 5⅜ x 8½.
20187-2 Pa. $6.95

THE DISCOVERY OF THE TOMB OF TUTANKHAMEN, Howard Carter, A. C. Mace. Accompany Carter in the thrill of discovery, as ruined passage suddenly reveals unique, untouched, fabulously rich tomb. Fascinating account, with 106 illustrations. New introduction by J. M. White. Total of 382pp. 5⅜ x 8½. (Available in U.S. only)   23500-9 Pa. $5.50

THE WORLD'S GREATEST SPEECHES, edited by Lewis Copeland and Lawrence W. Lamm. Vast collection of 278 speeches from Greeks up to present. Powerful and effective models; unique look at history. Revised to 1970. Indices. 842pp. 5⅜ x 8½.   20468-5 Pa. $9.95

THE 100 GREATEST ADVERTISEMENTS, Julian Watkins. The priceless ingredient; His master's voice; 99 44/100% pure; over 100 others. How they were written, their impact, etc. Remarkable record. 130 illustrations. 233pp. 7⅞ x 10 3/5.   20540-1 Pa. $6.95

CRUICKSHANK PRINTS FOR HAND COLORING, George Cruickshank. 18 illustrations, one side of a page, on fine-quality paper suitable for watercolors. Caricatures of people in society (c. 1820) full of trenchant wit. Very large format. 32pp. 11 x 16.   23684-6 Pa. $6.00

THIRTY-TWO COLOR POSTCARDS OF TWENTIETH-CENTURY AMERICAN ART, Whitney Museum of American Art. Reproduced in full color in postcard form are 31 art works and one shot of the museum. Calder, Hopper, Rauschenberg, others. Detachable. 16pp. 8¼ x 11.
23629-3 Pa. $3.50

MUSIC OF THE SPHERES: THE MATERIAL UNIVERSE FROM ATOM TO QUASAR SIMPLY EXPLAINED, Guy Murchie. Planets, stars, geology, atoms, radiation, relativity, quantum theory, light, antimatter, similar topics. 319 figures. 664pp. 5⅜ x 8½.
21809-0, 21810-4 Pa., Two-vol. set $11.00

EINSTEIN'S THEORY OF RELATIVITY, Max Born. Finest semi-technical account; covers Einstein, Lorentz, Minkowski, and others, with much detail, much explanation of ideas and math not readily available elsewhere on this level. For student, non-specialist. 376pp. 5⅜ x 8½.
60769-0 Pa. $5.00

THE SENSE OF BEAUTY, George Santayana. Masterfully written discussion of nature of beauty, materials of beauty, form, expression; art, literature, social sciences all involved. 168pp. 5⅜ x 8½.   20238-0 Pa. $3.50

ON THE IMPROVEMENT OF THE UNDERSTANDING, Benedict Spinoza. Also contains *Ethics, Correspondence*, all in excellent R. Elwes translation. Basic works on entry to philosophy, pantheism, exchange of ideas with great contemporaries. 402pp. 5⅜ x 8½.   20250-X Pa. $5.95

THE TRAGIC SENSE OF LIFE, Miguel de Unamuno. Acknowledged masterpiece of existential literature, one of most important books of 20th century. Introduction by Madariaga. 367pp. 5⅜ x 8½.
20257-7 Pa. $6.00

THE GUIDE FOR THE PERPLEXED, Moses Maimonides. Great classic of medieval Judaism attempts to reconcile revealed religion (Pentateuch, commentaries) with Aristotelian philosophy. Important historically, still relevant in problems. Unabridged Friedlander translation. Total of 473pp. 5⅜ x 8½.   20351-4 Pa. $6.95

THE I CHING (THE BOOK OF CHANGES), translated by James Legge. Complete translation of basic text plus appendices by Confucius, and Chinese commentary of most penetrating divination manual ever prepared. Indispensable to study of early Oriental civilizations, to modern inquiring reader. 448pp. 5⅜ x 8½.   21062-6 Pa. $6.00

THE EGYPTIAN BOOK OF THE DEAD, E. A. Wallis Budge. Complete reproduction of Ani's papyrus, finest ever found. Full hieroglyphic text, interlinear transliteration, word for word translation, smooth translation. Basic work, for Egyptology, for modern study of psychic matters. Total of 533pp. 6½ x 9¼. (USCO)   21866-X Pa. $8.50

THE GODS OF THE EGYPTIANS, E. A. Wallis Budge. Never excelled for richness, fullness: all gods, goddesses, demons, mythical figures of Ancient Egypt; their legends, rites, incarnations, variations, powers, etc. Many hieroglyphic texts cited. Over 225 illustrations, plus 6 color plates. Total of 988pp. 6⅛ x 9¼. (EBE)
22055-9, 22056-7 Pa., Two-vol. set $20.00

THE STANDARD BOOK OF QUILT MAKING AND COLLECTING, Marguerite Ickis. Full information, full-sized patterns for making 46 traditional quilts, also 150 other patterns. Quilted cloths, lame, satin quilts, etc. 483 illustrations. 273pp. 6⅞ x 9⅝.   20582-7 Pa. $5.95

CORAL GARDENS AND THEIR MAGIC, Bronsilaw Malinowski. Classic study of the methods of tilling the soil and of agricultural rites in the Trobriand Islands of Melanesia. Author is one of the most important figures in the field of modern social anthropology. 143 illustrations. Indexes. Total of 911pp. of text. 5⅝ x 8¼. (Available in U.S. only)
23597-1 Pa. $12.95

THE PHILOSOPHY OF HISTORY, Georg W. Hegel. Great classic of Western thought develops concept that history is not chance but a rational process, the evolution of freedom. 457pp. 5⅜ x 8½.   20112-0 Pa. $6.50

LANGUAGE, TRUTH AND LOGIC, Alfred J. Ayer. Famous, clear introduction to Vienna, Cambridge schools of Logical Positivism. Role of philosophy, elimination of metaphysics, nature of analysis, etc. 160pp. 5⅜ x 8½. (USCO)   20010-8 Pa. $2.75

A PREFACE TO LOGIC, Morris R. Cohen. Great City College teacher in renowned, easily followed exposition of formal logic, probability, values, logic and world order and similar topics; no previous background needed. 209pp. 5⅜ x 8½.   23517-3 Pa. $4.95

REASON AND NATURE, Morris R. Cohen. Brilliant analysis of reason and its multitudinous ramifications by charismatic teacher. Interdisciplinary, synthesizing work widely praised when it first appeared in 1931. Second (1953) edition. Indexes. 496pp. 5⅜ x 8½.   23633-1 Pa. $7.50

AN ESSAY CONCERNING HUMAN UNDERSTANDING, John Locke. The only complete edition of enormously important classic, with authoritative editorial material by A. C. Fraser. Total of 1176pp. 5⅜ x 8½.
20530-4, 20531-2 Pa., Two-vol. set $17.90

HANDBOOK OF MATHEMATICAL FUNCTIONS WITH FORMULAS, GRAPHS, AND MATHEMATICAL TABLES, edited by Milton Abramowitz and Irene A. Stegun. Vast compendium: 29 sets of tables, some to as high as 20 places. 1,046pp. 8 x 10½.   61272-4 Pa. $19.95

MATHEMATICS FOR THE PHYSICAL SCIENCES, Herbert S. Wilf. Highly acclaimed work offers clear presentations of vector spaces and matrices, orthogonal functions, roots of polynomial equations, conformal mapping, calculus of variations, etc. Knowledge of theory of functions of real and complex variables is assumed. Exercises and solutions. Index. 284pp. 5⅝ x 8¼.   63635-6 Pa. $5.00

THE PRINCIPLE OF RELATIVITY, Albert Einstein et al. Eleven most important original papers on special and general theories. Seven by Einstein, two by Lorentz, one each by Minkowski and Weyl. All translated, unabridged. 216pp. 5⅜ x 8½.   60081-5 Pa. $3.50

THERMODYNAMICS, Enrico Fermi. A classic of modern science. Clear, organized treatment of systems, first and second laws, entropy, thermodynamic potentials, gaseous reactions, dilute solutions, entropy constant. No math beyond calculus required. Problems. 160pp. 5⅜ x 8½.
60361-X Pa. $4.00

ELEMENTARY MECHANICS OF FLUIDS, Hunter Rouse. Classic undergraduate text widely considered to be far better than many later books. Ranges from fluid velocity and acceleration to role of compressibility in fluid motion. Numerous examples, questions, problems. 224 illustrations. 376pp. 5⅝ x 8¼.   63699-2 Pa. $7.00

CATALOGUE OF DOVER BOOKS

THE AMERICAN SENATOR, Anthony Trollope. Little known, long unavailable Trollope novel on a grand scale. Here are humorous comment on American vs. English culture, and stunning portrayal of a heroine/villainess. Superb evocation of Victorian village life. 561pp. 5⅜ x 8½.
23801-6 Pa. $7.95

WAS IT MURDER? James Hilton. The author of Lost Horizon and Goodbye, Mr. Chips wrote one detective novel (under a pen-name) which was quickly forgotten and virtually lost, even at the height of Hilton's fame. This edition brings it back—a finely crafted public school puzzle resplendent with Hilton's stylish atmosphere. A thoroughly English thriller by the creator of Shangri-la. 252pp. 5⅜ x 8. (Available in U.S. only)
23774-5 Pa. $3.00

CENTRAL PARK: A PHOTOGRAPHIC GUIDE, Victor Laredo and Henry Hope Reed. 121 superb photographs show dramatic views of Central Park: Bethesda Fountain, Cleopatra's Needle, Sheep Meadow, the Blockhouse, plus people engaged in many park activities: ice skating, bike riding, etc. Captions by former Curator of Central Park, Henry Hope Reed, provide historical view, changes, etc. Also photos of N.Y. landmarks on park's periphery. 96pp. 8½ x 11. 23750-8 Pa. $4.95

NANTUCKET IN THE NINETEENTH CENTURY, Clay Lancaster. 180 rare photographs, stereographs, maps, drawings and floor plans recreate unique American island society. Authentic scenes of shipwreck, lighthouses, streets, homes are arranged in geographic sequence to provide walking-tour guide to old Nantucket existing today. Introduction, captions. 160pp. 8⅞ x 11¾. 23747-8 Pa. $7.95

STONE AND MAN: A PHOTOGRAPHIC EXPLORATION, Andreas Feininger. 106 photographs by Life photographer Feininger portray man's deep passion for stone through the ages. Stonehenge-like megaliths, fortified towns, sculpted marble and crumbling tenements show textures, beauties, fascination. 128pp. 9¼ x 10¾. 23756-7 Pa. $6.95

CIRCLES, A MATHEMATICAL VIEW, D. Pedoe. Fundamental aspects of college geometry, non-Euclidean geometry, and other branches of mathematics: representing circle by point. Poincare model, isoperimetric property, etc. Stimulating recreational reading. 66 figures. 96pp. 5⅝ x 8¼.
63698-4 Pa. $3.50

THE DISCOVERY OF NEPTUNE, Morton Grosser. Dramatic scientific history of the investigations leading up to the actual discovery of the eighth planet of our solar system. Lucid, well-researched book by well-known historian of science. 172pp. 5⅜ x 8½. 23726-5 Pa. $3.95

THE DEVIL'S DICTIONARY. Ambrose Bierce. Barbed, bitter, brilliant witticisms in the form of a dictionary. Best, most ferocious satire America has produced. 145pp. 5⅜ x 8½. 20487-1 Pa. $2.50

THE ART OF THE CINEMATOGRAPHER, Leonard Maltin. Survey of American cinematography history and anecdotal interviews with 5 masters—Arthur Miller, Hal Mohr, Hal Rosson, Lucien Ballard, and Conrad Hall. Very large selection of behind-the-scenes production photos. 105 photographs. Filmographies. Index. Originally *Behind the Camera*. 144pp. 8¼ x 11. 23686-2 Pa. $5.00

THE COMPLETE NONSENSE OF EDWARD LEAR, Edward Lear. All nonsense limericks, zany alphabets, Owl and Pussycat, songs, nonsense botany, etc., illustrated by Lear. Total of 321pp. 5⅜ x 8½. (Available in U.S. only) 20167-8 Pa. $4.50

INGENIOUS MATHEMATICAL PROBLEMS AND METHODS, Louis A. Graham. Sophisticated material from Graham *Dial*, applied and pure; stresses solution methods. Logic, number theory, networks, inversions, etc. 237pp. 5⅜ x 8½. 20545-2 Pa. $4.95

BEST MATHEMATICAL PUZZLES OF SAM LOYD, edited by Martin Gardner. Bizarre, original, whimsical puzzles by America's greatest puzzler. From fabulously rare *Cyclopedia*, including famous 14-15 puzzles, the Horse of a Different Color, 115 more. Elementary math. 150 illustrations. 167pp. 5⅜ x 8½. 20498-7 Pa. $3.50

THE BASIS OF COMBINATION IN CHESS, J. du Mont. Easy-to-follow, instructive book on elements of combination play, with chapters on each piece and every powerful combination team—two knights, bishop and knight, rook and bishop, etc. 250 diagrams. 218pp. 5⅜ x 8½. (Available in U.S. only) 23644-7 Pa. $4.50

MODERN CHESS STRATEGY, Ludek Pachman. The use of the queen, the active king, exchanges, pawn play, the center, weak squares, etc. Section on rook alone worth price of the book. Stress on the moderns. Often considered the most important book on strategy. 314pp. 5⅜ x 8½. 20290-9 Pa. $5.00

LASKER'S MANUAL OF CHESS, Dr. Emanuel Lasker. Great world champion offers very thorough coverage of all aspects of chess. Combinations, position play, openings, end game, aesthetics of chess, philosophy of struggle, much more. Filled with analyzed games. 390pp. 5⅜ x 8½. 20640-8 Pa. $5.95

500 MASTER GAMES OF CHESS, S. Tartakower, J. du Mont. Vast collection of great chess games from 1798-1938, with much material nowhere else readily available. Fully annotated, arranged by opening for easier study. 664pp. 5⅜ x 8½. 23208-5 Pa. $8.50

A GUIDE TO CHESS ENDINGS, Dr. Max Euwe, David Hooper. One of the finest modern works on chess endings. Thorough analysis of the most frequently encountered endings by former world champion. 331 examples, each with diagram. 248pp. 5⅜ x 8½. 23332-4 Pa. $3.95

THE COMPLETE BOOK OF DOLL MAKING AND COLLECTING, Catherine Christopher. Instructions, patterns for dozens of dolls, from rag doll on up to elaborate, historically accurate figures. Mould faces, sew clothing, make doll houses, etc. Also collecting information. Many illustrations. 288pp. 6 x 9. 22066-4 Pa. $4.95

THE DAGUERREOTYPE IN AMERICA, Beaumont Newhall. Wonderful portraits, 1850's townscapes, landscapes; full text plus 104 photographs. The basic book. Enlarged 1976 edition. 272pp. 8¼ x 11¼. 23322-7 Pa. $7.95

CRAFTSMAN HOMES, Gustav Stickley. 296 architectural drawings, floor plans, and photographs illustrate 40 different kinds of "Mission-style" homes from The Craftsman (1901-16), voice of American style of simplicity and organic harmony. Thorough coverage of Craftsman idea in text and picture, now collector's item. 224pp. 8⅛ x 11. 23791-5 Pa. $6.50

PEWTER-WORKING: INSTRUCTIONS AND PROJECTS, Burl N. Osborn. & Gordon O. Wilber. Introduction to pewter-working for amateur craftsman. History and characteristics of pewter; tools, materials, step-by-step instructions. Photos, line drawings, diagrams. Total of 160pp. 7⅞ x 10¾. 23786-9 Pa. $4.50

THE GREAT CHICAGO FIRE, edited by David Lowe. 10 dramatic, eye-witness accounts of the 1871 disaster, including one of the aftermath and rebuilding, plus 70 contemporary photographs and illustrations of the ruins—courthouse, Palmer House, Great Central Depot, etc. Introduction by David Lowe. 87pp. 8¼ x 11. 23771-0 Pa. $4.95

SILHOUETTES: A PICTORIAL ARCHIVE OF VARIED ILLUSTRA-TIONS, edited by Carol Belanger Grafton. Over 600 silhouettes from the 18th to 20th centuries include profiles and full figures of men and women, children, birds and animals, groups and scenes, nature, ships, an alphabet. Dozens of uses for commercial artists and craftspeople. 144pp. 8⅜ x 11¼. 23781-8 Pa. $4.50

ANIMALS: 1,419 COPYRIGHT-FREE ILLUSTRATIONS OF MAM-MALS, BIRDS, FISH, INSECTS, ETC., edited by Jim Harter. Clear wood engravings present, in extremely lifelike poses, over 1,000 species of animals. One of the most extensive copyright-free pictorial sourcebooks of its kind. Captions. Index. 284pp. 9 x 12. 23766-4 Pa. $8.95

INDIAN DESIGNS FROM ANCIENT ECUADOR, Frederick W. Shaffer. 282 original designs by pre-Columbian Indians of Ecuador (500-1500 A.D.). Designs include people, mammals, birds, reptiles, fish, plants, heads, geometric designs. Use as is or alter for advertising, textiles, leathercraft, etc. Introduction. 95pp. 8¾ x 11¼. 23764-8 Pa. $4.95

SZIGETI ON THE VIOLIN, Joseph Szigeti. Genial, loosely structured tour by premier violinist, featuring a pleasant mixture of reminiscences, insights into great music and musicians, innumerable tips for practicing violinists. 385 musical passages. 256pp. 5⅝ x 8¼. 23763-X Pa. $5.00

TONE POEMS, SERIES II: TILL EULENSPIEGELS LUSTIGE STREICHE, ALSO SPRACH ZARATHUSTRA, AND EIN HELDEN-LEBEN, Richard Strauss. Three important orchestral works, including very popular *Till Eulenspiegel's Marry Pranks*, reproduced in full score from original editions. Study score. 315pp. 9⅜ x 12¼. (Available in U.S. only)
23755-9 Pa. $9.95

TONE POEMS, SERIES I: DON JUAN, TOD UND VERKLARUNG AND DON QUIXOTE, Richard Strauss. Three of the most often performed and recorded works in entire orchestral repertoire, reproduced in full score from original editions. Study score. 286pp. 9⅜ x 12¼. (Available in U.S. only)
23754-0 Pa. $9.95

11 LATE STRING QUARTETS, Franz Joseph Haydn. The form which Haydn defined and "brought to perfection." *(Grove's)*. 11 string quartets in complete score, his last and his best. The first in a projected series of the complete Haydn string quartets. Reliable modern Eulenberg edition, otherwise difficult to obtain. 320pp. 8⅜ x 11¼. (Available in U.S. only)
23753-2 Pa. $8.95

FOURTH, FIFTH AND SIXTH SYMPHONIES IN FULL SCORE, Peter Ilyitch Tchaikovsky. Complete orchestral scores of Symphony No. 4 in F Minor, Op. 36; Symphony No. 5 in E Minor, Op. 64; Symphony No. 6 in B Minor, "Pathetique," Op. 74. Bretikopf & Hartel eds. Study score. 480pp. 9⅜ x 12¼. 23861-X Pa. $12.95

THE MARRIAGE OF FIGARO: COMPLETE SCORE, Wolfgang A. Mozart. Finest comic opera ever written. Full score, not to be confused with piano renderings. Peters edition. Study score. 448pp. 9⅜ x 12¼. (Available in U.S. only) 23751-6 Pa. $13.95

"IMAGE" ON THE ART AND EVOLUTION OF THE FILM, edited by Marshall Deutelbaum. Pioneering book brings together for first time 38 groundbreaking articles on early silent films from *Image* and 263 illustrations newly shot from rare prints in the collection of the International Museum of Photography. A landmark work. Index. 256pp. 8¼ x 11.
23777-X Pa. $8.95

AROUND-THE-WORLD COOKY BOOK, Lois Lintner Sumption and Marguerite Lintner Ashbrook. 373 cooky and frosting recipes from 28 countries (America, Austria, China, Russia, Italy, etc.) include Viennese kisses, rice wafers, London strips, lady fingers, hony, sugar spice, maple cookies, etc. Clear instructions. All tested. 38 drawings. 182pp. 5⅜ x 8.
23802-4 Pa. $2.75

THE ART NOUVEAU STYLE, edited by Roberta Waddell. 579 rare photographs, not available elsewhere, of works in jewelry, metalwork, glass, ceramics, textiles, architecture and furniture by 175 artists—Mucha, Seguy, Lalique, Tiffany, Gaudin, Hohlwein, Saarinen, and many others. 288pp. 8⅜ x 11¼. 23515-7 Pa. $8.95

THE CURVES OF LIFE, Theodore A. Cook. Examination of shells, leaves, horns, human body, art, etc., in *"the* classic reference on how the golden ratio applies to spirals and helices in nature . . . . "—Martin Gardner. 426 illustrations. Total of 512pp. 5⅜ x 8½.   23701-X Pa. **$6.95**

AN ILLUSTRATED FLORA OF THE NORTHERN UNITED STATES AND CANADA, Nathaniel L. Britton, Addison Brown. Encyclopedic work covers 4666 species, ferns on up. Everything. Full botanical information, illustration for each. This earlier edition is preferred by many to more recent revisions. 1913 edition. Over 4000 illustrations, total of 2087pp. 6⅛ x 9¼.   22642-5, 22643-3, 22644-1 Pa., Three-vol. set **$28.50**

MANUAL OF THE GRASSES OF THE UNITED STATES, A. S. Hitchcock, U.S. Dept. of Agriculture. The basic study of American grasses, both indigenous and escapes, cultivated and wild. Over 1400 species. Full descriptions, information. Over 1100 maps, illustrations. Total of 1051pp. 5⅜ x 8½.   22717-0, 22718-9 Pa., Two-vol. set **$17.00**

THE CACTACEAE,, Nathaniel L. Britton, John N. Rose. Exhaustive, definitive. Every cactus in the world. Full botanical descriptions. Thorough statement of nomenclatures, habitat, detailed finding keys. The one book needed by every cactus enthusiast. Over 1275 illustrations. Total of 1080pp. 8 x 10¼.   21191-6, 21192-4 Clothbd., Two-vol. set **$50.00**

AMERICAN MEDICINAL PLANTS, Charles F. Millspaugh. Full descriptions, 180 plants covered: history; physical description; methods of preparation with all chemical constituents extracted; all claimed curative or adverse effects. 180 full-page plates. Classification table. 804pp. 6½ x 9¼. 23034-1 Pa. **$13.95**

A MODERN HERBAL, Margaret Grieve. Much the fullest, most exact, most useful compilation of herbal material. Gigantic alphabetical encyclopedia, from aconite to zedoary, gives botanical information, medical properties, folklore, economic uses, and much else. Indispensable to serious reader. 161 illustrations. 888pp. 6½ x 9¼. (Available in U.S. only) 22798-7, 22799-5 Pa., Two-vol. set **$15.00**

THE HERBAL or GENERAL HISTORY OF PLANTS, John Gerard. The 1633 edition revised and enlarged by Thomas Johnson. Containing almost 2850 plant descriptions and 2705 superb illustrations, Gerard's *Herbal* is a monumental work, the book all modern English herbals are derived from, the one herbal every serious enthusiast should have in its entirety. Original editions are worth perhaps $750. 1678pp. 8½ x 12¼. 23147-X Clothbd. **$75.00**

MANUAL OF THE TREES OF NORTH AMERICA, Charles S. Sargent. The basic survey of every native tree and tree-like shrub, 717 species in all. Extremely full descriptions, information on habitat, growth, locales, economics, etc. Necessary to every serious tree lover. Over 100 finding keys. 783 illustrations. Total of 986pp. 5⅜ x 8½. 20277-1, 20278-X Pa., Two-vol. set **$12.00**

GREAT NEWS PHOTOS AND THE STORIES BEHIND THEM, John Faber. Dramatic volume of 140 great news photos, 1855 through 1976, and revealing stories behind them, with both historical and technical information. Hindenburg disaster, shooting of Oswald, nomination of Jimmy Carter, etc. 160pp. 8¼ x 11. 23667-6 Pa. $6.00

CRUICKSHANK'S PHOTOGRAPHS OF BIRDS OF AMERICA, Allan D. Cruickshank. Great ornithologist, photographer presents 177 closeups, groupings, panoramas, flightings, etc., of about 150 different birds. Expanded Wings in the Wilderness. Introduction by Helen G. Cruickshank. 191pp. 8¼ x 11. 23497-5 Pa. $7.95

AMERICAN WILDLIFE AND PLANTS, A. C. Martin, et al. Describes food habits of more than 1000 species of mammals, birds, fish. Special treatment of important food plants. Over 300 illustrations. 500pp. 5⅜ x 8½. 20793-5 Pa. $6.50

THE PEOPLE CALLED SHAKERS, Edward D. Andrews. Lifetime of research, definitive study of Shakers: origins, beliefs, practices, dances, social organization, furniture and crafts, impact on 19th-century USA, present heritage. Indispensable to student of American history, collector. 33 illustrations. 351pp. 5⅜ x 8½. 21081-2 Pa. $5.50

OLD NEW YORK IN EARLY PHOTOGRAPHS, Mary Black. New York City as it was in 1853-1901, through 196 wonderful photographs from N.-Y. Historical Society. Great Blizzard, Lincoln's funeral procession, great buildings. 228pp. 9 x 12. 22907-6 Pa. $9.95

MR. LINCOLN'S CAMERA MAN: MATHEW BRADY, Roy Meredith. Over 300 Brady photos reproduced directly from original negatives, photos. Jackson, Webster, Grant, Lee, Carnegie, Barnum; Lincoln; Battle Smoke, Death of Rebel Sniper, Atlanta Just After Capture. Lively commentary. 368pp. 8⅜ x 11¼. 23021-X Pa. $11.95

TRAVELS OF WILLIAM BARTRAM, William Bartram. From 1773-8, Bartram explored Northern Florida, Georgia, Carolinas, and reported on wild life, plants, Indians, early settlers. Basic account for period, entertaining reading. Edited by Mark Van Doren. 13 illustrations. 141pp. 5⅜ x 8½. 20013-2 Pa. $6.00

THE GENTLEMAN AND CABINET MAKER'S DIRECTOR, Thomas Chippendale. Full reprint, 1762 style book, most influential of all time; chairs, tables, sofas, mirrors, cabinets, etc. 200 plates, plus 24 photographs of surviving pieces. 249pp. 9⅞ x 12¾. 21601-2 Pa. $8.95

AMERICAN CARRIAGES, SLEIGHS, SULKIES AND CARTS, edited by Don H. Berkebile. 168 Victorian illustrations from catalogues, trade journals, fully captioned. Useful for artists. Author is Assoc. Curator, Div. of Transportation of Smithsonian Institution. 168pp. 8½ x 9½. 23328-6 Pa. $6.50

CATALOGUE OF DOVER BOOKS

SECOND PIATIGORSKY CUP, edited by Isaac Kashdan. One of the greatest tournament books ever produced in the English language. All 90 games of the 1966 tournament, annotated by players, most annotated by both players. Features Petrosian, Spassky, Fischer, Larsen, six others. 228pp. 5⅜ x 8½. 23572-6 Pa. $3.50

ENCYCLOPEDIA OF CARD TRICKS, revised and edited by Jean Hugard. How to perform over 600 card tricks, devised by the world's greatest magicians: impromptus, spelling tricks, key cards, using special packs, much, much more. Additional chapter on card technique. 66 illustrations. 402pp. 5⅜ x 8½. (Available in U.S. only) 21252-1 Pa. $5.95

MAGIC: STAGE ILLUSIONS, SPECIAL EFFECTS AND TRICK PHOTOGRAPHY, Albert A. Hopkins, Henry R. Evans. One of the great classics; fullest, most authorative explanation of vanishing lady, levitations, scores of other great stage effects. Also small magic, automata, stunts. 446 illustrations. 556pp. 5⅜ x 8½. 23344-8 Pa. $6.95

THE SECRETS OF HOUDINI, J. C. Cannell. Classic study of Houdini's incredible magic, exposing closely-kept professional secrets and revealing, in general terms, the whole art of stage magic. 67 illustrations. 279pp. 5⅜ x 8½. 22913-0 Pa. $5.95

HOFFMANN'S MODERN MAGIC, Professor Hoffmann. One of the best, and best-known, magicians' manuals of the past century. Hundreds of tricks from card tricks and simple sleight of hand to elaborate illusions involving construction of complicated machinery. 332 illustrations. 563pp. 5⅜ x 8½. 23623-4 Pa. $6.95

THOMAS NAST'S CHRISTMAS DRAWINGS, Thomas Nast. Almost all Christmas drawings by creator of image of Santa Claus as we know it, and one of America's foremost illustrators and political cartoonists. 66 illustrations. 3 illustrations in color on covers. 96pp. 8⅜ x 11¼. 23660-9 Pa. $3.50

FRENCH COUNTRY COOKING FOR AMERICANS, Louis Diat. 500 easy-to-make, authentic provincial recipes compiled by former head chef at New York's Fitz-Carlton Hotel: onion soup, lamb stew, potato pie, more. 309pp. 5⅜ x 8½. 23665-X Pa. $3.95

SAUCES, FRENCH AND FAMOUS, Louis Diat. Complete book gives over 200 specific recipes: bechamel, Bordelaise, hollandaise, Cumberland, apricot, etc. Author was one of this century's finest chefs, originator of vichyssoise and many other dishes. Index. 156pp. 5⅜ x 8. 23663-3 Pa. $2.95

TOLL HOUSE TRIED AND TRUE RECIPES, Ruth Graves Wakefield. Authentic recipes from the famous Mass. restaurant: popovers, veal and ham loaf, Toll House baked beans, chocolate cake crumb pudding, much more. Many helpful hints. Nearly 700 recipes. Index. 376pp. 5⅜ x 8½. 23560-2 Pa. $4.95

ILLUSTRATED GUIDE TO SHAKER FURNITURE, Robert Meader. Director, Shaker Museum, Old Chatham, presents up-to-date coverage of all furniture and appurtenances, with much on local styles not available elsewhere. 235 photos. 146pp. 9 x 12. 22819-3 Pa. $6.95

COOKING WITH BEER, Carole Fahy. Beer has as superb an effect on food as wine, and at fraction of cost. Over 250 recipes for appetizers, soups, main dishes, desserts, breads, etc. Index. 144pp. 5⅜ x 8½. (Available in U.S. only) 23661-7 Pa. $3.00

STEWS AND RAGOUTS, Kay Shaw Nelson. This international cookbook offers wide range of 108 recipes perfect for everyday, special occasions, meals-in-themselves, main dishes. Economical, nutritious, easy-to-prepare: goulash, Irish stew, boeuf bourguignon, etc. Index. 134pp. 5⅜ x 8½. 23662-5 Pa. $3.95

DELICIOUS MAIN COURSE DISHES, Marian Tracy. Main courses are the most important part of any meal. These 200 nutritious, economical recipes from around the world make every meal a delight. "I . . . have found it so useful in my own household,"—N.Y. Times. Index. 219pp. 5⅜ x 8½. 23664-1 Pa. $3.95

FIVE ACRES AND INDEPENDENCE, Maurice G. Kains. Great back-to-the-land classic explains basics of self-sufficient farming: economics, plants, crops, animals, orchards, soils, land selection, host of other necessary things. Do not confuse with skimpy faddist literature; Kains was one of America's greatest agriculturalists. 95 illustrations. 397pp. 5⅜ x 8½. 20974-1 Pa. $4.95

A PRACTICAL GUIDE FOR THE BEGINNING FARMER, Herbert Jacobs. Basic, extremely useful first book for anyone thinking about moving to the country and starting a farm. Simpler than Kains, with greater emphasis on country living in general. 246pp. 5⅜ x 8½. 23675-7 Pa. $3.95

PAPERMAKING, Dard Hunter. Definitive book on the subject by the foremost authority in the field. Chapters dealing with every aspect of history of craft in every part of the world. Over 320 illustrations. 2nd, revised and enlarged (1947) edition. 672pp. 5⅜ x 8½. 23619-6 Pa. $8.95

THE ART DECO STYLE, edited by Theodore Menten. Furniture, jewelry, metalwork, ceramics, fabrics, lighting fixtures, interior decors, exteriors, graphics from pure French sources. Best sampling around. Over 400 photographs. 183pp. 8⅜ x 11¼. 22824-X Pa. $6.95

ACKERMANN'S COSTUME PLATES, Rudolph Ackermann. Selection of 96 plates from the Repository of Arts, best published source of costume for English fashion during the early 19th century. 12 plates also in color. Captions, glossary and introduction by editor Stella Blum. Total of 120pp. 8⅜ x 11¼. 23690-0 Pa. $5.00

CATALOGUE OF DOVER BOOKS

THE ANATOMY OF THE HORSE, George Stubbs. Often considered the great masterpiece of animal anatomy. Full reproduction of 1766 edition, plus prospectus; original text and modernized text. 36 plates. Introduction by Eleanor Garvey. 121pp. 11 x 14¾. 23402-9 Pa. $8.95

BRIDGMAN'S LIFE DRAWING, George B. Bridgman. More than 500 illustrative drawings and text teach you to abstract the body into its major masses, use light and shade, proportion; as well as specific areas of anatomy, of which Bridgman is master. 192pp. 6½ x 9¼. (Available in U.S. only) 22710-3 Pa. $4.50

ART NOUVEAU DESIGNS IN COLOR, Alphonse Mucha, Maurice Verneuil, Georges Auriol. Full-color reproduction of *Combinaisons ornementales* (c. 1900) by Art Nouveau masters. Floral, animal, geometric, interlacings, swashes—borders, frames, spots—all incredibly beautiful. 60 plates, hundreds of designs. 9⅜ x 8-1/16. 22885-1 Pa. $4.50

FULL-COLOR FLORAL DESIGNS IN THE ART NOUVEAU STYLE, E. A. Seguy. 166 motifs, on 40 plates, from *Les fleurs et leurs applications decoratives* (1902): borders, circular designs, repeats, allovers, "spots." All in authentic Art Nouveau colors. 48pp. 9⅜ x 12¼. 23439-8 Pa. $6.00

A DIDEROT PICTORIAL ENCYCLOPEDIA OF TRADES AND INDUSTRY, edited by Charles C. Gillispie. 485 most interesting plates from the great French Encyclopedia of the 18th century show hundreds of working figures, artifacts, process, land and cityscapes; glassmaking, papermaking, metal extraction, construction, weaving, making furniture, clothing, wigs, dozens of other activities. Plates fully explained. 920pp. 9 x 12. 22284-5, 22285-3 Clothbd., Two-vol. set $50.00

HANDBOOK OF EARLY ADVERTISING ART, Clarence P. Hornung. Largest collection of copyright-free early and antique advertising art ever compiled. Over 6,000 illustrations, from Franklin's time to the 1890's for special effects, novelty. Valuable source, almost inexhaustible.
Pictorial Volume. Agriculture, the zodiac, animals, autos, birds, Christmas, fire engines, flowers, trees, musical instruments, ships, games and sports, much more. Arranged by subject matter and use. 237 plates. 288pp. 9 x 12. 20122-8 Clothbd. $15.95

Typographical Volume. Roman and Gothic faces ranging from 10 point to 300 point, "Barnum," German and Old English faces, script, logotypes, scrolls and flourishes, 1115 ornamental initials, 67 complete alphabets, more. 310 plates. 320pp. 9 x 12. 20123-6 Clothbd. $16.95

CALLIGRAPHY (CALLIGRAPHIA LATINA), J. G. Schwandner. High point of 18th-century ornamental calligraphy. Very ornate initials, scrolls, borders, cherubs, birds, lettered examples. 172pp. 9 x 13. 20475-8 Pa. $7.95

GEOMETRY, RELATIVITY AND THE FOURTH DIMENSION, Rudolf Rucker. Exposition of fourth dimension, means of visualization, concepts of relativity as Flatland characters continue adventures. Popular, easily followed yet accurate, profound. 141 illustrations. 133pp. 5⅜ x 8½.
23400-2 Pa. $2.75

THE ORIGIN OF LIFE, A. I. Oparin. Modern classic in biochemistry, the first rigorous examination of possible evolution of life from nitrocarbon compounds. Non-technical, easily followed. Total of 295pp. 5⅜ x 8½.
60213-3 Pa. $5.95

PLANETS, STARS AND GALAXIES, A. E. Fanning. Comprehensive introductory survey: the sun, solar system, stars, galaxies, universe, cosmology; quasars, radio stars, etc. 24pp. of photographs. 189pp. 5⅜ x 8½. (Available in U.S. only)
21680-2 Pa. $3.75

THE THIRTEEN BOOKS OF EUCLID'S ELEMENTS, translated with introduction and commentary by Sir Thomas L. Heath. Definitive edition. Textual and linguistic notes, mathematical analysis, 2500 years of critical commentary. Do not confuse with abridged school editions. Total of 1414pp. 5⅜ x 8½.
60088-2, 60089-0, 60090-4 Pa., Three-vol. set $19.50

Prices subject to change without notice.

Available at your book dealer or write for free catalogue to Dept. GI, Dover Publications, Inc., 31 East 2nd St. Mineola., N.Y. 11501. Dover publishes more than 175 books each year on science, elementary and advanced mathematics, biology, music, art, literary history, social sciences and other areas.